WHO AM I?

Yoga, Psychedelics
& The Quest for
Enlightenment

Allowah Lani

"Allowah Lani has written an incredible book combining deep insights from the teachings of yoga, psychedelics, and *A Course in Miracles,* each of which provides us with doors and windows into what is possible for us including an awakening back into the heart of God. Though I've had no experience with psychedelics since the 1970s, I know how incredible that experience can be. Each of these disciplines are 'alchemies.' Let them 'cook' inside and you will see another world your body's eyes could never find."

—Jon Mundy, Ph.D. Author of *Living A Course in Miracles*

"Incredibly well-written, highly personal and throughly researched, Allowah Lani's new book *Who Am I?* explores the links between Shamanism, Rituals, Plant Medicine and Yoga. Shamans and Yogis were the original explorers of evolutionary consciousness, healing and communication with the Spirit Realms. Nature and all its tools have been their guides since the emergence of the human race. Ancient Egypt was one of the first great centers of the mystic and healing arts including early forms of what would later be refined in India as Yoga. The Egyptians developed sophisticated spiritual initiations and practices that are still alive in different forms today throughout the world. Read this book and you will learn of many of the possibilities that have existed throughout time for Humankind's evolution and how they relate to you."

—Danny Paradise, Ashtanga yoga master

"Good read. Well written and held my attention, up after midnight a few nights not wanting to put it down."
—Carey Turnbull, Veteran TM teacher and yoga scholar

"Allowah Lani's book, *Who Am I?*, is a tome whose time has come. Part autobiography, part confessional, part interview smorgasbord, part historical inquiry, part pop-spirituality and counterculture catalog—this book dives headfirst in the question of how psychedelics relate to yoga and spiritual practice in general. With the disastrous and misguided 'War on Drugs' coming to a timely end around the world, many are now exploring how psychedelic substances can contribute to health, wellbeing, spiritual development and awakening. Though largely dismissed in the burgeoning Western yoga community, psychedelics have both a past, present, and potential future in relationship to yoga and meditation practices, as explored in this book. *Who Am I?* is a must-read for anyone interested in this question and presents a thorough overview of the various perspective of yogis, historians, gurus, researchers, practitioners, and more."
—Martin W. Ball, Ph.D., Author of *The Solandarian Game: An Entheogenic Evolution Psy-Fi Novel*

"Thank you for sharing this… I felt a familiarity in your writing style that I have not felt elsewhere. Clearly this is a labor of love that you've truly put your all into. In India we say 'The harder I work, the luckier I get.' You will get lucky yet, I tell you."
—Jagadish Anand, Yoga professional

"Your insights of the Yoga tradition are original and unique. I truly hope you can make this happen."

—Estella Arias, Literary Agent, New Chapter Editions

"The author's new book dealing with an important topic on the history of yoga is a very engrossing read and a very unique book. In exploring its topic areas with the author, we feel as if we are falling down the rabbit hole hand-in-hand with him. He treats his exploration with the intellectual honesty, respect, and open-mindedness it deserves and the reader is drawn into the narrative by the lucidity of his prose and by his ever-expanding exploration of this fascinating area of study. Drawing upon a wide array of 'seekers' who have come before him, the author presents a straightforward and engaging narrative that investigates his topic for anyone and everyone on the road to enlightenment. The fact that there are no other books on the market that engages this specific subject makes this book's appeal that much greater."

—Anne Dillon, Project editor, Inner Traditions,
Bear & Company, Rochester, Vermont

"Wow brother… just after a couple pages I'm hooked… I really really like it and your writing style. Please understand that I'm not just trying to make you feel good… it's really really excellent."

—Joe Marshalla, Author of *Repeatlessness*

Truly Helpful Books
210 Willoughby Dr.
Naples, FL, 34110

WHO AM I?

Yoga, Psychedelics & The Quest for Enlightenment

Cover by: Alexander Ward
Book design by: Beata Acs

ISBN-13: 978-0692732137
ISBN-10: 0692732136

www.whoami.love
allowah@trulyhelpful.love

Printed by CreateSpace, an Amazon.com Company

DEDICATION

To my Mother ~
Who always supported the next new phase of my quest.

To my Father, who often told me:
"There are no answers, only questions."

To all of my teachers, and especially ~
Neem Karoli Baba & Ram Dass,
guiding lights for so many.

And lastly,
To YOU, dear reader ~
Namasté.

Here's to our all arriving at that mind-blown state
of nirvana where there are, if but only for a moment,
"No more Quest-ions"

Thanks for listening… to your heart.

AHO ~ AUM ~ AMEN

Contents

Introduction

The book you hold is an all-encompassing work that seeks to shine light on the use of psychedelic substances from the perspective of the yoga tradition.

Over the span of three sections, ranging from ancient rituals to current practices, this book explores the mysterious term "Soma," its meaning and its long history within the heritage of yoga. This is a compelling topic of exploding interest to both the yoga practitioner (past or present) and the unaffiliated spiritual seeker who is on his or her own journey.

Because the author seeks to be inclusive of all those who are interested in the deeply human question of "Who am I" and "What am I here for," every effort has been made to make this book accessible and user-friendly. Towards that end, woven through each of the book's three subsections is the author's autobiography subtitled *Who I Am: Autobiography of a Gen-X Yogi*. This section hopes to illuminate how the author's own personal journey prepared and qualified him to create this work. You will find detailed interviews with experts and people of note on this timely issue, as well as journals and accounts of various experiences involving psychedelics and yoga practice.

Also included is a *Glossary of Terms and Personages* which will help the reader identify and/or reference any terms or persons with which they may not currently be familiar. And lastly, for further research, a detailed *Bibliography* is also included.

The Main Questions this Book Explores

- ◎ How are yoga and Soma related? Is it possible to see psychedelics as a legitimate part of the yoga tradition? Is it possible to view these substances as a legitimate tool in one's toolbox of yoga methods and practices?

- ◎ Can one successfully combine yoga and the use of psychedelics in a way that will optimize one's physical, mental, and spiritual capacities. Or, is it a case of "never the twain shall meet?"

- ◎ What were the psychoactive ingredients in the Vedic brew Soma, and how might that be important in how we view our first questions?

How else have psychedelics influenced the yoga community, both in the East and the West?

◎ Are there more "natural" ways of "getting high and staying high"—chanting, ecstatic dance, meditation, breathwork, etc.—that are more preferable than the use of psychedelics? Which begs the question: What is "natural," and what does it mean to "be high" or "stay high," and is that even something that is desirable?

◎ Is taking psychedelics… 1) "Cheating," in the current sense of "performance enhancing;" 2) An artificial substitute or "false Samadhi;" 3) Harmful to one's health and well-being; 4) Detrimental to one's mental and spiritual development, and/or unable to promote true, lasting transformation?

◎ Given that psychedelics had a large influence on the Sixties generation, perhaps especially on those who later became practicing yogis, Buddhists, and so on, why is it that there has been relatively little discussion on these subjects in the yoga community?

◎ Where are we now in terms of the current debate on this subject in the yoga world, if there is one?

◎ What has brought about the recent upsurge of interest in both yoga and the use of psychedelics?

◎ What is the difference between a yogi and a shaman?

◎ What are the differences between the synthetic psychedelics—LSD, mescaline, MDMA, etc.—and the natural plant medicines—Ayahuasca, Iboga, Psilocybin and Amanita muscaria mushrooms, etc.

◎ Just how important is set and setting in use of these substances, and what can we learn from yoga in this regard?

◎ In what sense are psychedelic experiences "real?"

◎ What is "ego" and how do these substances create the feeling of "ego death?"

◎ How are psychedelic phenomena similar or different to Kundalini phenomena?

How to Read this Book

With an open heart and mind.

If you are coming to this book with an agenda, subtly or not so subtly leaning toward one side of the yoga and psychedelics issue or the other, you will probably find only what you want to find and disregard the other side of the argument. Please bear in mind that I am not championing one side or the other, but simply hoping to present both sides of the issue in a balanced fashion to allow readers to reach their own conclusions.

You might ask yourself here at the outset: What is your purpose in reading this book, and what are you hoping to find? On one hand, do you want me (or someone else quoted herein) to give you license to take psychedelics? I will not. On the other, do you want to see me debunk their usefulness or damn their legitimacy in the spiritual realm? I also will not oblige. If anything, my intention here is to suggest how we might clarify our thinking about such controversial subjects as this, for it is the asking of clear, pointed questions that seems most essential in these matters, and will serve us best in any inquiry.

That said, this book does not necessarily need to be read straight through from beginning to end as it is not so much a linear presentation as a holographic one. Each chapter stands alone, including within it various perspectives on the one basic question here: Can psychedelics in any way be seen as a legitimate tool on the yogic path—why or why not? In presenting the material holographically, there is some necessary overlap and repetition. I view this as a plus, not a liability, for most learning is aided by a circular review of all major themes and ideas.

Even though, based on my own experiences, I may speak positively regarding some psychedelics, I also want to again make clear at the outset that I in no sense intend to be seen as an advocate or endorser for them. Because, simply put, what works for one person cannot be guaranteed to work in the same manner for another, and judicious caution seems to be the wisest approach to all such substances.

A Final Word About Word Choice

Throughout the text, I have chosen to use the term "psychedelic(s)" to refer to all mind-altering substances, despite the fact that some readers may no longer be comfortable with this word. I have made this choice with the awareness that the word carries certain pejorative connotations carried over from when these substances were outlawed in the Sixties. The neologism "psychedelic" was first coined in 1957 by Humphrey Osmond as a combination of two Greek words, *psyche* (mind or soul), and *deloun* (to manifest), with the translation "mind manifesting," meaning the revealing of the contents of the mind of which one is not consciously aware. Another word that has gained much currency of late, is "entheogen," literally meaning "God within us," or "that which causes God to be with or within an individual." I feel this term begs the question of whether these substances truly give access to the world of Spirit, or spirits, a serious point that this book addresses in various ways. To use the Sanskrit term "Soma" as synonymous with "psychedelic" similarly assumes that the psychoactive substances of today are the same as the original Soma, yet this, too, is an open question. Thus, I have decided after considerable reflection, to stick with the more conservative, and perhaps less debatable term, "psychedelic," and occasionally use "Soma" in a broader, looser, more figurative sense.

Acknowledgments

I would like to especially acknowledge
the kind assistance of the following people:
Nathan at Six Gallery Press, Marie Colandrea,
Nadine Naia Newlight, Gerry Segal, Sufey Chen,
John-Allen Gibel, Ganga White, Tom Law,
Eve Neuhaus, Danny Paradise, Greg Sanders,
Roman Gomez, Edward Lowenschuss, Bruce W.,
Tim I'ses, Allison Gardella, Gretchen Ross,
Marvin Glover, the Maui tribe, the Evolver and
Reality Sandwich tribe, and my wonderful editor
Brian Francis Heffron. And to the many others
who lent their support over the years to this project.
Special thanks to Angel D'Amore who was a
great inspirer and supporter of this project, to
Alexander Ward for creating the brilliant cover
art for this book, and to Bea Acs for doing such an
amazing job of proofreading and book design.

Preface

"If things are ever to move upward, someone must
take the first step, and assume the risk of it…"

—William James

This has been a challenging book for me to write. Yoga and the use of Psychedelics has been a subject fraught with public controversy for over 50 years, and probably even more so *within* the yoga community. Perhaps this is why there has not been a single book confronting the ambivalent relationship between yoga and psychedelic substances. The truth of the matter is that, as in the broader community, these things are being used and talked about, though discreetly. Some of the leading yoga people of the Sixties generation whom I interviewed for the book hesitated to even be involved with a project such as this. One veteran teacher told me frankly that he feared the branding and possible isolation from the yoga community that might result if he came out *publicly* on this subject.

As a yoga teacher, I too have experienced this reaction on the few occasions when I openly broached this matter with my students. Mentioning the topic in class one day, one of my female practitioners from the sixties generation seemed quite shocked that a yoga teacher would even mention the possibility that "drugs" could be enlightening in any way, shape, or form. As a child of that era, she had come to practice yoga as a safe alternative to the "mind-expanding" modalities that were blooming all around her back then. From that moment on, I could tell she didn't look at me in quite the same light, and not long after, she left my program.

The controversy may lie in how yoga has been "marketed" to the Western World. Since the Sixties there has been a huge influx of gurus and swamis to Western shores. In the beginning, yoga was targeted to the *Hippie* community as a natural way to "get high and stay high." Their drugs, they were told—primary among them LSD, mescaline, psilocybin, and DMT—were no longer necessary given the practices of posture, breathwork, meditation, and chanting. These practices along with the philosophical and spiritual insights of the yoga tradition, pointed the way to a whole new way of life.

Interestingly, this sudden rapid influx of Eastern spirituality to America was happening at the very same moment that psychedelic drugs, particularly LSD, were made illegal (1966). While for the most part psychedelics were still the rage for many young people, there was a marked movement away from them that was partly due to the anxiety of having to acquire them in an increasingly hostile environment.

Perhaps one of the most fascinating and enduring documents of this era is found in the movie, *Woodstock*, where a young hippie leads a crowd in an advanced yogic *pranayama* (breathwork) session. Before they start, he tells his peers that this breathing technique is a way of raising their Kundalini, like drugs do "*only drugs do it for you, and this way you can do it yourself...*"[1]

Indeed, Swami Satchidananda, who became known as the "Woodstock Guru" for his presence at that now historic festival, was only one of several yoga masters who had approached the hippie community with his "yoga as a natural high" message. As with most of his Indian peers who came to America at that time, Swami Satchidananda did not have positive things to say about psychedelics. Even LSD guru Richard Alpert, fresh back from India on pilgrimage, was spreading the message to the flower children that his guru, Neem Karoli Baba, was so naturally high all the time that LSD had absolutely no effect on him. Largely as a result of such developments, by the mid-Seventies there was a marked shift away from psychedelics to what were seen as more "natural" practices such as yoga. Practices that were legal and safer forms of achieving the same states of expanded consciousness that came along with psychedelics, even if this consciousness came in a slower and more methodical fashion.

Fast-forward 20 years.

By the mid-90s, when Generation X, came of age and helped to make yoga the mainstream workout and practice that it has become in the West, these "taboos" against drugs were still in full effect. As a young yoga student in my mid-20s, I was certainly influenced by the idea that this ancient technology was a natural alternative to drugs. It made perfect sense to me as the "natural high" had been my whole purist ideology since day one of my journey.

Yes, I was already inclined to this belief, as I had long been zealously opposed to the use of all drugs, including alcohol. In fact, until my mid-30s I only had a handful of experiences with any *substance*. I'd tried pot a couple of times with no effect (and yes, I did inhale!). And I had once got giddily drunk with my college roommate on his birthday, an experience that only taught me about the pain of a gruesome hangover.

These few-and-far-between experiences only confirmed for me that I didn't really care much for mind-altering substances, psychedelic or otherwise. I was truly a purist at heart, so when yoga came into my life, it effectively squelched any curiosity I had towards experimenting with LSD or any other drugs

Truth be told, in the early days of my yoga quest, it would have been overkill to use drugs as I was positively swimming in bliss much of the time—my ego boundaries faithfully dissolving on a regular basis. It was a 2-year honeymoon during which I couldn't get enough of yoga, an ancient spiritual discipline which my Indian teachers informed me was aimed at nothing less than the total transformation of one's consciousness.

Indeed, yoga radically altered my life. In fact, like many yoga people I have spoken with, I would not hesitate to say that yoga actually *saved* my life, and by this I mean in the sense of saving me from a lot of wasted time, effort, and life force. I would even suggest it saved me from using psychedelics before I was ready to do so, as we will see.

Once the initial honeymoon with my beloved yoga was over and I came back down to earth, I began to lose the perfect faith I had in my practice, in my teachers, and in myself. I was beginning to feel that even after all of the work I was doing, I wasn't seeing the results I should. I wanted more spiritual experiences, viewing them as milestones on any "successful" spiritual journey. For some reason, it seemed as if my early, tantalizing visions of a world beyond myself, experiences that whet my appetite for deeper explorations, had now all but dried up.

More accurately, I wanted not simply just new and deeper experiences, but something that would have more staying power—a stable, steady knowledge that was demonstrable; a solid recognition that I had truly "arrived." Needless to say, this was not forthcoming, and though I clearly continued to make progress, it just wasn't enough.

And so, not five years after I began my yoga practice, I chose to sever all contact with my teachers from India, a decision that I did not make lightly and one about which I had grave doubt and apprehension. At this same point in time, I also moved to Florida where I began to teach yoga. In doing so, I re-entered the workaday, time-bound world where teaching became my practice, and my former intense *sadhana* (yoga practice) became a thing of yesteryear. I slowly began to lose my connection with the magical, mystical, timeless world I had joyfully inhabited during my Twenties, and was now solidly entrenched in a kind of depressing "Flatland." I was well aware of the phenomenon of the "Dark Night of the Soul," and assumed this was it.

Fast forward another five years, when after doing due diligence and research, I allowed myself the experience of using pure MDMA. More commonly known by its street name, "Ecstasy," MDMA is not the adulterated form used by kids at raves, but is the drug in its purest form.

This was a tremendous turning point in both my life and my perspective on the spiritual. The main thing MDMA showed me was a glimpse of what it is to be free of the ego-mind, to be brought into a state of what I would call "pure presence." Had I ever experienced this state before? Not as far as I could remember, at least not to that degree. Indeed, the experience went far deeper than anything I had ever imagined. But, enlightening as it was, there was still a nagging, gnawing doubt within me as to whether such experimentation was valid from a yoga perspective (or any perspective, for that matter). I was also concerned as to the potential corrosive effects on my gray matter! My conscience raised issue after issue, yet something more than mere curiosity seemed to be propelling me further on in my own search.

As I continued to explore, next with plant substances (San Pedro, Magic Mushrooms, Ayahuasca, Iboga, DMT, Cannabis, even GABA), I encountered further experiences that I had been hearing and reading about for years, but had given up hope of ever actually witnessing myself.

Through all of this and despite my reservations, I felt that, given the degree of evolution and maturity I had attained in my spiritual journey, these plant satori if you will, were useful tools for understanding the inner workings of the mind. Yes, they were ephemeral experiences, as all experiences are (including our own material existence itself!). Yet certain deeper core lessons and truths remained after these experiences and still continue to inform my everyday existence and spiritual practice. It's been rightly said that once having taken the *Matrix's* red pill and gone down the rabbit hole you will never see the world or yourself again in quite the same way. This has been confirmed now by studies showing that psychedelic experiences are generally rated the most profound experiences of one's lifetime; they certainly have been for me.[2]

There is now a general consensus that we have come full circle since the Sixties—from an era of growing acceptance of the use of psychedelics, followed on by a reactionary "War On Drugs" which proved to be both wasteful and pointless. Only now are we moving back into a period of cautious, but growing interest in the responsible use of the substances under consideration. Some have even used the word "renaissance" to describe recent developments in the medical use of controlled substances, as well as the significance of these substances in the psycho-spiritual realm.

I feel it is worth highlighting that as a member of Generation X who grew up during the "War On Drugs," I did not come to yoga by way of psychedelics, but rather the reverse. As such, I feel that yoga prepared me for psychedelics. I sense the same is true for others of my generation, and this is certainly one audience this book is for: my peers.

I am just one of not a few now who have opened Pandora's Box and discovered, like Jake Sully in the movie Avatar, that we no longer know what the "real world" is. We are seeking deeper insight into what psychedelics can potentially teach us, how they might inform our lives and yoga (spiritual) practice, and how they might even help heal our fractured minds and bodies.

All this being said, having lived in yoga settings with masterful teachers, having had certain experiences occasioned by my yoga practice, and having deeply considered the perspectives on psychedelics from *inside* the yoga tradition, I must in good conscience propose that we not jump to hasty conclusions, but rather that we duly reflect on what actually may be a deeper wisdom regarding these substances. Perhaps, just perhaps, the path of yoga—the *true* path of yoga—calls us to a truer way of living, one that does not require any kind of external tool or technology to bring us to the deepest insight into the nature of reality. I thus humbly, but with some concern, present this book to you as light shining onto the path to a deeper, richer and more complete understanding of "yoga, psychedelics, and the quest for enlightenment."

Getting High and Staying High:
Yoga and the Woodstock Generation

"I personally arrived at the kind of states we've been talking about via the yoga of using psychedelics, and while I recognize that psychedelics might be just an astral analog of the real thing, at least they gave me a glimpse of what It must all be about. They gave me some purchase on those other states of being."

—Ram Dass[3]

"Nobody stopped thinking about those psychedelic experiences. Once you've been to some of those places, you think, 'How can I get back there again but make it a little easier on myself?'"

—Jerry Garcia[4]

"From the standpoint of the gods this world is less than child's play; it is a seed in the earth, a mere potentiality. Our whole world of consciousness is only a seed of the future. And when you succeed in the awakening of Kundalini, so that she begins to move out of her mere potentiality, you necessarily start a world which is a world of eternity, totally different from our world."

—Carl Jung[5]

"Well, dog my cats!" says Baba Fats.
"Here's one more burnt-out soul,
Who's looking for some alchemist to turn his trip to gold.
But you won't find it in no dealer's stash,
or on no druggist's shelf.
Son, if you would seek the perfect high—
find it in yourself."

—Shel Silverstein[6]

Who was that hippie at Woodstock telling the crowd that simple breathing exercises could get them as high as drugs?

One of the little known histories of Woodstock is that the opening "act" was not Richie Havens singing "Freedom," but friend of the Hog Farm and former Yogi Bhajan student Tom Law leading the crowd of 400,000 in a modest yoga "set," consisting primarily of deep breathing exercises. Many people fondly remember the late Swami Satchidananda as "the Woodstock Guru,"[7] but it may well be that Yogi Bhajan's tradition of Kundalini Yoga as translated via Tom Law had a more far-reaching influence on the hippies during the 3-day "Aquarian Exposition" on Max Yasgur's farm in Bethel, New York, August, 1969.

A recent émigré from the Punjab, Yogi Bhajan had only been teaching yoga in the States for less than a year when Law brought the newly-minted guru's yoga to Woodstock. Clearly Yogi Bhajan's influence was already very strong, and the word spread quickly in the hippie community in those days. This was not surprising for the well-connected counterculture, nor was the phenomenon of gurus from the east reaching out to the flower children with a message of "get high without drugs."[8]

Indian Sikh Yogi Bhajan teaching Kundalini yoga class, summer solstice,
Tesuque Reservation, New Mexico, 1969 (Courtesy of Lisa Law)

And the young people were listening. Even early on in the phenomenon we now marvel at as the Sixties, some members of the counterculture were rejecting drug use in favor of mind and spirit expansion through yoga, meditation, chanting, and other such practices.[9]

If you have seen the Woodstock movie, you might have been as intrigued as I was by the short scene of Law leading a small group of fellow hippies in a breathwork (in Sanskrit, pranayama) session.[10] In it, Law begins by telling his peers what by then would have been well known counterculture wisdom—that yoga could potentially do the same thing for them that their drugs were doing:

"Yoga means union... it's the same energy that drugs give you to force a rush on with, right... it's the same channels, only drugs do it for you, and this way you can do it yourself. You can do it when you want to, and you don't have to score to be able to do it, all you gotta score is some clean air..." [11]

What's curious from our vantage point now is that the pranayama practice does not look anything like what you would find in a conventional yoga class today, or even a 3HO Kundalini class. It more closely resembles Rebirthing or Holotropic Breathwork, those being two distinct modalities that were developed in that same era by Leonard Orr and Stanislav Grof, respectively. The latter was developed partly as a substitute for LSD when it became illegal in 1966. [12] As with those therapies, in the scene from Woodstock we see participants lying on their back, most with legs to chest in a fetal position, breathing very intensely and quickly through their noses. This breath technique is a traditional yogic form of *pranayama* called "Bhastrika," which translates as "Bellows." It is known widely in English as "Breath of Fire." [13] While this pranayama has been a staple of 3HO Kundalini classes, the selling point that day at Woodstock was the possibility that the Kundalini energy might rise so rapidly it would produce a rush equivalent to a psychedelic experience. As Law explained to the assembled crowd:

"The Kundalini nerve, it's called the nerve of awareness, you can't dissect it, it's a current that runs up the center of your spine... I don't know if any of you have ever sat down and crossed your legs and smoked DMT and watched what happens, but what happens to me is this big thing goes "Roooaaaarrrr!" and runs up my spine and flashes in my brain, right? Well, apparently that's what is gonna happen if I do this stuff and learn it... It takes years I guess, but this is the beginning of it. These exercises are exercises to create those channels in your body, and to free your body of blocks..."

The scene concludes with Law instructing his peers:

"Go within yourself, meditate on each breath, make each breath a complete breath, and if you do it right, you'll be flashing... momentarily."

This interesting word "flashing" was hippie slang for having visions or rapid fire insights, [14] and it also here seems to be a reference to Law's earlier remark about the effects of DMT on his brain, suggesting—even if somewhat tongue-in-cheek (as Law said, it takes years to learn)—that some of those gathered could potentially have such an experience. Whether any of the young people that day did have illuminating journeys is unclear as the scene ends with the group just beginning the practice. Even without this testimony, from my experiences with this kind of breathwork, I feel we can safely assume that some Woodstockians did enjoy some adventures in non-ordinary states of consciousness that day.

Woodstock was and is an event of profound importance for our culture on many levels, it both encapsulated the spirit of the Sixties, and at the same time foreshadowed and inspired world-changing events and movements to come. Its cultural significance and impact raises many of the important issues that this book seeks to address. Because of the movie Woodstock, the "yoga" scene in question had a major impact on Western counterculture, as well as on the burgeoning yoga movement both here and abroad.

Let us not underestimate the importance of this scene at Woodstock extolling yoga to half a million stoned youth. As one commentator put it, "…Woodstock was the ultimate declaration of dope, not as an incidental euphoria, but as some kind of necessary virtue." [15] In fact, the 29-year-old Tom Law spent most of his time at Woodstock not teaching yoga, but giving aid and comfort to hundreds of kids who were having "bad trips" from the now legendary "brown acid."

And yet, Law's yoga revelations to his hippie brethren at Woodstock were old news on the West Coast. Many important moments in yoga and psychedelic history had already passed. Most notably, in 1967, the Beatles had gone to India on retreat with Maharishi Mahesh Yogi. There they had made public statements that meditation could potentially be better than LSD. [16] And former Harvard professor Dr. Richard Alpert, now calling himself Ram Dass, had just returned from India preaching that yoga could get you higher than drugs. Nevertheless, such high profile developments only gave fuel to the fire of trends that were already happening. By the Summer of Love in 1967, the hippie community had split into those doing hard drugs like heroin, cocaine, or speed and those opting for a more "natural" path using marijuana, LSD, or even a totally drug-free spiritual quest.

In other words, Yoga at Woodstock was a sign of the times. A sign that the East Coast counterculture was getting hip to what was already *avant-garde* on the West Coast. Still, like the movie Woodstock itself, the scene of Tom Law saying that yoga could get you as high as drugs encapsulated and defined both a moment and a movement.

Tom Law instructing yoga newcomers at his
farm in Truchas, New Mexico in 1971.

Following the Life magazine article, a steady stream of pilgrims
and the curious visited the Law farm.[17] (Courtesy of Lisa Law)

One of the paramount issues this book confronts is to what extent was the early promise of yoga in the Sixties, as promoted by the Indian holy men coming to the West, fulfilled? Did all of the promise and assurances of awakened Kundalini, transformation, and enlightenment, end in disillusionment? What happened when enlightenment failed to materialize? What happened when the "masks of authoritarian power"[i] fell away? (These are not rhetorical questions, mind you, they are open ones…)

This book seeks to re-evaluate the usefulness of psychedelics as a spiritual tool. It will examine the use of psychedelics at a time when the "guru" had become suspect. In a time when those who were once considered wise elders are now suspected of being nothing more than an altered form of authoritarian figure, seeking self-aggrandizement rather than being true guides to enlightenment. In a time of doubt when more and more spiritual seekers are once again turning to psychedelics for answers.

Picking up our scene from Woodstock once again, let us begin with a basic yet fundamental question: Can deep breathing exercises, as taught by Tom Law and which we find in the yoga tradition, grant one the same kind of experiences that psychedelics can and do? Well, yes… and no… and maybe.

The answer is a categorical "yes" to the question of whether breathwork techniques actually can produce what feel like spiritual or mystical states. This has been well-known for ages. The real question is whether they are the identical experiences

---

i   The reference is to Joel Kramer's "Guru Papers: Masks of Authoritarian Power," a work which I will discuss.

that psychedelics engender. Is the "flashing" in the brain produced by a DMT rush the same as what one might experience from practicing intense *pranayama*? This is an open question.[18] As is how both of these modalities, psychedelics and breathwork, compare to the experiences received during a state of deep yogic meditation, or "*samadhi*." No one has a satisfying answer for all this, yet such are the questions we will be considering here.

• • •

Four decades after Woodstock, a small group of yoga teacher trainees convene at a yoga retreat center in Costa Rica to, among other things, explore essentially the same breath practice that we have just been discussing, albeit a more recently developed variation called "Transformational Breathwork," by Judith Kravitz.[19]

Most of the students, a mixture of men and women from age 20 to 50, have never done this practice before, and the facilitator does not tell them what they might expect. One of them, Matthew, is a former Pentecostal minister who is also, coincidentally, on the path to becoming a teacher of 3HO Kundalini, a style of yoga that he has found speaks to him more than any other he has yet encountered. Matthew has done plenty of breathwork in the context of Kundalini classes, but not to this degree of intensity or length of time.

The session is a solid 45 minutes, and the participants are asked to continue breathing throughout that entire period. Most do, and the results are overwhelmingly positive—everyone finds the practice helpful, with several of the students having what they describe as spiritual experiences. Matthew's experience, however, seems the most dramatic. He has what appears to be a classic "Kundalini awakening" wherein he feels an energy running up and down his spine. In Matthew's own words:

"After about 5 minutes I began to feel tingles all through out my body with a concentration in my hands and arms, feet and lower legs, and lower abs and groin. The feeling began to get too intense so that I would have to slow down my breathing, for about 30 seconds to a minute, and during this time the laughter was uncontrollable. It felt like waves of Joy; they would hit and laughter would burst out of me.

"After the full 45 minutes of breathing we had time to breathe normally and process what just took place, but for me, the real experience was about to begin. I could literally feel energy pulsing in my hands, and for some reason I decided to connect my right pointer finger with my left pointer finger, and my right thumb with my left thumb and laying my hands right on top of my belly button/naval center. The second my hands touched my stomach, I could feel energy shooting from my hands to the base of my spine, like my hands were some kind of connector of power/energy. Then I raised my

hands and lay them on my heart and BOOM—instantly the energy coursed from my heart to the base of my spine. After experiencing this, I placed my hands on my throat, and forehead and experienced the exact same thing... Finally, I thought, 'I wonder if this is Kundalini energy?'... I slowly placed my hands on the top of my head and it was like a live wire was connected to me. I could feel a strong vibration of energy traveling from the base of my spine to the top of my head and back down, vibrating my entire body. This energy was so powerful, that I would literally hear it, making a wal wal wal wal wal noise really fast.

"I felt completely drunk from the experience, every emotion was rushing through me. I was laughing and crying at the same time!! This lasted for about an hour or two, I remember trying to sit up and a wave would hit me and almost knock me down, and to be honest, I didn't mind it at all, it was an ecstasy that was out of this world."

Now, I can personally attest to Matthew's report as I was the facilitator for the breath-work session in Costa Rica. I want to reiterate that while Matthew's experience was exceptional, it was not completely out of the ordinary. I have myself done these kinds of breathwork sessions in which I had what felt like profound shifts in awareness, experiences of what I can only call "heavenly" states, and even moments of feeling in a state of blissed-out breathlessness, perhaps a kind of samadhi. These experiences have seemed to me similar, and yet somehow different in kind and degree from my previous yogically-induced experiences.

When I first got into yoga in 1996, I received Shaktipat initiation from Anandi Ma, a Kundalini Yoga teacher of another Kundalini tradition. Shaktipat is literally an energy transmission from master to disciple. From the time I received Shaktipat, I began to experience subtle movements of Kundalini and chakras, and spiritual experiences like improbable synchronicities and ecstatic feeling states became regular occurrences in my life. I also witnessed many others having Kundalini experiences, some quite dramatic, and not too dissimilar, I might add, from the "holy rollers" in a Pentecostal church.

My point is to make clear that Kundalini is a real phenomenon: an experience that people can and do have of an actual, embodied energy that fits traditional descriptions and other firsthand reports of what Kundalini is and does. As Tom Law suggested at Woodstock, there seems to be a similarity between Kundalini phenomena (whether produced via breath-work, shaktipat, or otherwise) and psychedelic experiences. How similar these phenomena are is a question this book will address in a later chapter.

• • •

To return now to the question of what has happened to the hippies since the Sixties in regard to the issue at hand… Of course, this is a broad and complex question. The hippie community was then, and is now, not monolithic. It is as diverse as any other community. Nevertheless, here is the story of one young person's journey from that period to now that seems a rather telling sign of the times…

Edward was a college student in the late Sixties, and like many of his peers, was experimenting with psychedelics, primarily LSD and mescaline. Through a friend he heard about Transcendental Meditation and, also like many of his peers, decided to give *it* a try. He did and was impressed enough to stay with it, but now he had a decision to make—he was told that in order to make the most progress with his TM practice, he would have to get off all drugs. Feeling this was a worthwhile sacrifice if it might ultimately establish him in a permanent state of "cosmic consciousness," Edward signed on, as did his soon-to-be wife. The year was 1970.

It wasn't long before Edward rose up the ranks to become a TM teacher himself, and his position took him all around the globe offering TM courses. Edward found this fulfilling through the Seventies and even the Eighties, but late in the Nineties, Edward began to become skeptical about the claims made by Maharishi about the experiences TM might produce. He soon thereafter left the movement, and it was only in recent years that this former international TM teacher formally stopped his actual practice of TM.

A couple of years later, Edward made a momentous decision—he finally realized that he deeply wanted to return to his exploration of psychedelics, but to now look at them through the lens of the yoga tradition and his meditation practice. He called Randolph Hencken at MAPS (the Multidisciplinary Association for Psychedelic Studies)[20] to see if he knew of anyone he could speak to on the subject. Randolph did not know of anyone, but wait… there was a guy who had emailed him just a week earlier to say he was writing a book on that very topic…

Maharishi Mahesh Yogi, the Beatles, and friends in India in 1967

Not long after, I received a call from Edward, and we've been in communication about "yoga and psychedelics" ever since.

Several months after we connected, Edward was invited to participate in a traditional peyote ceremony in New Mexico with some members of the Native American Church. Edward had not taken a psychedelic for forty years, and never of the plant variety. So he was hesitant at first, but then realized it was an opportunity he couldn't pass up.

He told me he spent a tortuous night eating peyote buttons while sitting cross-legged on the wet floor of a cold teepee until the break of dawn—and having no experience whatsoever. It was only when he went back to his room to rest that he suddenly discovered the peyote was finally beginning to take effect. What follows is a relevant excerpt of that experience:

"And then a little later, its hard to say how long, but maybe twenty minutes, I realized with a bit of a start that I was still lying there awake, loving myself infinitely. OK, I thought, now I am tripping. I lay there for a while and began to think, 'all those years, decades have gone by, and I have spent so much time in disciplined meditation environments, and really trying to experience just this... All that meditation and all of those lectures and studying and reading, and now I am experiencing loving myself infinitely, ananda chit sat, is there anything I can do intellectually, anything I can know, that can capture this in some way...'

"A few minutes later, now that I was clearly having a 'classic psychedelic experience', I wondered if there were any hallucinations, so I opened my eyes for the first time since lying down. Nothing, just the room, no hallucinations. I thought I would get up and look in a mirror because sometimes that foments hallucinations, a distorted picture of oneself. There was a mirror across the room but when I looked in it—just me, and nothing unusual about the visual experience at all. Then I thought, that's strange, here I am, fifty-seven years old, what a long strange trip it's been, my life flashing before me, a quick review. But the interesting thing is that there I was, fifty-seven years old, but the self that was loving itself infinitely, that wasn't fifty-seven. In fact it wasn't old or young. Not a man or a woman and not old or young. More of that attribute-less self of the Upanishads. Very cool, I thought. Who'd have thought it.

"Decades of meditation and discipline with the best of intentions, and now I eat a plant and here I am seeing this. Seeing in the way of understanding, of 'I see what you mean.' So I thought 'okay, here I am now seeing this; if all that reading and studying and practicing didn't do what eating a plant did, then that just is what it is, no harm; but is there anything I can know from this time forward that I can take with me?"

"I started slowly pacing around the room and the question I was thinking about

was what am I? I had just read an Advaitic biography, someone posing that archetypal non-dual question 'What am I,' Ramana Maharshi or Ramakrishna or Gangaji or someone of that sort. I was thinking 'What am I? If I can 'see' this other stuff now, I should be able to see what I am, and then take it home with me.' Pacing around thinking that, it suddenly struck me that I don't know what I am. A pretty funny answer to the classic question 'What am I?'—'I don't know.' Not like I don't know and I need to find out, or I don't know but somebody else might, but just I don't know. What we are or why we are here. And just that it is what it is. And I love myself infinitely."

Edward is an example of a Sixties youth who put down psychedelics and took up yoga with the understanding that, as Tom Law related to the hippie assemblage at Woodstock, it was a discipline that might take years to master and actually experience a full-fledged awakening. In Edward's case at least, the early promise of TM was not fulfilled as he had hoped it would, as he had been told it *could*. He ultimately returned to psychedelics for the reason many do—they provide a window on things that even many years of disciplined spiritual practice do not. The above experience clearly attests to this.

Now, some would maintain that Edward (like myself) gave up, failed—that he fell away from the path, that "razor's edge" path of which the Upanishads speak. They would say he's cheating, taking the cheap and easy way, but ultimately a misguided and fruitless way…

Certainly for all of the ones like Edward who ultimately went back to psychedelics, there are perhaps as many or more who never left TM (or whatever yoga path they were on) and have been quite satisfied with their yoga practice, or practices.[21] As noted, some of them look askance at those who mix their "medication" with meditation. Many will tell you they took up yoga to get clean of "dope" and that whole lifestyle in the first place. Others, as Jerry Garcia put it (in the quote above), wanted to get back to those psychedelic highs in a way that would "make it a little easier on myself."[22] Because, as those who have taken them will assure you, *psychedelics are really not such an easy path*—they require preparation, fitness, mental stability and discipline, courage… Or, they require, to put it bluntly, *youth, or a certain youthfulness*. Yes, they are for the most part the province of the young in mind and body, those whose systems can, like the young Garcia, handle the psychonautical terrain.[23] So this is one very valid response that has been made to psychedelics by many of the Baby Boom generation—that they created certain openings that were necessary to catalyze a spiritual search, but now there are so many other safer and saner ways of "getting there," it's just too risky, not to mention impractical and hard on the body (as Cathy Change told me on Penn's campus when I asked her if she still took LSD).

Granted that, my interest here is not so much in arguments against psychedelics because they are challenging, and more in those that would say to Edward that there should be no mixing a discipline like yoga with the use of substances that alter one's consciousness; and on the other side of the fence, those who would maintain that psychedelics may be more helpful and beneficial once well-established in a practice like yoga, and used in conjunction with yogic techniques.[24]

Let's now consider the latter possibility, for there is one other broad category to consider here, namely, those Sixties youths whose gurus told them not to continue to use psychedelics, or at least made clear that they are not the highest path, but who continued to experiment and explore anyway, in the context of their yoga practice. Interestingly enough, one very high profile figure in the yoga community falls into this camp, one who has been extremely influential in both the worlds of psyche-delics and yoga. That someone is Ram Dass, formerly Dr. Richard Alpert, Harvard professor turned-LSD-guru turned Yoga-disciple, turned Baba Ram Dass, spiritual voice of a generation.

By this time many of us know the story: On a journey to India in 1967, Dr. Alpert gave a very high dosage of LSD to his soon-to-be guru Neem Karoli Baba. Alpert was amazed to see that "nothing happened." On a return pilgrimage to India, Alpert (now "Ram Dass"), harboring a doubt, once again gave his guru a high dose.[25] Once again it had no effect on him. When Alpert asked Neem Karoli Baba whether it would still be okay for him to use these "chemicals," his guru's famous response was:

"If you were to take it in a cool place, and your mind was feeling much peace, and if you were alone and turned toward God, it could be useful. It would allow you to come into the room and pranam [bow] to Christ... But you can only stay two hours, and then you have to leave again. It would be better to become Christ than just to pranam to him, but your medicine won't do that for you. It's not the ultimate samadhi."

Now, for someone new to Hinduism or the yoga tradition, this statement might require an explanation: "What! *I* can become Christ?" But the Baba's essential mes-sage to Ram Dass was that psychedelics are not able to create a *permanent* state of liberation. That only meditation, true love, deep devotion, and complete surrender can do that. And yet *he was nonetheless giving his disciple permission to explore them*!

As Ram Dass later put it, it might well be that psychedelics only serve as an "astral analog of the real thing," providing a temporary glimpse of where his yoga practice might be taking him, but no more. And he was okay with that because he recognized that psychedelics could take him places and give him insights that his yoga practice alone could not.

Ram Dass with Neem Karoli Baba in India

What is especially interesting and not as well-publicized in the case of Ram Dass, is that prior to his first trip to India, Dr. Richard Alpert was deeply influenced by another "Baba Fats."[26] Also a powerful Sixties guru who, unlike Neem Karoli Baba, actually came to the United States to spread his messianic message. I refer to self-proclaimed "Avatar of the Age," Parsee holy man Lord Meher Baba.[27]

Meher Baba poster on a telephone pole from
the 1970's documentary Woodstock

"If God could be found in a pill,
then God isn't worthy of being God."

—Meher Baba

Though not as well-known today as some of the other Sixties gurus, there is a case to be made that Meher Baba was the most influential guru of that decade. Certainly his message that psychedelic drugs, particularly LSD, are harmful "physically, mentally, and spiritually" was quite controversial, and it apparently lost him many would-be followers among the youth. Yet it gained him some influential ones, such as Pete Townshend, mastermind and heart of the rock band The Who, who based parts of his now classic rock opera Tommy on the teachings of Meher Baba, as well as the song "Baba O'Reilly."[28] Clearly Ram Dass was also deeply affected by Meher Baba as his 1971 seminal classic "*Be Here Now*," which tells the story of his meeting Neem Karoli Baba, has cameos of Meher Baba in at least a few places, and also includes picture drawings of him. These passages suggest to the reader that this new messiah Meher Baba, who passed in 1969 at the time Ram Dass' writing his book, was to be numbered among the great masters.

In actual fact, Drs. Richard Alpert and Timothy Leary had been in communication with Meher Baba since the mid-Sixties. Dr. Alpert wrote first to him around 1965, and his letter is rather telling, expressing as it does how Alpert truly felt about LSD at that time, his personal unsettledness and spiritual yearning. Here is an intriguing excerpt from that letter:

"*I am confused and would value your counsel. In 1961, as a professor at Harvard, I had the opportunity to ingest a chemical derived from the Mexican mushroom, which has been treated as a sacrament by the Mexican Indians through their recorded history. For my colleague, Timothy Leary, and I it appeared to pierce the veil of illusion that our limited reality was indeed the only reality and show us, albeit briefly, the possibility of man's true identity. Because we were social scientists interested in helping our fellow man, we set about a systematic exploration of psychedelic chemicals, including LSD. At first it appeared as if the chemical would do it all—truly and everlastingly bring one to God. With time, however, we realized that the chemicals but showed one a possibility experientially when previously there appeared to be no possibility, or at best only an intellectual one…*

"*Inside of me I feel that LSD has been a major influence in my own life of a positive nature and that the work I have been doing in the United States is humanly good. I also hear your message and understand that you probably do know. At first I entertained the possibility that you did not understand that LSD is quite different and, in fact, quite opposite from the opium derivatives. But reflection and communing with you via your written word, has failed to support my initial reaction. Thus, at present, I feel you do understand. I should like to understand also. Can you help me?*"

Some years prior, Meher Baba had taken a vow of silence, and so he was communicating through his secretary, Adi K. Irani, who sent the following telegram on the master's behalf:

"Your letter made me happy. I know you are a sincere seeker of Truth. My love will help you. My love blessings to you and those with you..."

Later, the following letter was sent to address Dr. Alpert's concerns:

"No drug, whatever its promise, can help one to attain the Spiritual Goal. There is no short cut to the Goal except through the grace of the Perfect Master, and drugs, LSD more than others, give a semblance of 'spiritual experience,' a glimpse of the false reality.

"The experiences you elaborate in your letter and book are as far removed from Reality as is a mirage from water. No matter how much you pursue the mirage you will never reach water and the search for God through drugs must end in disillusionment.

"To a few sincere seekers such as yourself, LSD may have served as a means to arouse that spiritual longing which has brought you into contact with Meher Baba, but once that purpose is served further ingestion would not only be harmful, but have no point or purpose. Now your longing for Reality cannot be sustained by further use of drugs, but only by your own love for the Perfect Master, which is a reflection of his love for you.

"Meher Baba has pointed out that the experiences derived through drugs are experiences by one in the gross world of the shadows of the subtle planes and are not continuous. The experiences of the subtle sphere by one on the subtle planes are continuous, but even these experiences are of illusion, for Reality is beyond them. And so, although LSD may lead one to feel a better man personally, the feeling of having had a glimpse of Reality may not only lull one into a false security, but also will in the end derange one's mind… Only the One who knows and experiences Reality, who is Reality, has the ability and authority to point out the false from the real. Hence, Meher Baba tells those who care to heed him that the only real experience is to see God continuously within oneself as the Infinite Effulgent Ocean of Truth, and then to become one with this Infinite Ocean and continuously experience infinite power, knowledge and bliss."[29]

A later communication added the following interesting addendum, stating clearly that LSD has no value whatsoever, except in certain extreme medical cases:

"Meher Baba indicated that medically there are legitimate uses of the drug LSD. LSD could be used beneficially for chronic alcoholism, for severe and serious cases of depression, and for relief in mental illnesses. Use of LSD other than for specific medical purposes is harmful physically, mentally and spiritually. LSD is absolutely of no use for any kind of spiritual awakening. Use of LSD produces hallucination, and prolonged use of this drug will lead to mental derangement, which even the medical use of LSD

would fail to cure. Proper use of LSD under the direct supervision of a medical practitioner could help to cure insanity. It could lead to insanity if used for purposes other than strictly medical." [30]

All this surely had a profound impact on the young Dr. Alpert, it perhaps being one of the main inspirations for his original India trip in 1967 where he met Neem Karoli Baba. Yet he wasn't the only LSD researcher interested in what India and the yoga masters could teach him. Indeed, "Mr. LSD, Sr.," Dr. Leary, went on pilgrimage to the Motherland first…

We don't usually associate Timothy Leary with yoga or India or spiritual guides (in many respects, he seemed the "anti-Ram Dass"), but he actually had a deep interest in all things Eastern, as his autobiography, *Flashbacks*, attests. The winter of '64-'65 found him and his then wife, Nanette, and colleague, Ralph Metzner, in the Himalayan foothills with Tibetan Buddhist philosopher and scholar Lama Govinda, to whom Leary, Metzner, and Alpert had just dedicated their new book, *The Psychedelic Experience*. This seminal book reexamined the revelations of the *Tibetan Book of the Dead* in the light of recent psychedelic experiences and had a very large impact on the psychedelic community at the time.

Prior to his arriving, Metzner had guided the German-born Lama through an LSD session during which, according to Leary, he experienced states of being he had never prior in all of his years of practice. *"For the first time, after thirty years of meditation, the Lama had experienced the bardo Thodol [realm between lives] in its living, sweating reality,"* [31] Leary later noted. If this is true, it is a remarkable testimony to the power of these substances, even for a highly trained mystic like Lama Govinda, and it also perhaps highlights the uniqueness of the effect it had on Neem Karoli Baba.

German-born Lama Govinda

My point here is to reveal Dr. Leary's obvious interest in the systems of yoga found in the east, and to show that, unlike his friend and colleague Dr. Alpert for whom psychedelics became subsumed under the umbrella of his yoga practice, for the "High Priest of LSD" psychedelics always remained the primary focus.[32] Thus when Meher Baba wrote him around this time asking him to cease all positive messages to the youth regarding LSD due to its harmful effects, Leary did not take his warning as much to heart as Alpert. In fact, Leary does not make so much as a mention of Meher Baba in his autobiography.[33]

Timothy Leary at the Human Be-In, San Francisco in 1967

To return now to Dr. Alpert… Even considering the influence of Lama Govinda, Meher Baba, and surely other gurus and yogic masters, let us not underestimate the impact that LSD had on his consciousness. By this time, Alpert had done LSD over 300 times, and had received many profound insights into the nature of reality, or so he felt. What follows is but one telling story that he was to later recount about his experiments with LSD…

"After one of our sessions, when I finally got back into my body, I… went upstairs to the kitchen. There was a woman in the kitchen who had arrived at the house the day before.

"She'd come up from the south by bus to get a job in the north; she had come to our house, and was thinking of working there. She was sitting in the kitchen, drinking a cup of coffee, when I came up from the basement. She took one look at me, and whatever it was she saw must have blown her mind, because the coffee cup went flying, and she came running over and fell at my feet. Well, that completely freaked me—I mean, here was this woman, in her fifties, very solid, straight, conservative-looking, kneeling at my feet; it drove me running out of the room. Later, she told me that when I came up the

stairs from the basement, all she saw was a radiant, golden light."

Ram Dass concludes this fascinating anecdote in his usual humorous, endearing way: *"As you can see, we had some pretty good LSD in those days!"*[34]

This story is remarkable in that the effects of the LSD here were inter-subjective, whereas in many if not most reports it is purely subjective. These and other similar accounts in the literature show the potential power of psychedelics to at the very least mimic psycho-spiritual phenomena. It also leads me to feel that the young Alpert could not take Meher Baba's near blanket condemnation of LSD completely to heart; he needed to go to India for a second opinion, and that "opinion," from his guru—that he could continue using LSD under certain conditions—was exactly what felt right and worked for him. Indeed, in the years following his "conversion" to yoga, Ram Dass continued to lecture about and use psychedelics, though by his own report, not nearly as often as he had.

For Ram Dass, clearly this issue has not been an "either/or" thing; it's not yoga *or* psychedelics, but how these two tools might be integrated in order to optimize their evolutionary/involutionary potentials. Ram Dass' own personal answer was to focus mainly on his yoga practice (primarily Bhakti Yoga), and to use psychedelics only occasionally to "check in" on his progress. He understood, correctly, that the lessons received from his often high flying journeys needed to be given time to be incorporated into and embodied in real, every-day, "be here now" realities in order to find their fullest expression and greatest value. Once the lessons are absorbed, then one might again check back in with them to see how well the integration process has gone, and what one further needs to work on.

[Note: In his recent books, *Be Love Now* and *Polishing the Mirror*, Ram Dass has made clear that psychedelics are no longer a part of his spiritual practice.]

• • •

In this age of mass information, it's not too difficult to track down public figures. Actually, it's sometimes as easy as friending someone on Facebook—if they happen to be one of the 300 million people now with profiles. That's how I found Tom Law…

It actually all started the day after that breathwork session in Costa Rica when I showed the scene of Tom at Woodstock to our little yoga group. At this point, I had no idea who the young hippie was, but curious to find out who he was and what happened to him, I did a Google search for his name and found a very interesting piece about Tom from a 3HO Kundalini Yoga perspective. So now I knew his name was Tom Law. Dead, or alive? There are several Tom Laws on Facebook. After a quick glance through the profile pictures, I decided that the one of a 60-something looking gentleman at a rally with a sign saying "Reclaim America" was probably my man. It didn't matter that, 40 years later, the guy in the picture did not much resemble the young yoga teacher at Woodstock—I knew it had to be him.

Tom Law's Facebook profile picture

Tom was a little hesitant to talk at first, but when I fully explained my project and what I do, he very kindly took a good half hour to speak with me by phone, even offering to do a longer interview I could record. Tom clearly is at the place where he wants to share his story now, and he's got quite a story to tell. There were some very interesting revelations that came forth.

One such revelation, something I had already surmised, is that Tom did not stay with Yogi Bhajan or continue his Kundalini yoga practice. In fact, not too long after Woodstock and subsequent to becoming something of a yoga celebrity and showing up at various Woodstock spin-offs, Tom cut off his association with his teacher's community in disgust. As he related to me, he was appalled, among other things, by the guru's having sex with so many of his young women followers. So when, in the afterglow of Woodstock and a 4-page spread in Life magazine about him, Yogi Bhajan offered him $100,000 to go on the road and promote 3HO and his form of Kundalini Yoga for one year, he declined and gracefully bowed out of the whole scene. Tom told me he had already heard enough about the yogi's behind the scenes affairs, and "wasn't interested in foreign religion with all its trappings that Bhajan was foisting off on his following." It was Yogi Bhajan's authoritarian control of the young flocking to him as well as his devotion to materialism that turned Tom away. Besides, he now had a growing family to care for and support, and he preferred returning to organic farming, carpentry and building "as a means of living an uncompromised life."

Even though Tom did not continue practicing and teaching yoga past the early Seventies, in just those few brief years he had a rather big impact on the yoga world. One example: At a festival in Atlanta in 1971, a very young David Williams heard Tom speak about and demonstrate yoga and was so inspired that he went to India, found K Pattabhi Jois, and was the first westerner to bring Jois' now world-famous Ashtanga Yoga to the West.[35] Williams himself influenced some of the biggest names in yoga today: David Swenson, Bryan Kest, Tracy Rich, Chuck Miller, and Danny Paradise, among many others. Tom seems very humble about it all, though, saying he was just an "instrument"—he just happened to be the one through whom it flowed.

As far as smoking DMT is concerned, Tom also did not continue his use of psychedelics past the Sixties. He also wanted me to know that he "never took psychedelics to have fun, it was always very serious." And I get that about him, and it comes across on film—this is a no-nonsense, grounded person who was a truth seeker, and still is.

Tom Law demonstrating the "Ego Eradicator"
in LIFE MAGAZINE in 1970

Tom just turned 76 and is now a 13-year survivor of stage four cancer. He is currently reconsidering returning to a type of "Elder Yoga" along with breath work that he has used frequently throughout the years, finding it the key to mastering unreasonable emotions. Tom told me he is now "far more interested in progressive politics and salvaging what is left of our democracy." He studies history, politics, writes poetry and gardens on his roof in NYC, has raised 5 children and has, currently as of this writing, 5 grandchildren with his wife and business partner, Caroline. Together they created and have maintained a successful "design and build" business in the heart of the Big Apple for the past 30 years.I didn't ask, but I gather that what Tom saw with Yogi Bhajan and a lot of the Hindu gurus who crossed over left a bad taste in his mouth and he didn't want the association. He early on saw the human-all-too-human nature of these teachers, and he could no longer be an innocent follower "selling" their philosophy, however ancient or useful it was, in re-packaged form for the modern West.

I would not hesitate to suggest that for Tom's generation, and my own, Generation X, there is something of disillusioned cynicism, or at least a cautious skepticism, now about Indian gurus. With the rise of the Internet, many of us, perhaps the more thoughtful of us, can no longer retain our original naïve faith in these teachers. We have by this time read too many lurid tales of cultish behavior, sex scandals, power trips, spiritual materialism, etc., that our faith is tainted and we can't go back. Many have by now, for instance, read "Stripping the Gurus," an online expose of many of the most famous gurus from the last century.[36] Others have gone on the various cult-watch sites such as Rick Ross' to get insider information on what's really going on in these groups, or read the popular blog "Guruphiliac." I have personally looked in-depth into the controversy surrounding yoga titans like Sai Baba, Swami Rama, Amrit Desai, Baba Muktananda, Andrew Cohen, and Ammachi and my mind had been blown a thousand times already before I ever went near a psychedelic.

To be clear, this "stripping" of gurus is not a recent phenomenon. As far back as the Thirties, British journalist Dr. Paul Brunton wrote a *A Search in Secret India,* which expressed grave doubts about some of the yogis, fakirs, and even saints then popular in India, including, interestingly enough, a young Meher Baba. Brunton seemed shocked by the audacity of the self-proclaimed messiah, Meher, famously writing: "Some men are born great, some achieve greatness, and others appoint a press agent. Meher seems to favour the latter course."[37] By the end of his search, it is clear that Brunton feels he has found a true guru in the more unassuming Ramana Maharshi. Generally regarded today as one of the greatest sages of modern India, Ramana tells him to meditate on the quintessential spiritual question *Who am I?,*" proposing that this is the quickest and most direct path to "Self-realization."

Now, surely the young Dr. Alpert was aware of such criticisms of Meher Baba, but he was willing to overlook or accept his apparent foibles, as he would later those of Neem Karoli Baba. From stories in Ram Dass' book, *Miracle of Love,* we learn that his guru apparently had sexual relations (or at least uninvited physical contact) with some of the young Western women devotees who stayed at his ashram in the late Sixties. Not that Ram Dass didn't have doubts about his guru, at least initially, apparently he did. You will recall that after returning to the States, he began to question whether Neem Karoli Baba had really ingested the LSD he had given him, or perhaps palmed it (as Terence McKenna would later suggest). Ultimately, though,

Ram Dass has remained loyally connected to his guru, as have most of Neem Karoli Baba's followers from that era.

Because yoga is about balance, if anything, which means not throwing the proverbial baby out with the bathwater, let me now suggest a few ways to look at the guru that might help to salvage the concept, for those of us who are still open to listening. First, it may be possible to *separate the teaching from the teacher.*[38] As Tom acknowledged about Yogi Bhajan, even though he feels he was a "con man from the beginning," he did "have a lot of good things to say." Indeed. Clearly after all the dust has settled on the Sixties, when, admittedly, there was a lot of free love and hippie capitalism happening, we can actually admire Yogi Bhajan's legacy and movement, and some can clearly even fully embrace it. Many people now, including myself, are discovering the benefits of the 3HO Kundalini Yoga method and are even receiving healing from it. You will recall that Matthew, the young man who had the Kundalini awakening from our breathwork session, says that he got into yoga in the first place after he received a healing from a 3HO Kundalini class, and his is by no means an isolated case. Certainly there is a sense in which we can see Yogi Bhajan, too, for whatever faults he might have had as an "instrument" in the creation of a very powerful spiritual technology.

I would further suggest that it is possible to separate the guru from what in the yoga tradition is known as the "guru tattva," or "guru principle." This essentially means that a human guru, even with what we perceive as "faults," can yet embody or express something in their teaching that transcends the limited ego and work in a salvific mode. This guru principle is "beyond good and evil," to borrow Nietzsche's phrase, and it at once perfectly balances what on the Kabbalistic Tree of Life is "Hesed" and "Gevurah," or loving-kindness and strict judgment. Sri Yukteswar, Paramahamsa Yogananda's guru, is a good example of a teacher whose teaching was very stern, but at the same time absolutely grounded in compassion and committed to his disciple's success. I have personally experienced this principle at work with my teachers; it's both humbling and an ego-bust, but also ultimately liberating.

Yet, what about those who are not necessarily ready, willing, or able to devote themselves to a human teacher? A small and growing percentage of the yoga community has now also experienced this guru tattva with a non-human teacher, and that is a plant medicine from the Amazon known variously as yagé, or Ayahuasca (sometimes "ayawaska"). From my own work with it, I can say simply that Ayahuasca, like the guru, sheds light on the darkness within oneself, clarifying what one's negative tendencies and weaknesses are, and thus helping to release these unconscious layerings of ego. It seems to me to be not much different from what my human gurus have brought out in me.

I have been using Ayahuasca for the past 2 years under the guidance of a master shaman from Peru who is also grounded in the yoga tradition. At his ceremonies, the shaman asks that everyone sit up and be as still as possible with backs straight and concentrated attention for the entire 4-6 hour ceremony, just as one might be expected to do at a yoga meditation retreat. (This can be especially difficult as the Ayahuasca will often instigate bodily movements that seem to me very similar to those "kriyas," or cleansings, found in Kundalini yoga settings. For more on this, please see the chapter on Kundalini & psychedelics.)

This particular shaman also speaks of finding the unchanging, undying "Self" behind the buzz and bloom of the Ayahuasca visionary experience, this "Self" being a common translation of the Sanskrit word "Brahman" or "Atman" (with possible roots itself in the Sanskrit word, "swa," meaning "self"). He also regularly chants, not only the traditional icaros, but also Sanskrit mantras such as the Maha Mrtyunjaya mantra, an invocation of Shiva. It is a rare hybrid of yoga and Amazonian shamanism that is perhaps not so unique at all, as we shall see.[39]

• • •

Ayahuasca was not widely used yet in the Sixties, though it was known of,[40] and certainly one of its most active ingredients, DMT, was and still is a staple psychedelic of the counterculture. But traditional use of Ayahuasca with a shaman was still a rarity at that time. In the last 10-20 years, however, things have shifted radically, at least in the yoga community, with use of plant medicines like Ayahuasca, Peyote, mushrooms and Iboga in a shamanistic context on the rise, and somewhat of a decrease in use of synthetic drugs like LSD, Mescaline, and MDMA. There have been many reasons for this shift, and later in the book I will discuss them more at length, but one key change has been in literature that has come out in recent years, particularly the more popularly read books by Terence McKenna, Ralph Metzner, and Daniel Pinchbeck.

In the world of yoga literature, one book that certainly influenced my decision to explore plant medicine was Ganga White's Yoga Beyond Belief, in which White briefly touches on their potential for promoting health, wellness, and spiritual growth.

Here is the passage that most captured my attention:

"There are neural pathways in the brain that are more ancient than our beliefs, philosophies, and religious proscriptions. There are keys to the doorways of the rich interior landscape that open dimensions of beauty, order, intelligence, immense complexity, and sacredness beyond measure. These realities can be so powerful, brilliant, and intense that, while visiting them, our world seems like a distant hallucination, in the way that these other realities can seem hallucinatory from this one. Seeing and being touched by these mystical experiences can change us and help us in positive ways with insights into self-healing, enlightened living, and the wholeness of life. Our bodies and brains operate on chemical messengers and information exchange systems in nature. Some scholars and evidence show that medicinal plants were probably at the origin of religious and mystical experience. To say plant sacraments are unnatural, and practices, rituals, and belief systems created by man are natural, is an absurdity. It is a shame that fear and conditioning can preclude the greatest journey... within."[41]

Ganga White, author of "Yoga Beyond Belief"

Having now been exposed to the wider literature on this subject, I can't help but wonder what Meher Baba might have said about plant medicines like Ayahuasca, as well as White's arguments on their behalf. As noted, in the Sixties these substances were not as well known, or at least used on the popular level; LSD was the primary psychedelic. Was Meher Baba speaking, then, only or mainly in regard to LSD, or was he categorically saying of all such substances that they essentially have a "Schedule 1" status; i.e., no value whatsoever, except for certain extreme medical conditions? If so, that gives me pause, but in any case, I wonder—where today is the avatar or master who would come forward to issue a very clear message to the world that Ayahuasca (or iboga, mushrooms, peyote, etc.) is to be absolutely avoided at all costs by the spiritual seeker? I have not heard such a clarion call by anyone in recent years, but I am curious to know if there has been one, and whether this book you are reading might invite (incite?) such a statement. That said, there are spiritual teachers today who, while not making a blanket criticism, are advising students not to explore Ayahuasca if they want to continue learning with the teacher.[42]

A recent book on the modern history of Hatha Yoga, *Yoga Body*, by Mark Singleton, argues that the contemporary system of Hatha Yoga as we know and love it in the West is really not an ancient system of practice at all, but one somewhat artificially created in the early part of the 20th century by Hindu reform movements in India. Prior to that, Singleton argues, Hatha Yoga had a very poor reputation in India, and most traditional gurus, like Vivekananda and Yogananda, did not consider it to be the highest form of yoga.[43]

Drawing on the possibility that Singleton's thesis is correct, I would here suggest that perhaps a similar phenomenon has occurred in regard to psychedelics. In the Sixties when there was a very big influx of Eastern teachers to the United States, primarily due to the lifting of the Asian Exclusion Act in 1964, many Indian teachers wanted to establish themselves here and abroad. In order to do that, they had to do two things: gain the acceptance of the counterculture youth who were the most receptive to them at the time; and at the same time, distance themselves from drug use of any kind, primarily because it was illegal and would have tarnished their image among the "Establishment." So there had to be a strong "say no to drugs, say yes to yoga" message being given at that time. And now, perhaps, in an era when interest in plant medicine is growing, and these things are again being studied under government auspices here and abroad, the time has come to again bring psychedelic exploration under the broad wing of the yoga tradition. I say "again," because there is very good reason to believe that these substances were used by yogis in ancient times under the name of "Soma" (and certainly many Indian yogis still use them), an idea which will be explored in an upcoming chapter.

Tom Law at Woodstock in 1969 (Courtesy of Lisa Law)

2

Journey Into Naked Awareness: My Initial Experience with the Ayahuasca Analogue Jurema

*"True nakedness is the one and only sign of truth. Yes, only truth
is naked. So that you may rise within yourself to the place where
truth is laid bare, each of you must become free of everything
inside that is opaque and impervious to the divine world. When
you achieve this nakedness, you can go very high and receive
messages, advice, wisdom, love and God's help. You must stand
quite naked before heaven, that is to say, stripped of your greed,
your self-interest and your false ideas. The more you strip away,
the higher you rise. Then, when you come back down—and you
always do have to come back down, because as long as you are
on the earth you have to perform your earthly tasks—you dress
yourself again, that is to say, you again take up your activities,
your projects, your relationships with your family, friends and
neighbors and so on. It is necessary to clothe oneself for the
world, but not for heaven: heaven loves only 'naked' beings."*

—Omraam Mikhaël Aïvanhov

In the spring of 2004, I had the opportunity to teach a short course I called "The
Varieties of Spiritual Experience" at the Florida Gulf Coast University's Renaissance
Academy in Naples, Florida. The course was eight sessions and met once a week for
two hours. For purposes of better dialogue and interaction I asked all the students
to read two books, William James' *Varieties of Religious Experience*, and the newly
published *Rational Mysticism*, by John Horgan.

For the first class about 15 people showed up. Because most had no background
in mysticism or spiritual experience, we had a very interesting initial discussion.
There was just one guy, an older man in his late forties who had been attracted to
the course and who was obviously quite seriously into the subject even more than

myself. So, when I broached the subject of "mysticism," and asked the mostly older, retired Naples audience what it meant to them, one conservative-looking fellow raised his hand and said, "I associate that with what primitive people used to do…" Needless to say, once I got going that first session, that guy never came back. But it was somewhat remarkable that many of the others did return for the subsequent sessions, and were open to hearing me out.

During the course of our sessions, a couple of interesting changes occurred that shed light on my later explorations of "entheogens."

[Note: When I wrote this journey report several years ago, I was referring to these so-called drugs as "entheogens," or "god-inspirers"—at the time, I preferred this term over "hallucinogens or psychedelics." It was also more accurate than "plant medicines" because some substances, like MDMA and LSD-25 are chemically synthesized in a laboratory. Two other useful terms are "shamanics," in the sense that these substances take one on a shamanic journey into the nature of consciousness; and "consciousness expanders," because they do seem to expand one's consciousness beyond the normal, everyday "waking-state" consciousness. Perhaps these other terms are preferable to "entheogens," because certainly not everyone who trips has an experience of God. But "entheogens" is a term many are using to distance these substances from the pejorative connotations of terms from the past like "hallucinogen" and "psychedelic."]

At one point, maybe halfway through the course, I dropped a bombshell and made it known that I was open to exploring such substances myself (as William James had done a century earlier with nitrous oxide, as well as John Horgan, who had been a materialist science writer before taking Ayahuasca), and I invited a response from the students. Everyone seemed opposed to the idea, including my mother, who was also sitting in for the course! All except for that one guy, who it seems was a very experienced user of plant medicine. At this point, please note, I didn't even know how to pronounce "Ayahuasca" so he corrected me several times. For most of the course he had been just listening intently and basically holding back, but now he felt the pressing need to say some things.

In essence, he went on to explain at some length that plant medicines opened doors to other dimensions of existence that might otherwise take years of meditation and/or other spiritual practice to reach. He argued that those who feel a desire to explore these dimensions, but who have not found meditation, etc., to be effective, be allowed to explore realms through God-given plant medicines.

And he also defended my point of view, saying that obviously all of my research and searching had led me to the same conclusion. Still, all of the others in the class, especially my mother, expressed grave concern and reservations about my proposed choice; perhaps this was because I seemed so pure and innocent, compared to this other guy who, by comparison, seemed like a hardened veteran. Or I should say, softened veteran. There was a softness and glow in his face and eyes that were hard to mistake for anything other than that of an initiate into a more awakened state of being. Couldn't everyone see what I saw, I wondered?

It's interesting that I didn't try to befriend this man and ask him to basically "hook me up" with some of that stuff I couldn't pronounce. Nor did he approach me. There was a part of me that wasn't ready to go there. From what I'd read of Horgan's mixed experiences and somewhat frightening description of Ayahuasca, I wasn't completely convinced that I should try it anyway. But the real reason was that, at that point at least, I didn't want to ingest anything that might hurt my body in any way, or that might radically change myself. In theory, of course, I was open to entheogens, but there was a part of me that was just not prepared to go there yet.

At least, that's what I'm hypothesizing now in retrospect. Let me just backtrack a moment and tell you a little bit about my past history with drugs.

Until I was in my early twenties, I had no drug history at all. I had never used any drugs. This was because, at 14, I made a conscious decision that I wasn't going to do any mind-altering substances.

The ironic thing was, because of the way I looked and acted, many of my peers thought I was on drugs all the time! That was easy to understand as I was a long—haired kid who looked kinda freaky, played electric guitar, and seemed out of it most of the time.

That was just for a couple of years, though.

Once I got into distance running, I began to look and act quite differently. In a sense, distance running was my drug-of-choice for many years. I prided myself on being self-possessed of a natural high and not having to use any drugs to get my happy on.

As time went on, I became adamantly opposed to all drugs and alcohol. This was partly due to messages from my parents and the media, but I was also becoming a control freak. Essentially I was a purist who would never do anything that might make me do something crazy, or out of my control, or anything that would damage my body or psyche, not to mention take away from my running performance.

It's interesting that the same year that I said "no" to drugs, I also: quit the guitar, stopped listening to music, quit masturbating, ended my love affair with the "Boob Tube," started long distance running, and became radically antisocial.

I even stopped talking to my closest friends. I never dated or partied or hung out, and decided—no, I swore—that I was never going to ever use another swear word ever again.

Without knowing anything about Nietzsche, I was well on my way to becoming an *ubermensch*. I had chosen the ascetic path, or it had chosen me, and it was a path I more or less kept on for much of my post-adolescent life.

So basically, in straight world terms, I was a pretty straight arrow, on the path of the straight and narrow. Even when I began to loosen up a teensy bit towards the end of college, I had the attitude of "I'll try anything once, but only once." So I got drunk—once. And I smoked pot—once. And that was it. Then I got into Yoga, and all of the teachers I was following were saying that drugs were a no-no, and so I just continued on the hyper-disciplined ascetic path I had already set for myself.

Well, except for one relatively brief but notable period in Graduate school when, I had been open to trying psychedelics, particularly LSD. Yes, at the age of twenty-five I went through a drug-free hippie period (I couldn't find a holding company), but then Yoga, the path of discipline, took me away from all that. (More on this in a later chapter).

Coming back to the story at hand, by this point I had been living as a yogi for years, I was now becoming open to the possibility that my yoga practice was lacking something important…

And so, a couple of years after teaching that course at the Renaissance Academy in Naples, I became friends with two wonderful old souls, big-hearted beings who eventually guided me through journeys with MDMA (aka Ecstasy). It was the beginning of my "shamanic journeying" and I quickly realized what I had been missing.

Not that I hadn't had beautiful entheogen-free experiences in my life, especially a spontaneous heart-opening at the age of nineteen, but this was something completely new and different.

What I also appreciated about these "journeys" was that they allowed me to cut to the chase, without ritual or other conventional trappings of religion that are usually requisite of the spiritual seeker. Or, we could create our own rituals, and individualize the process more. We didn't have very strong doses of Ecstasy, but it still brought me into a state of blissful *Presence*, beyond ego thought and mental conditioning—no past, no future, and no need to do anything or be anything in particular, just Be. Just Be the Love that I Am, that We Are. That was E for me. I have since done it 3 more times.

There was one little problem with all of this: MDMA is an illegal substance, a Schedule 1 drug meaning the FDA has deemed it to have no medical value. While this is a designation that may be changing due to the studies that are currently being done, this could take years. San Pedro cactus, however, can be very similar in its effects to E, plus it's legal, you can even buy it at Home Depot. So that seemed the obvious next choice for me to try. My first time using the cactus I had a fairly deep experience (which you can read about in the Appendix). The second time I tried San Pedro, this time with a higher dosage in hopes of blasting off into the mescalito empyrean, I basically never left the ground, but it was still a positive experience overall.

After I did San Pedro the second time, I got into reading Ganga White's "Yoga Beyond Belief" in which he talks about taking Ayahuasca, Ralph Metzner's book on Ayahuasca, "Sacred Vine of Spirits," and Daniel Pinchbeck's "2012" and "Breaking Open the Head." These books began to get me considering taking the "Vine of the Dead," as Ayahuasca is often translated. I asked my friend and mentor who had been guiding me, and he thought it was a good idea as well. He did some research and told me that I should try an Ayahuasca Analogue (known as "Jurema") prepared with Mimosa Hostilis Root Bark, and Pegamum Harmala (Syrian Rue). I did quite a bit of research too, and discovered that this is one of the better Ayahuasca Analogues, perhaps not quite as potent as Ayahuasca itself, but quite effective. I was all for doing this, but my concern grew when I saw that one of the ingredients has the word "hostile" in it, and another, "harm!" Still, I wasn't scared…

The materials were ordered from one of the several online plant medicinal companies available at the time. Once it arrived in the mail, I let the stuff sit in the fridge for a couple of weeks until the fated day I was to prepare it and go on my journey. But before I relate my experience, I want to talk about Timothy Leary's now universally recognized wisdom in preparing oneself for such an experience, what Leary called "*set and setting*." This is based on the observation that one's *mindset and the circumstances* where one takes a psychedelic journey can be extremely important in the *outcome* of one's journey.

Taking this to heart, I knew that before embarking on this inner expedition I needed to speak with my father. I wanted to call him because we hadn't talked for some time, and I wanted to let him know that I still loved him, and to possibly try to heal some rifts with him. I didn't want to push any buttons, or confront him too much on anything as I had in the past, just to check in with him. I don't want to go into a lot of details, but one thing he said to me, which I feel was important and possibly symbolic, was, "You're thinking a lot better now."

This was significant because I used to be much more naïve, impractical, and idealistic, so he was basically affirming that I was now more grounded in reality. Previously he used to ask me "What planet are you on?." I'm not judging his opinion of me as good or bad, right or wrong, though I had often in the past been quite disturbed by what I felt to be his judgment of me. The important thing here is that when you do these kinds of inner journeys it is imperative to be grounded and focused and soulfully calm. Simply put: to have one's wits about one. By speaking with my father I was settling in for the journey to come and wherever it took me. I was now ready for this new experience.

But I also felt that there were other forces at work—despite my previous choices with regards to not taking drugs, I feel, and have felt for some time, that I must have some guide, higher force, or principle, which is protecting me from myself, and which is leading me to take these journeys at just the right time and in the right place.

That's just my sense. I could be wrong. But there have been so many instances when I seemed to have been saved from some tragic fate by an unseen hand. And when I was going through the journey that night, I could definitely clearly see how my entire life had led up to taking Ayahuasca at just that moment in time.

Indeed, it felt like everything before had just been a preparation for this incredible experience. I had been prepared for it by non-material entities, call them spirit guides, angels, ascended masters… or what have you. I'm still open, to the idea that my experience was all just a delusion caused by the plant medicine (something Daniel Pinchbeck discusses in some detail in his book, "2012")…. But I'm getting ahead of myself…

When I had done San Pedro the second time, I recited all of my intentions in front of my video camera, recording them for posterity. While I didn't do that this time (nor did we capture anything on video), my intentions were essentially the same: healing, opening my heart, connecting with higher realities, exploring other dimensions, gaining more insight into my life and life's purpose, receiving answers to all or at least some of my burning existential questions, and… meeting *God*. Actually, I didn't have any preconceived notions or expectations, especially in regard to *that* concept.

My "set" was, at least on the surface, very good, very steady, very ready—I was mentally prepared. I had done lots of studying and reading on the subject, and had watched many YouTube videos of people having this experience. I had fasted, clarified my intentions, and felt I knew what to expect. As to the setting—my Guide, who I will call "A," invited me to use her beautiful temple as a safe place to make this first journey. This "setting" had the additional benefit that A would be available to help me if I needed it during the experience, which, as it turns out, I did…

As for the preparation of the brew, I used a few different recipes I had gotten from the internet, not being quite sure which would work best. From my notes:

First, I put about 10-15 grams (I used a small kitchen scale that probably wasn't too exact) of the Mimosa bark into the blender with a couple inches of water and blended it on low for a couple of minutes, putting that mixture in the fridge for later. Then, I boiled about 5 grams of the Syrian Rue, chewing and swallowing a small bit of it raw. I boiled it for about 15 minutes, straining it once and then re-boiling it for only 5 more minutes. It actually smelled pretty good, and it was making me hungry. So I enjoyed drinking two golden chalices full, as I prepared the Mimosa.

I boiled the Mimosa also for about 20 minutes, straining it once during that time. I drank this second mixture approximately 20 to 30 minutes after consuming the Syrian Rue. The Mimosa was a brownish liquid that resembled the San Pedro I had consumed one month before. Fortunately, it didn't taste nearly as bad.

Still, at a certain point, I simply couldn't drink any more. This might have been because the Syrian Rue had begun to take effect.

This left me with a whole chalice-full of left over Mimosa, and I mistakenly thought that I might be able to drink it later if nothing happened.

In retrospect, given that my forthcoming Syrian Rue experience rated a 7 in intensity on a scale of 1 to10, and given that once the Mimosa I did drink kicked in, I was freaking out, it was probably a very good thing that I wasn't able to drink the second cup of Mimosa.

That's one of the reasons I feel I was being protected during these experiences with the unknown. Who knows what would have happened to my psyche if I had forced myself to drink the second cup "to the dregs"…?

(Please note that the time was approximately 9pm when I had finished consuming everything.)

The Syrian Rue began to take effect first as I felt my body begin to become more calm and relaxed. After jumping on the trampoline outside for several minutes, I went in and sat in my little room which had a guitar, a blanket, a video camera, and not much more. I didn't use a candle, just a little incense. At first, I had no music, but a few hours later, "A" put on a lovely CD of Tibetan Bells which played for the rest of the night.

Soon I began to see visuals, yet at first not very distinctly, and felt concerned that this experience might turn out ineffectual and indecisive, just like my experiences with San Pedro.

But it wasn't long before my sense of visual space changed dramatically. Opening up into a huge 3-D theater-like visual, everything became clearer, more pristine, and distinct. At first. I found myself witnessing a tacky, kind of kitschy, cartoonish, Disney-like visual realm. In the course of my research, I had actually read several Ayahuasca trip reports that discussed this particular stage of the journey, particularly one where the journeyer was thinking exactly as I was, something along the lines of: "Gee, I hope this doesn't go on for the duration…"

Well thankfully, it didn't for him, and it didn't for me. It could be that for the dose I took, that's what was going to come in first regardless of "set and setting." I actually was seeing this weird pre-teen world, with cartoon cut-out kids floating by, as well as cartoonish geometric forms. It came to me that this was perhaps what children who pass on see as a way of comforting them before they transition on to other realms. It also occurred to me that perhaps this was just a mirror reflection of my own consciousness at that point in the journey (and/or the consciousness that most of us are in most of the time!). Because I didn't know whether I would be stuck in this cheesy, kiddie realm for the rest of the night, I began to speak my intentions aloud, saying things like, "I'm seeking guidance… Is there anyone who can guide me?" I was asking for true spirit guides, though, I wasn't open to just anyone or anything joining me.

Nothing much was forthcoming, disappointingly.

Indeed, as far as I can recall, my entire journey was free of any and all power animals, shamans, guides, aliens, clowns, fairies, deities, or anything personal like that. I actually was very open to these things and so somewhat let down that nothing like that came through. That being said, I don't recall the entire experience in anything near perfect detail. There could very well have been visitations that night which my psyche is blocking me from consciously remembering. From both my experience of DMT and other people's trip reports, it appears that this whole strange new world it brings you to is extremely ephemeral, much like a waking dream. So, if you don't make a strong conscious effort post-trip, to immediately write down or otherwise record your experience, you will almost immediately forget 80-90% of what was revealed to you, as with our dreams at night. And fortunately or unfortunately, I didn't record any audio or visuals during this initial spiritual journey—all I had to go on was memory and post facto journaling.

So next, still quite myself enough to play scientist, I decided to go outside to see if anything would be different if I communed with nature. Not noticing much of an observable difference besides being devoured by mosquitoes, I quickly went back inside.

Back indoors, I suddenly felt like I was going to be sick to my stomach. To prepare myself for what seemed like the inevitable, I quickly went to the bathroom and knelt in front of the toilet. I hadn't vomited for decades and the only time I *almost* did was for a unique yoga practice that requires vomiting (*Gaja karani*); then, as now, I found it hard to go through with it.

This may be partly due to squeamishness, but also no doubt, I have a strong stomach. I had never been sick to my stomach as a kid, yet my older brother D. was vomiting all the time. So I wasn't that surprised that even though it felt like my body needed to expel the foreign material within, and even though I actually began to have pre-convulsions, they never actually came, and after a few minutes I left the bathroom.

Please note that I hadn't eaten for five hours prior to ingesting these two substances, so by this point it had been seven hours since I had put any food in my stomach. Later, my guide told me that my body was excreting a horrible smell at this time, so perhaps this was my system's way of releasing what it could not expel by vomiting.

The next phase of the journey began when I asked "A" if she would lie down in the bedroom with me. I'm just guessing about when this happened, perhaps an hour or two into the experience? I wasn't keeping track of time very well by this point, having graduated out of the Kiddie City visuals into a more adult cosmos replete with sacred geometry and other expressions of complexity that I can't recall. I sat up in bed and began to relate to "A" exactly what I was experiencing. I remember being amazed that I could be in two distinct worlds at the same time and where my sense of time was different in both worlds.

The Ayahuasca world opened up to me *very, very slowly,* seeming to take me all the way down to the molecular level. And yet, coming back from that a bit, I was still able to talk to "A" about what was going on within me and my perception of what was happening around me.

I kept repeating things like, "This is just amazing!" (Jerry Garcia, aka "Captain Trips," used to say, "What a trip!") Not sharing my enthusiasm, "A" expressed the desire to go to sleep. Leading me back by the hand to the other room, she told me she was happy I was having such a great experience, but it was hard for her to relate to it as she had not ingested anything and was now very tired.

About this point I began to go so deep into this other realm that it became much more real for me than the physical dimension. For seconds, perhaps even longer, I was completely losing all awareness of my own body. I was no longer even "conscious" of the fact that I was having an Ayahuasca journey at all.

And it wasn't like I was lying down, either. I was standing up, and, according to "A," my eyes were pinned wide open and bulging out. At several points when I did "come to," I began to get very worried that I might get lost in this other world that now seemed so real, and not ever come back.

Connected to this was a thought even more disturbing: I was becoming convinced that everything I had previously thought was real up until that point in my life had actually been a total *illusion*—something I had dreamed, or It was dreaming me. I wanted "A" to hold me, to comfort me, to reassure me, but I wasn't even sure she was real.

As a kind of reality check I got in the shower, but wasn't convinced that it was real, either, that I wasn't just imagining it. I kept wandering back into the bedroom and "A" kept leading me back to the other room so the repetition made me feel that I was trapped in a weird time loop from which I would never escape. I felt that I might stay completely trapped in this multi-dimensional Ayahuasca world.

I began panicking.

I asked "A" to call my mentor, "K." I kept saying: "I'm really concerned, I'm RE-ALLY concerned, please help me!"

So "A" called "K" and it was good to hear "K's" grounded voice on the speaker phone. With K's strong presence and "A's" comforting words, I began to sense that I would make it through this experience unharmed. Essentially, "K" said that this was simply a stage in the journey and it would probably last only a little while longer. He said I was experiencing the dissolution of my ego, and the Aya was showing me all the places where I hold tension, and what I needed to let go of.

One thing that "K" said to me at that point particularly sticks in my memory. He asked, "This is what you wanted, isn't it?" And I was feeling, "Yes, and no." Because not many people would willingly, knowingly seek for their ego boundaries to be blasted apart, especially if they knew what a harrowing ride they would be in for… somehow I was thinking it was going to be more fun than this!

But I needed to hear what "K" said because I had forgotten that it was the DMT that was creating and causing this experience, and that once it had run its course, I would return to life as I knew it. It may seem amazing that I would forget that fact, but what I was experiencing was so real to me that it seemed completely plausible that I might not return from that consciousness.

At this point, I could hardly speak, getting out only a few words at a time and with long intervals in between sentences. Both "K" and "A" wanted to know what I was experiencing, but there was no way I could describe it, particularly as I wasn't even there half the time! All I could say was, "I feel rooted." The Syrian Rue made me feel like a tree powerfully rooted to the earth. (The San Pedro had been a much smoother sensation, although it did make my body feel "puffed up.")

Please note that there were moments of lucidity during my experience when I could think rationally in our 3D world. And yet most of the time my consciousness was completely and totally absorbed in another dimension where I was experiencing something like an intensely vivid dream. Sometimes when "K" or "A" would say things to me, "I" just wasn't there any more to answer them. Other times I would hear their questions, but they seemed so very, very far away. There were also instances where, because time had slowed down so much for me in this other realm, it would take me an extremely long time to answer a simple question.

Once, when I came out of this multi-dimensional other world for a spell, I recalled a humorous and relevant story that I had heard told by Ammachi, one of my greatest inspirations on the yoga path: *Three yogis are deep in meditation in a Himalayan cave. This goes on for a while, and then finally the first one says to the others, "Hey, did you see that horse?" A few months or years pass and the second one says: "Yeah, that was awesome!" Finally, after another very long interval, the third one pipes up, "If you two guys can't shut up, I'm leaving!"*

It occurred to me at that exact moment in my Ayahuasca journey that I finally understood this tale on a fundamental and experiential level.

Several times I requested that "K" come over to where we were, and I recall him saying that even if he were to do that there wouldn't be much he could do to help as he didn't know what I was experiencing. So with that, "K" and I hung up, and "A" went back into the bedroom to try and sleep. She told me the next day that she didn't sleep at all because she was so worried about me.

The next part of the experience took me into spaces I could only go on my own, so in retrospect, it was a good thing that I spent the rest of the journey alone. Perhaps the experience would have been quite different if someone else had been with me.

It must have been around midnight. I had been journeying for approximately three hours. As awesome and awe-inspiring as this had all been thus far, the next four hours were to be the most revealing of all. Simultaneously, these hours seemed to both last an *eternity*, and yet also, to have passed in an *instant*.

As William Blake once famously wrote:

"To see the world in a grain of sand, and to see heaven in a wild flower, hold infinity in the palm of your hands, and eternity in an hour."

And this one from Blake also seems pertinent:

"He who binds himself to a joy
Does the winged life destroy;
But he who kisses the joy as it flies
Lives in eternity's sunrise."

"Eternity's Sunrise"—that's a great way of describing the space I now ultimately moved into. I had allowed the *ego death* process to run its course. I didn't fight it or get freaked out by it. Now I felt myself coming into purer and purer realms of consciousness, driven at warp speed into new hyper-realities of exploding rainbow colors and geometries.

Finally, I came into a feeling of total naked *being-ness*. I had no body awareness at all. It was the closest I have ever came to feeling "Pure Awareness." By the end of my journey, I was only a point of Awareness, existing in a realm of pure Light and Love. Before getting to that point, I felt like I was in what has been described as the "Light Body." Visionary artist Alex Grey's artwork made complete sense from this vantage point. Occasionally I could even see and feel this spiritualized body that I was now in. I felt stripped down to my essential nature, a newborn, naked to the entire universe, devoid of all earthly garments and their limitations. My actual visual and mental experience was even richer than any words could possibly depict and beggars my mind's abilities to describe anything like it. (Synchronicity: the Omraam Mikhaël Aïvanhov quote which begins this chapter showed up in my email box the day after my journey).

In my more lucid moments, I had no doubt that this was Enlightenment, though I didn't think of that word, but rather "Pure Awareness." I was convinced I was enlightened and that there was nothing more for me to do but to "Allow More Love to Be," a phrase which kept coming to my lips over and over again over the course of that morning. It wasn't my own personal voice though, repeating these words, it was like the Universe was speaking through me, expressing its intention to "Allow More Love to Be," and to "Release All Limitations."

I was simply the vessel through which this message was currently emerging. In some ways it did also feel like my own personal message, but it was also like I was joining a part of all Life in this movement towards more and more Love. And, that there was no end to how much Love could be created, and that my entire reason for being was for the creation and sustenance of more and more Love.

Over the course of those early morning hours, I also realized how my whole life had led perfectly up to this point in time and space. Everything else had simply been preparation for this experience of Awakening to the essential nature of both myself and of all life.

Everything now made complete sense. The timing for this experience had also been perfect. Nothing could convince me that I had not now fully "arrived" and would henceforward be recognized as a Spiritual Master. Of course, not everyone would recognize this, but other seekers with a similar experience would immediately see their own reflection in me. So now my work was to remove my light from under a bushel and let it shine with my new awareness, to shout about what I had experienced from the proverbial rooftops in the pages of this book. Because if I didn't share this experience, I would be rejecting and insulting a Universe that had gifted this experience to me. And, for all I knew, this experience might be a once-in-a-lifetime opportunity with no further revelations forthcoming in my future.

Delusions of Grandeur induced by DMT? No doubt. But I'm not the only one. I recalled how Daniel Pinchbeck struggled with this himself in his *2012* book. After taking Ayahuasca, he feels like a messianic, prophetic ("Quetzlcoatl") who has been given the role of being a kind of savior of humanity. My question is: Does everyone feel this way on Ayahuasca? Or is it that you will only have this Enlightenment experience if you have been sufficiently prepared for it? Not everyone reading these words will grasp the full import and meaning of them. So too, not everyone that has an experience with Ayahuasca will necessarily "get it" either.

So, did I fully "get" my experience? From my perspective a few days later, the answer seemed to be the negative. When I was resting there in Pure Awareness, I assumed that feeling would stay forever, and, to some degree, the experience has certainly shifted me, and continues to do so. But in many other ways, I realize it is only the beginning (which is, of course, what "initiation" means). Now it is up to me to conform and reform my life to this Experience, to ground myself more in accordance with its message on a daily, moment to moment, basis.

After experiencing Ayahuasca, I didn't think I would ever need to ingest another entheogen ever again. But now I feel that entheogens may still be useful for me. That as long as I'm living and working in the "real world" and not in a cave or in an ashram, that experiencing Enlightenment through the use of entheogens may be beneficial to my spiritual enfoldment.

Because the universe is composed of both Yin *and* Yang, I can't remain in a Yin state of being too long. I must keep exploring consciousness. But during all my journeys I must keep the primary thought that, as Walt Whitman once wrote, "Love is a keelson of creation."

• • •

Postscript

It's five nights later, Friday, 3:30 in the morning and I just had five straight hours of tripping in my sleep! It wasn't just that I was dreaming—and I was dreaming—but that these were entire dream scenarios based on taking DMT and the visions it produces. And these scenarios felt very similar to the actual experience itself.

I have no idea why this happened. Or maybe I do. Could it be because my Ayahuasca experience has been so heavy on my mind that it consumes all my waking thoughts? Was this "scenario" a flashback? Is this going to happen again? Will it become a normal occurrence now? I am sensing that it would be a good thing to again keep a dream journal, writing down everything I dream as soon as I awaken. I haven't done this for years, but it seems like an important step to sorting things out. "K" suggested a good analogy on the phone: my Ayahuasca experience was an earthquake and these are the tremors that follow the quake, yet they will subside over time.

Parting thoughts: The Ayahuasca Analogue that I ingested, Jurema, brought on what was certainly the most transformative entheogenic experience of my entire life. Perhaps the most transformative experience I have ever had, period. I would recommend it more highly than either MDMA or San Pedro, though again, the doses of E or San Pedro that I took were not as high as the Ayahuasca dose I ingested, so it's not a fair or equal comparison. I can only say that for me, Jurema gifted me with the most profound experience of all.

• • •

Synopsis

The entire Jurema experience lasted 8 hours. In the last 4 hours I experienced the dissolution of my physical body, and was taken into a space of Pure Loving Awareness.

The experience does not seem to fit neatly into any one category, and names like "Godhead" seem too ambiguous. I am left with more questions than I'd expected… Did I experience the Godhead? Was it a death/rebirth experience? A union with everything? It felt like a little of each of these, yet also none of these things. Did I experience fear at first because the worlds which opened to me seemed more real than this one? At times it did seem that I would never return to my physical body. (Timothy Leary put it so well: "Trust your nervous system.")

But, as I let go of that fear, I was given greater and greater insight into what Unity Consciousness truly is: a feeling of being, at essence, pure, bodiless awareness. The words that kept returning to my lips seemed to be of Cosmic import: "Release All Limitation, and Allow More Love to Be." It was as if I was being told this personally, a message for myself, yet I was no longer myself (limited self), and thus it was also the same message that encompassed the entire progression of our Universe, the Cosmos, and of all Life itself. I felt that I now had attained Enlightenment, or touched its face, and that I was now completely awakened spiritually. But I also realized then, and now, that I had entered a seemingly ever-expanding process, a continuous movement back to Oneness. Next time, if there is a next time, I plan to record all or part of the session.

3

The Search for the Elusive Soma, Nectar of the Gods, Fountain of Youth

"Soma, Soma, devamritam, parama jyoti, namo, namah."

*"To Soma, nectar of the gods, who reveals the
divine light, salutations, again salutations!"*

*"a ápāma sómam amŕtā abhūmâganma jyótir ávidāma devân c
kím nūnám asmân kṛṇavad árātiḥ kím u dhūrtír amṛta mártyasya"*

*"We have drunk Soma and become immortal;
we have attained the light the Gods discovered.
Now what may foeman's malice do to harm us?
What, O Immortal, mortal man's deception?"*

—The Rigveda (8.48.3, tr. Griffith)

*"…The Vedas derive, more than from any other single identifiable
source, from Soma. Would it not be useful, then, to know what Soma
was? Not particularly, India herself seems to have answered, judging
from her scholars' lack of interest in identifying the lost plant."*

—Huston Smith

*"The Soma sacrifice was the focal point of the Vedic religion. Indeed,
if one accepts the point of view that the whole of Indian mystical
practice from the Upanishads through the more mechanical methods
of yoga is merely an attempt to recapture the vision granted by
the Soma plant, then the nature of that vision, and of the plant,
underlies the whole of Indian religion, and everything of a mystical
nature within that religion is pertinent to the identity of the plant."*

—Wendy Doniger, Psychedelics

"I was told she was manifesting amrit, nectar, from her feet..."

I first was drawn into the yoga fold during the Spring and Summer of 1996. During that time, I had the rare opportunity to meet no less than four truly re-markable women saints from India. These encounters were due to the gentle, but insistent prodding of a colleague in my religious studies graduate program, an In-dologist-in-training, who recognized that I was on a spiritual quest and decided I was ready to meet the masters. It was a wild ride for a guy who just two years earlier had been a born-again Orthodox Jew in Jerusalem! But now I actually *was* ready. There was a clear sense in which I took all four women to be my teachers. However, it was with only one of them, Śri Karunamayi[ii], that I developed a more traditional guru-disciple relationship, traveling to see her in India no less than five times in as many years.

The basic hagiographical account of Śri Karunamayi's life I knew from both verbal stories and writings about her. Prior to her birth in 1958, Śri Karunamayi's mother went to see Ramana Maharishi, revered both East and West as the greatest sage of 20th century India. At their meeting, the great sage told her she would soon give birth to an incarnation of the Divine Mother.

Indeed, from birth onward Śri Karunamyi did display signs that the great seer's prediction was true. Her deeply compassionate nature inspired the name "Karuna-mayi," or "Goddess of Compassion."

A major turning point came in her first year of college, when she began meditat-ing for longer and longer periods in her family's worship room. Finally, one day she locked herself in the room for an entire month, emerging, according to her family, clearly transformed. With her mother's blessing, the young saint-in-the-making left college and lived for the next 12 years in a remote forest outside of Bangalore "ab-sorbed in meditation for hours, days, or even weeks at a time."[44] At the conclusion of her *tapasya* (austerities) in the early 1990s, a temple was built for the now recog-nized saint in Bangalore, and she began offering regular worship services there.[45]

When I met Śri Karunamayi in the mid-'90s, she was just beginning to establish a presence in the States. The first time I went to see her was, ironically enough, in a synagogue in Philadelphia built by Frank Lloyd Wright. At first, I didn't know what to make of the diminutive, plump woman I soon came to call "Amma" (a word for "Mother" in South India); she seemed so soft-spoken and unassuming. I knew she

---

ii   There are many ways of addressing a saint in India, from the formal to affectionate. For most, Karunamayi was affectionately known as "Amma," meaning Mother, or "Karunamayi," Goddess of Compassion. Slightly more formally, she's known as "Śri Karunamayi," Śri being a term of high respect. Even more formally, Karunamayi's name is "Śri Śri Śri Vijayeshwari Devi," signifying that she is an incarnation of Durga, born on Vijayadashami, the 10th day of the Navaratri festival.

was gifted. I just wasn't feeling especially called to follow her.

Nevertheless, my colleague-mentor strongly felt that Śri Karunamayi had IT, and as I trusted her opinion completely, I went along for the ride. In 1998 this ride took me to Amma's temple ashram in Bangalore, India, which I visited daily for nearly a month.

While I was certainly amazed and touched by my teacher's loving, motherly presence, if I was going to devote my life to her service, the skeptic in me, the critical analyst developed over years of academic training and Torah study, was always searching for more "proof." As with Ram Dass and the Westerners who entered the orbit of Neem Karoli Baba, that proof came for me mainly in the form of the unconditional love and compassion I felt from this obviously saintly being, and often within myself when around her.

But I wanted, I needed, more. If Amma truly was omniscient, I wanted to experience that she was. If she really could do miracles, I wanted to see one. If she could inspire profound meditation, I wanted to feel that. I got glimpses and heard other people's miraculous stories, but I wanted more than just glimpses, more than just stories. I needed to see/hear/feel these things for myself. (I realize now this was my problem, not hers, yet it was what it was.)

Now one *siddhi*, or yogic power, that Śri Karunamayi is said to have is the ability to manifest various sacred substances from her feet. I actually was in her Temple in Bangalore during the Navaratri Festival when she began to produce the red vermilion powder known as *kumkum* that many Indian women place on their foreheads. At the moment this was happening, however, I was absorbed in meditation and moments later when I finally sensed the commotion all around me, all of the Indians in the room had already rushed to the front and I couldn't actually catch a glimpse of the "feat." When Amma left the room and the crowd simmered down, I did see the powder settled in heaps around where Amma's feet would have been. On another occasion, I came into the room only after it happened to witness the same sight.

This all had been preceded back in the States by another devotee friend giddily relating how on the 7th day of a 9 day meditation retreat with Amma in India, he and the others were aroused from their meditations to witness *amrit* (also, *devamritam*; cognate with the Greek "ambrosia"), the "nectar of the gods," pouring from Amma's feet. They even got to taste it. He said it was essentially the same stuff that miraculously comes out of a wall at Sai Baba's ashram, Whitefield, just outside of Bangalore, and he gave me some to sample. But as for the actual production of it, I never got a chance to see this, and again, though I was extremely impressed by Amma in so many ways beyond such yogic powers, the living proof continued to elude me.[46]

Śrī Karunamayi

I bring all of this up partly because, as we will see, this *amrit* is very pertinent to the discussion of Soma that follows.

Soma, Why & Wherefore?

By this time, most of us have heard the word "Soma," whether via Aldous Huxley's *Brave New World*, by the steroid of that name (aka, Carisoprodol), or simply because it has entered the lexicon to mean a hallucinogenic substance. So it's at least on the periphery of the collective consciousness, as it was with me until I discovered that there has actually been some controversy over the actual identity of the Vedic Soma.

Curiously, while Śrī Karunamayi would discourse at length on the ancient Vedic way of life, she rarely spoke of Soma. Soma is first spoken of in the Vedic texts as both a *deva*, or deity/god, no less; the most revered of the Hindu pantheon, *and* an intoxicating drink (among other things).

Perhaps this omission is due to the fact that the term Soma is such a complex one, and the exact identity of the Soma brew so elusive. Or perhaps Amma was only doling out what she felt we, her "little children," could grasp. Whatever the case may be, Soma has remained one of the most hotly debated subject among Western scholars and researchers of entheogens (Huston Smith's preferred designation), and many lay users of psychedelics are interested and well-versed in this debate. For those new to this subject, let's begin the discussion by considering the core of the controversy.

First it seems appropriate to ask: Why should we care about Soma at all? Why is its identity all that important, anyway? Isn't Soma a part of ancient history that has no bearing on our lives now?

Yes, and no.

No, because given the widely-ranging and diverse views on what Soma is, a definitive answer as to its true identity seems highly unlikely; and in any case, we also have our own modern "Somas," the plant-based psychoactive substances that are the subject of this book, to consider. But yes, too, and for several reasons…

First, if it could be shown that ancient religions, such as "Hinduism" (traditionally referred to as *Sanatana Dharma*, or "Eternal Religion"), were inspired by ingesting sacred plant concoctions, then this would have a profound effect on our understanding of religion generally, and the Hindu/Sanatana Dharma tradition, very specifically.

Second, if we could get a better idea of what Soma was, and determine if it still exists today or could be re-produced, we might then make use of it as a technology or tool that would better inform our understanding of the Yoga tradition.

Finally, a deeper study of the Vedas and its "Soma," regardless of what it is or was, can only help to enlarge our understanding of this time-honored spiritual tradition.

There is another reason to probe the identity of Soma. Soma is currently part of a broader debate regarding whether Western scholarship has been fair and accurate in its descriptions and analyses of India's origins, history, and culture.[47] In the case of our mysterious substance, the issue in particular is over the extent to which R. Gordon Wasson's thesis, which claims that Soma was a brew concocted from the *Amanita muscaria* mushroom (also known as "The Fly Agaric"), is to be privileged over the views of those who speak from within an "authentic" Indian tradition.

Wasson's Thesis

R. Gordon Wasson was a banker who was also the founding father of "ethnomycology," the study of the cultural use of mushrooms. In 1927 Wasson happened upon some wild mushrooms on his honeymoon with his wife, Valentina Pavlovna Guercken. They published their first book, *Mushrooms, Russia, and History* in 1957, the same year that they became the first westerners to participate in the Mazatec sacred mushroom ritual with the now legendary shaman, Maria Sabina. This ritual involves the ingestion of psilocybin mushrooms (widely known as "Magic Mushrooms"), and the resulting ecstatic voyage Wasson was taken on deeply inspired him to continue to immerse himself in the fields of ethnomycological and entheogenic studies.

Wasson's work had a profound impact on many subsequent users of psychedelics. An article he and his wife penned for Life magazine that year, "Seeking the Magic Mushroom," was the catalyst for the subsequent psychedelic quests of many diverse and notable people, including Aldous Huxley, Anthony Russo, Michael, Bowen, Timothy Leary, and Richard Alpert.

Although eventually Leary became best known as the "High Priest of LSD," it was his participation in the Mazatec magic mushroom ritual in 1960 that inspired his Harvard research.

Leary famously commented that he "learned more about my brain and its possibilities, and more about psychology in the five hours after taking these mushrooms, than I had in the preceding fifteen years of studying and doing research in psychology."[48] A remarkable statement, for sure. Although Leary later became known for his dramatic and hyperbolic declarations, in this case, I suggest, he was not exaggerating.

Wasson's famous limited-edition book on Soma

I first was exposed to Wasson's research via Huston Smith's work, *Cleansing the Doors of Perception: The Religious Significance of Entheogenic Plants and Chemicals*

(Tarcher, 2000). Smith presents Wasson's thesis and then summarizes his main arguments, adding that despite the recent controversy surrounding them, they are still "the strongest in the field."[49]

These arguments essentially boil down to Wasson's thesis that *Amanita muscaria* best fits the descriptions of Soma in the Vedas, in regard to its genus, color, shape, geographical location, and psychoactive properties. Another interesting fact that makes Wasson's argument stronger is found in a passage in the Vedas suggesting that Soma was also drunk via the urine. This is because its psychoactive properties survive metabolic processing. This practice was also known to have been used in other cultures, too, most notably the shamans of Siberia, about whom there is interesting speculation that their drinking *Amanita muscaria* through the urine of reindeer may have been the real origin of the Santa Claus myth.

On a first reading of Smith's presentation of Wasson's work, and knowing something of the Vedas and Vedic science, I was impressed by Wasson's research, but not persuaded beyond a reasonable doubt about his thesis. Wasson had just not provided any truly convincing proof that Soma was a mushroom, let alone *Amanita muscaria*. It just seemed like so much scholarly conjecture.

Yet I was given pause by the number of top scholars supporting his thesis, including the well-regarded Indologist Wendy Doniger O'Flaherty, as well as Evans Schultes, Albert Hofmann & Christian Ratsch.[50] Could all of these great scholars be mistaken?

Perhaps. After all, as Smith himself acknowledged, much was to be gained from discovering the original identity of Soma, first and foremost a permanent place in the history of scholarship. Smith also added that "*most ranking scholars had abandoned the quest as hopeless*," a statement which should tell us something about how difficult the task was.[51]

Moreover, because Wasson was such a mycophile (mushroom lover), might there have been an element, even if only just a tad, of attempting to fit the evidence to a prior and preconceived conclusion?[52] Needless to say, perhaps, Wasson has had his critics.

Contra Wasson

If Wasson's thesis found moderate support among Western scholars, including Smith, there has been far less sympathy toward his views from inside the tradition. When I queried American-born sadhu Baba Rampuri, who has been living among the psychedelic-savvy Naga Babas for the past 40 years, he confirmed what I already felt, although he took things quite a bit further:

"Wasson paid a couple of Sanskrit scholars (incl. Wendy O'Flaherity) to find amanita in the Vedas. His hypothesis is ridiculous. It makes no sense whatsoever to people, like myself, who actually know about these things. I WISH it were true!! It would be great! But all this research and writing was done by people who spent very little if any time in India, and people who have never even met a shaman, let alone took a trip with one. Wasson was very generous with Maria Sabina (he was a banker, you know), and he may have been very well informed about Mexican shamans, but certainly not Indian ones. I met him once, and he was a gentleman. But I'm afraid he and many others, especially today, miss the point. It's not the chemical formulas—it's the deities. And Dr. Hofmann knew this well, it just took him many years to come to grips with his first meeting with LSD."

Baba Rampuri at the 2008 World Psychedelic Forum
(sharing words with Alex Grey)

Rampuri's deeper concern here is essentially the same as the one he stressed at the 2008 World Psychedelic Forum in Basel, Switzerland, namely: how is it really possible for Western scholars to speak with any authority about a culture that is not their own and which they have not even experienced in any depth from within its fold?

Indeed, turning this question back on myself: how is it possible for me to write about yoga, and yoga's view of psychoactive plants from outside of the Indian tradition? To this, I can only answer that by letting the twain of speakers from both East and West meet within these pages I am simply attempting to let both sides speak for themselves and thereby allow the reader to reach their own conclusions.

Today there are Western-born Vedic scholars, like Dr. David Frawley (Vamadeva Shastri), who do know Indian culture intimately and are very highly regarded within both worlds. Frawley has also been one of the most vociferous spokespeople for the view that Western scholarship has greatly misunderstood and misrepresented Indian culture and tradition.

Dr. Frawley's view is that Soma is an umbrella term for many substances, including even water. His thesis is that it probably referred to several plants that were used sacramentally in Vedic times and afterwards. He sums up his research in this area as follows:

"My view—based upon more than thirty years of study of the Vedas in the original Sanskrit, as well as related Ayurvedic literature—is that the Soma plant was not simply one plant, though there may have been one primary Soma plant in certain times and places, but several plants, sometimes a plant mixture and more generally it refers to the sacred usage of plants. Soma is mentioned as existing in all plants (RV X.97.7) and many different types of Soma are indicated, some requiring elaborate preparations. Water itself, particularly that of the Himalayan rivers, is a kind of Soma (RV VII.49.4). In Vedic thought, for every form of Agni or Fire, there is also a form of Soma. In this regard, there are Somas throughout the universe. Agni and Soma are the Vedic equivalents of yin and yang in Chinese thought... Soma is also connected with marijuana, suggesting that mind-altering plants were regarded as different types of Soma." [53]

Dr. David Frawley

While Frawley does not rule out the possibility that *Amanita muscaria* may have been used after the Vedic period, he holds that *"the main Rig Vedic Somas were probably certain reed grasses, some of which do have nervine and nutritive properties."* [54] This, of course, would certainly argue against Wasson's notion that *Amanita muscaria* was *The* Soma of the Vedas.

Another highly regarded American-born Indologist and Ayurvedic physician, Dr. Robert Svoboda, has also suggested that Wasson's thesis misses the mark. In *Aghora*, Dr. Svoboda's fascinating exploration of Tantra, the author quotes his guru, Swami Vimalananda, as having said:

"The Rishis [great yogi seers] used to take Soma, which is a type of leafless creeper. Some people today think Soma was the poisonous mushroom Amanita muscaria, but that was also merely a substitute for the real thing. Only the Rishis know what the true Soma is, because only they can see it. It is invisible to everyone else." [55]

So, among those who are deeply acquainted with Hindu culture, spirituality, and scholarship, it appears that the claim that Soma was *Amanita muscaria*, as Wasson and others stated, simply does not hold water. Rampuri, Frawely, and Svoboda have all leveled arguments against such a claim, as have others from within the Indian tradition. Additionally, certain Western researchers outside of mainstream academic circles have challenged Wasson on this point, most notably the late Terence McKenna.

Amanita… or Psilocybin?

Not long after reading Smith and Wasson, I discovered McKenna's 1992 work, *Food of the Gods*, and found his critique of Wasson's thesis that Soma was *Amanita muscaria* very persuasive. Of course, being Terence McKenna, the Psilocybe champion bar none, he was willing to acknowledge that Wasson was *"brilliant in advancing the notion that a mushroom of some sort was implicated in the Soma mystery,"* he just wasn't convinced that mushroom was *Amanita*! It was Psilocybe Cubensis (aka "Magic Mushrooms"), of course.[56]

McKenna's main points are as follows:

1. *Amanita muscaria does not produce "a reliable ecstatic experience… the rapturous visionary ecstasy that inspired the Vedas… could not have possibly been caused by Amanita muscaria."*[57]

2. *Wasson himself considered the possibility that Soma was in fact Stropharia cubensis (Psilocybe cubensis), raising but not answering his own question: "Is Stropharia cubensis responsible for the elevation of the cow to a sacred status?" Which is a question that also came to my mind during my first experience with magic mushrooms. Other mycophiles have suggested this idea to me as well, in addition to the idea that Krishna's famous theophany in the 11th chapter of the Bhagavad Gita appears to bear strong resemblance*

to a psychedelic experience. McKenna suggests it was Wasson's aversion to the Hippie cult of psilocybin, including "self-styled psychiatrists" that he himself inspired, that would not allow him to accept such a conclusion.

3. Connected with this last point, Wasson appears to have avoided the obvious fact that Soma in the Vedas seems to be inextricably linked to cattle, particularly the bull, which makes sense for Stropharia cubensis because it grows on dung, but not for Amanita. McKenna doesn't say it, but I would answer Wasson's question by suggesting that it would certainly help explain the sacredness of the cow in India!

4. Perhaps the most damning evidence McKenna brings is a letter Wasson wrote to him which expressed doubt about his own thesis and seemed to favor Stropharia cubensis, a possibility which, McKenna notes, Wasson eventually contradicted.

Even given the amount of conjecture involved, McKenna certainly presents a very strong argument against Wasson's thesis, if not a completely compelling case in favor of *Stropharia cubensis*.

Terence McKenna

The tentative nature of all of these conjectures aside, what I find most compelling in *Food of the Gods*, is McKenna's overarching theory of the stages through which the human relationship to the Divine via Soma has been degraded over time.[58]

He proposes that there are four distinct stages to this devolution: 1) In the first stage, there was a substitute made for the original Soma, a substitute which is still a psychoactive plant, but a less potent one, such as Ephedra; 2) In the next stage of devolution, due perhaps to climactic changes, a completely inactive plant is substituted for the active one; 3) In the third stage, there are no plants whatsoever, and in their place are merely "esoteric teachings and dogma, rituals, stress on lineages, gestures, and cosmogonic diagrams," as we find in today's major world religions; 4) And finally, we have reached the fourth stage today in our modern secular West. A state in which we find ourselves in a "complete abandonment of even the pretense of remembering the felt experience of the mystery."[59]

While it is doubtful that such a hypothesis would carry much weight in mainstream academic circles, let alone those sympathetic to the Hindu tradition, McKenna does raise some interesting points. Key among them are questions as to why no one knows the original identity of the *Vedic Soma*, and why the use of Soma-like psychoactive substances in India has largely been downgraded to the status of "Left-Handed Tantra." The latter is considered a less-than-pure path to God, a province occupied primarily by *Shaivite* sadhus yogis who are followers of Shiva.

Could it be that the ritual ingestion of sacred plant extracts was what formed the basis of some major current world religions? Perhaps this may seem like a *conspiracy theory*, or revisionist history, but for a moment, let's entertain the possibility that we have been robbed of our spiritual birthright by doctrines and dogmas created and enforced by a *priestly caste*, rules and regulations that diminish and degrade the once sacred value of these natural plant admixtures. Is it possible that we have surrendered our power to this *priestly caste*: A human institution that has secured spiritual and physical power for itself at the expense of an opiate-intoxicated, and thus numbed, citizenry?

I hope it is clear that these are questions from the heart of this book. Here we are seeking answers to questions:

◎ Is a human Guru or other intermediary really necessary, or can sacred plant medicine be as good, if not better than a teacher?

◎ How is plant Samadhi the same or different than the Samadhi that comes through spiritual practices such as meditation, and can we say that one is higher or lower, worse or better than the other?

◉ Do psychoactive plant medicines "level the playing field," as McKenna and others have suggested, allowing each and every individual to find their own spiritual truth within themselves?

Such questions are directly connected to this whole debate over Soma. I touch upon them here in an attempt to make the reader aware of the deeper connections involved between yoga-induced expanded consciousness, and expanded consciousness achieved through the use of plant extracts.[60]

McKenna's Critique

An entire book could be written on McKenna alone in regard to the above questions, particularly relating to the period just prior to his life-changing trip to the Amazon basin with his brother Dennis in 1971. For, like so many young seekers of his generation, McKenna had first journeyed to Mother India in search of the divine.

Yet unlike many spirit-questers, McKenna came away disappointed. He expressed his feelings about India candidly on a number of occasions, not least his critique at the outset of his work *Food of the Gods*:

"I had traveled India in search of the miraculous. I had visited its temples and ashrams, its jungles and mountain retreats. But Yoga, a lifetime calling, the obsession of a disciplined and ascetic few, was not sufficient to carry me to the inner landscapes that I sought.

I learned in India that religion, in all times and places where the luminous flame of the spirit had guttered low, is not more than a hustle. Religion in India stares from world-weary eyes familiar with four millennia of priest craft. Modern Hindu India to me was both an antithesis and a fitting prelude to the nearly archaic shamanism that I found in the lower Rio Putomayo of Colombia when I arrived there to begin studying the shamanic use of hallucinogenic plants."[61]

On another occasion, McKenna put it like this:

"[Psychedelics] are democratic. They work for Joe Ordinary. And I am Joe Ordinary. I can't go and sweep up around the ashram for eighteen years or some rigmarole like that."[62]

This seems to have been a recurring theme for McKenna. Interviewing Ram Dass in the early '90s, he made a very similar point:

"The idea is not to come up with something that the best among us can make hay with, but a democratic... something that addresses the species. The thing that seemed to me so important about the psychedelic experience was that it happened to me... So I assumed that I am a very ordinary person, therefore if it happened to me, it could happen to anyone, and that's unquestionable."[63]

It's not clear if McKenna's issue was with the degradation of Indian religion, *per se*, or more his own, and by extension, most humans' unwillingness to submit to the long, hard discipline of a spiritual practice. He seemed to be conceding that the discipline of yoga alone could take you there, but why work that hard if we don't need to? So McKenna was asking: "Why take the ox cart when the hyper-space shuttle is available?" His concern was not just personal, but global. In the above interview, McKenna asks Ram Dass *"Do you think this* [the return back to *Source* consciousness] *can be done without psychedelics fast enough to have an impact on the global situation?"*

This dialogue between these two psychedelic pioneers is particularly interesting because of McKenna's skepticism of India's traditional religious doctrine and practices, and of gurus in particular. Most notably, McKenna was one of the chief critics of Ram Dass' story about nothing happening when Neem Karoli Baba took LSD; McKenna suggested that he had possibly palmed the dosage, or perhaps thrown it over his shoulder.[64]

At times McKenna may have overstated his case, but hyperbole aside, his critique of Indian religion is valuable because it causes us to keep our eyes open and to question what is happening right in front of our eyes, without any veil of spiritual devotion.

For those of us who haven't witnessed these things, it is reasonable and forgivable to ask whether "miracle stories" about yogis and saints are indeed just variations of a central "Big Lie"; Could a fog of ritual and spiritual devotion be put forth to dupe the masses? A lure to attract the spiritual seeker to some particular cult and then keep them in perpetual servitude?

In my own case with my guru Karunamayi, part of me was always wondering why I never had the amazing mystical experiences that others seemed to be having around me. Why wasn't I witnessing the miracles that I heard described hundreds of times? Was I *personally* blocked? Was I just not prepared for mystical experiences yet? Was it my negative karma that was preventing me from being privy to such amazing grace? Was this dark karma manifesting itself in the form of "sour grapes"? Or was it *Fear*?

I will not offer the fruit of my ponderings on these questions just yet, but simply affirm the wisdom of carefully considering and weighing every possibility and experience we encounter in life.

Soma—Still Kickin' After All These Years?

In a synchronistic way, not long after I wrote the above, a fellow yoga teacher gifted me Stanislav Grof's book, *When the Impossible Happens*. A book in which Grof speaks at length about… synchronicities! Grof also talks about his teacher, Swami Muktananda, describing some of the more remarkable "coincidences" that occurred between and around him.

It should be mentioned that synchronicity isn't a characteristic unique to Muktananda. We find this phenomenon associated with many Indian gurus. I myself experienced synchronicity too many times to count.

One notable synchronicity Grof recounted was that immediately prior to meeting Muktananda for the first time he had been speaking with his wife, Christina. He was describing to her how in the course of his LSD experiences he had some profound encounters with Shiva, all without ever having any prior conscious connection to this particular Hindu deity. Then, upon the occasion of meeting Muktananda he received a *darshan* from him, a blessing usually transmitted through a gaze. After looking at him long and hard, the first thing this heir to the tradition of Kashmir Shaivism said to him was: "I see that you are a man who has seen Shiva." Grof was impressed. So was I. But I remained cautious. Did the guru want to impress this highly respected psychologist? If so, why?

Grof goes on to relate some dialogue from that meeting which is particularly relevant to this discussion:

"I understand you have been working with LSD" said Muktananda. "We do something very similar here. But the difference is that in siddha yoga we teach people not only to get high, but to stay high. With LSD you can have great experiences, but then you come down. There are many serious spiritual seekers in India, Brahmans and yogis, who use sacred plants in their spiritual practice…"

He talked then about the need for a respectful ritual approach to cultivation, preparation, and smoking or ingesting Indian hemp… and criticized the casual and irreverent use… by the young in the west. "The yogis grow and harvest the plant very consciously and with great devotion."

In the course of the discussion, I asked Muktananda about Soma… mentioned more than a thousand times in the Rig Veda and that clearly played a critical role in Vedic religion. This sacrament was prepared from a plant of the same name, the identity which was lost over the centuries…

Talking about Soma Muktananda dismissed the theory that this plant was Amanita muscaria, the fly agaric mushroom. He assured me that Soma was not a mushroom but a 'creeper'. This seemed to make sense and did not particularly surprise me because another important item in the psychedelic pharmacopeia, the famous mesoamerican ololiuqui was a preparation containing the seeds of morning glory (ipomoea violacea), which would qualify as a creeper plant...

But what came as a surprise to me is what followed. Muktananda not only knew what Soma was, but he assured me that it was still being used in India to this very day. As a matter of fact, he claimed that he was in regular contact with Vedic priests who were using it in their rituals. And according to Baba some of these priests actually came every year down from the mountains to Ganeshpuri, a little village south of Bombay, to celebrate his birthday... Baba extended his invitation to Christina and me to visit his ashram at the time of his birthday and promised to make arrangements for us to participate in this ancient ritual.[65]

Stanislav Grof (right) with Fritjof Capra and Baba Muktananda

Intrigued, I contacted Dr. Grof to ask him whether he ever participated in the Soma ritual, and if so, what that was like? Dr. Grof told me that he never got a chance to participate in the ceremony. Then Muktananda passed in 1982 and Grof never pursued the subject further. However, more recently Grof told me of a Parsee woman friend who attended a ceremony in India where the priest said that the Haoma, which is the Zen Avesta name for *Soma*, is still used in Iran by the Parsees...[66]

While awaiting Dr. Grof's response, I got back in touch with one of my first and most influential teachers on the yoga path, Swami Satyananda Saraswati (whom I call "Swamiji," a term of affectionate respect, plus it's shorter!). I sent him the above passage and asked if he knew anything about the modern day Soma ritual to which Muktananda referred. Swamiji's response was quite interesting:

"*Yes. We were traveling in Maharashtra a few years ago, when we were invited to attend a large Vedic yajna being performed for the initiation of a Vedic Pathshalla or Sanskrit University. They were making ahutis, offerings to the sacred fire, with a substance they called Soma. They claimed that it was the real Soma, handed down by tradition through the generations.*

However, neither did the participants display any overt signs of enlightenment, nor did the members of our group who all participated in drinking the Soma, reflect any changes in their attitudes or behaviors. I, too, drank the Soma juice, and did not feel any different because of having partaken."

Swami Satyananda Saraswati's account leads me to doubt that the priests in question were using the original *Soma*. Perhaps they were using an inert, ritual stand-in?

As we have seen, any number of other psychoactive substitutes have claimed to be the elusive *Soma*, but if the original Vedic *Soma* were still in existence, surely it would have come to the attention of the scholarly community by now?[67]

Swamiji interestingly concluded his response to me with the words:

"*Therefore, I remain much more interested in the inner Soma—which we define as the nectar of Pure Devotion.*"

I can certainly attest to the power of the "nectar" of which Swamiji speaks, as I experienced it on numerous occasions while on tour with him and Shree Maa, a great woman saint from Bengal, in the late nineties.[68]

Swami Satyananda Saraswati and Shree Maa in Varanasi, India

The Inner Soma:
Khecarī Mudrā and the Remarkable Case of Prahlad Jani

Swamiji's words to me echo what we find elsewhere in the yoga tradition. As Swami Muktananda similarly told Grof: *"In siddha yoga we teach people not only to get high, but to stay high."* Clearly this is one of the most remarkable assertions of this entire quest; that through the practice of yoga alone, it is possible to live in a more heightened, blissful, peaceful, harmonious state most or even all of the time, rather than just when we are doing our spiritual practice or "under the influence" of one substance or another.

Dr. Frawley affirms this potentiality explaining in depth how the *"real Soma"* is a byproduct of yogic *sadhana*, or disciplined spiritual practice:

"…We must remember that the real Soma is a secretion in the brain from spiritual practices of Yoga, pranayama, mantra and meditation (an elixir prepared from the Tarpak Kapha or form of Kapha lubricating the nervous system in Ayurvedic thought). Soma at a yogic level refers to the crown chakra, which is opened by Indra (yogic insight) and releases a flood of bliss throughout the body. This inner Soma is the main subject of the Vedic hymns, though outer Somas were also important…"[69]

According to Dr. Frawley, *outer Somas*, like the psychoactive plant mixtures we are discussing here, may be helpful in preparing one for the *inner Soma*, a secretion produced in the brain as a byproduct of yogic sadhana. But these plant mixtures are still only that: an external means to this authentic *inner Soma*;

In light of a yogic practice mentioned in the 14*th* century yogic manual, the *Hatha Yoga Pradipika* (which translates as "Light on Hatha Yoga"), the brain secretion to which Frawley refers is worth noting. The practice is called Khecarī Mudrā (*kay-charee moo-drah*), and it is the unusual technique of cutting the *frenum linguii* of the tongue. This is done to allow the tongue to stretch back far enough into the throat cavity to seal it (some persons can do this without cutting).

The point of this unusual practice is to close off the "three paths," into the body, the olfactory (nose), ocular (eyes), and oral (mouth). Then, with the seeker's tongue blocking his throat exit, this same seeker is able to "catch" the nectar, or *amrit*, that is said to be secreted by the brain. Here it will be instructive to consider the relevant verses from the *Hatha Yoga Pradipika*:

(32–37) When the tongue is bent back into the gullet and the eyes are fastened upon the point between the eyebrows, this is khecari mudra. When the membrane below the tongue is cut, and the tongue is shaken and milked, one can extend its length until it touches the eyebrows. Then khecari mudra is successful.—Take a clean, shining knife and cut the breadth of a hair into the fine membrane that

connects the tongue with the lower part of the mouth [the froenum lignum]. Then rub that area with a mixture of salt and turmeric powder. After seven days again cut a hair's breadth. Follow this for six months. The membrane is then completely separated. When the yogi now curls his tongue upward and back he is able to close the place where the three paths meet. The bending back of the tongue is khecari mudra and [the closing of the three paths] is akasha chakra.

(38) The yogi who remains but half a minute in this position [with upturned tongue and imperturbable calm] is free from illness, old age and death.

(39) For him who masters this khecari mudra there will be no more [physical helplessness in bodily conditioned situations such as] illness, death, mental sluggishness, hunger, thirst, or cloudiness in thinking.

(40) He is free from [the laws of] karma and time has no power over him.

(41) The mudra is called khecari by the siddhas because the mind as well as the tongue remains in "ether" for the duration of the practice.

(42–43) Once he has closed the throat in khecari mudra he cannot be aroused by the most passionate embrace, and even if he were in the state of an ecstatic lover he still could negate the result through certain practices.[70]

(44) He who with upcurled tongue and concentrated mind drinks the nectar conquers death in his days—provided he masters yoga.

(45) The yogi who daily saturates his body with the nectar that flows from the "moon" is not harmed by poisons even when bitten by the snake Taskshaka.

(46) Just as fire burns as long as there is wood, as the lamp burns as long as the oil and the wick last, so also the life germ [jivan] remains in the body while it is regulated by the "beams of the moon"

(47–49) Daily he may "eat the flesh of the cow" and "drink wine," still he will remain a son of noble family.

(50–51) When it remains pressed in the throat passage, the tongue is able to receive the nectar "beams of the moon," which are [simultaneously] salty, hot, and pungent, but also like milk, honey, and ghee. Then all diseases are eliminated, and also old age. Thus he will be able to teach all the Vedas and the Shastras; and he has power to attract the damsels of the siddhas.[71]

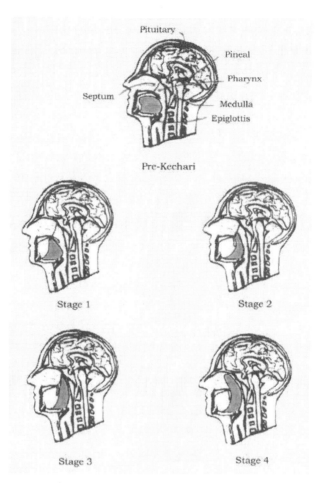

The Stages of Khechari Mudra[72]

Early on in my yoga practice I recall being fascinated by a point made by one of the four women teachers I had the pleasure to meet in '96, Mata Amritanandamayi, who is popularly and affectionately known as "Ammachi," or "The Hugging Saint." Ammachi explained that this is what is meant in the Hindu scriptures when it says the gods quaffed nectar: it is a completely internal process of drinking this brain secretion.[73]

The story Ammachi was referring to is the Puranic tale of how gods and demons churned the "Ocean of Milk" in order to get the "nectar of immortality," which is *amrita*, or *Soma*.[74]

In his commentary to the *Hatha Yoga Pradipika*, Hans-Ulrich Rieker makes the following interpretive remarks regarding the puranic mythology:

"We recall the legend of the churning of the ocean of milk where from this ocean, with the aid of the world mountain, the nectar of life was to be produced. The mountain

of the world, so we learned, is, in the human universe, the spinal column, the carrier of the life centers. The snake, wound around the mountain, is Kundalini, the potential divine force of nature. The gods who pulled on one end symbolize the higher life forces; the demons on the other end represent sheer physical forces. The tortoise that support-ed the mountain is the power of yoga, of divine origin and universal. But what is the ocean of milk, and what is the nectar?...

We hear at the beginning that the kapha current of the life force is called nectar (Soma)... The cosmology of the "Puranas," the ancient Indian garland of legends (and a treasure trove of the secret teachings, if one knows how to read it) tells us that the ocean of milk lies between the Isles of Shaka and Pushkara (Bhagavata Purana V, 20). Shaka is the mythological name for ajna chakra, between the eyebrows, and Pushkara that of the sahasrara chakra at the crown of the head. Between these two centers lies the ocean of milk, the source of the nectar. That is where the kapha current originates.

This shows that kapha, the nectar, is not just any kind of secretion, for the primary functional and structural elements cannot be delineated so simply. True, the expla-nation that the inversion of the tongue diverts the kapha current, i.e. the biological process of evolution (or at least part of it) is not evident; we have to accept this as a given fact. Irregularities in the course of this current or process, which as a rule lead to illness, are produced at will and utilized for positive purposes. Through supreme spirituality, a physical process is transmuted into a spiritual one.

No one can tell what this fluid is, if indeed it is a fluid. Is it a glandular secretion? Possibly. Most likely, yes. But this should not tempt us to make fruitless speculations. In any case, the tip of the upcurled tongue touches a point on the mucous membrane and through this touch some process of endocrine secretion is altered....

You may think as you like about khecari mudra, you may consider the matter of the "nectar" naive or ridiculous; the fact remains that there are countless yogis who can take even large quantities of deadly poisons without any harm to their bodies. This fact has been verified by medical authorities." [75]

This is certainly an amazing claim: Yogis being able to consume poison and survive. Although this may be accepted by India researchers, it has not been verified in the West. Nevertheless, throughout the relevant literature there are numerous anecdotal accounts of this phenomenon, such as the following fascinating paren-thetical "addendum" to Ram Dass' story about giving LSD to Neem Karoli Baba (aka "Maharajji"):

"I once told one of Maharajji's Indian devotees the story about giving Maharajji the acid and he said to me, 'That's nothing.' He told me that a couple of years before, a sadhu had come to see Maharajji. In India, some sadhus take arsenic for devotional

purposes. They take tiny, tiny amounts of it, and in those doses it's not lethal, but instead it acts like a psychedelic; it gets you high. This sadhu was carrying something like a two-year supply of arsenic, which would be a lethal dose for maybe ten people. Maharajji said to the sadhu, 'Where's your arsenic?' The sadhu said, 'Oh, Maharajji, I don't have any arsenic.' Maharajji said, 'Give me your arsenic!' The sadhu fished around in his dhoti and handed over the packet. Majarajji opened it up and swallowed the whole thing. Everyone started to cry and wail… and nothing happened."[76]

Although this is certainly a compelling, well-told story, it is impossible to verify. Yet, what about all the yogis who have submitted themselves to the rigors of scientific scrutiny and monitoring? Is there any hard evidence to support the miraculous reports of India's "holy men"?

One of the oldest claims made by yogis is breatharianism. This is the claim that they live on *prana*, or life force, alone.

From the above description of *khechari mudra* it would seem there would be no need to consume foodstuffs if one was living on the nectar of *kapha*. Such has been the claim recently of an 82-year-old yogi named Prahlad Jani, who says that he has not partaken of food or drink for the past 70 years. How does he do this? He maintains that he was blessed by a goddess at the age of 8, and now, *"I get the elixir of life from the hole in my palate, which enables me to go without food and water."*

The "elixir" the yogi refers to is of course none other than the mystical *amrita* we have been discussing. When doctors at Sterling Hospital in Ahmedabad were able to study Jani for 10 days in the summer of 2010, they were apparently very favorably impressed. But others remain critical, arguing that many yogis have made such a claim, but none has ever proven these long term fasting claims under rigorous laboratory conditions.[77] What is most interesting is that the doctors who studied Jani have yet to verify his claim of having a hole in his palate, which would seem to be an easy feature to identify.[78]

Whether Jani's claim is true or not, my purpose is to understand the yogic view of how *Soma*, which is also referred to as *amrita* or *kapha*, is produced within the body as a brain secretion through the practice of yoga.[79]

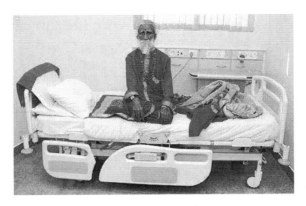

Prahlad Jani at Sterling Hospital in Gujarat, 2010

Maharishi on Soma

Could it be that there is some middle ground between those who say that the real *Soma* is a plant admixture, and those who maintain that it is alchemized in the body via the catalyst of yogic practices?

Since our first phone conversation, Edward (who we met in Chapter 1) and I had been exchanging emails every day, sending each other work we've written, suggesting interesting books, relevant websites, etc.[80] One day Edward sent me a fascinating artifact. It was an item which only came to light in December, 2008, after gathering dust in an archive for over four decades: An audio file of a question and answer session at the 1966 Kumbha Mela festival in Allahabad, India, wherein Maharishi Mahesh Yogi was seriously questioned as to the value of psychedelics in regard to "transcendental consciousness."

The meeting with the Maharishi (his name means "Great Seer," the rishis being the yogis of Vedic times) begins with queries from the mainly British audience about meditation and the meaning of the Sanskrit word "*tapas*," often translated as "austerity." After some discussion about this, one woman in the audience finally gathers the courage to ask:

"Would this be a good time to talk about how psychedelic drugs work?"

The woman goes on to explain why she's asking:

"The fact is that you don't have this problem in Germany, but we have it in Canada and the United States...

Strait-laced students are taking LSD and mescaline drugs and enjoying the dreams and hallucinations they have, and I know from what Maharishi has said, that it's only a dream or hallucination, but I'm interested in going into what part of the nervous system is triggered that it produces this dream or hallucination?"

It's clear from the Maharishi's reply that he doesn't have any more knowledge of this subject than his audience, who all seem to be familiar with Aldous Huxley's groundbreaking work on the psychedelic experience, "*The Doors of Perception.*"

Maharishi's first response is that because such drugs as LSD and mescaline do not produce "transcendental consciousness" to any lasting degree, they are not "acceptable" substitutes for yogic discipline. At one point in the discussion, Maharishi even goes so far as to say, playing on the famous phrase of William Blake and later used by Huxley, that these drugs cause a *retardation of perception... and that can only be the closing of the gates of perception.*"

Yet some audience members are persistent: "Wait," they say, "Huxley's experience on mescaline was certainly transcendental, and there's a London pediatric physician who has been successfully using a potentized homeopathic form of mescaline with wonderful results...?"

This leads the Maharishi to ultimately make the following concession:

"We could accept that there could be some drugs which could influence the nervous system to reflect real transcendental consciousness. It could be possible... the possibility exists. Only we say that from the effect that we hear—from these mescalines and such things as are known today—they don't seem to meet the requirement... Otherwise there could be medicines which could set up the nervous system to that level... And when that consciousness is achieved, it would be real transcendental consciousness which will transform the life of a man, as is done through meditation."

An objection is raised:

"But if transcendental consciousness is produced by a drug—an external influence—would that have the same culturing effect as yogic discipline?"

The Maharishi thinks this a good question, and he agrees, but interestingly, he holds fast to his new view, expanding it as follows:

"...there could be that gradual application of the medicine, so that as the mind keeps on retiring from the gross and becoming more subtle and more subtle, naturally all those intermediary steps are naturally fulfilled... The use of that could also be to that value. There could be that manner of taking that drug could such like that like that like that... So if it is done in this way, then we could accept the possibility of transcendental consciousness through drugs."

Q: *"Could meditation produce from inside something similar to what the drug does from outside?"*

Maharishi: *"Right. It may be that always changing self and this, this, this... always changing... it gets surcharged with such an element being produced in that state, that the decay stops. In order to stop the decay, there must be some chemical change in the body—has to be. So when that consciousness is gained, simultaneously some element must be produced, some chemical must be produced all over the body which will disallow decay..."*

Q: *"Yes, and that's why Soma is called the drinking of eternal life..."*

M: *"Mmm, if Soma is that, then we could accept that—then that Soma Rasa is produced in every stroke of transcendental consciousness. Then the saying that they used to drink Soma Rasa means that they used to meditate and gain the Samadhi."*

Q: *"Or it could also be thought that they really found something to drink as chemical also..."*

M: *"Yes, as chemical also, as a drug also."*

Q: *"Isn't that the next logical step, when this meditation is lost and this Kali Yuga goes deeper and deeper, that there will be something still simpler, still more mechanical than this meditation and that will be the next thing: the drug..."*

M: *"But then... the knowledge to use the drug properly would be by far greater difficulty than learning this meditation [laughter]."*

To summarize and clarify what is being said here: The Maharishi is suggesting that, in theory, there could be a plant substance, or a drug, a *"Soma Rasa,"* which could produce a lasting "transcendental consciousness," *even if this substance had to be taken on a regular basis to continue to produce this effect.* Now, this drug does not seem to be LSD or mescaline or anything specifically known at that time by Maharishi, but is a hypothetical substance. However, when asked if this substance that he describes as *"Soma"* might be what the ancient Vedic rishis (or *seers*) drank to "see" and hear the Vedic hymns, Maharishi (the "Great Seer," recall) answers affirmatively. Note also that for the Maharishi this *Soma* is something that the body itself could produce both *in response to* activation by an external substance, *and by* a discipline like meditation. Theoretically, then, this drug could produce the same biochemical changes in the body as meditation.

This is simply an amazing admission on Maharishi's part, even if it is a hypothetical one. And it clearly brings to the fore the issue that meditation is obviously not a one-shot deal for most and must be practiced again and again to receive the fullest benefit. If so, why is this different from ingesting a substance on a continual basis?

We must keep in mind that all this was being discussed in 1966, before LSD was declared illegal in the USA. So these comments were made before the government's official "war on drugs" began, and the ensuing paranoia struck deep into the culture. In any case, keep in mind this was all very much a hypothetical discussion. Not long after making these comments, Edward told me, Maharishi required that anyone taking his meditation program be "clean" and off drugs for at least 2 weeks prior to beginning. So, far from being an endorsement of psychedelics, the underlying meaning of Maharishi's comments on *Soma* need to be emphasized: he was advocating for meditation, not drugs.

I appreciate the Maharishi's openness to the possibility of a transcendent consciousness produced by a drug, but this was clearly not a path that he was promoting, or even recommending.

But for us, here and now, we can take what the Maharishi said so long ago, and apply it to the currently burgeoning examination of psychoactive plant derivatives and their relationship with the spiritual quest. In particular, we will now turn our lens on DMT (Dimethyltryptamine), a substance produced naturally in the body, and which therefore *may* be the mysterious link between psychoactive plants, such as Ayahuasca, and spiritual practices, such as meditation.

Soma & Ayahuasca

In the mid-Sixties when the above dialogue with the Maharishi took place, Ayahuasca and DMT were not very well known. Certainly not as well known as the "designer" psychedelics in those days: LSD, psilocybin, and mescaline.

Since that time, there has been speculation regarding how DMT might play a crucial role in spiritual experience, most notably in the work of Terence McKenna and Dr. Rick Strassman. Dr. Strassman has the distinction of being the first scientist to be awarded government-financed research on psychedelics since such funding was cut off in the Sixties.

McKenna was one of the first to suggest that *Soma* might just have been an Ayahuasca-like brew, similar to the one used today in the Amazon basin. After the *S. cubensis* mushroom, which was McKenna's first choice for *Soma*, he warmed to *Pegamum Harmala* (Syrian Rue), found abundantly in northern India.[81]

Syrian Rue is both psychoactive and a MAO inhibitor. McKenna speculates that Syrian Rue might just have been combined with a DMT-containing plant, perhaps the giant river reed *Arundo donax*, for example. Together Syrian Rue and Arundo donax emulate a chemical concoction very much like that of Amazonian Ayahuasca. So, once again Ayahuasca and *Soma* are found to be linked at the molecular level. Perhaps that is why so many people on spiritual quests, many of them yoga practitioners, are currently ingesting plant mixtures under the guidance of experienced shamans.[82]

McKenna refers to are what are known as "Ayahuasca analogues," a subject not completely academic to me, as we have already seen in Chapter 2. On several occasions I explored the most well-known of these analogues, *Jurema*. Jurema is a combination of Pegamum Harmala and Mimosa Hostilis root bark. These experiences were, without a doubt, the most profound of my life, ecstatic and in some cases terrifying, on one occasion resulting in a full "ego-death" experience. I can certainly see how this particular concoction, or something like it, might have been the original *Soma*.[83]

Dr. Strassman has acknowledged that his DMT research was partly influenced by McKenna's.[84] Dr. Strassman' first FDA study was at the University of New Mexico where he was a tenured Associate Professor of Psychiatry. The study involved reporting the effects of intravenous injections of DMT into willing participants: about 400 doses to 65 participants in 5 years. Strassman has since published his findings in two very widely read and discussed books.[85]

Dr. Rick Strassman

One of Strassman's central and most influential theories in *The Spirit Molecule* is the concept that our pineal gland contains an endogenous DMT created *within* the body, or what Dr. Strassman interestingly refers to as "Soma Pinoline."

Dr. Strassman's theorizes that when internal production/supply of DMT is increased through any number of external influences, such as meditation, breathwork, or even an injection of DMT; the pineal gets flooded with DMT and the result is what is referred to as a "mystical experience."

DMT is similar to the neurotransmitter, serotonin, a brain chemical involved in feelings of well-being. Do Serotonin and DMT target the same receptor sites in the brain? Could this naturally occurring pineal DMT be the exact spot we need to look for an answer on how we might link the "inner" and "outer" *Soma*?[86] Could it be that a DMT-containing brew, perhaps an "analogue" of Ayahuasca was the original *Soma* that stimulated the creation of this endogenous DMT, Strassman's *Soma Pinoline*?

Dr. Strassman seems convinced that it is not the external *Soma* which is of primary concern here, but rather the context and intention (Leary's "set and setting") of the person who consumes it.

In a mid-'90s interview, he said the following about using Ayahuasca in a religious setting:

"In Brazil, I met and spent some time with members of the Uniao de Vegetal, an Ayahuasca-using church. Ayahuasca, as you know, is a combination of two plants, one of which contains DMT, and the other contains a compound that allows DMT to become orally active. Thus, it is a 3 to 5 hour, slow onset, slow offset, DMT experience. Their ceremonies were beautiful, moving, emotionally cleansing, and spiritually uplifting. The members were kind, the elders were powerful, wise, and inspiring. The Ayahuasca was an integral part of their ceremonies. However, I don't believe the psychedelic brew informed the church. I think it was the other way around: the church fashioned the psychedelic experience. Or if you still want to believe that there is free-standing information that comes from DMT, and not from the person who takes it, I will put it another way. The church setting maximized the chances that one would selectively receive certain types of information 'from' the DMT.

The tea powered and strengthened the processes that could have taken place without the tea; it was jet fuel, rather than weak coffee. Put weak coffee into a 747, and you stay on the ground; put in jet fuel, and away you go. The tea increased emotions, suggestibility, and heightened thought processes, but the information, rules, teaching and ethics came from the people, not the drug. In the triad: drug, set and setting; the one that is least important, or most dispensable, is drug. The UDV church experience made this point even clearer to me."

This suggests that it is the belief system and tradition that is the prime directive force behind the Ayahuasca experience, and that the plant brew itself only serves to help reveal that to the participant.

This may be true, yet Ganga White, who authored *Yoga Beyond Belief*, has suggested that it is important to let the plants speak for themselves as much as humanly possible, uncolored by any pre-set human belief systems. Or, as he put it to me, "letting the plants communicate and open doorways without overly pre-programming the journey." White's view comes after years of working directly with the Unaio de Vegetal church, participating in conferences and summits in Brazil and the US.[87] He is open to the possibility that such "plant teachers" were the primary inspiration for some of the world's religions, including what we now know as "Hinduism." If this is so, then we might well ask if it is fact that psychoactive plant brews like Ayahuasca are actually "teaching" humanity something, or are they simply revealing what is already in the mind?

The Way Out as the Way In

Oh, East is East, and West is West,
and never the twain shall meet,
Till Earth and Sky stand
presently at God's great Judgment Seat;
But there is neither East nor West,
Border, nor Breed, nor Birth,
When two strong men stand face to face,
tho' they come from the ends of the earth!

—Rudyard Kipling

The principal question this book seeks to clarify is whether psychoactive plants might be an aid to the yoga practitioner seeking spiritual union. Is it possible to see plant medicine and yoga not as an either/or proposition, but as a both/and possibility?

Over the millennia, of all the cultures in the world, India has clearly demonstrated perhaps the greatest tolerance of diversity and religious freedom, absorbing and incorporating countless cultures, philosophies, and creeds into its fold. There is a tentative and uneasy acceptance of its Shaivite *Soma* users, to be sure, but they are still part of Mother India's greater family, and have no fear of legal repercussions for their approach to the divine.

I once saw this tradition of openness and tolerance at work at a public *darshan* when Karunamayi was pointedly asked whether the path of Hatha Yoga alone could lead one to *moksha*, or liberation.

At first Amma's answer seemed an evasive and roundabout way of saying "no," which is consistent with how many traditional Indian saints and gurus respond to this question. But, when pressed by the persistent questioner, Karunamayi finally did give her blessing to the possibility that Hatha Yoga alone could lead to moksha, and the issue was dropped.

I have no idea what Karunamayi would say about our subject at hand—it would seem to be more of a stretch for her to allow the kind of uses of plant material on discussion here! But I will note the following observation: I had the opportunity to spend time at Karunamayi's forest ashram in Penusila, located right outside the same forest where she spent a decade meditating and performing other austerities. One day Amma led us on a tour through the forest, lovingly explaining to us the properties and uses of every plant, flower, and tree along the way. I can only wonder the extent to which use of these plants played a role in her own *sadhana*…[88]

We can also see this tradition of tolerance in the fascinating dialogue with the Maharishi, quoted above. At first, Maharishi's inclination was to say "no" to the question of whether drugs could be a path to God, but when pressed and offered a well-reasoned argument, he opened up to at least a "hypothetical" possibility that a *Soma*-like substance could be used as a disciplined spiritual practice over a period of time.

More recently, Dr. Frawley has also echoed this tradition of "accommodation." As he put it to me when I asked him in general about how Yoga views the use of psychedelics:

"Intoxicants may be helpful on an outer level for some yoga practitioners, particularly to open them up to higher possibilities. Many ancient and tribal cultures have their sacred plants that can be used for such purposes."

Thus, Frawley's view is that plant materials are permissible if they are used as a sacramental tool, but that they are only that—a tool to help the inward process—and should not be mistaken for being more than that.

This does not appear to be a universally shared perspective among more traditional yoga teachers, even among Western-born seekers as is Frawley. Take Swami Satyananda Saraswati, for example, who was born in California and lived for much of the Sixties in the USA. He takes a far more uncompromising view of external additives, a view that seems more consistent with what other traditional teachers have said. As Swamiji wrote to me recently,

"Once we understand the nature of the various levels of consciousness, and we are sincere in our desire for that experience, then there is no other need of external stimulation in order to attain that experience. Once we have proved that existence, then all that is required is the will to enter into that state of awareness and the knowledge of how to shift our consciousness. No physical substance will take us there.

An external substance creates a dependency. Sadhana promotes freedom; freedom through discipline—not freedom from discipline.

I do not take nor promote the use of psychedelics. Sadhu means efficient—someone who has become so efficient at doing whatever he or she does, that they need not repeat the experience again.

Ingesting an external substance almost invariably inspires us to try to repeat the experience, to take the substance again. Meditation enhances spiritual power, empowers us to pay attention, creates efficiency, so that whatever we chose to do, we can perform with minimum mistakes, with proper utilization of energy and resources, without wasting time, and at some point we can look back on life and say I am proud of the contributions I have been privileged to offer to make this world a better place because of my having been here.

When we pay attention, we learn. When we pay attention, we respect. When we pay attention, we love. When we pay attention, we worship. Meditation is the cultivation of the skills by which we pay attention. By practicing meditation, we learn how to learn, we learn how to respect, we learn how to love, we learn how to worship.

No external substance will grant us such empowerment."

A powerful statement, and no doubt true for those with a high level of discipline, fervor, and focus. This is for the spiritual seeker prepared to commit himself 108% to the rigors of the yoga path, and only that path.

But what of the average "John Does" of our world? McKenna's crowd of "Everyman" among whom he numbered himself? And what of all of the Sixties youths who initially got into yoga through the use of psychedelics?

Isn't all yogic *practice* by definition a repetitive, every day application, whether asana, meditation, or breathwork? Ganga White made just this point in a recent essay, "Yoga and Psychedelics," published in MAPS:

" I mainly want to suggest that many of the arguments against psychedelics have as much validity, or the lack thereof, when aimed back toward organized religion. I heard a Zen master once lecture that if psychedelics provided authentic awakening or spiritual experience, one would not ever have to approach them again. This is a common point of view. I would ask why the same isn't said of the Zen cushion or approaching the Zen master or guru? Is wisdom and realization a destination we arrive at, or a constant journey in ever unfolding possibility? If it is an ongoing process, a journey of constant vigilance, awakening and reawakening, then tune ups, from life, from teachers or plant friends are welcome along the way."

McKenna's rant-response to the same issue is characteristically humorous (but *not* tongue-in-cheek):

"People say, 'Don't you think you ought to be able to do it 'on the natch?'"[i.e., without the use of plants] And I love this question because the answer is: No, you can't do it 'on the natch.' That's the entire message of the last 10,000 years of human history. The self is insufficient. The ego will not suffice… you must humble yourself to the point where you admit that you can't do it without the help from someone whose idea of a good time is growing in a cow flop."

This is an interesting twist on the idea that "you can't do it alone, you need a guru;" in McKenna's world, you need a plant!

On a more serious note, Dr. Strassman was expelled from the Zen Buddhist monastery with which he had a relationship for nearly 2 decades over issues surrounding his research with psychedelics. This was particularly surprising given the care and sensitivity with which he had approached the subject; not to mention the fact that Dr. Strassman was far from advocating drug use, and often seriously questioned their value. Consider Dr. Strassman's words in the following interview from that time:

"If drugs are to have any use at all (and this is by no means a given), they should be part of an overall life dedicated to self-knowledge and a more compassionate life. This partakes of the perennial question: do drugs have spiritual/religious import?"

Strassman continues, echoing Huston Smith's point that it is "traits" not "states" that are to be considered primary:

"How many of us really are willing to take the next step, and live a life fully informed and influenced by the psychedelic experience? Very few, and those who do, generally stop taking psychedelics..." [89] [90]

That said, Dr. Strassman still acknowledged that under certain conditions and for a certain kind of person, a psychedelic experience might be of value:

"Dedicated Buddhist practitioners with little success in their meditation, but well along in moral and intellectual development, might benefit from a carefully timed, prepared, supervised, and followed-up psychedelic session to accelerate their practice. Psychedelics, if anything, provide a view that—to one so inclined—can inspire the long, hard work required to make that view a living reality."

Perhaps the exact same statement might also apply to the dedicated yoga practitioner?

*For more information on Soma please visit "Yoga & Psychedelics: A Select, Interpretive Chronology" on page 352 for "A Select, Interpretive Chronology"

4

Who I Am: Part 1

Autobiography of a "Gen-X" Yogi

From childhood's hour I have not been
As others were; I have not seen
As others saw; I could not bring
My passions from a common spring.

—Edgar Allan Poe, Alone

My Bally 'n' Me

I am 4 years old and on the beach with my family in Atlantic City, New Jersey. It is summertime, 1974, and the beach is crowded with vacationers. My three older brothers are in the ocean, playing, and my mother and father are relaxing on two inflatable rafts on the sand, somewhere nearby. I am alone by myself, throwing a tennis ball up into the air.

I've been tossing the ball up and down and catching it for some time, and now suddenly I get this great notion to throw the ball up as high as I can. I give it my best underhand throw and see it go way up, and then, to my amazement... stick in sky! I see it, my yellow tennis ball, just there above me, as if the sky has caught the ball and is holding it. Whaaa?

Now, though I am of tender age, I have learned enough about the laws of physics to understand that this is a highly unusual event. I run over to where my parents are resting and excitedly tell them what has happened to my "bally." They listen to me, and then laugh, remarking on how cute I am. "You were just seeing the moon," they say.

Later, I tell my brothers about what happened, and they, too, laugh. For a long time after that, whenever we see a full moon, everyone kids me, saying, "Hey A., look, there's your bally!" I laugh along with them, but I also feel put down—I know what I saw...

I begin this autobiographical section with the above story because I find it expresses, in microcosm, a dynamic between myself and my family that played itself out on numerous occasions over the years. The dynamic is essentially that I would have some kind of unusual experience like the one related above, and then not be believed or fully understood. As a result, I began to have a sense of being "different."

In the case of the story above, from my perspective now, 3 and a half decades later, I'm open to all possibilities—maybe it *was* the moon that I saw; or maybe in the process of throwing the ball up, I entered an altered state of consciousness (ASC); or it could be I had looked into the sun and was seeing spots… Whatever the explanation for what happened, it doesn't matter, because I'm more concerned here with what it felt like to me at that moment, and with the interplay between my family and myself. And the truth is: I was already different to begin with.

Without becoming too speculative, I wonder if when children receive messages such as this, they are less likely to have such magical experiences. And I wonder, in my own case, if this was perhaps a pivotal event in my childhood that dampened my natural connection to other realities…

Who Am I?

I thought to begin this book with a personal retrospective, because it seems so essential to get at who I am (on the level of "personality") and why I've been passionately exploring these deep, existential questions all through my life, starting from a very early age. I also see that people who have gotten to know me also have wondered about me. "Who is this guy?" is a thought that crosses their minds. "Why does he seem so different? And how *does* he do those things with his body? He's 40 years old? He looks like he's in his mid-to-late Twenties…"

I wonder these things myself. Why do I seem to be different? Why do I seem to have "God on the brain"? Why have I been so driven in certain areas of my life?

As I've looked around me more, I've recognized that, yes, I'm a rather strange bird, but I'm not the only one. There are other dreamers and freaks like me, many of them my kindred yoga peers. We may be a minority, but there are many others whose lives have had a similar trajectory as my own. Perhaps there is at least one in each family group, an individual who feels a certain calling of Spirit, let's say, a Prophet in their own lands. They go through a period of trial and tribulation in their early years, a period of incubation and gestation, to emerge later from the chrysalis as spiritual guides and teachers. We'll meet some of them later in the book, and we'll wonder together about all of this.

The Estrangement

Despite what I wrote about my family dynamic, my childhood was a pretty charmed one. Yes, overall there was a preponderance of love and caring and good times in our family—we had a lot of happy moments as a family unit of mom, dad, grandma, and four fun-loving, rambunctious little guys. I, for one, didn't want it to end, and actually never thought it would. In my innocence, I just took it for granted that we'd always be together and live happily ever after.

But, alas and of course, the fairy tale did come to a cataclysmic, crashing halt when my parents went through what was for me a very ugly and traumatizing separation, and eventually, divorce. The year was 1981. In that same devastating year, age 11, I hit puberty. As fascinating and exciting as that was on a certain level, it was also deeply disturbing and even shocking to be entering this new world where, just because of my adolescent appearance, I was no longer being treated as this cute little guy, but now as something else entirely.

Literally overnight, people just began to treat me differently, especially my peers who would not go through the same maturation process for 2-3 years. Suddenly girls would go "Ewww!" whereas before they would flirt or just treat me like one of the boys. People had no problem commenting on my newfound gawkiness. I recall one girl saying to her friend right in front of me as if I weren't there, "Yuck, he's so greasy!" Another time a kid from a couple grades up came right up to me in the hall, pointed his finger at me and said quite matter-of-factly, "Geek," and walked on.

I don't know why I took this all so hard and to heart, but I did. It marked the beginning of a withdrawal from the world into introversion and introspection, which manifested itself as a painful shyness due to feelings of inferiority. Suddenly I felt as if there must be something dreadfully wrong with me, and me alone. My family situation didn't help. I blamed myself on some level for the war that was unfolding, partly because the blame was passed around by family members.

I realize that many adolescents go through this "awkward" stage, yet not all adolescents retreat within themselves as a result. Rather, many find a peer group through which they learn to make some sense of their teenage angst. I did not choose that course, though, and without a support group, I had very little recourse to comprehending the rapid changes my body and consciousness were undergoing. As a result, there was a part of me that began to reject the world now for rejecting me, and feel a deep longing to return to the paradise of childhood's carefree simplicity.

A Seminal Discovery…

Now, it was just around this time that I made an important discovery that many young boys and girls with raging hormones make. Well, maybe if someone had told me about it, I would have discovered it a lot earlier! But because I had really no one to talk to about these things, I just unearthed it on my own one night. (You know all those wet dreams? Well I can do the same thing without having a dream!) After that, like most boys, I was hooked. At that point, I really didn't have the sense that there was anything really wrong with it. It brought me pleasure (more than anything else, even my guitar), so it couldn't be that bad, my pre-rational mind figured.

Yet as I grew increasingly dorky looking, I began to wonder if perhaps there might be some connection to masturbation, my sorry appearance, and social decline. Could it be…? I began to get superstitious almost… Maybe…? Keep in mind, at the tender age of 13, I knew nothing of Victorian ethics, and perhaps I was only vaguely aware of any Christian puritanical teachings on the subject. On the fringes of my consciousness were slightly older adolescent male terms of derogation like "jack off" and "jerk off," and later, a classic Bill Cosby segment on the subject (he discovered it much as I had, and probably as most boys do); but beyond that, I was really just putting two and two together—somehow my current geek status seemed to be connected to orgasm.

So I tried to get off the onanistic kick for a while and see what would happen. And it wasn't long before things seemed to shift. People were noticing, and not just people—girls were noticing. So I knew I was onto something. When I quit masturbating for a while, my complexion seemed to change, and I even felt a certain power in my body. I noted that, for example, my athletic abilities improved. Even though I didn't even have the concepts or vocabulary yet, I felt almost, dare I say, god-like when I refrained from "it."

The only sticking point, of course, was the fact that eventually I would again succumb to the old habit. It might be months or even a year or more, but for all of my teens and even up until my mid-Twenties, I struggled with this whole issue. Had I allowed myself to actually be sociable and have a girlfriend, perhaps things would have been different. But as it was, I was on this crazy pendulum swinging from hedonism to asceticism and back.

Psycho

By the tender age of 14, I was entering a period where I basically disdained everything and, like the kid in the movie "Little Miss Sunshine," was rapidly becoming a Nietzschean ubermensch (without having read any of the German philosopher—it filtered through by way of the Jim Morrison bio "No One Here Gets Out Alive"). That summer, I impulsively decided I was giving up everything: music, masturbation, meat and most other food, friends, television… I had been living with my mother and grandmother and moved back to live with my father and eldest brother. Essentially I was becoming an ascetic, without knowing what that was. I "flagellated" myself (as my father put it), eschewed anything "soft," and became almost hyper-masculine, making up for the few years when I had no male role model. My dad sometimes commented that I looked like I was carrying the world on my shoulders, and I was in denial then, but he was right.

I had been so into my electric guitar since my parents' separation, and had a beauty—a jet black Gibson Les Paul Custom (BB King's "Lucille") that my mother had bought me when my guitar teacher saw how precocious and serious I was. That summer I had attended an exclusive music camp in Maine, but now I just stuck my black beauty in the closet, not to take it out again for years. Music was for the soft, my world had no need for it. I was a rock, an island unto myself. Same with my two closest friends—I just stopped talking to them completely. They were weak; they were uncool. So they were out of my life, and one of them has never forgiven me.

I started running, long distance running, of course. I didn't just run though, I ran as hard as I could every time, as if my life depended on it. Pacing? Pacing oneself was for wimps. I gave it my all, or not at all. I did join the track and cross country teams, which was a compromise, but I kept to myself—kept the loner thing going, hardly ever speaking to my teammates, who clearly wondered what I had stuck up my ass.

At this point, I ran partly because I loved the feeling when I was done (I was in the early stages of addiction), but found the actual training tortuous. Races were the worst. I would literally go over the race a hundred times in my head, nearly paralyzed with fear and trembling. Years later I would see that same look in the face of a young kid who was preparing for a competition—that narrow, tunnel vision look that revealed an unimaginable terror-ridden angst. I was essentially seeing myself as I had looked like at his age. I felt for him.

I also ran because I was driven to be better, to perfect myself. To be superhuman? I think that was it, though I don't know that I ever really thought of it in those terms. If someone had put it in terms of uncovering my innate divinity, I probably wouldn't have understood what that meant. But I could certainly understand the superhero concept. I wanted to transcend anything human, and at the same time, I wanted to be recognized for it too. Being acknowledged, being seen, of course, was one of the big things that drove me, and paradoxically, it's what made me push people away too. There were times when I even considered suicide, if only because then I thought however delusional, that I would be understood at last; no matter that once deceased, "I" would probably never have any idea of it to rejoice at the victory.

To a certain degree, I was recognized and respected, but it wasn't until the end of high school. Before that, there was a two year period when people were either scared of me, and/or concerned for my mental health. Some of my peers called me "psycho" behind my back (as I found out later), never directly to my face, because with my gritted teeth, curled Elvisian lip, and intense gaze, I no doubt scared the shit out of people (funny thing is, I would never had used the word "shit" at that point as I had also forsworn all swear words!). One young woman asked one of my few remaining friends, "Does he need to see a psychiatrist?" The answer, of course, was "Yes, desperately," but what was amazing was that no one in my family ever did any formal therapy.

My form of therapy, of course, was running. Running was quickly becoming my world, my everything. It was my therapy, it was my religion, it was my identity, my best friend; and it was my way of clearing my head and thinking clearly, of getting my happy on. I planned my day around running, and if I missed a day, I felt lousy, depressed, guilty, and weak. I actually would go through withdrawal. Obsessive-compulsive as it was, if it weren't for running, I don't know if I would have made it through my teens alive, or with my sanity intact.

It's not at all surprising, then, that I "walked on" to the cross country team at Bucknell University, the only school that accepted me.

Puke in a Cult

I always thought I would write a book about my experience at Bucknell that year, it was that fascinating. You see, I didn't just walk on to a Cross Country team that fall, I walked into a freakin' cult scene. Next to my own father, who was quite the authoritarian, it was my first real encounter with a Guru figure, in the person of our Coach.

Coach was for the first part of the year a Great Mystery. Every day we'd get to the locker room by 3pm. Our workout would be written out, and we'd just go and do it without question. We never knew when the hard workouts were coming, and to some degree our lives hung in the balance. We might be all psyched up for a killer training day, only to find we were off the hook—which was a let down, as we were so up for it. Other days we didn't see it coming and we were slammed.

Now, to most of the team, Coach elicited unquestioning obedience and devotion. His word was the word of God. The few guys who dared to air any kind of grievance whatsoever, let alone mutinous sentiments of any kind, were immediately silenced by the senior runners. The coach ruled by fear and intimidation—at least that was the way I saw it at first, because later I came to view him as a kind person who had just chosen to coach with an iron hand because it made for a better team.

What ended up happening that year was the team split into factions: The majority faction was the pro-Coach guys, which included the team captain and co-captain. The renegade group was led by these two crazy dudes who had been kicked off the team the previous year and who now lived off-campus in almost like a Delta House set-up where they partied, smoked, drank, and devil knows what else. What was interesting was that despite the fact that these wild pranksters had been booted, and that there was a good deal of animosity between them and the captains and some of their peers, they would still run with us for the really hard workouts. Even though they'd been suspended, they were on probation; and because they were actually two of the best runners (with scholarships), they had to keep training.

One of these two mutineers was one of the most charismatic people I have ever met. I felt a magnetic attraction to him from the moment I sat near him at lunch one day and heard him rambling on, and at that point I didn't even know who he was. He was probably the best runner on the team, and I could tell stories about him that would sound like legends and they're all true. His charm and charisma lasted largely on a most insanely funny sense of humor that came out in his quick one-liners and all the ingenious nicknames he gave to all the guys on the team (all except me—I never found out why, nor did I ask, though chalked it up to being, again, the outsider).

So essentially what was going on was that there was this power struggle between Coach and this young charismatic (to some, "hot shot") talent. I watched the whole thing come to a head and explode one night toward the end of the season when we all (renegades included) got together with Coach for a team meeting. Suffice it to say, it was a highly charged event!

Slowest Man on the Totem Pole

Me, I was just a naif along for the ride. There was a sense in which I had no place being there because I wasn't a recruit—I was one of the "pukes," the new guys. It was out of the kindness of Coach that I was kept on, though it was also true that some of the better runners on the team started off as walk-ons.

I became almost like the team mascot in a way. Because I wasn't involved at all with all the politics and the power struggle, and because I was a very young 17 and far from a competitive threat to anyone (slowest man on the totem pole), I became privy to all sorts of things I wouldn't have heard otherwise. And I also got treated in an avuncular way, particularly by the older guys. There were some very sweet moments…

One day we were training indoors on the track. Now, in high school my fastest mile time was just 5 minutes, which for most people is unthinkable, but for these guys was like an easy jog—not really exactly, but just go with it. So there I am, now at the back of the pack, and we start going 5 minute pace. Most days this is a little fast, but this day I'm actually hanging in there, and when we finally come through, Coach calls out our time: "4:52." "Wow, okay, not bad," I think, feeling pleased. Just then the team captain jogs up next to me—a guy who spoke to me directly maybe 3 times that whole year and who I secretly idolized—and he pats me on the back and says with a smile, "4:52—nice work, kiddo; your personal best, huh?" That blew me away!

At the end of the year we had a little "graduation" party at which all of us received a gag gift by the captain, and I'll never forget the captain reading mine with a smile on his face: "To you we give a few fast twitch muscle fibers—just a few!"

[Note: By the way, I never did puke that year, but I did pass out on one particularly hot 12 mile run at 6 minute pace, which is interesting in light of my plant medicine journeys, which we're getting to…]

Out of the Garden

I didn't feel that from all of the guys, however. A couple of the guys were very Christian, and I, the sole Jewish guy on the team (and one of the few at B.U. that year), was looked upon by them as someone who needed to be saved. One day towards the end of the first term, I accepted their invitation to come to a Bible study meeting. The meetings were led by the son of a preacher man, who clearly had learned well the art of the fire and brimstone sermon from his dad. It wasn't long before I was seriously worried that I would be eternally damned because we Jews had apparently never accepted Jesus as the messiah. This was news to me at that time, as was much of the "chapter and verse" quoting to prove to me how my whole tribe had gone astray. I'll never forget some of the things the preacher's son said to me that first meeting—to me only, because it was just me, him, and my two teammates sitting there in his dorm room! He would point his finger at me and say, "What are you going to do with your sin?" Because Jews no longer sacrifice in the Temple as of old, he explained. "Do you expect Jesus to write you a blank check?" In other words, I had to believe in Jesus to be saved, and that's all I needed to do.

When I went back home that winter, I asked my father point blank at the dinner table one night if he believed in God, and his answer was, "I would like to think there's a God…" That kind of shook me at that point because I had always thought we as a family believed in God, or at least that my Dad certainly did. This was rather disturbing; I needed a firmer expression of faith. I also asked my dad about Jesus and how he felt about Christianity. In so many words, he said he thought the biblical stories were all too fantastic to be true, and he included the Old Testament stories. He concluded by saying: "To me it's all bullshit, but if I'm anything, I'm a Jew—I'd rather be Jewish than anything else."

When I got back on campus that Spring, I set up an appointment to meet the campus rabbi whom I had first met during Yom Kippur services that fall. This whole thing was weighing on me greatly and I desperately was seeking resolution to it. I told the rabbi what my father had said, that he didn't really believe in God and that I was thinking about converting to Christianity. The rabbi took my father's side: "Your father said he would like to believe that there is a God—that doesn't mean he doesn't believe in God—he would like there to be a God!" From where I am now, I liked the way the rabbi handled that (and my dad's response to my question), but back then the rabbi's words didn't satisfy me either, because I sensed there was stronger faith on the side of the Christians. Or maybe it was that I just wanted to be loved and to fit in, and I was scared that if I didn't accept Jesus, I wouldn't be accepted. I hated that feeling!

The ironic thing is that when I finally did accept Jesus as my Lord and Savior, I was suddenly accepted by the two teammates and preacher's son—but now I had completely alienated my family, particularly my father. When I called him on the phone to tell him the "good news"—with much fear and trembling, mind you—he said the following unforgettable words to me: "Do you remember what God said to Adam after he ate the forbidden fruit?" Then a pause, with no response from me. "Well, you're out of the Garden!" That was truly shocking and scary to me, but I later learned that was my father's way of getting me to come back to the fold, and that he had no intention of disowning me. On the other hand, our relationship, though strained before, was never quite the same after that. I began to be seen by my family as this religious freak. Over the years to come, I certainly lived up to that image, and I have to say that this seminal moment as a freshman in college really was a huge catalyst spurring me on to really find "The Truth."

Veteran of the Psychic Wars

Due in large part to the Jesus incident at Bucknell and with my dad's help, I transferred to Penn for the next term. I walked on again to the Cross Country team, but it wasn't the same. They were a great group of guys, but it seemed like less of a family (however dysfunctional). It just wasn't the same!

I also struggled with academics. While I had done very well at Bucknell, I found Penn's classes to be more challenging for me and I got straight Cs my first semester.

I had started out pre-med at Bucknell because I had no idea what I wanted to do with my life and I listened too much to what my elders were suggesting (becoming a veterinarian was a big suggestion). Then I fell in love with philosophy, or more specifically, Plato's Socrates, and I switched majors after just one semester of an intro Philosophy course.

The figure of Socrates intrigued me on many levels, and perhaps you can understand why. Like me, I felt, he was an outcast who went against the grain, challenging the norms and mores of his fellow Athenian citizens all in the name of seeking Truth. He didn't claim to have all the answers (as he famously said, "All I know is I know nothing"), but he knew he could show his fellow citizens that maybe, just maybe, they didn't know either. For this, the Delphic oracle proclaimed him the wisest man in Athens. He was my first encounter with a Guru-figure who was a teacher of *Sophia*, wisdom.

Alfred North Whitehead once famously said that all Western philosophy is just footnotes to Plato, and certainly that's what the academic study of philosophy was for me—all downhill from there! I connected most with Socrates, because he didn't just spout about wisdom and the good life, he seemed to embody it.

Besides Soc, if I had one other hero at that time it was Carl Jung, who I discovered that summer when I took an 8 week intro Psych course. In the context of discussing the Freud-Jung split, the prof mentioned Jung's memoir, "Memories, Dreams, Reflections." I was really getting into Jung's ideas, so I immediately bought a used copy and started reading it in my usual OCD way. I was still a bit young to really understand a lot of it, but not too young to know I was digging Jung way more than Freud, and I was also amazed at some of his own psychical/metaphysical experiences that helped lead to their split. It's not an understatement to say that reading Jung was opening my mind and heart in ways that I never knew possible, and in ways that I was not fully understanding yet.

Suffice it to say that Jung was suddenly my boy, and I began scouring bookstores for his writings. Soon I was digging into my copies of *Modern Man In Search of Soul*, as well as *Man and His Symbols*. As the Psych course that summer came to a close,

I asked the prof if I could do a paper on Jung. He said sure, and I really let loose on that one, writing this overlong, intense and somewhat inspired paper on the man. At the end, the title came to me: *Carl Jung, Veteran of the Psychic Wars* (from the title of a Blue Oyster Cult album.) The professor liked it, but I think he only gave me a B or B+, which was fine with me because I was just grateful to have made the connection.

A Return to Love

After summer school was over, my father, two of my brothers, and I took a trip out to California. All I really remember right now is that we were staying in a hotel in LA near Universal Studios, and I was reading Jung's *Man and His Symbols*. Some of the major things that were in my consciousness at that point were:

I wasn't running for the first time in years as I had slightly injured my foot. This was very hard for my ego, but I made sure I walked at least an hour a day (and I timed myself, too). The fact that I wasn't running is actually highly significant and telling for what was to happen. Even though I hated not running, somehow I also realized that my body needed it, and that walking was actually healthier, balanced, and felt better. And I finally could relax in some deep sense, not having to run or train competitively.

Yet I was still eating the same huge amounts, due to stress and habit—something that stressed me out even more.

And I secretly hated myself for masturbating, even though I kept getting messages from the outside that it was okay, that it was healthy, that most males my age did it, etc. Something about it still felt very wrong, and I didn't know it but I was about to get insight into why I felt that way. Suffice to say, I was doing it all during the initial part of our stay in California, and feeling very torn about it.

The other major thing that was going on inside of me at that point was that a young woman friend from high school was very much on my mind. There was something about her that I had always felt and known was very special to me, but it was only now that it suddenly was hitting home just how dear she truly was to me. Essentially, it was something about her feminine nurturing, accepting, kind qualities that I felt I sorely needed, particularly in the midst of all of this "guy" energy I had had around me for so long. I was tapping into the Divine Mother Goddess energy (Jung's feminine archetype, or anima) and realizing how much I needed it, indeed was starved for it, even though at the time I was just vaguely aware of this.

One night after a rather traumatic episode between my father, my brothers, and myself, I went to bed and thought about this young woman for a while. She was like this precious haven for me, and I realized what I truly loved about her: she always made me feel loved and special. Suddenly, as I was thinking about her, I felt something move up my body and enter my heart space. It was this incredibly blissful feeling. I lay in that blessed state for I don't know how long before finally falling asleep. The next morning I awoke early to find that I was still in the same beatific state from the night before! I felt joyful like I hadn't felt for the longest time, not since childhood. My heart was full. It was not long before I fully realized I was in love for the first time.

"Love is the Strongest Medicine"

In the days that followed, I thought about my beloved constantly—journaling and writing letters and poems to her in my head. I just couldn't stop thinking about her! It was my first experience of what in Bhakti Yoga is called "Bhava Samadhi," which is one-pointed devotion towards someone or something. I had entered this state somehow, and I wasn't relinquishing it too readily!

What were most interesting to me were the physiological changes that were taking place in me. I suddenly was hardly eating or sleeping—at the most I needed four hours of sleep a night. I no longer felt the need to exercise compulsively, but when I did train, I found I was actually physically much stronger. For instance, suddenly I could bench press a whole lot more than I used to, and when I ran it felt like I was flying! (This wasn't all in my head: When I got back on Penn's campus and started working out again with the team, the "walk-on" suddenly was able to keep up with the runners he had never kept up with before, and the coach noticed—but I no longer felt the need to run or exercise so much, so I stopped going to practice.) And perhaps most importantly, I had no desire whatsoever for sex or to engage in masturbation—that ego-based urge just totally fell away, and I do mean totally.

The other amazing thing that happened as a result of "falling in love" was that suddenly music, which since quitting the guitar at 14 had taken a backseat in my life, was now the most important thing next to my beloved friend. Why had I denied myself of it for so long?! Of course, it was songs about love or ones coming from that vibration that really moved me the most. I suddenly found myself really tuned in to Cat Stevens, for one, James Taylor, and certain individual songs like "Peaceful Easy Feeling" by the Eagles, "Turn Turn Turn," by the Byrds, and especially "Blue Sky" by the Allman Brothers. I found myself crying bittersweet tears listening to music, thinking of my friend, in a state of blessed-out okay-ness with everything, including my previously tortured, splintered self.

As soon as we got back home, I called my friend. Once I finally got her on the phone, she agreed to meet me at our home. That wouldn't be for a couple of weeks.

In the meantime, I was inspired to take my Gibson Les Paul out of the closet and start playing again. When I did, it was from this completely different place than years before. Without knowing what I was doing, suddenly I started playing all of these "open chords" (chord structures where a lot of open strings are played) that felt more to be in that love vibration I was tuned into. There was this one A chord especially in the middle of the guitar that I really felt expressed how I was feeling. That chord led to another and then to another... And so it was that day that I began writing the first song of my life!

For the next two weeks, I worked day and night on the song in the basement, and when my friend finally, finally came over, we sat down in the basement and I played it for her. The song was about some moments my friend and I had spent together and how she seemed so sad, and essentially it was me trying to cheer her up. It had all of these parts to it and even a little guitar solo. I don't know if it changed or meant anything for her, but I felt that she appreciated my writing the song. Then we went outside and sat on this little bench we had in our backyard, and I told her, somewhat stumblingly, that I loved her. And she said something at that point which was really true but which I was not fully getting at that time. She said, in the kindest way possible, "I don't know who you're talking to when you say that." I didn't understand. I loved *her*, I had fallen in love with *her*! It took me quite a few years actually to fully understand that really, truly I had not fallen in love with her, per se, I had fallen in love with Love, and with a part of myself—the deepest, truest part that had been lost for many years. She was merely the catalyst for this grace to occur, and I was projecting onto her a love which was truly only emanating from within myself.

Maybe on some level I just wasn't quite ready for the spell to wear off, because I lived with that illusion for the greater part of the next 3 months, all the way up until Thanksgiving. I still held out some hope that my Muse would requite my love, and as I sat "studying" in my college dorm room, I would often pull out her picture, write her romantic poems and letters, dance for her, make music for her, long tearfully for her... I had these visions of us marrying and living together in this secluded forest home by a river, etc... It was crazy. Believe it or not, with all this seemingly distraction, my grades actually started to improve that year. Was all this making me smarter, too? It appeared so. My life had been transformed on all these different levels. People noticed, too, though not so much my family, oddly enough. But isn't it just like Jesus said: those with spiritual gifts are never fully understood, heeded, or appreciated amongst their own kin? For my part, I could have used some transcendence of my own sense of specialness!

In retrospect, the thing must have needed to run its course, and as I said, the river ran dry around Thanksgiving with a phone call I placed to my beloved. I had been trying to get in touch with her for all those months, but she wasn't answering my letters or returning my calls. And now, at long last, she did! And essentially, her message to me was the same as it had been a few months earlier: "I don't know who you're talking about when you say these things. It couldn't possibly be me." That's something close to her exact words. Then I got the courage to finally ask her point blank if she did not want to be together? Her answer was a kind but firm "No."

So there it was. We hung up and I was devastated, my love unrequited! I still didn't fully get it, you see—*this wasn't about her; it was about me.* Had I known that then, perhaps I could have kept that beautiful state of being going indefinitely... As it was, I had no idea that once my *raison d'être*, my cause for celebration was no longer there, the whole thing would just come to a crashing halt! And that it did, though with one big difference: now I really knew that this state existed and that it can be accessed naturally. What I didn't realize is how difficult it is to re-access it, to stuff the proverbial genie back in that bottle!

As is noted in the book, Ram Dass says that he took LSD some 300+ times in the Sixties in a vain attempt to see if he could actually permanently maintain the "high" state of consciousness. His search ultimately took him to India where he met a highly revered yogi saint, Neem Karoli Baba, gave him a high dose of LSD, found it had no effect on the Baba, and concluded that Yoga was what could keep one "high" all the time. Neem Karoli later famously told Ram Dass: "Love is a stronger medicine than LSD" (which later became shortened to "Love is the Strongest Medicine"), and having had this experience, I can certainly see that, if only for the reason that LSD lasts 8 hours and at most the high lingers for a few days, while my experience kept me blissed out for months, allowing time for certain permanent changes in my character.

Bring Back that Lovin' Feeling

So interestingly and surely enough, having become somewhat attached to this state now, I desperately tried to keep from coming down from the "high" by finding someone else to whom I could devote myself! And soon enough, she appeared, only it quickly became apparent that this young vixen was expecting something more than a purely pure and platonic relationship. After seeing each other for a bit, the young lady wanted to take a little jaunt to New York City around Christmas (she had never been), and so that we did, taking Amtrak into Penn Station. We had a nice little time, except for the fact that I had all day to cuddle and possibly make out with this girl and I didn't make any move (nor did she). By the time we got back,

I suddenly found myself dumped, with no real explanation why (I surmised the "why" after the fact).

At this point, I really struggled between KNOWING that the state I had just been in for the last 4 months was a truer, purer, more delightful way of being than the state of mere physical attraction, and dealing with the usual 19-year old male horniness. I think we all know the former is true on some level, which is why love is love, and lust is, well, lust, ego-based. Even if we've never experienced true love, we at least sense this is true. For myself, I wanted to stay true to an ideal I now had, which is the way life and love can be, and not rush into sex with just anyone, which is probably why I was to not even kiss a woman for the next seven years. The facts on the ground though, were that this girl was hot and I was very physically attracted to her. She no doubt sensed that and was wondering why I was such a loser that I wouldn't take the initiative and kiss her...?

As I say, I really struggled with all of this. Even when I eventually succumbed to masturbation again that term, I was plagued by this strong feeling that I was really doing it out of weakness, and that it was dishonoring to women, or at least the Goddess in each woman. But suddenly it all hit me—having not even thought about the lower half of my body for months, now there was this girl I wanted to have sex with but wouldn't allow myself, and there was also that hot girl next door who had been trying to get my attention for all of those months, and there was this calendar of nudes my roommate had on his wall, etc. etc. I couldn't handle it, my will power wasn't strong enough. And so once again, I was out of the Garden...

A Brief Digression to Consider the Upshot & Implications of All This

I feel it's important to say a bit more about all of this, to get at what this experience was and was not, because it does get to the root of the subject at hand here. Let me first say that what happened to me that summer and fall a quarter of a century ago did not come without a lot of preparation. Although I called it "Grace," I do not feel that the Universe grants us these things without a struggle and a discipline of some sort. As I said, my inner turmoil due to my family's situation and other adolescent concerns led me to a life of increasing self-denial and worldly withdrawal. I would not allow myself pleasure for many years, even shunning music at times. My inward torment ultimately found resolution in a "savior" to whom I devoted myself, a young woman who became my ideal to emulate. Whether my initial experience of "falling in love" was a Kundalini awakening is perhaps beside the point. The point is that my heart was suddenly opened, and when it opened, I truly knew unconditional love for myself, and from that, I began to be able to really fully see and love others in the same way. Not that I did this perfectly, mind you, especially once the experience was over and I returned again to my usual fractured self—but it was a beginning, a source point to which I could see where I was falling short of the mark. Once being granted experiences such as these, one can never really go back to "business as usual."

What I Have Learned

I learned from the experience that there are these states of true love and joy that exist and can be accessed. I learned that music can be a gateway to these states, and that musicians are often the gatekeepers. I learned that one-pointed devotion to an ideal is a way of staying in these states. I learned that other states, such a lust and anger, can effectively block these experiences. I had now a newfound love and appreciation for nature and all things natural, and I longed for a deeper connection to "Mother Earth." I discovered that my memory had become unblocked and I now was able to recall much of my past and accept it. I realized that when the heart is full, physical sustenance in the way of food is not nearly so essential, nor is sleep, nor much exercise. I was in effect learning what the yogis know: you don't need much to be happy! In fact, ultimately, I am beginning to realize, you need Nothing!

From my vantage point now, I will offer that experiences such as these, much as one would like them to, can never be repeated in exactly the same way. They are dramatic and transformative because they need to be to break through all of the layers of contraction that veil the "true Self." Beautiful as they are, it is wise not to become too attached to them, but rather to learn the essential lessons from them and apply them to one's moment-to-moment existence. What will happen over time is that slowly, slowly the initial experience of love, joy, wonder, etc. will become a more constant part of your existence, without the somewhat illusionary romantic love projection. In other words, no longer will you be in love with someone outside of you, but you will be Love, unconditionally loving to all, and you will express that love in everything you do and to everyone.

I have to say that as amazingly profound as my psychedelic experiences have been, and even all of those that have come via yoga, the simple experience I had at the age of 19 was the most divine and dear to me. (I say "divine" in the sense of wonderful, because at that time I didn't necessarily connect this experience to "God," although it did awaken certain questions within me, such as how given the fact of Love there could be anything truly "evil" or "bad"). There were moments when I felt I could die right there and my life would be fulfilled, it was so beautiful. In the Jewish tradition there's a wonderful word/idea, *dayyeinu*, meaning: "If I had lived just for this, it would have been enough!" That was my feeling then, yet later I also felt that had I died then, I wouldn't have lived to experience the next wondrous evolution of my consciousness, and the next, and the next... This journey of life back to love seems never-ending! So even though I never really have been able to get that genie back in the bottle, I have gained an invaluable perspective on this whole experience and life over the years.

The "Natural Awakening" vs. The "Rude Awakening"

Having said all that, I feel it would be helpful at this point to put on the table an issue which no book like this could disregard, namely the question of how the mystical experiences granted via psychedelics are similar or different to those which are, shall we say, more organic? I will refer to this issue throughout the book as the difference between the "natural awakening" and the "rude awakening," and I recognize, of course, that these terms are loaded—"natural" has the connotation of "good and wholesome," while "rude" seems pejorative—but I do not mean it that way. Indeed, now that I have experienced both sides of this debate, I find it much more challenging to pass judgment either way, and this entire book can be seen as a means of getting some clarity in regard to what really can be said on this matter, if anything.

Certainly it has been true that up until now, the Yoga community as a whole has tended to disdain use of psychedelics as a path to spiritual evolution, and this is due in large part to what the young people of the Sixties were told by many of the saffron-robed gurus who came to these shores at that time. If I may re-phrase this whole issue in a way in which it has been passed on by Yogis and Gurus for the past 4 decades:

"Yoga teaches how to get high and stay high naturally, without the use of drugs, which are artificial crutches, obstacles to true spiritual practice and growth."

This is what I always had been told, in so many words, and it was just confirmation of what I had thought and felt myself, as my early experiences all came without ever putting a drug in my body. Now, I say "putting a drug in my body" as opposed to saying "by altering my chemistry via an external source," because clearly there are chemical changes that take place in the brain and body when one person inspires love in another, for example. In any case, I will just say that from the vantage point of the person who has done years of disciplined practice and is granted a spiritual experience of some sort, there is a tendency to view a seemingly less disciplined way of approaching that experience, like taking a drug, as "cheating" at best, and a sham at worst. Such was essentially the way I viewed things. Drugs were for those who wouldn't, or couldn't, do the work on their own. And there was a certain feeling of superiority and elitism that went along with that sentiment (which, I noted, ran high in the yoga community).

At this point, I would like to mention that this hot button issue was brought to the surface for many worldwide when Oprah interviewed Eckhart Tolle on her show in 2008. In the very first of ten installments, Tolle brought up the fact that, after some urging, he had agreed to try LSD ("acid"). This in itself I am sure was a bit of a surprise to many out there who are familiar with Tolle, but what was not so surprising perhaps was Tolle's perspective on LSD. What follows is a brief transcript of what was said after Oprah asked Tolle how his LSD experience compared with his awakening experience:

Tolle: *It's not quite the same thing because what I experienced [in his awakening experience] was much more subtle and beautiful. The acid I experienced was almost a violent thing where violently the perceptions, sense perceptions, became so magnified that there was no room for thinking anymore. But I could see why people say, for some people it's a glimpse of what it means to perceive the world without this continuous interference of mental noise.*

Oprah: *Yeah, but your trip without acid was better.*

Eckhart: *Much better.*

There is much that could be said in response to Tolle's response, and again, this entire book is primarily dealing with this very issue. For now though, my purpose is simply to get these ideas to you, the reader, and then keep moving forward, so let's do that...

5

Light in the Yoga Sutras and Psychedelics[91]

*"In addition to the LSD, there were a number of other pills for this
and that—diarrhea, fever, a sleeping pill, and so forth. He asked
about each of these. He asked if they gave powers. I didn't understand
at the time and thought that by 'powers' perhaps he meant physical
strength. I said, 'No.' Later, of course, I came to understand
that the word he had used, 'siddhis,' means psychic powers."*

—Ram Dass on Neem Karoli Baba, from Be Here Now

*"The beatific vision, Sat Chit Ananda, Being-Awareness-
Bliss, for the first time I understood, not on the verbal level,
not by inchoate hints or at a distance, but precisely and
completely what those prodigious syllables referred to…"*

—Aldous Huxley, Doors of Perception

*"The fourth method of awakening is through the use of specific
herbs. In Sanskrit this is called aushadhi, and it should not
be interpreted as meaning drugs like marijuana, LSD, etc.
Aushadhi is the most powerful and rapid method of awakening
but is not for all and very few people know about it."*

—Swami Satyananda Saraswati, Kundalini Tantra

"You want to eat organic food, right? So why not organic Samadhi?"

—Attributed to Swami Satchidananda

We've now established that *Soma* can be defined as both a plant, meaning psychoactive flora, and an "implant," if you will, meaning that it is also produced naturally within all of us, and can be accessed through yogic discipline.

Leaving the plant metaphor aside for a moment and switching now to an arboreal motif… One traditional view is that yogic discipline has a number of "limbs," like a tree, and that all must be taken into account in order to churn one's inner

"Ocean of Milk" to discover the *Soma* implant within oneself. These limbs include conscious living (ethics) and self-care, physical cultivation, breath control, mental discipline, and meditation. When practiced on a consistent basis, the result is an ever-deepening connection to one's true nature, which is none other than God. This "classical" concept is according to a tradition set forth in the *Yoga Sutras*, a collection of aphorisms on Yoga dating anywhere from 200 BCE to 500 CE, after the Vedic corpus, and attributed to a sage named Patanjali.

In the West today, the *Yoga Sutras* have become one of the primary sources on Yoga, oft-quoted and referenced… and yet there's reason to think that perhaps this text has been a tad overrated.[92] Certainly the *Yoga Sutras* wasn't all that important to my own Indian gurus. None of them ever quoted or referred to it, though they did refer to other various time-honored scriptures, like the Vedas (Sri Karunamayi), and of course the Bhagavad Gita. But much of what my traditional teachers were imparting to their disciples was still very much consistent with what is found within the *Yoga Sutras*.

First and foremost, what is known as *Ashtanga Yoga* (aka Raja Yoga), which is laid out in the Sutras, was implicitly assumed by all of my teachers. The Sanskrit word "*ashtanga*" translates as "8 limbs," and these limbs are as follows:

Limb 1) *Yama*: The Five Abstentions

◎ Ahimsa: non-violence

◎ Satya: truth in word & thought

◎ Asteya: Non-stealing

◎ Brahmacharya: Conservation of Sexual Energy

◎ Aparigraha: Non-possessiveness

Limb 2) *Niyama*: The Five Observances

◎ Shaucha: cleanliness of body & mind

◎ Santosha: satisfaction/contentment

◎ Tapas: austerity/physical & mental discipline

◎ Svadhyaya: Self-study (Introspection) and Study of Sacred Texts

◎ Ishvarapranidhana: Surrender to (or worship of) God

Limb 3) *Asana*: Discipline of the body

◎ Rules and postures to keep one's physical vessel disease-free and for preserving vital energy. Correct postures are a physical aid to meditation, for they control the limbs and nervous system and prevent them from producing disturbances.

Limb 4) *Pranayama*: Control of breath

◎ Specific exercises that lead to greater mastery of the breath, as well as awareness of prana, or life force

Limb 5) *Pratyahara*: Withdrawal of senses from their external objects

[Note: The last three levels are called internal aids to Yoga (antaranga sadhana)]

Limb 6) *Dharana*: Concentration of Mind

◎ Focusing the mind on one specific object

Limb 7) *Dhyana*: Meditation

◎ When Dharana (concentration) becomes undisturbed flow of thought toward the object of meditation

Limb 8) *Samadhi*: Oneness with the object of meditation,

◎ with a resulting experience of oneness with everything. *Samadhi* is also translated, inter alia, as "*mystical union*," "*cosmic consciousness*," "*ecstasy*," "*enstasy*," "*absorption*," "*integration*."

My preceptors all implicitly followed the above "8-limbed Path" (*Ashtanga Yoga*), and all emphasized the primacy of meditation and *Samadhi*. They all recommended the other limbs only as a "preparation" for meditation and *Samadhi*. Sri Karunamayi, for example, though she acknowledged the beginning steps, would downplay the importance of Hatha Yoga and pranayama, as well as even singing and chanting. Instead she exhorted us to "*Meditate, Meditate, Meditate!!!*" And if she had had her way, we would all be sitting still and silent in lotus position day and night. Once her Swami told us of how Amma had put him into a state of *samadhi* for 24 hours straight, to which Amma added:

"Children, the day will come when you, too, will be absorbed in meditation for 24 hours in a day."

I'm sure a lot of us present were wondering, "Really? In what lifetime?" but we took the point that meditation is the most important of all practices.

Now, please note that Karunamayi wasn't saying the day will come when you will all be doing one-finger handstands! Or finally master that sick AcroYoga transition! There even seemed to be a distaste expressed for physical culture—a distaste which you will find throughout all yoga literature, from Vivekananda to Yogananda to Ramana Maharshi and on—the idea being that Hatha Yoga focuses too much on the body, making it more challenging to release attachment to it and deepen in our meditation and spiritual life.[93] Swami Satyananda Saraswati similarly told me that for my personal progress, I would need to place far less importance on Hatha Yoga, relating to me the following story:

As a young disciple of his guru, he quickly became very proficient in asana practice, easily putting his legs behind his head, etc. One day his teacher had him "perform" some very advanced asanas for his Indian students, who were far less adept. At the end of Swamiji's show, everyone was very impressed, and he was glowing. But as he sat there basking in the glory afterward, his teacher told him he would no longer be doing Hatha Yoga—he no longer needed to—and that was that. And it was. In all the time I was with him, I never saw Swamiji practice asanas. Nor did I see any of my other Indian teachers practice or put much emphasis on Hatha Yoga.

However, at one time or another, I did see nearly all of them go into *Samadhi*. Invariably, when in this state, they appeared not to be present like they were "not at home," perhaps even dead. Definitely not visibly breathing. This was always very inspiring to me, giving me a sense that I, too, through diligent and devoted practice, might one day attain such a lofty and profound state of being.

Lord knows I tried.

Yet if I am honest, I will tell you that I never had an experience of *Samadhi* beyond a taste of the lower *samadhi*s, such as "*Bhava Samadhi*," which is a trance state involving feelings of ecstasy and bliss, and sometimes of joyful tears dissolving one's ego boundaries.

Most of these experiences came in my initial exposure to Yoga, and it was largely due to them that I continued on the Yoga path. I had always heard that spiritual experiences so early on in one's yoga practice are gifts of grace and signs to the seeker that the practice is indeed bearing fruit. Thus they draw the aspirant increasingly inward on his quest.

Certainly this was the case with me, but over time these experiences became fewer and farther between. I was left wondering if I was doing something wrong? Or maybe I should try harder? Or is this just a passing stage on my journey? How I eventually dealt with this perplexity is why you are now reading these words…

• • •

Besides spiritual experiences, another notable milestone and by-product of the 8-limbed path, is what is known as "*siddhis.*" Siddhi is often translated as "a yogic power," and sometimes "psychic power." When I originally began my yoga practice, I must honestly admit to you that I was attracted to the idea of gaining such special powers. This was partly because I desired physical proof that my practices were bearing fruit, just as I sought such proof from my teachers. Spiritual experiences were not enough for me. I needed to know that I wasn't just wasting my time and struggling in vain; but even more, I wanted something demonstrable, something that I could actually show others.

Of course, with all of yoga's little "aha" enlightenment moments and all of the positive changes it brought to my life, no further proof of yoga's value to me was really needed. The only problem was, even though I knew I was a completely different person on the inside, the changes were not always so apparent on the outside. My family, especially, wondered and worried about my somewhat cloistered and cultish behavior. They became concerned that I was wasting my precious Twenties doing impractical things, like meditation, that were inconsequential in terms of real world values.

My eldest brother, for example, would sometimes say things to me like, "Instead of meditating so much, I would like to see you really begin to develop a body of work as a singer/songwriter," to which I would respond, "Well, meditation is about going to the *Source* of all creativity, so it may seem like a waste of time, but it's actually a very wise investment of my time." I was heard of course, but not really understood or believed, and as I discuss later, there was also that part of me that still wanted to be Bob Dylan… And yet, yogic powers and enlightenment presented an even more tempting attraction. So I felt that once I was able to show my family and the world that this wasn't just nonsense, they would think differently about me. Certainly this was not the choicest reason for practicing (nor was the drive to have spiritual experiences), but I was a neophyte and put it down to spiritual immaturity.

Now, you may wonder: did I ever attain any of these *siddhis*? I cannot say for certain. I feel that I began to see glimpses of them (such as clairvoyance), and if I had continued with my intense *sadhana* (yogic practice), who knows? At this point, I feel like I've lost much of whatever I had, but that's due to the choice I made to come back down to earth a bit and meet the "real world" halfway, though I realize this could be seen as succumbing to worldly desires (what is called a *yogi bhrashta*, or "fallen yogi" in the *Bhagavad Gita*).

As noted, I did come into the presence of teachers, like Amma, who seemed to possess such *siddhis*, and who would sometimes display their powers, though usually only along the lines of clairvoyance, which is often referred to as "omniscience." I was fascinated, and an ongoing question for me was: what is the process for developing such yogic powers, and what is their true purpose?

To begin to get some clarity to this, we must look inside the Yoga Sutras. For our purposes here, there is a relevant sutra regarding the *siddhis* that begins the 4th and final chapter (*pada*) of the text, known as "Kaivalya Pada," or the chapter on liberation. The sutra reads as follows:

Janmaushadhi Mantra Tapah

Samaadhi Jaah Siddhayah

Janma = birth

aushadhi = herb, medicinal plant, drug, incense, elixir *mantra* = incantation, charm, spell

tapah = heat, burning, shining, an ascetic devotional practice, burning desire to reach perfection, that which burns all impurities

samadhi = profound meditation, total absorption

jah = born

siddhayah = perfections, accomplishments, fulfillments, attainments, psychic powers

Translation: *"Siddhis are born of practices performed in previous births, or by herbs, mantra repetition, asceticism, or by samadhi."* (Sutra 4.1)[94]

As far as this study goes, this sutra essentially says that via "*aushadha*" (also "*aushadhi*") or herbs/drugs/plants, yogic powers can be attained. While this is fascinating information, unfortunately the sutras say nothing more about the subject, leaving us with many questions.

Questions such as:

◎ To what does *aushadha* refer exactly?

◎ To which yogic powers do these herbs, *aushadha*, give rise?

◎ How, exactly, do *aushadha* give rise to *siddhis*?

◎ Is this sutra suggesting that it is permissible for a yogic aspirant to make use of *aushadha* as a means toward attaining success in Yoga?

◎ Are all of the methods of attaining *siddhis*—past lives, herbs, mantra, tapas, and *samadhi*—of equal value, or are some better than others?

◎ Why is the term *aushadha* suddenly mentioned at the outset of the 4th and final chapter of the Yoga Sutras, and then not referred to again?

Fortunately, while we don't have a way of finding out the original meaning of sutra 4.1, at least we can refer to the considerable body of commentary on the Yoga Sutras, including the opinions of contemporary teachers. As for the latter, let's first consider Neem Karoli Baba's words to Ram Dass, previously quoted at the outset of this chapter:

"In addition to the LSD, there were a number of other pills for this and that—diarrhea, fever, a sleeping pill, and so forth. He asked about each of these. He asked if they gave powers. I didn't understand at the time and thought that by 'powers' perhaps he meant physical strength. I said, 'No.' Later, of course, I came to understand that the word he had used, 'siddhis,' means psychic powers."[95]

Neem Karoli Baba, an advanced yogi and guru, who some say was enlightened, is asking his disciple, Ram Dass, if his LSD gives the person who ingests it *siddhis*. Now, many of those who followed Neem Karoli Baba or were around him, felt/believed/knew that he himself possessed such yogic powers. Yet as far as anyone knows, they were not derived from any kind of pill or drug, but from his *sadhana* and *tapasya*, meaning his yogic practice and discipline. In fact, one of the *siddhis* he was believed to possess was the ability to know anything that he chose to know at any time (again, *omniscience*) so perhaps he already knew the answer to the question he put to Ram Dass. He was apparently a bit of a trickster.

For our purposes, it is enough to know that Neem Karoli Baba linked drugs to *siddhis*, and that is exactly what Sutra 4.1 appears to do. From this, we can speculate that yogis like Neem Karoli Baba are well aware of this passage in the Yoga Sutras and its implication. Yet even if they are not aware of that specific passage, or even the text itself, there appears to be a common *understanding* among yogis that yogic powers can be also be obtained via plant material and/or their derivative drugs. You will also recall that Neem Karoli Baba ultimately told Ram Dass that "yogi medicine," such as LSD, can give one a glimpse of *Samadhi*, but not the "highest *Samadhi*" (or "not a true *Samadhi*"—see Chapter 1). This will become more relevant as we proceed.

Now, regarding sutra 4.1, what do traditional commentators on the Yoga Sutras have to say?

First, let us consider the words of Vyasa, a revered *rishi*, or seer-sage who is credited as the author of the "*Yoga Bhashya*," a highly regarded and referenced commentary on the Yoga Sutras dating to circa the 5*th* century CE. Though Vyasa's comments on Sutra 4.1 regarding *aushadha* are cursory and ambiguous, like the sutra itself, we can still get some sense of his general approach. The text reads as follows:

"By herbs, as for example with chemicals in an Asura's (demon's) abode, medicinal powers are acquired."

Swami Hariharananda Aranya notes the difficulty in Vyasa's passage:

"The commentator has mentioned about the abode of demons but nobody knows where it is, but it is certain that supernormal powers on a small scale can be acquired by the application of drugs." [96]

Swami Hariharananda further comments that the "supernormal powers" acquired through drugs "have nothing to do with Yoga," and are "insignificant."

"Some in a state of stupor through the application of anaesthetics like chloroform etc. acquire the power of going out of the body. It has also been reported that by the application of hemlock all over the body similar power is acquired. Witches were supposed to practice this method. These powers are insignificant." [97]

Swami Satyananda Saraswati of the Bihar School (not to be confused with the "Swamiji" quoted in the previous chapter, who shares the same name) differs with Swami Hariharananda Aranya's view. He holds that *aushadha* does indeed produce powerful *siddhis*. He also states that such "psychic powers" are true *siddhis*, not insignificant, different, or inferior. However, these spiritual herbs do not include modern "herbs" like LSD and ganja (marijuana), which have a deleterious effect on the body. In Swami Satyananda's own words:

"Psychic powers can be obtained in five ways… Siddhis can also be had from herbs, but things like LSD and ganja are not to be included here because they cause disease and nervous disorders. These things cause depression of certain nerve centers and give rise to effects like samadhi, but they are not to be included in the herbs causing siddhis because they are of a lower type. Traditionally, aushadhi means the juice of certain herbs, such as anjana, rosayana, etc., but not LSD or ganja. Only a few responsible persons know the method of preparation. These herbs are available in the Himalayas and nowhere else and bring about supramental states of consciousness.

"The effects of these herbs can be controlled through higher mental phenomena. There are certain preparations of mercury which are of great importance." [98]

In another context, Swami Satyananda Saraswati makes the interesting remark that:

"Aushadhi is the most powerful and rapid method of awakening… There are herbs which can transform the nature of the body and its elements and bring about either partial or full awakening… [but this is] a very risky and unreliable method."

He further mentions *Soma* and other substances that may have been the same or similar in other cultures, such as the Persian brew *Hoama*; mixtures that could allow the ingesters to *"enter a state of samadhi, and awaken their Kundalini,"* but due to improper use by unqualified people, the knowledge about these substances has been closely guarded for centuries. The Swami concludes:

"Everyone is craving Kundalini awakening, but few people have the discipline and mental, emotional, physical and nervous preparation required to avoid damage to the brain and tissues. So, although no one is teaching the aushadhi method of awakening today, its knowledge has been transmitted from generation to generation through the guru/disciple tradition. Perhaps some day, when the nature of man changes and we find better intellectual, physical and mental responses, the science will again be revealed."[99]*

  *(Please note that this last point intersects with our discussion of Kundalini and psychedelics in the following chapter.)

Swami Satchidananda, the "Woodstock Guru" we met in the first chapter, differs from this view in that he suggests that modern psychedelics like LSD and marijuana are indeed to be classed among the *aushadha*. Still, he does agree with Swami Hariharananda and others that *siddhis* obtained via herbs, any herbs, are of inferior spiritual value. He writes:

"Patanjali… gives us some clues about the people who get some experiences through their LSD and marijuana. The so-called "grass" is an herb, is it not? Mushrooms could be considered herbs also… So, there are various ways of accomplishing the psychic powers. But normally it is recognized that all the others except samadhi are not natural. For example, using herbs means inducing siddhis by the use of certain external stimuli. It's not an "organic" siddhi. It may come and then fade away. So, siddhis should come in the regular process of Yoga, not through external stimuli."[100]

Swami Satchidananda's basic point is that *siddhis* acquired through "unnatural" non-organic means such herbs are only temporary, and thus should not be taken seriously by the yoga aspirant.

A friend on Maui who was close to Swami Satchidananda for many years often reminds me of her guru's words: *"You eat organic food, right? Well, why not organic Samadhi?"* In other words: Why take psychedelics if both the experience and its psychic powers fade, then disappear, once the drug wears off? Don't you want the real thing and not a cheap imitation?

Yet is it really the case that such powers never last? Certainly there are reports of shamans who are capable of retaining these psychic powers obtained from their plant medicine. There are also similar personal reports from lay people and psychonauts. The question then is whether such powers truly are authentic and lasting?

The late BKS Iyengar provides an answer to this question. His commentary on sutra 4.1 echoes Swami Satchidananda's view that those *siddhis* gained via *aushadha* are inferior to those gained via yogic practice. They are inferior because they can be lost due to a fall from grace. Writing his commentary on the Yoga Sutras in the mid-Sixties, Iyengar first spells out in greater detail the five ways of becoming an accomplished yogi (*siddha*):

1. *By birth with aspiration to become perfect (janma)*

2. *By spiritual experience gained through herbs (or as prescribed in the Vedas), drugs or elixir (aushadha)*

3. *By incantation of the name of one's desired deity (mantra)*

4. *By ascetic devotional practice (tapas)*

5. *By profound meditation (samadhi)*[101]

Iyengar then goes on to note why all five of these classes of siddhas are not equal:

"There is an important distinction between these means of spiritual accomplishment. Followers of the first three may fall from the grace of Yoga through pride or negligence. The others, whose spiritual gains are through tapas and samadhi, do not. They become masters, standing alone as divine, liberated souls, shining examples to mankind...

Sage Mandavya and King Yayati developed supernatural powers through an elixir of life. Today many drug users employ mescaline, LSD, hashish, heroin, etc. to experience the so-called spiritual visions investigated by Aldous Huxley and others. Artists and poets in the past have also relied on drugs to bring about supernormal states to enhance their art."[102]

Iyengar's mention of Huxley is interesting, particularly as the latter referred to psychedelics as "moksha medicine," moksha being a Sanskrit word meaning "Liberation."[103] Had he lived to read Iyengar's commentary, Huxley would probably have been chagrined by Iyengar's "so-called spiritual visions" put-down. Of course, Huxley had certainly heard this from numerous other sides, not least of which is his contemporary, another scholar of mysticism, R.C. Zaehner. Zaehner wrote of mescaline as "unable to produce the *natural mystical experience*."[104] Huxley's life and work will be considered shortly, but for now, you should note Iyengar's view well: truly great yogis do not attain their enlightened status through the medium of *aushadha*.

Iyengar's point has also been echoed by numerous other commentators. I.K. Taimni, whose book on the Yoga Sutras "*The Science of Yoga*" has become one of the most well-regarded in English, translates "*aushadhi*" as "drugs," and similarly notes:

"Of the five methods given [to attain siddhis] only the last based upon Samadhi is used by advanced Yogis in their work because it is based upon direct knowledge of the higher laws of Nature and is, therefore, under complete control of the will."[105]

Taimni's point is that the Yoga Sutras, after all, are all about attaining *Samadhi* through yogic discipline, not via *aushadha*. Indeed, he notes that all of the *siddhis* mentioned in the third chapter of the Sutras are obtained via what is known as "*Samyama.*" Samyama is the combination of concentration (*dharana*), meditation (*dhyana*), and absorption (*samadhi*). Like Iyengar, Taimni privileges the *siddhis* attained via *Samyama* above those obtained otherwise:

"The Siddhis, which are developed as a result of the practice of Samyama, belong to a different category and are far superior to those developed in other ways. They are the product of the natural unfoldment of consciousness in its evolution towards perfection and thus become permanent possessions of the soul, although a little effort may be needed in each new incarnation to revive them in the early stages of Yogic training. Being based upon knowledge of the higher laws of Nature operating in her subtler realms, they can be exercised with complete confidence and effectiveness, much in the same way as a trained scientist can bring about extraordinary results in the field of physical Science."[106]

Taimni concurs with Swami Hariharananda that such yogic powers aren't of much importance. Even when they are "remarkable":

"Psychic powers of a low grade can often be developed by the use of certain drugs. Many fakirs in India use certain herbs like Ganja for developing clairvoyance of a low order. Others can bring about very remarkable chemical changes by the use of certain drugs or herbs; but those who know these secrets do not generally impart them to others. Needless to say that the powers obtained in this manner are not of much consequence and should be classed with the innumerable powers which modern Science has placed at our disposal."[107]

This last point reminds me of the story of the guru who chides his student for showing off how he can walk on water. "Why would you bother yourself with that," the guru laughs, "when the ferry works just as well, and might even be quicker?!!" Needless to say, in the Yoga tradition, such overt displays of one's psychic/spiritual prowess are generally not considered a wise course of action.

Two slightly more contemporary commentators have something quite similar to say regarding sutra 4:1. Krishnamacharya's son, TVK Desikachar, in his relatively more recent book, *The Heart of Yoga*, remarks:

"The Vedas describe various rituals whereby the taking of herbal preparations in a prescribed way can change one's personality... Only the practices described in earlier

*chapters [of the Yoga Sutras] to reduce and render the five obstacles [to yoga] ineffec-
tive can guarantee the end of these tendencies. Genetic inheritance, the use of herbs,
and other means cannot be as effective.*"[108]

The well-known scholar of Yoga, Georg Feuerstein, also mentions the ancient
Vedic Soma ritual, implicitly accepting their validity, though downplaying their ultimate value:

*"The use of herbal concoctions may seem surprising. Yet this tradition goes right
back to Vedic times and ritual quaffing of the Soma (fly-agaric?). At any rate, nowhere
in the Yoga Sutra or any other Yogic scripture do we find the claim that drugs can
replace the years of self-discipline and commitment demanded of the yogi.*"[109]

One other traditional teacher who added to this overall consensus on the superiority of *Samadhi* via meditation was Swami Prabhavananda, who commented on
Sutra 4:1 as follows:

*"Certain drugs may produce visions, but these are invariably psychic, not spiritual,
as is commonly believed. Furthermore, they may cause prolonged spiritual dryness
and disbelief and may even do permanent damage to the brain… Concentration [sa-
madhi] is the surest of all the means of obtaining the psychic powers.*"[110]

Swami Prabhavananda makes a compelling point: We have all encountered
people with "chemical burnout," a mental malady that comes from years of taking
psychedelics in an undisciplined manner. While the long-term effects of psychedelics on the human brain are still not fully known, it is clear that for some they have a
debilitating and decaying effect.

Even I, a spiritual seeker who has almost exclusively ingested plant extracts in a
sacramental way, wonders whether my ecstatic experiences are truly a *corrective* to
my own spiritual dryness, or are in fact *corrosive*.

My plant journeys inevitably left me with many doubts and questions: Were my
experiences even real? Where was a personal God, or gods, or even guiding spirits?
Where was anything of a personal nature, for that matter? Had my exploration of
psychedelics forever spoiled the beautiful little "natural awakening" experiences I
had previously? Or… had they just brought things to a whole other level?

For true enlightenment to occur, what is needed, it seems to me, is a constant,
everyday, moment to moment spiritual practice. One that is ultimately not dependent on any outside influence, including a drug or herb or elixir or other concoction.
On this, I am in agreement with the traditional commentators above.

The path of *aushadha* may be a viable one for some already advanced souls, but
for others, including myself, it can also be a trap, a distraction, and a dead end.

Yet the fact that herbs that give rise to *siddhis* are mentioned at all in the Yoga

Sutras is clearly significant, and once again clearly reveals a link between psychoactive plant materials and the practice of yoga.

One wonders what the ancient traditions of *aushadha* really are, and if this might even be a viable yogic path on equal standing with the practice of the "*samyama*" that the Yoga Sutras seem to prefer? What about Soma? And what about the preparations of the juice of the herbs "*anjana*" and "*rosayana*" which Swami Satyananda Saraswati mentioned? To answer these and other questions I turned to the work of more recent commentators on these subjects, including my teacher, Dr. David Frawley. I also sought out the thoughts of Dr. Robert Svoboda, and the Director of the Himalayan Institute, Pandit Rajmani Tigunait

In his book, *Inner Quest: Yoga's Answers to Life's Questions*, Pandit Rajmani Tigunait discusses at some length the use of herbs in connection with spiritual practice. He notes the connection of herbs not so much with the path of Raja/Ashtanga Yoga, but with that of Tantra and Kundalini:

"According to Ayurveda, especially the tantric version, herbs are the embodiment of the living goddess. If applied properly they release divine energies—to heal not only the physical aspect of our being, but the mental and spiritual aspects as well... [Using herbs as part of one's spiritual practice] is briefly introduced in the first sutra of chapter four of Patanjali's Yoga Sutras. It is greatly elaborated in the tantric scriptures, as herbs play a significant role in the advanced practices of Tantra and Kundalini yoga."[111]

Admittedly, I know very little of Tantra, much less the tantric scriptures. Again, this is as a result of who my gurus were—decidedly not tantric gurus, or not "left-handed" tantrics at any rate. In fact, Amma herself would occasionally strongly caution us against reading any tantric books! My other teachers also never had anything much to say about Tantra, and if they had, it probably wouldn't have been anything good.[112] Like many others, I had only vague images of fantastic and lengthy sessions of "tantric sex," and so Tantra appeared to me to be a path for only the wildest, and probably impure, spiritual seekers. And at that point, at least, I was not at all tempted to take a walk on the wild side.

Interestingly enough, on my first trip to India to visit Amma, my Australian friend Billy advised me to purchase a copy of Dr. Robert Svoboda's *Aghora: At the Left Hand of God*, which is all about the tantric path. This book served as my port of entry to the subject of Tantra. The most important things I learned from Svoboda's book is that just as there is white and black magic, Tantra is also divided into "right-handed" Tantra (*Dakshinachara*), and "left-handed" Tantra (*Vamachara*). It is really only the latter which involves the notorious "5 M's," namely: 1) Madya (wine); 2) Mansa (meat); 3) Matsya (fish); 4) Mudra (gesture); and 5) Maithuna (sexual intercourse). Still, both right and left-handed Tantra are considered legitimate paths, though both Drs. Frawley and Svoboda suggest that the Vamachara path is but a means to the Dakshinachara path, and not an end in itself.

Dr. Frawley has put it this way:

"Tantra is divided into the right-handed and left-handed Tantras. The right-handed or Dakshinachara adheres to the Yamas and Niyamas of the Yoga system, including following a vegetarian diet. The left-handed or Vamachara system includes the use of intoxicants, including alcohol and psychedelic or mind-altering drugs, and the eating of meat, but sanctified in a ritualistic context to make them spiritually beneficial. The Vamachara system uses the more overt sexual Yogas, though the Dakshinachara tradition is not opposed to sex in a sanctified relationship.

Generally speaking, the right-handed Tantra is more for those in whom Sattva guna predominates. The left-handed Tantra is for those in whom Rajas and Tamas predominate.

There are some Tantric teachers today who do claim that a meat diet and other Vamachara practices are a better and quicker way to reach Self-realization. They may claim that the Dakshinachara or sattvic approaches are not possible for people to really do today and only result in repression. This tradition does exist for those who want to follow it. Yet while the Vamachara done sincerely can be a valid path, particularly in the modern cultural context, it is a stepping stone to Dakshinachara, not a substitute for it."[113]

Dr. Svoboda's teacher, Swami Vimalananda, likewise suggests that the goal of Vamachara Tantra is *sattva*, purity of body and mind. In a section on the subject of intoxicants and the "Left Hand Path," Swami Vimalanda says:

"This is the true test of an Aghori: from full-blown Tamas he must graduate to pure Sattva, love for all."[114]

In the end, Swami Vimalananda says he gave up intoxicants when he experienced the sweetness of the divine name, what you will recall Swamiji (Swami Satyananda Saraswati) referred to in the last chapter as the "nectar of devotion":

"I realized that the greatest intoxicant there is exists within me at all times. It is free, easy to use, harmless, and never gives me a hangover. It is the name of God. It gives the best concentration of mind. The effects of alcohol or marijuana or whatever will wear off by the next day, but the intoxication caused by God's name just goes on increasing; there is no end to it. I use it all the time, and it always works for me. No matter what has been my problem, the holy name of God has always been my solution. This is true Aghora. Forget all the externals; only when your heart melts and is consumed in the flames of your desire for your Beloved will you ever come close to

qualifying to learn the true Aghora."[115]

This means that psychedelics are not the be-all end-all of yoga, but merely a stepping-stone to a clearer, more pure realm of being. They are part of a process that ultimately involves graduating from psychedelics to a more *sattvic* path involving vegetarianism, sexual moderation, austerity, meditation, and other "chemical-free" practices.[116]

It is a misconception that the yoga path forbids intoxicants and mind-altering drugs. As we have seen, this is simply not the case. Rather, it is a matter of an ideal path vs. a less ideal path, where the path of chemically-enhancement is considered less ideal. This misconception is so widespread that even I was surprised when Dr. Frawley wrote me the following:

"Intoxicants may be helpful on an outer level for some yoga practitioners, particularly to open them up to higher possibilities..."

Dr. Robert Svoboda, author of the "Aghora" books

I had thought that Dr. Frawley would give me a much more hard-line, response more like, "Psychedelics and Yoga do not mix—period!"

But clearly, it's all in one's intent. If one's intent is to use plant material or a chemical in a sacramental way, in a quest from the illusory to the Real, or to catch a glimpse of the road ahead for the purposes of bolstering one's faith, then that is permissible.

That said, as Dr. Frawley puts it, the user must then remember that once they have been "opened up to higher possibilities," then it is advisable for them to move on to a slower, steadier, and more reliable spiritual practice, practices such as uttering "the name of God," as Swami Vimalananda suggested.

Now it may be asked: Although this makes perfect sense, on paper, how does it actually play out in the hurtling pace of postmodern life? Does this make sense for the individual living in the world as it is today?

From my own experience, I seemed to have reversed the usual process: starting out on a *sattvic* path, and maintaining it for years, but more recently taking a distinct turn towards *left-handed Tantra* practices, including the use of psychedelics.

Did I fall from my path? Am I a *yogi bhrashta,* a fallen yogi? Did I just become too impatient for ecstatic experiences and lost faith I ever would using only yogic practices? Had I digressed and devolved to using psychedelics, or were they a necessary step in my own "soulular" evolution?

And what about Terence McKenna? McKenna went as far as to declare that practices like chanting and meditation don't make sense except in the context of a shamanic journey. [See previous footnote] Could someone like McKenna ever reach a place where they might forgo psychedelics in favor of, say, *vipassana* meditation?

Now about these *siddhis,* or yogic powers… Such powers are traditionally seen as "milestones" along the path to enlightenment or Self/God-realization. The Yoga Sutras themselves suggest that they are not to be sought or abused, that they are not an end in themselves, but rather merely by-products of the quest for awakening.

Yogananda famously raises this point in his classic *Autobiography of a Yogi,* noting that some yogis abuse such powers, demonstrating them merely for the sake of fame or fortune. Paul Brunton agrees in *A Search in Secret India.*

More recently, however, in his book entitled *Yoga, Power, and Spirit: Patanjali the Shaman*, Alberto Villodo, Ph.D. maintains that according to Patanjali,

"The siddhis are essential to achieving samadhi, which is the true power… to deny them [the siddhis] is to deny your ultimate freedom. You can only step beyond these powers once you've acquired them. Renouncing them beforehand, as many practitioners of yoga do, mimics yet forestalls the true liberation… In addition, renouncing the siddhis, as some yoga teachers today advocate, keeps you powerless, and perpetuates your suffering as a victim."[117]

This is a point well-taken, considering that the Yoga Sutras does go out of its way to describe a number of these *siddhis,* ranging from clairvoyance, knowledge of past and future events (including one's past lives), the power to make oneself minute or even invisible, superhuman strength, conquest of hunger and thirst, among others. Again, these all result from the practice of "*Samyama.*" But what of *siddhis* that arise through other means, such as use of *aushadha*—are they at all comparable?

We have already seen that Iyengar and others hold that while such *siddhis* might be equivalent to those gained via *Samyama*, they are generally not permanent, but rather subject to loss due to a "fall from grace," or other means.

This is an interesting proposal, and to really check its validity would require a careful study of shamanism (see the following chapter), or better yet, personal experience. For the time being, let's consider some anecdotal evidence, the first a personal anecdote:

I recently met a woman who had a traumatizing LSD experience in the Seventies and was never the same afterwards, not only because of the trauma, but because the LSD "trip" had given her the ability to perceive unseen levels of reality. Today, some 3+ decades later, she offers shamanic healing through "soul retrieval." She also works in other therapeutic modalities that require access to hidden dimensions. For her, at least, the effects of the psychedelic experience have remained quite a long time, and show no signs of abating. Whether they would carry over into future lifetimes is another question…

Dr. Rick Strassman told me that he knows of a similar case in which a woman's psychic powers went away once she became a Christian. Dr. Strassman wrote,

"I recently got an e-mail from a Christian woman, who when younger, was slipped some PCP, which "opened the portals" for her to have all kinds of paranormal, psychic, experiences. She's a reasonable sounding woman, so I don't think she was psychotic. She and her husband became serious Christians and the portals seem to have closed.

It would be helpful to look into other "accidental" ways of acquiring such "psychic powers," such as through Near-Death Experiences (NDE). It seems a significant portion of those claiming to have had such experiences also maintain that the experience left them with psychic powers. Astral projection, or out-of-body experiences (OBE), are also another avenue for exploring this issue.

Still, such claims remain difficult to prove or disprove; and in most cases of psychedelic experience, whatever psychic powers are acquired during the "trip" usually disappear once the experience fades. Or, if not all at once, then eventually.

Such has been my own experience thus far: As real and as powerful and transformational as my psychedelic experiences have been, it is amazing that so little of them have actually stayed with me.

Perhaps if I did more, and in an even more disciplined way, my case might be different. But for now, I am left with the sense that these ecstatic experiences are ephemeral to the point of being almost unhelpful in regard to actually developing *siddhis*, or attaining *samadhi*.

Please don't misunderstand me: I don't mean to diminish the value of getting a glimpse, however paltry, of *Samadhi*, including the invaluable lessons that went along with the whole psychedelic experience. But it seems to me that psychedelics must be approached in a disciplined way and *as a discipline*, or the deeper, more abiding lessons of these plant "teachers" will be missed. In subsequent chapters, we will meet individuals and groups who are doing just that.[118]

6

What's the Difference Between a Yogi and a Shaman?[119]

"While our modern secular culture denies the existence of a spiritual dimension to life, many of our popular post-secular movements of mysticism still refuse to address the question of spirits. Philosophers such as Ken Wilber tend to reduce them to psychological tropes or delusions. Based on my on experiences, I strongly suspect we need to attain a more sophisticated understanding of how spirits may operate, as well as a set of techniques for dealing with them, before we can approach higher states and stages of development. We cannot have "Spirit" without spirits."

—Daniel Pinchbeck

I begin this chapter with Pinchbeck's quote because not only did it speak to me personally when I first read it, but I also sense this idea holds some deep resonance for those of us engaged with Yoga and Shamanism right now. Perhaps you also wonder how the paths of Yoga and Shamanism intersect. And wonder, too, how accessing non-ordinary states of consciousness (NOSC), or what shamans call "the spirit world," and what Grof calls "Holotropic States," might be helpful for yoga practitioners in the West.

You might also have wondered what use psychoactive aids, or "plant sacraments" have for the contemporary yoga practitioner. Particularly for those of us who have been told that "plant medicine" is not a "pure" yogic path, one leading to the ultimate goal of *Moksha* (liberation).

Let's begin by looking at how Yoga and Shamanism might be seen as distinct disciplines. The late great yoga scholar, Georg Feuerstein, did much research on this very subject. Feuerstein's current published view on the relationship between Yoga and Shamanism is as follows:

"The development of Yoga's heritage spans at least five millennia and may go back

into the dim past of the early Neolithic age. Conceivably, Yoga emerged out of the Shamanism of the Paleolithic, but at this point in our knowledge of Yoga's history this is mere speculation. Certainly Yoga and Shamanism have many features in common, though the final purpose is quite distinct: Whereas Yoga aims at spiritual liberation (moksha), Shamanism is primarily concerned with what in Yoga would be called the "subtle dimension" and with so-called magical feats and healing service to the community." [120]

Despite this assertion, Feuerstein did acknowledge that a form of shamanism is still widespread in India today, especially among the Shaivites, or yogis who follow the tradition of Shiva. In the 2005 film, "Origins of Yoga: Quest for the Spiritual," Feuerstein makes the following assertion:

"Many yogis also fulfill the role of the shaman, whereby they serve the community as healers, magicians, wise men, and so on."

One only need look at the values and practices of the most radical Shaivites, the Naga Babas, to see unmistakable signs of shamanism. These include:

- ◎ Use of psychoactive herbs such as ganja, datura, etc.
- ◎ Ecstatic dance and song
- ◎ A firepit (*dhuni*) which confers healing and blessing upon the community
- ◎ Asceticism
- ◎ Magical powers (*siddhis*)
- ◎ Initiation rites [121]

Dr. Wolf-Dieter Storl, writing in his book *Shiva: The Wild God of Power and Ecstasy*, comments that:

"When confronted with the image of Shiva, an anthropologist will most likely think of a Super-Shaman."

This is because Shiva, in the form of Nataraja, Lord of the Dance, carries a drum in one hand, and fire in the other as he engages in his cosmic dance of dissolution. The Naga Babas certainly embody this image of Shiva in their lives and practices, striving to emulate their beloved deity.

Feuerstein's reply to this is that, yes, it is true that many yogis fulfill the role of the shaman, yet the domain of the yogi (or "yogin," as he prefers) extends beyond that of the shaman:

"The yogin's ultimate purpose, however is to go beyond the subtle levels of existence explored by the shaman, and to realize the transcendental Being, which is trans-dimensional and unqualified, and which the yogin knows to be his innermost identity.

Thus, whereas the shaman is a healer or miracle-worker, the yogin is primarily a tran-
scender. But in the spiritual ascent to the transcendental Reality, the yogin is likely to
gather a great deal of knowledge about the subtle realms (sukshma-loka). This explains
why many yogins have demonstrated extraordinary abilities and have long been looked
upon by the Indian people as miracle workers and magicians. From the yogic point of
view, however, the paranormal abilities possessed by many adepts are insignificant by
comparison with the ultimate attainment of Self-Realization, or enlightenment." (The
Yoga Tradition, *p. 95)*

To use the language of Ken Wilber, the role of the yogi "transcends and includes" the role of the shaman. The role of the shaman is part of the yogi's job description, agreed, yet the yogi also explores the causal realms, not solely the shaman's high astral planes.

It is important to note here that Feuerstein does not discount the importance of the yogi consciously familiarizing himself with the subtle realm of existence. From such astral travels, a yogi can sometimes serve as a healer or intermediary for the community, much as a shaman would.

In other words, while not the goal, for Feuerstein there's certainly a place for shamanism in Yoga.

But what of Feuerstein's suggestion that the shaman does not access the causal dimensions, while the yogi can and does? Is there any evidence to support such a claim? This brings us back to the original quote from Pinchbeck, and into a scholarly debate that has been going on between Stanislav Grof and Ken Wilber.

I'm not sure to what degree Pinchbeck was aware of this debate when he made his criticism of Wilber, but Grof and other Transpersonal psychologists have been leveling similar critiques for years. In his critical essay, "Ken Wilber's Spectrum Psychology," in which Grof confronts Wilber on a number of key points, Grof makes the following statement, almost as if directly responding to Feuerstein as well:

"Shamanic literature, as well as the personal experiences of many anthropologists
with shamans, leaves little doubt that they regularly have spiritual experiences not
only of the subtle realms, but also of the causal realms."[122]

Feuerstein would argue that we're talking here about the over-arching goals of shamanism and yoga, not what some yogis or shamans might access in their own personal experience. Both Feuerstein and Wilber hold the great Indian sage, Ramana Maharishi[123] in very high esteem, and would no doubt maintain that there isn't a comparable figure in the world of shamanism.

Yet Grof is suggesting that, in fact, shamans are on the self-same path of integration as yogis, and access the same levels of consciousness in their journeys. Using

Ramana Maharishi as our example, he apparently did not reach enlightenment in one day in the sense of permanently attaining God-realization, it was a process. Only after years of patient integration of his initial awakening experience did he become the universally honored sage he was later recognized to be.[124]

Admittedly, I am not as familiar with the wide world of shamanism as I am with yoga, and so I cannot point to any personage in shamanism who, like Ramana Maharishi, has unambiguously reached the same pinnacle in their own evolution.[125]

Yet I will add this personal note: During my own initial *Ayahuasca* experience—the most harrowing, hallowing episode of my entire life—I had the sense that it was a kind of shamanic initiation. This feeling involved traveling through various astral realms and eventually having the sense that the entire ego/body-mind complex was being dismembered and ultimately reconstituted. Once the final re-integration was complete, I experienced myself (Self) as "pure awareness" devoid of ego. To use the language of the Yoga Sutras, there were no more "*vrittis*," or mental fluctuations. I was truly in the state of Yoga, experiencing the causal ground of simply Being. In other words, at that point, I was not in an astral dimension but a "transpersonal" state of consciousness.

Put simply, my shamanic journey took me through the astral into the causal, and ultimately back into a sense of "*ahamkara*," or narrow self-consciousness, "The Box," though a considerably expanded box, to be sure.[126] (Please keep in mind, these are merely words straining to express what truly cannot be expressed.)

Ken Wilber does not deny the reality of these experiences for the experiencer, but he does distinguish between what he calls "back door," or "regressive," transpersonal experiences, and "front door" experiences. "Back door" therapies include Holotropic breathwork, rebirthing, psychedelics, hypnosis, etc., while "front door" experiences come about spontaneously through practices such as meditation and other "consciousness disciplines."[127]

Let's "listen" to an excerpt from an informal talk with the Integral philosopher. Here Wilber's droll and somewhat derogatory designation, "druggies" are essentially the "back door" men, and "meditators" are those who do It through the "front door":

"My sense is that the people I know that have done it responsibly, have gained a lot from using psychedelics to open up a certain space. But there are downsides. Particularly in this movement, you find there are two general approaches to consciousness studies. One is the druggies, and one is the meditators.

And the druggies are into altered states, and the meditators are into stages. And the meditators believe that you have to actually discipline and work and it's four years, ten years, fifteen years, to reach a stable realization of these higher states and stages.

And the psychedelic or drug side is much more into altered states, Ayahuasca, LSD, any sort of number of altered states, and they don't tend to get into permanent realizations based on these things.

I happen to believe that both of these models—I use states and stages—I believe both of them are required. But there's kind of an acrimony between these two groups. There are very few people that do drugs and are serious meditators. And the people that only do drugs, I think eventually it kind of tends to catch up in away. I don't see permanent realization coming from these things, I don't see permanent access to some of these higher states, and I think at some point the simple neurological noise of the ingredients starts to almost outshine the luminosity that was there, perhaps, at the beginning.

And so the people I know that I've watched over thirty years, that have done only drugs, have become increasingly, frankly, unpleasant people, and disillusioned, and sad, in certain ways. It's not to say that meditators do all that much better, but there is at least a chance with meditators that you can have a permanent realization that is enduring and not merely a transitory state.

I think people do better if they either have a judicious combination of the two, or if they do mostly meditation. And my recommendation is don't just do drugs, because people tend to get into trouble, and the theories I see coming out of people that just do drugs are frankly pretty wacky theories. They don't take enough evidence into account, they are not inclusive enough, they don't include other types of data and evidence, and I think they're very partial."

Although Wilber doesn't mention Grof or McKenna by name, one wonders whether they are to be numbered among "the druggies" whose theories are "pretty wacky."[128]

This interview with Wilber took place in April of 2001, a year after McKenna's death from brain cancer, which some have speculated was caused by his taking high doses of psychedelics. Terence himself suggested it was due to his cannabis use.[129]

Today there is general support for the Pinchbeck-Mckenna-Grof view in the psychedelic community, but I think Wilber's view is worth serious consideration. Specifically, that a combination of psychedelics *and* meditation just might be the wisest route to reaching a permanent state of enlightenment. Let "back door" elements such as Ayahuasca cleanse one's "doors of perception," but for deeper, more lasting expanded states of consciousness, a seeker should also practice a slower, more stable "front door" meditative discipline.

That said, I don't feel it's fair or helpful to make sweeping judgments about so-called "druggies," such as McKenna. I don't see him as having been unpleasant, disillusioned, or sad, as Wilber suggests (nor Grof, or other psychedelic pioneers).

Actually, I have felt more inspired by McKenna and Grof than by Wilber. I sense my reason could be that Wilber's use of psychedelics is rather limited: he openly acknowledges that one long LSD experience in college pretty much turned him off of drugs, until he got into MDMA in the early '80s. He also makes the point that MDMA was still legal then. And we must also keep in mind that though "E" or MDMA is not a true psychedelic, though if not "mind expanding," it is heart-expanding.

I also feel that it is a cardinal principle of open debate that one shouldn't theorize about what one has not personally experienced in a direct and intimate way. How can Wilber really talk about these *Transpersonal* therapies without actually having taken them for a spin himself? Test out an actual plant sacrament like Ayahuasca with a shaman guide, explore the spirit world as "primary source," otherwise stand accused of armchair philosophy!

To be fair, perhaps Wilber is right is suggesting that many in the psychedelic community have not done their "om-work," if you will, in terms of having a core spiritual discipline or serious meditation practice that they can use as a framework to inform their own models of reality. It might also be that they thus would not be able to fully comprehend what Wilber is getting at. The same might be said for those of us who would throw out the guru model, and all eastern metaphysics without actually ever having had any deep encounter with them. I sense that this may be one of the greatest blind spots of the current psychedelic community.[130]

For myself, though, I appreciate that neither McKenna nor Grof were ever bent on establishing a Kosmic "theory of everything" as Wilber has been. I see that rather, they have always been intent on pointing to the *Mystery*, and showing us ways that we may become more wonder-filled by invoking and evoking the *Mystery*. To invoke Ken Kesey's immortal words:

"The answer is never the answer. What's really interesting is the mystery. If you seek the mystery instead of the answer, you'll always be seeking. I've never seen anybody really find the answer—they think they have, so they stop thinking. But the job is to seek mystery, evoke mystery, plant a garden in which strange plants grow and mysteries bloom. The need for mystery is greater than the need for an answer."

Theories and models will always have their use, but I believe that the need for a personal *experience* of the *Mystery* is what we should be seeking. Only an *experience* plus *understanding* will bring about a true change in personal perspective. Talk is cheap—the hard work is to take the plunge into the *Unknown*, returning to earth and actually living and embodying the wisdom with which you've been gifted.

Bringing This All Back Down to Earth

To bring this all down into our own intense present moment, there is a shift happening in the world of yoga. This change is in connection to shamanistic practice, particularly the use of plant sacraments like Ayahuasca. This shift has actually been taking place for some time now, but it's only in the last few years that the older generation of yoga teachers have begun to speak out about their use openly. One example is Ganga White, one of the top yoga teachers in the world, who quite openly broached the subject in his recently published book, *Yoga Beyond Belief*.

"I touch on the topic of plant sacraments because it is a timely subject and something I am repeatedly asked about." White continues, *"There are neural pathways in the brain that are more ancient than our beliefs, philosophies, and religious proscriptions. There are keys to the doorways of the rich interior landscape that open dimensions of beauty, order, intelligence, immense complexity, and sacredness beyond measure. These realities can be so powerful, brilliant, and intense that, while visiting them, our world seems like a distant hallucination, in the way that these other realities can seem hallucinatory from this one. Seeing and being touched by these mystical experiences can change us and help us in positive ways with insights into self-healing, enlightened living, and the wholeness of life. Our bodies and brains operate on chemical messengers and information exchange systems in nature. Some scholars and evidence show that medicinal plants were probably at the origin of religious and mystical experience. To say plant sacraments are unnatural, and practices, rituals, and belief systems created by man are natural, is an absurdity. It is a shame that fear and conditioning can preclude the greatest journey... within."*

Now, these are the words of a master Hatha yogi who has been on the yoga path for over four decades and has himself studied with some of the great Yoga gurus. White's book was influential in getting me to explore plant medicine further, as well as to write the book you are now reading.

Using plant medicine was not an easy decision for me. Like many Hatha yoga practitioners, I was extremely careful about what I allowed into my body. Using "strange' plant medicines gave me great fear of causing permanent damage to my body. The possibility of it messing with my beloved yoga practice was also a grave concern. As was disobeying my teachers, and the traditions I held dear.

But, interestingly enough, what I subsequently learned from my plant journeys, is that it is precisely the over-identification with the body, bordering on obsession for some, that needs to be released in order for one's ego boundaries to be bridged. This realization would be of utmost value to those who are utilizing the technology of Hatha Yoga as a means of self-transcendence.[131]

There are many reasons why a yoga practitioner might find Ayahuasca helpful, both personally, and also for the healing of our communities and planet. As for the latter, I appreciated Daniel Pinchbeck's comments on the subject during a dialogue with Jivamukti Yoga co-founder Sharon Gannon on Ayahuasca.[132] His points regarding the elitism and narcissism within the yoga community were particularly relevant. Pinchbeck suggested that our era calls for those yogis who are already familiar with moving through uncomfortable spaces in their yoga practices to consider that plant sacraments might have a timely value for us, both personally and globally.

I've personally, first and foremost within myself, experienced firsthand the elitism and narcissism of modern yoga. That kind but superior look accompanying a sad shaking of the head whenever the subject of "drugs" is mentioned. And I have also seen for myself how an Ayahuasca experience can move one through very difficult and uncomfortable psychic spaces, thus making it easier to deal with real world events and issues once the experience is over.

Of course, this is also exactly what yoga work "on the mat" does, albeit in a less dramatic way. Still, some Hatha Yoga practice, a Bikram or Kundalini class for example, can be very intense for some!

But, there can be no doubt that a guided plant medicine journey accelerates one's quest for enlightenment. That was my experience. To paraphrase Timothy Leary's famous quote about LSD: "I learned more during my first session with Ayahuasca than I had in all my 13 years on the yoga mat."

Look at it this way: Many of us have spent years disciplining our bodies in an extreme physical way to prepare our physiology for intense moments of "Samadhi." We have quested to become fit vessels to "hold" these moments of intense energy, to navigate the "uncomfortable" spaces of our own psyches in a fully conscious way.

But from whence do such experiences come? They won't come from Hatha Yoga alone, and almost certainly not even from the path outlined in Patanjali's Yoga Sutras, Raja Yoga, unless you are an *extremely* devoted and disciplined meditator.

No, it seems that such unique experiences for most of us come through shamanic journeying. Particularly through the use of shamanic rituals using psychoactive plants in a sacramental and yogic way. Could it be that this is why we have all been doing all these intense physical practices and contortions for so long?[133]

Here's a wonderfully expressed statement from a Yoga teacher that uses Ayahuasca as a sacrament. She was influenced to do so by an internationally recognized yoga teacher of the previous generation. In a private email interview, I had asked her what Ayahuasca meant to her as a yoga teacher and practitioner, and here's how she so eloquently replied:

"Like many yogis, I am very interested in the nature of consciousness. Isn't that why we do yoga? As such, I've explored both traditional and less traditional ways to shift my perception of reality—and, yes, that includes working with various entheogens in a sacred setting. Without getting into the details of when, where and with whom, I'd say I have done a reasonable amount of work with Ayahuasca and I've always experienced it as a powerful medicine—healing, transformative and liberating on the most profound levels. I so appreciate the fact that the work I do in ceremony builds on, and is harmonious with, the work I do on my mat. For me, Ayahuasca is a teacher who speaks poignantly to the challenges of the Kali Yuga [the so-called "dark age of materialism"]; little wonder she is slowly finding her way into the mainstream."

Let's speculate about Pinchbeck's ideas on exploring what Yoga calls the astral or subtle realm: we live in a materialistic era where even yoga people need reminders that within our work-a-day materialist culture there's more going on than we can perceive through our five senses. One of my own personal encounters in the astral realm led me to consider the possibly that the earth's spirit, or even perhaps beings from other star systems wanted to communicate with us via plant medicines. Perhaps we are we meant to consciously alter our DNA as part of the next stage of evolution? Could plant sacraments be the true and original teachers of humanity? Are plant spirits endowed with the power to save humankind from ourselves, precisely at this point in time and space.

There is evidence that suggests that some of the above may just be the case, but ultimately we really don't know. Mystery remains.

All the above ideas connect us with an original sense of human awe and wonder—sublime feelings that we are all here to attend to some deeper purpose and meaning—a feeling with which we all truly desire to connect, or perhaps re-connect. So we should be cautious here and not come to any rash conclusions on any of these points. We simply don't know and this is why we are on this quest.

So to sum up this introduction to yoga and shamanism: There is now and always has been a place in yoga for shamanic practices, including the use of "plant sacraments." Even beyond that ancient tradition there might currently be a call for yoga and plant medicines in terms of healing our fractured selves, communities, and planet. Yoga alone is perfectly positioned to be one of the most effective disciplines for preparing the spiritual ground for both individual and worldwide healing and harmony among peoples. For those wanting to quicken the awakening process, the plant teachers, particularly Ayahuasca, might just be a complementary accessory to yogic discipline.

7

Kundalini and Psychedelics

Pharaoh's Magicians or:
My Experience Was...
I Didn't Have An Experience

"Trumpets and violins I can
Uh, hear in the distance
I think they're callin' our name
Maybe now you can't hear them,
But you will, ha-ha, if you just
Take hold of my hand
Ohhh, but are you experienced?
Have you ever been experienced?
Not necessarily stoned, but beautiful..."

—Jimi Hendrix

I am sitting on the floor of a private home in New Jersey, chanting and singing Sanskrit mantras and verses, taking part in an advanced training with a Kundalini Yoga group that I was initiated into one year previously. There are approximately 40 students, and two teachers—a husband and wife team from Northern India, who are sitting on a divan in front of us. As our singing and music making crescendos, some of my fellow students begin to go into altered states of consciousness, in which they do any one or more of the following: laugh, cry, yell, dance or sing ecstatically, adopt special hand or facial gestures (mudras), spontaneously go into yoga postures, and more. Although I personally am feeling quite uplifted and even blissful, there is a part of me that feels as an outsider, observing all that is happening, and wondering why I have yet to have these kinds of seemingly ecstatic experiences.

At a climactic point in the midst of this whole melee, our primary teacher, who is the better half of the husband and wife team, begins to dance ecstatically. She, too, is in another state of consciousness, and her dance seems completely spontaneous and effortless. Before our eyes (those of us who are still "there"), she takes on aspects of the all-embracing Divine Mother, and then Shiva, her consort, doing his Cosmic Dance, and next Krishna, with his flute, and… just one divine archetype after after another. Although others in the room are having similar movements of Kundalini energy, none are having it to this degree, or in such fullness of expression and beauty. Our teacher stands apart, unapproachable, and seemingly, from my perspective, unattainable.

As the guru dances, a woman in our group begins to make the most horrifyingly inhuman, wounded animal sounds—bellowing, throaty yells, grunts, and groans that seem to emanate from the deepest recesses of her being. It is actually frightening to listen to, and some of us are feeling the need to assist her in some way. Some devotees gather around her, and I feel relieved that she has help. Meanwhile, the teacher is now flat on her back on the floor, motionless, in a very deep state of Samadhi, mystic absorption. Those who are not assisting the other woman are now up close to our teacher, ready to receive the blessing of the Divine.

Later, the woman who had seemed to be in such terrible torment earlier, remarks to several of us, "Did anyone have as much fun as me?"

Apparently not I.

Over the course of several years involved with this group, I witnessed several similar proceedings, and each time I left feeling amazed, energized, and transformed. But I also left with a sense of having missed something.

Why did I seem to be blocked from going deeper? Where was my *ecstatic experience*? Where was that blissful, unconditional, love I had experienced when I was nineteen? There was an incredible urgency to this question that was driving me forward on my quest.

Originally, I had become involved with this group through a friend and colleague specializing in Indology. She had recognized that I was sincerely searching for answers through authentic mystical experiences. She befriended me and began to introduce me to some of the contemporary masters from India, most of them were women either touring or based in the United States. My new friend assured me that if I sought genuine mystical experiences, *these* were the teachers I should get to know. This was in the Winter–Spring of 1996.

At this same time, a passionate young man in his mid-twenties strongly encouraged me to get involved with his Kundalini Yoga. This group was based in the Philadelphia area and was also organized around a woman teacher from India.

This is how it happened…

In December, 1995, in collaboration with the local Hillel, I co-organized an interfaith dialogue on ecology at the University of Pennsylvania. We invited a priest, a rabbi, and an imam to speak on ecology in the context of their religious traditions. Our intent was to see if there might be greater cooperation among faiths on these issues.

Coincidently, the room we were using for the occasion was to be used by the Kundalini Yoga group directly after our program. As we were concluding, this young man, whom we'll call Brad, approached me and excitedly began telling me about this amazing Kundalini Yoga path he had found. He also sang the praises of his guru to the point of deification: She was his God!

Recognizing the sign, I got involved with not one, but two Kundalini Yoga groups simultaneously. With the one, led by the woman guru in the story above, I received a traditional Shaktipat initiation. With the other, I was shown practices that were to raise my Kundalini, but had no contact with the actual teacher herself. Only a very few friends knew I was involved with both groups. For my part, to avoid conflict, I played dumb and kept mum.

All that Winter, Spring, Summer and into the Fall, I interacted with both groups intimately, learning a great deal not only about their organizations, but also receiving an initiatory education into all things Indian.

Of course, my grad school colleague-mentor also helped me immensely. We would speak for hours about all that I was experiencing. I asked my friend many questions, and because she was both a scholar and veteran Yoga practitioner, she was able to provide me with an enormous amount of helpful guidance.

Why was I spending all my waking hours doing yoga? Well, I had been burning with questions most of my adult life and now I finally found something that could quench my thirst. Indeed, I was discovering that many of my most existential doubts and questions were being answered via this new "I-Thou" encounter with India and Yoga. For the first time in my life, I was meeting genuine master teachers who could enter at will into deep states of consciousness. From these profound depths of awareness, these teachers could guide souls like myself who were just beginning to awaken and flower.

Like many other seekers when they first encounter their life's true calling, I had a strong sense of "This is It!" I had at last found what I had been searching for, unconsciously and consciously, all of my life. I had come home.

One gnawing issue that was being healed through this encounter was in regard to my sexuality. I had a lot of confusion and anxiety about it, and no one I felt I could really relate with about my feelings and concerns. I had never been in a relationship with a woman, and it was a subject about which I was very ambivalent. Even though I had a very strong libido, I had always felt that a relationship would be too restrictive. In any case, I had always been looking for just the right person, but in retrospect, my standards were unrealistically high.

Also, I had been torn for years over the issue of masturbation, and now from Yoga I was finally learning and deeply understanding the wisdom behind conserving and transmuting one's vital essence (termed "brahmacharya" in Sanskrit). No one had ever been able to explain masturbation to me before without bringing in "sin" or "guilt" on the one hand; or that it was "perfectly normal" behavior on the other. Now it was hitting me as an amazing revelation, a kind of gnosis, or salvational Knowledge. A part of me had always known there was deeper wisdom out there, but the truth is, it was already inside of me. As the saying goes, "When the student is ready, the teacher appears."

Brad from the Kundalini Yoga group explained that any physical orgasm is but a paltry imitation of the Cosmic "O." And once you experience the latter, or even glimpses of it, the sex act takes on much less importance. He also told me that before having his own awakening experience from his teacher, he had been heavily into partying, drugs, alcohol, etc. The Kundalini Yoga teachings and practices had helped him wean himself away from his addictive behavior.

Not a few times, Brad related a story about how, not long after he had gotten his teacher, a friend convinced him to go to a rock concert where they took LSD together. As usual, he began hallucinating almost immediately. But then, out of curiosity, he decided to meditate on his Kundalini energy to see what would happen. Immediately, the hallucinations vanished and did not return, even though LSD usually takes

8-10 hours to wear off.

Though interesting, Brad's story seemed far-fetched; and in any case, anything having to do with drugs didn't resonate with me at that time as I had always been a purist when it came to putting anything foreign into my body. Also, I had no context to appreciate the enormity of what Brad was getting at. So, like much of what Brad was sharing with me, I was skeptical…

Almost from the start, I had a strong sensation that Brad's Kundalini group was a cult, or at least cultish, and that I should play a participant-observer role and nothing more. But because I was so new to all of this, I was challenged by his insistence that their path was the only true one. The group actually believed that their human teacher was God, and that all of the other Yoga teachers who had come to the West were all false gurus. They were particularly against a few of the women teachers I was meeting at that same time, especially one of my favorites, Mata Amritananda-mayi, or "Ammachi," "the Hugging Saint."

Mainly I thought all this was preposterous, but it did make me wonder: "Well, what if they're right? Could they be right?" This wasn't an academic exercise for me, this felt like a divine test I was being given to learn how to be discriminative in spiritual matters, to learn how to follow my heart and intuition. This was especially challenging as I was being asked to doubt and question my own heart and conscience…

And here's what my heart and conscience were telling me:

The other Kundalini group felt like a breath of fresh air in comparison. It was all about the heart, and really quite understated and pure. It didn't feel cultish at all, but more like a self-selected coming together of experienced souls who were seeking a true path to liberation. I felt a lot of love and joy amongst them, and even had some of my first mystical experiences, which included movement of chakras, precognitive dreams, clairvoyance, telepathy, and synchronicity.

At the same time, because it didn't seem like an exact fit, I was still inwardly singing Bono's line, "…*But I still haven't found what I'm looking for…*"

I sought more depth of experience, and for my Western mindset and Jewish education, Kundalini was a bit of a stretch. Could I really follow this Hindu path? Wouldn't I feel forever a stranger in a strange land, both in this new community and in my own native culture and society? How long did I want to keep up this intense discipline without going much deeper?

Meanwhile, Brad told me that the difference between his path and all the other, false paths is that his Teacher gives each student a genuine Kundalini awakening right from the very beginning.

His challenge to me was: Have you ever had a powerful, authentic experience of Kundalini from any other teacher? And my answer, of course, was that I had not, but I hadn't felt very much from Brad's path either. He asserted that was because I had never actually met his Guru, and that when I did, I would get it. And it just so happened there was soon going to be a big gathering in New York presided over by Brad's Teacher…

So, not long after that conversation, we road-tripped up there with some of the group from Philadelphia.

To put it simply, that excursion only served to intensify my distaste for this group, and for Brad's Teacher. Not only was the group feeling more and more cultish—devotee after devotee seemed both spiritual neophyte and budding missionary—but the Teacher herself did not seem to demonstrate very enlightened behavior.

This was a big, annual event in celebration of the Teacher that attracted many devotees from around the world, including contingents from each major city in the US. There was a very heightened sense of expectancy in the air, a feeling that something earthshaking would be revealed at that night's program. For many, this sense of anticipation was all the more palpable, for some obscure reason, when the Teacher arrived at the hall hours late.

From my perspective, this behavior was simply inconsiderate, at best. Brad's Teacher had kept hundreds waiting and guessing as to what was going on. To make matters worse, the ceremony began with gift giving, and the Teacher actually began to grumpily criticize some of her devotees for their offerings! The amazing thing was that no one seemed to think there was anything amiss. The Empress had no clothes, and no one was willing to call her on it.

Up until this point, I had kept most of my deeper reservations to myself. I had given no one any indication of the battle raging in my own mind and heart. But at the end of that weekend, I finally had it out with Brad.

We argued passionately all the way back to Philadelphia. Sometimes Brad's reaction to me became ugly. At other times I thought I glimpsed a glimmer of understanding. At another point, after I had stated some of my innermost feelings and criticisms—things which he had no real inkling that I had been weighing in my mind and heart—he blurted out, "You're a great seeker!" and I couldn't detect any irony or sarcasm in his face or tone.

Still, we kept arguing… and arguing. This went on even after we returned. Shortly after this incident I parted ways with the group. After I departed, I began getting "talked to" about my leaving, as often happens with cults. It didn't matter. I was through. While it wasn't easy leaving that group, leave I did. I have never looked back.

• • •

During that first year of my "passage to India" my mentor would inevitably ask me what my experience of a given group or event or program was. "My experience," I unfailingly noted with a laugh, "was that I didn't have an Experience." To that, she would rhetorically reply, "Well, aren't you so glad you got into all of this anyway?" to which I always unhesitatingly agreed. Then she was off to India again for a year of study, and I was left alone without my trusted friend and guide.

I wept when she left.

Cheap Thrills… and Imitations?

"Vanity of vanities, all is vanity."
—Ecclesiastes

"I returned, and saw under the sun, that the race is not to the swift, nor the battle to the strong, neither yet bread to the wise, nor yet riches to men of understanding, nor yet favor to men of skill; but time and chance happeneth to them all."
—Ecclesiastes 9:11

One core truth I've learned on my quest is that life is short, but just long enough to experience everything we wish to experience in this body… or at least, to experience the things we want to experience.

Let's take the example of sex: for many years, my mind was craving sex. It was such a strong desire that, even though there was guilt and shame attached, eventually sex happened. And when it did happen, I recognized it was not all that I had imagined and hoped it would be, but a fleeting pleasure.

So, too, with spiritual experience. My mind craved "mystical experience," so eventually that came… and went. Clearly it wasn't IT either. When I finally received these things, I realized that they were no big deal and I had been, as Solomon put it in the Book of Ecclesiastes, chasing in vain to catch the wind. Perhaps it has been the wind of Spirit pushing me forward all along on my quest?

Ten years after participating in those Kundalini groups, I found myself in the Ayahuasca circle under the guidance of a Peruvian-trained shaman. I took this very seriously and kept a journal, even taking fervent notes in the dark of what the shaman counseled us right before we all partook of his medicine, Ayahuasca. I will now relate just a little snippet of relevant material from my journey report:

"…the energy began to move me into what in Kundalini Yoga is called "kriyas," or automatic bodily postures and movements. For example, I suddenly realized I had my arms raised in the air ecstatically. And then I became conscious to the fact that my

upper body was being circled around in the exact same movements I teach at the outset of most of my yoga classes, movements made popular by Yogi Bhajan's 3HO Kundalini Yoga. It's not that these didn't feel good, they did. And these were the kinds of experiences I had always wanted to have 10 years ago when I had been in a Kundalini yoga group, but never had. Now the realization came that although these were "fun," they also were the result of unconsciousness, of my own asleepness...

So Let's Get One Thing Clear Here

The experiences to be had through psychedelics are quite similar to experiences engendered via substance-free practices such as breathwork and meditation.

Which begs the question: They look the same and feel the same, but *are* they the same? And then, even if we could establish that they are indeed not the same qualitatively, the next question is, does it really matter?

Exhibit A: An actual research study of psychedelics and Kundalini by a man named Donald J. DeGracia entitled, "*Do Psychedelic Drugs Mimic Awakened Kundalini? Hallucinogen Survey Results.*"[134] As the title suggests, DeGracia's point is merely to show that psychedelics instigate experiences that appear on the surface to be very similar to non-psychedelic-based Kundalini phenomena. And to my mind, DeGracia does succeed in establishing this point.

The nagging question for me is why I had no Kundalini experiences after receiving shaktipat initiation (they're called "*kriyas*"), yet I have now had numerous Kundalini-like *kriyas* from psychedelics, particularly Ayahuasca. There are two main possible explanations for this: One is the possibility that in the ten years since first getting into yoga, there had developed in me certain blockages and impurities that come with living in the body and the world, as well as blockages from yoga itself. These things were absent in my twenties but present in my thirties. So the psychedelics had to work through more "stuff" within me, more layers, before the truest, most authentic self, or Self, could be revealed. The other possibility is the opposite of the first: That after all of my earlier yoga initiations and practices, there were *less blockages,* and so I was able to surrender more to plant medicine experiences without fearing a loss of control. Another possibility, and one that has been a criticism of psychedelics, is that they often bulldoze right through all of one's armoring, but miss all the subtleties along the way. Much the way a prescription drug wipes out bad cells, but also destroys many good cells in the process. While Ayahuasca has often been described as a wise and gentle teacher, this might depend on dosage. I once had a dose that had me writhing on the floor like a snake almost immediately and ended up being a complete "ego death" experience.

Could it be that Ayahuasca was able to penetrate deeper into my blockages than could the *Kundalini Shakti* energy? And does that mean one is better or worse?

Or would it simply be better to lay such value judgments at the feet of the One who knows…?

And now for Exhibit B: A journey report of one Yogi Zen, a contemporary spiritual guide who some 2+ decades ago had what he felt was a Kundalini awakening via a psychedelic compound. Yogi Zen is one of the most wild and crazy beings I have ever met: a sacred fire bearer of the Shaivite lineage and also the creator of the increasingly popular Yoga Swing. One afternoon, just prior to spending the night together around the fire with a tab of lysergic each, Zen related to me the following story about an early mushroom experience that awakened him to his true calling in life:

"Yeah what happened to me was I went to a hippie gathering and I started eating raw foods and salads and stuff, and I started feeling better. And I got lots of mushrooms and took 'em at 'Reggae on the River.' I was getting a massage from this woman and somehow the 'shrooms came on. She finished the massage and my Kundalini started to awaken. I'm starting to get off and all of a sudden a rush of heat goes up my spine, pushing, pushing and it pushed up to my brain and it was such a pressure I felt the snake—it was a snake—the serpent, the Kundalini just came up to the crown, the top of my head, all over the top like: Jingggg. And then I felt like I had to open my mouth and then the snake came out and hissed, HSaahhhhh, and all this energy released. I felt really high, elevated. So the energy just started moving, moving and moving—and then I got off the massage table, went out to the river, and then I just started chanting mantras and mantras."

Q: Did you know the mantras?

No, nothing, nothing. I saw some mantras on my arm painted inside the skin, and I could see energy and auras, you know, and the two arms became serpents, and the fingertips became eyes, you know you can see through your fingers. It was so clear. So I was doing all these mudras, brother, and fucking everything was aligned and powerful and like nothing I've ever done in my entire life, ever, ever. I was putting on The Show in the water, and I was looking at people and Vammmm! Sending that energy and they were like, "Dude, rocking." I played in the water and did this for hours, man, the temperature was perfect, and swam with the snake and the nagas [divine serpents]. See, once they came out was one thing—then, they wanted to come back inside me. Meaning they were inside me but then… a snake came out, danced with me, and then I had to eat the snake again, so the snake tried to kill me under water—I actually felt it trying to kill me, drown me, and I let that happen. And then I became resurrected, I became Lord Shiva, the highest embodiment of Shiva in a human body for sure, the energy was there, BAM! And then from then on I was a changed human being…"

My response to this was so that's *why* Yogi Zen is who he is. The mushrooms seemed to have unblocked some esoteric knowledge that was lodged deep in his psyche. Or perhaps his subconscious mind activated those subtle grooves in the mind called *samskaras,* places that had lain dormant awaiting that exact moment in time to become activated. Zen was 24. I was also around the same age when I got yoga "activated." Prior to that I had been ignorant and uninterested in India or yoga. Again, "*When the student is ready, the teacher/teaching appears…*" [135]

Another particularly relevant aspect of Yogi Zen's story was his description of heat rising up his spine like a snake which then comes right over the top of his head.

This is a common description of Kundalini energy that we see depicted in Buddhist iconography. Perhaps you recall this exact image in the film, Little Buddha, with Keanu Reeves.

Additional confirmation that this is a common experience came a few days later when Yogi Zen and I sat down with a local shaman. Let's call him "D." D was around my age, mid-forties, and offered both Ayahuasca and Kambo, or frog medicine, ceremonies. He told us that he once did a combination of mushrooms and Syrian Rue which produced the same experience: a serpent of energy rising over his head like a cobra spreading its hood. Neither he nor Zen had ever seen or heard of this phenomenon before they experienced it personally.

Śri Jimi-Ji ~ Note the cobras above the heads

Now, having conclusively established that psychoactive plant medicines can at least *mimic* the activity of Kundalini, we may well ask: Well, are they the same thing?

Consider the answer given by a young Osho, when he was still going by "Acharya Rajneesh," from the early 1970s. A woman asked him whether an experience she had of Samadhi while on LSD was genuine or not, to which he replied:

"It was not genuine. It was not Samadhi, but a chemical change. The mind can project anything it likes to project, even an unconscious desire of Samadhi! So whatsoever you have known about Samadhi and have read about it, will be projected through the chemical help of LSD. LSD or any other chemical drug is nothing but a help to make the mind more projective. All the hindrances, all the ordinary hindrances are withdrawn. The ordinary reason and conscious mind are withdrawn. You are completely in the hold of the unconscious. But the unconscious itself will not bring Samadhi through

LSD. It can only be possible, if the unconscious has been fed with conceptions, colors and vital experiences. Everything that has been put into it can be projected.

If you have not known anything about Kundalini, it is impossible to feel it through LSD. A person who is suffering from any Phobia will project his phobia. A person who is under some suppressed fear will feel the actual phenomenon to take place. So LSD will bring different experiences to different persons.

LSD can only be a help to project whatsoever is in the seed form of your unconscious mind. If it is love, then love will be projected—if it is hatred, then hatred will be projected. LSD is an expanding drug; whatsoever is in the seed form will be expanded into a tree. You could feel Kundalini, you could feel Chakras, and you could feel harmony or the totality, only because these are the seeds already in your unconscious mind. If they are not there, then LSD will not project these.

The projection is because of LSD, but this is not Samadhi. Samadhi comes from your unconscious longing. If you have longed for it, then LSD will help you. LSD can be a help to anything unconscious, to be psychically realized, but it is not a spiritual revelation. What you have seen is something which you wanted to realize, projected on the psychic canvas, so it is not Samadhi and it is not genuine. It is neither; and it is nothing else than dreaming. It is just a dreaming phenomenon.

At this moment, I can really see Osho's point.

Let me explain…

Since we're on the topic of Kundalini, or the "Serpent Power," we might compare psychedelics to the serpents in the biblical story of Pharaoh's magicians. The Pharaoh's magicians could turn their staffs into serpents at will, as could Moses' brother, Aaron. But Aaron was working through the genuine power of God, so his serpent swallowed up all of the magicians' serpents. This is because the magicians could only create an imitation of this powerful serpent, a fake that could only fool the casual, unschooled observer [see Exodus 7:10ff].

Similarly, while through the use of psychedelics I have experienced or witnessed a number of Kundalini-esque phenomena, I now think these experiences may just have been an imitation of the far more difficult-to-achieve activation of true Kundalini energy.

Or perhaps these two things are similar in nature and purpose, but still different. Perhaps we should also leave any value judgments about plant medicines aside. My experience of Kundalini in my twenties was decidedly different than anything I have ever had from plant medicines, and yet both experiences were very *similar.* Many of the kriyas I witnessed with envy at those early Kundalini yoga retreats, I actually experienced later in the context of my own psychedelic journeys. Were both experiences the same? I don't know, but they certainly looked the same.

Let's now consider a similar cautionary piece by a personage who has been one of the most inspirational spiritual teachers for me, Omraam Mikhail Aivanhov. Aivanhov no doubt aimed the following words partly at the youth drug culture of his time:

"In antiquity, during the celebration of the mysteries, the initiates attended sacred dances performed in the temples by young virgins, who were not allowed to show themselves to the uninitiated and whose whole life was consecrated to purity. Others wished to imitate them, disciples who had been expelled from the temples for their weaknesses and who created schools where they gave so-called initiations into the great mysteries, symbolized by Isis unveiled. Those who are not sufficiently elevated to attain heavenly beauty make do with gross imitations.

So, the crowds we see these days in nightclubs, watching strip-tease shows and contemplating Isis unveiling, are just disciples from the past who failed true initiative examinations and are now preparing for them in places of debauchery. And they all pass their diploma with flying colours, since this Isis unveils herself much more easily than the great goddess in the ancient temples! And it's a pity, for anyone who knows how to contemplate true beauty is able to ascend all the way to the throne of God."

While the above could possibly apply to the current usage of psychedelics in the name of spirituality, I want to point out that the people I have met who are using plant medicines and psychedelics have been among the most sincere spiritual seekers after truth I've ever encountered. It's also important to note that greatly respected teachers in the yoga world have also promoted the spiritual use of psychedelics. Gurus such as Ganesh Baba, and Prem Baba, and other yoga people like Ganga White have supported the use of plants medicines and psychedelics. Are they all misguided?

Many of the "Old Guard" spiritual teachers have answered with a definitive yes! *We are on the wrong track*, and we need to get the train off this track now before getting derailed and finding it that much harder to make our way back home. Consider the following words of Gopi Krishna, world famous for his books on Kundalini in which he related his own Kundalini awakening through meditation alone:

"What happens to the individual during the course of transformation is now purely a matter of speculation. Before our time, illumination denoted an encounter with Divinity or an anthropomorphic God. Now, in the eyes of many scholars, it means a peculiar psychological condition, a trip to deeper regions of the mind or autointoxication brought about by altered chemistry of the body. This leads to the mistaken view that the drug experience has something in common with or is parallel to mystical

ecstasy or enlightenment.

If we believe in the absolute wisdom, absolute knowledge, and absolute justice of the Godhead, can we heap a greater insult on Him than to suppose that He would demand of those who strive to reach Him an abnormal, unhealthy or eccentric way of life and behavior, irrationally different from other people?"[136]

A big put-down of the psychedelic movement, for sure!

But could there be sour grapes in such denouncements? Is Gopi Krishna really saying something like: "Listen, *I* reached enlightenment solely through my own hard work, and you, *you* debauched people think you can get there just by sitting around drinking Ayahuasca together?"

I have no definitive answer. There always seems to be two or more sides to any practice or theory seeking spiritual enlightenment, and in the above I'm simply observing all of them without passing judgment.

In another place, Mr. Krishna felt he had to bring William James into the mix to make a similar point:

"There is still a great deal of confusion about the phenomenon known as mystical ecstasy. The general impression is that it is just an altered state of awareness, comparable to the states brought about by intoxicants, mind-altering drugs, hypnosis, biofeedback, hypnagogic conditions, and the like. Even an authority like William James was in error in the comparison he made between mystical ecstasy and the states induced by wine and nitrous oxide."[137]

Yes, a good half-century before Leary and Alpert ever even *got* to Harvard, William James was there, mixing up the medicine and lecturing about his findings. These lectures became the classic, *The Varieties of Religious Experience*, a recommended read for any new explorer of mysticism and religion.[138]

Taking all the above into consideration, all those on a spiritual quest must recognize the following: Mystical experiences engendered by psychedelics look the same and often feel the same as substance-free mystic states, although it is true that there is no undeniable proof that they are the same. And if they seem to be the same, but one is genuine and one is not, does it really make a difference? Maybe meditation and plant medicines do not produce identical states of consciousness. Yet if the overall positive effect on one's life after a psychedelic experience is more or less the same as after years of meditation, can we really say that one method is superior to the other?

Based on my experience and the research available thus far, I would say that you get what you pay for... If you put in the disciplined work, you get a more durable and enduring change in consciousness. If you *only* use plant medicines, you have to keep taking them in the hope that somewhere along the line the experience will stick more permanently. And research suggests that it doesn't generally seem to become a permanent and enduring fixture as it does with meditators. This is supported by Huston Smith's oft-quoted distinction: "altered traits" vs. merely "altered states," meaning essentially that to really make it stick, one would need to combine use of psychedelics with a spiritual discipline like yoga.

Again, though I seem to be taking a stance, I'm not making definitive conclusions one way or the other, but merely playing devil's advocate and saying: let's look at all sides here.

Can't Touch This!

Personally, I sense that many who use psychedelics probably would not have the discipline to meditate to the point where they got down to the root of things, and psychedelics do provide an almost immediate access to that realm. That access may only be for a flashing instant, or even a few hours, but however long, it may be all that is needed for psychic healing to take place.

Also, because I have had my doubts about *gurus*—to the point of never being able to be "experienced" by them—I therefore have felt more comfortable with a plant showing me certain things. I didn't have to fully surrender to a human being who could possibly take advantage of me.

And yet, I've also had Ayahuasca journeys where I sensed a missionizing impulse on the part of the Vine. A Muhammed Ali-like "I Am the Greatest" proclamation. The Vine seemed to be challenging me: "Have you ever experienced anything like this before from your human gurus? They ain't got nothing on me! Can't touch this!" There was an uncomfortable sense that I had dropped the guru/disciple dynamic only to unwittingly become a devotee, or worse, a slave of a plant teacher. Had I been initiated into the cult of Ayahuasca?!? Had I been led into some strange place of no return by my desire for the mind blowing "spiritual experiences" that I had always craved? Talk about "The Seduction of Spirit"—*Ayahuasca* has got it going on!

The story of Adam and Eve's Fall in the Garden of Eden can be read in two basic ways: The straightforward, traditionalist way, where Adam and Eve were seduced by the serpent, sinned, and so we find ourselves in the sorry state we're in, suffering the separation from God. Or it can be read the Gnostic way, where the serpent is the bearer of salvific knowledge that opens Adam and Eve's eyes to what's really going on: that Yahweh is not the true God but a megalomaniacal Demiurge intent on enslaving them. I can see *Ayahuasca* as both the snake and the Demiurge, both enslaver and liberator, endarkener and enlightener.

My spiritual quest has helped free my mind to the point where such either/or dichotomies no longer matter to me. I see truth on all sides of Truth's multi-faceted diamond. My mind recognizes its limits and becomes still, content in the fullness of "knowing nothing."

If I were to come out of this stillness, my thought would be this: It's not a question of Yoga *OR* Psychedelics; one is not necessarily better than the other. Both are tools that can work effectively, both together and separately. But psychedelics can also be ineffective, depending on the needs of the seeker in any evolutionary moment.

In other words, as usual: it's very complicated and depends on the particular person, the "set and setting," and other unknown factors, so go figure it out for yourself!

This book is at least open to the possibility of Yoga *AND* Psychedelics being a combination that is most effective for the spiritual seeker. The underlying thrust of all of this is to observe that this is the way things seem to be headed, and at the same time to step back and ask: well, is this really a good direction?

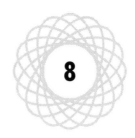

8

The Sixties: A Brief History of Sex, Drugs, Rock 'N' Roll... and Yoga

To a few sincere seekers, LSD may have served as a means to arouse that spiritual longing which has brought them into my contact, but once that purpose is served, further ingestion would not only be harmful, but have no point or purpose. The longing for Reality cannot be sustained by further use of drugs, but only by the love for the Perfect Master, which is a reflection of his love for the seeker.

An individual may feel LSD has made a "better" man of him socially and personally. But one will be a better man through Love than one can ever be through drugs or any other artificial aid. And the best man is he who has surrendered himself to the Perfect Master irrespective of his personal or social standing.

—Meher Baba, God in a Pill

"It is also true now that the culture has shifted and different kinds of realities are now accepted in everyday life. There are many young people who never took acid and never smoked grass whose consciousness are free to float, in the midst of this culture, in and out of planes, and that's partly because of the Rock and Roll movement; and, too, it's partly a result of the cultural shift which resulted from the usage of acid in the Sixties. Don't underestimate the social changes that have occurred as a result of the acid phenomenon."

—Ram Dass, Grist for the Mill, 1977

A Little Bit Rock & Roll…

"You've got to be a little bit rock & roll to do Ayahuasca…"
—Jan Kounen, paraphrase[139]

I was born in January, 1970, just 6 months after Woodstock. The Sixties were officially over and both cultural and countercultural attitudes were changing rapidly, not least in regard to drug use. By the time I could watch television and understand what I was seeing, my malleable mind was constantly fed and bred on anti-drug messages. Indeed, like most Gen Xers, I grew up in the era of Nancy Reagan's "Just Say No" campaign, and later the ubiquitous Partnership for a Drug Free America campaign, *"This is your brain on drugs…"*

It wasn't just media messages that informed my early view on drugs. I was hearing the same warnings everywhere, and especially from my father. He often told us boys at the dinner table, in no uncertain terms, that we were to *never drink, smoke, or take drugs*. Of course, it was okay for him to drink Coors beer and smoke Cuban cigars. It just wasn't okay for us—he was already beyond help. I kid.

Partly as a result of this constant bombardment, I became anti-drug myself, especially once I got into long distance running. From that point on, I prided myself on being able to get high naturally. My "mantra" became: "I don't do drugs, I get high on life!" I didn't realize I had jumped onto the mainstream bandwagon.

The truth was, all through my teens and twenties, I did get high on life, but with the help of a healthy dose of endorphin-releasing exercise. Indeed, I was quite literally a running addict. If I didn't get my fix, didn't run for even a day, I would experience withdrawal symptoms. But it was a socially acceptable and *"healthy addiction!"*

Prior to getting hooked on running, at age eleven, I began listening to rock music. At first, I couldn't get into it as it sounded quite foreign to my pop-music bred ears. But I thought it was the cool thing to do, and I really wanted to be cool and fit in. So soon I had my little radio constantly tuned to WYSP or WMMR, the two major rock stations in Philadelphia, never listening to anything else. It wasn't too long before I acquired the taste and fell in love with those radio sounds and the people that produced them. My ambition in life now was to be like them, to become a rock star.

One morning while listening to The Who's Pete Townshend play the opening riff on the song "I'm Free," my prepubescent brain became so excited that I scoured the house for a cheap old acoustic guitar I remembered my grandmother had stashed somewhere. I finally found the thing in a lonely corner, missing a couple of strings and completely out of tune. It didn't matter. By ear and on the spot, I taught myself that Townshend riff—at least I thought I did!

So I began playing my riffs for anyone who would listen: "Smoke on the Water," "Iron Man," later "Stairway," etc.—you know, the usual suspects. And thus began my fascination with guitar and the "rock gods," who quickly replaced my parents and teachers as my heroes.

Mind you, I was not totally new to music: I had played trumpet in band for five years, and was still taking lessons with one of the lead trumpet players with the Philadelphia Orchestra. I still recall the day I sat with him and my mother and made it known that I was going to quit lessons so I could focus on the guitar—the electric guitar. That trumpet and his orchestral music were just no longer cool in my world.

Now please note that even though I had grown my hair long and was into Rock music, I never did drugs. Even so, everyone seemed to think I did, just by the way I looked! Looking back at pictures of me from that time, I must admit I did look kind-of stoned. I attribute this at least partly to the music. Day and night I listened to Rock at unreasonable decibel levels.

Although, at that pre-yoga juncture I knew nothing of the Shaivite lineage, in retrospect one might surmise that I was a descendant of that line of yogis even before I knew it. A point I will return to in a moment.

Mr. Mojo—Kundalini Risin'—Shiva-Dionysus

"Come on baby light my fire."
—Jim Morrison/Robbie Krieger

All of the above is to emphasize the dramatic effect rock music has had on my consciousness from an early age. It wasn't just about listening for me—I delved deeply into the lives of the great rock artists, especially Jimi Hendrix, Jim Morrison, and later on, Bob Dylan.

Jim Morrison, in particular, held a deep and abiding fascination for me. Danny Sugarman's 1981 biography *No One Here Gets Out Alive* is one of the few books I read cover-to-cover several times over. This intense fascination ultimately found expression in a research paper on the "mythos" of this "rock god," one I submitted for a Folklore class at the University of Pennsylvania.

I wanted to explore the linked mythology of Shiva and Dionysus which the late scholar of yoga, Alain Danielou, had brought to light. Taking Danielou's lead, I began to view Morrison and the Doors, and rock music in general as part of a re-emergence of ancient Indian and Greek archetypes. An "archaic revival," to use Terence McKenna's phrase, that was clearly being fueled by drugs, particularly psychedelics.[140] In my research, I focused on exploring the figure of the rock star as a shaman, a term often used to describe Jim Morrison. Morrison was certainly a consummate "showman," and consciously brought in elements of shamanism to his stage performances.

After reading every book I could find about Morrison, I began to realize how little I had understood the man. One thing that I felt could have been highlighted more in all the books I read is the effect that LSD had on the young Morrison's consciousness. LSD played a particularly important role in Morrison's development during the summer of 1965, just prior to the formation of the Doors, when he was living on a rooftop and taking "acid" (LSD) regularly. Interestingly, Morrison later told an interviewer that during that time he heard a whole "mythic concert" in his head, during which the early Doors songs came to him. This could also be described as a shamanic vision. Morrison's words:

"Those first five or six songs I wrote, I was just taking notes at a fantastic rock concert that was going on inside my head."[141]

One can also note the remarkable change in Morrison's physiology during that summer: He went from a baby-faced college kid, to a trim, muscular "Alexander" with flowing locks. It was a transformation which his bandmate and collaborator, the late Ray Manzarek, often commented on. Even after his initial initiation, and long after the other three Doors stopped using psychedelics, Morrison continued to use LSD. The others opted for Maharishi Mahesh Yogi's Transcendental Meditation instead, as did the Beatles and other rock musicians of that era.

Morrison's psychedelic journeys into the "end of the night" certainly influenced the Doors' music—the Oedipal section of "The End" is a well-known example. It was apparently composed spontaneously on stage after coming down from a particularly intense LSD trip.

If Morrison's early songs were inspired and informed by his acid journeys, he was no different than many of the rock artists of that period. During the years '65-'68, LSD and other psychedelics were in vogue and psychedelic songs were in heavy AM radio rotation. These stations played what is now called "Classic Rock," though back then it was called "Acid Rock," meaning LSD-influenced. Many bands of that era produced a form of Acid Rock, perhaps most notably the Beatles, the Grateful Dead, Pink Floyd, and the Jimi Hendrix Experience. But there were also bands of that era who, while imitating some of the sounds of psychedelia, were not so much into taking psychedelics: Janis Joplin, the Who, and the Rolling Stones, for example. Yet even if these other artists did not do psychedelics, they were still heavily influenced by the *Zeitgeist*, which was heavily informed by this new culture of drugs and the promise they seemed to hold.

It is still an open question to what extent the music of the Sixties was influenced by psychedelics, and certainly in retrospect, artists like the Beatles had an investment in psychedelics NOT being seen as a primary source of their creative output. Nevertheless, I feel it would be a mistake to underestimate the role of psychedelics in the creative process, just as it would be unwise to consider the influence of drugs on the batting averages of professional baseball players, for example. In which case, we might ask whether these substances were "performance-enhancing" for these artists and musicians?

In other words, how much did psychedelics affect the music and the musicians of the Sixties? There is a very strong case to be made that, as illustrated by the case of Jim Morrison, psychedelics had a profound influence on the artists of that seminal era for music. And perhaps far more of an influence than the bands of that time seem willing to admit in their later years.

I am not necessarily referring here to playing music while on a psychedelic. Many musicians will tell you that while it's fun to create in that space, and though the music might sound cool and interesting to you *while* you're creating whatever you're creating, you would never want most of those performances to see the light of day. A prime example of this is Jerry Garcia's comments about how the Dead learned early on at the Acid Tests that making music while tripping on acid was fun, but not conducive to creating listenable or marketable music.

Another famous example: Carlos Santana's had to perform at Woodstock earlier than expected while he was still tripping on mescaline. He did, and while that was certainly a classic moment (especially "Soul Sacrifice" with that wild drum solo), the more memorable parts of the Santana's performance happened after the effects of the drugs wore off a bit.

On the other hand, Hendrix played many a show while high on LSD. It might be that he had a higher tolerance for LSD, or that he could better handle the performance-enhancing potential of the substance than other artists. Getting back to the analogy with baseball, Pittsburgh Pirates pitcher Dock Ellis famously pitched a no-hitter while on LSD. My point here is mainly that psychedelics informed the production of much of the great music of the Sixties much more than we might think.

> *"If you don't think drugs have done good things for us, then take all of your records, tapes and CDs and burn them. Cause you know what? The musicians that made all that great music that's enhanced your lives throughout the years? Real fucking high on drugs. The Beatles were so fuckin' high they let Ringo sing a few songs."*
>
> —Bill Hicks

"I think basically the Grateful Dead is not for cranking out rock and roll, it's not for going out and doing concerts or any of that stuff. I think it's to get high. To get really high is to forget yourself. And to forget yourself is to see everything else. And to see everything else is to become an understanding molecule in evolution, a conscious tool of the universe. And I think every human being should be a conscious tool of the universe."

—Jerry Garcia

Picking up on the chapter-opening quote from Ram Dass, I would like to consider the idea that music, particularly rock music, is in itself an addictive drug. That rock music has the ability to effect physiological changes in the human body purely via the medium of vibration, a music that produces an actual physical "body rush" from head to toe. There is no doubt that the "rush" from some rock songs sometimes compel young people to play that same song over and over again, trying to recapture the initial "rush" they felt upon first hearing it. But the first time we hear a song is unique and that exact "rush" can never be repeated. Yet, we listen again and again to see if the song still has the power to effect us; we're "hooked on a feeling."

Again following Ram Dass, we can also recognize how life informs art, and art life. In this case, "Acid Rock" was both inspired by the psychedelic experience while simultaneously attempting to re-create that experience, both for the "experienced," and for those like myself who were not open to ingesting such a substance. Thus, through the vehicle of this genre of music, I was unwittingly initiated into the world of psychedelics.

For me, then, rock music was a kind of preparation for the actual psychedelic experience itself. Perhaps this is why my first mushroom journey, which occurred many years later at the age of thirty-six, helped me understand the cultural phenomenon of psychedelia. It was a completely new culture that emerged directly from the psychedelic experience. At age thirty-six, all those Wavy-Gravy posters, the strange combinations of hippie apparel, the spiritual intensity of rock—it all made sense! And it all felt so familiar! I had become "experienced," to use the term made popular by Jimi Hendrix. Even now when I listen to certain music, I often think: that song could not have been created but by someone who has explored psychedelics. I also wouldn't hesitate to propose that most rock musicians have used psychedelics.

Which brings us to an even deeper consideration: Why do some young people, like myself, develop such an intense interest in music, particularly rock music? Could rock music assist people who are seeking higher states of consciousness? Might rock stimulate the deeper levels of our psyche? And why do some people react to this music more than others? Given my abiding interest in "Classic Rock," perhaps it was inevitable that I would ingest a psychedelic.

> *"It's better to burn out than it is to rust."*
> —Neil Young

> *"LSD burst over the dreary domain of the constipated bourgeoisie like the angelic herald of a new psychedelic millennium. We have never been the same since, nor will we ever be, for LSD demonstrated, even to skeptics, that the mansions of heaven and gardens of paradise lie within each and all of us."*
> —Terence McKenna

Yoga and Psychedelics from the Sixties Onward

Aldous Huxley—Cleansing the Doors of Perception

It is very interesting that the popular usage of psychedelics in the West began in the Sixties and coincided with the influx of gurus from the East. This influx of spiritual teachers was partly due to the lifting of the Asian Exclusion Act in 1963. And prior to the early Sixties, psychedelics, like yoga, were primarily the domain of a small group of research scientists, artists, writers, and spiritual seekers—many of whom wanted to keep it that way. But by mid-decade, the use of psychedelics had percolated out into the broader society, particularly the youth culture, as did yoga. We have already discussed two of the most well-known *agent provocateurs* on the East Coast: Harvard professors Timothy Leary and Richard Alpert. On the West Coast, there was Ken Kesey, who had achieved national fame for his book, *One Flew Over the Cuckoos Nest*. Kesey publicly asked "Can you pass the Acid Test?" and organized gatherings at which LSD was available to anyone who sought a "trip."

Prior to all of this, one figure who informed and inspired the Baby Boomer generation with regards to psychedelics and the wisdom of the East perhaps more than any other was Aldous Huxley. Huxley had become famous for his novel, *Brave New World*, in which "Soma" was actually a kind of pharmaceutical "opiate of the masses." But this was written before he was introduced to mescaline under the guidance of Aleister Crowley in the early Thirties (others say it was Humphry Osmond who initiated Huxley). Following his initiation into psychedelics, Huxley became one of its biggest promoters and eventually went on to pen his now classic study, *The Doors of Perception* while under the influence of the mescaline. In the book, Huxely related his moment-to-moment observations of what he was experiencing. Here is one famous example:

"The beatific vision, Sat Chit Ananda, Being-Awareness-Bliss, for the first time I understood, not on the verbal level, not by inchoate hints or at a distance, but precisely and completely what those prodigious syllables referred to..." [142]

When *The Doors of Perception* was published, Huxley was criticized for romanticizing psychedelics. Yet others considered him elitist because of his position that psychedelics could really only be fully appreciated and understood by intellectuals, scientists, or artists. Today some even claim that Huxley was a supporter of the *New World Order*, a cabal of mega-wealthy bankers and secret bloodline families intent on world domination. Far-fetched as this is, there is a kernel of truth in that Huxley did feel most lay people were not prepared for the psychedelic experience.

This is reflected in his last work, the Utopian novel *Island*, in which Huxley envisioned an ideal society that ritually ingests mushrooms from an early age as a sacrament. The novel had a powerful impact on the hippie movement, particularly on a secret group of spiritual seekers whose story is only now coming to light: The Brotherhood of Eternal Love. A whole book could be written on this group alone (and books have), but for now I'll just note that the Brotherhood's drug smuggling exploits are legendary and may have been largely responsible for the Nixon administration's massive crackdown on drug trafficking, including the creation of the Drug Enforcement Agency (DEA). This, of course, subsequently led to the making of many of those anti-drug public service announcements I heard growing up.

Swami Satchidananda—The "Woodstock Guru"

Even in the Sixties, it was recognized that if used only by themselves, psychedelic drugs posed potential dangers; yet if they were ingested in conjunction with a discipline like yoga, then they could be used more safely and might even be an aid to one's yoga practice. This was partly due to the influence of gurus like Swami Satchidananda, who offered his brand of Yoga to the fledgling hippie movement experimenting with psychedelics.

Consider the report of Ken, who was interviewed by Ralph Metzner (a close colleague of Leary and Alpert) for his book *"The Ecstatic Adventure,"* on the connection between LSD and Yoga. After taking LSD regularly for about 3 years, Ken found Swami Satchidananda's yoga institute in Manhattan and began practicing yoga.

Ralph Metzner: *You do this every day?*

KEN: *Yes, sometimes a lot, and I work with the Institute on West End Avenue: Swami Satchidananda. There are lots of nice people there and lots of conflicts have* been happening about LSD with people who don't fully understand. We've had some strong arguments at times, but I try not to get bung up there, because things are working out too well. I'm working with the yoga, combining it with LSD, to sustain it. The thing about LSD—it's a beginning, I'm finding, but it's not enough alone. Because you can take a trip and it can change you, but you can also fall into a lot of bad things if you trip that much and if you don't continually work on yourself. So I've been combining them. Just body postures make it a better trip. I've lost about thirty pounds in the past few months.

Another young person, Joan, also found that Yoga was helpful to her during her sessions with LSD...

RM: *Joan, when were you first interested in LSD?*

JOAN: *About three years ago, when I was nineteen. I smoked pot for about two or three years before that. The first thing it did was... it showed me what it was to be a girl and then a woman. I had only sort of felt maneuvered before; before that I really didn't know what I was or what role I was supposed to play. So I—it showed me how to play that role. With love, and I didn't know what love was before that, on a personal level or a total level anyway, being one with everything. The greatest good I think it did was I used to be very strongly into possessions and things and people, and it showed me that that just was keeping me back from being part of everything and having everything and giving everything. And—I don't know—that's about it.*

RM: *How often do you take it?*

JOAN: "*Well, I used to turn on—when I first started taking it, I turned on twice a month. That was about the end of the summer. Then I went to yoga and I didn't take it for three months. I took it again recently, and it was just so much better, even physically. I was able to control the tremors that I used to get at one part that would divert me from the whole trip that would take me into—being held—by somebody, or fear. The acid changed my life. It brought me to yoga, and now they're both still changing me.*"[143]

This is a results report that I have heard many times by now. Simply put, psychedelic experience helps yoga, and conversely, yoga assists in the journey. Yoga and the psychedelic experience complement and enhance one another.

Here's another relevant passage on this theme: an "acid aphorism" from Stephen Gaskin's "*Amazing Dope Tales*"...

"*There were hidden subtleties that people who took acid regularly shared as a lore among them... real experiences from the street. Folks would say things like, 'Well, I usually trip once a week because I can stand it if I trip once a week. If I went two weeks, I'd grow enough ego in two weeks that it would just devastate me, blow me to pieces. But, if I go a week between trips, and really yoga in between, it's bearable, and I can stand it. I hate to skip a week.*"[144]

Of course, Swami Satchidananda didn't see his Integral Yoga as a supplement or aid for those taking psychedelics. He saw Yoga as a tool these misguided flower children could use to wean themselves away from drugs entirely. As he famously pronounced:

"*The problem with drugs is that while they elevate you, they immediately drop you back down again… Yoga gives you a "natural high.*"[145]

Like most of the other Eastern gurus of the Sixties, Swami Satchidananda did not see the possibility of combining yoga and psychedelics. For these teachers, it was either one or the other, not both. Huxley's vision of "Sat Chit Ananda" under the influence of mescaline would better come through yogic discipline alone, for only then would it be real and enduring.

The "Psychedelic Yoga" of Sri Brahmarishi Narad

There were exceptions, however. It is not well known, but even at that time (late Sixties) there were yogis and gurus who taught Yoga specifically as a tool for assisting in the psychedelic experience. For example, there was Sri Brahmarishi Narad, a teacher I first discovered while doing a web search for this book. Sri Brahmarishi Narad is credited with the authorship of a widely circulated document detailing how yogic meditation can serve the psychedelic explorer.

The document begins:

The following article originally appeared as an uncopyrighted set of mimeographed sheets sometime during the late 1960s, which was freely distributed on a limited basis, probably in San Francisco. Feel free to make copies of this article and to distribute them to those interested to keep this information alive; otherwise it will disappear into antiquity.

At the outset of this document, Sri Brahmarishi Narad explains the purpose of writing it:

"*The fact that entheogenic drugs induce a greater sensitivity to subtle spiritual and psychic energies, and speed up the influx of impressions from deeper levels of consciousness, raises the immediate question of how these energies can be properly understood and handled. Obviously, if these energies are not guided, they can do more harm than good. The application of traditional Yoga meditation techniques while under psychedelic experiences, provides a constructive solution to this problem.*"

So who was this Sri Brahmarishi Narad? Thus far I have not been able to find anything more about him. It could be a pen name for another guru, perhaps someone like the psychedelic swami, Ganesh Baba? Or perhaps he was a Western hippie who was into both yoga and psychedelics, though this seems doubtful due to the authoritative language and nature of his essay. It also could have been written more recently—certainly the use of the word "entheogen," which is a recent coinage, is suspicious. If it *was* written by an Indian teacher of that era, it clearly demonstrates that there were more formal attempts to use yoga as a tool to navigate and stabilize the psychedelic experience.

In any case, Sri Brahmarishi Narad's document presents an important argument in favor of the *combination* of yoga *and* psychedelics.[146]

"Nothing's Gonna Change My World"
The Beatles, the Maharishi , and the Hare Krishnas

> "If people take any notice of what we say, we say we've been through
> the drug scene, man, and there's nothing like being straight."
> —John Lennon, The Dick Cavett Show (September 24, 1971)

> "STAY HIGH ALL THE TIME!
> CHANT TO KRISHNA!"
> —Hare Krishna sign in the Sixties

It is well known that the Beatles were heavily influenced by both Hindu spirituality and psychedelics. John Lennon was "turned on" by Timothy Leary's work, and by his own accounting took LSD over a thousand times in just a few years. Lennon said he often read Timothy Leary's book, The Psychedelic Experience, while high on LSD, and he even composed a song based upon it, the highly psychedelic *"Tomorrow Never Knows"* (on Revolver).[147] Even the comparatively *pure* Paul McCartney went through an acid phase, telling Life magazine that LSD *"...opened my eyes... It made me a better, more honest, more tolerant member of society."*[148]

From an artistic standpoint, it's clear that regardless of what the Beatles later claimed, if it weren't for LSD, works of genius like Revolver and Sgt. Pepper would never have come into existence. And the same can probably be said for much of the "Classic" Rock music of that era.

Yet despite LSD's transformative highs, it wasn't long before the Beatles felt they had passed the "Acid Test" with flying, double rainbow, kaleidoscopic colors and were now prepared to graduate onto other, possibly more natural means of personal and societal transformation. As George Harrison declared at that time:

"Acid is not the answer... It's enabled people to see a bit more, but when you really get hip, you don't need it."[149]

Harrison's thoughts reflect the general sentiment of the Beatles and many of the youth of that era. It was becoming clear for a number of young seekers that psyche-delics alone simply could not produce lasting changes in consciousness. There was a growing sense that a psychedelic revolution was not going to be the harbinger of world peace, nor a Golden Age of enlightenment.

Yet there was still ambivalence about revolution, *any* revolution, whether it was radically changing the world or changing one's consciousness about the world. This ambivalence was reflected in the lyrics of John Lennon's initial version of the song "Revolution" which was released in 1968:

"But when you talk about destruction, don't you know that you can count me out (in)."

Lennon was clearly not ready to put himself completely in the yogi and peace-maker camp just yet.

The Beatles first met Maharishi Mahesh Yogi in August of 1967. They were so impressed with the Transcendental Meditation (TM) guru that the following year they went to a TM teacher training retreat at the Maharishi's ashram in Rishikesh. The band was beginning to see the possibility that meditation might be a more use-ful tool for lasting, evolutionary change than psychedelics. And most admirably, they were open to putting that pregnant possibility to the test.

What happened next is particularly of note for us: Not long into the retreat, word got around that the Maharishi made sexual advances toward Mia Farrow, Lennon's girlfriend at the time. Lennon promptly denounced the guru, putting an abrupt end to the Beatles yoga and meditation idyll in India.

John recounted the story to Jann Wenner in their famous 1970 Rolling Stone interview:

"Yes, there was a big hullaballo about him trying to rape Mia Farrow or somebody and trying to get off with a few other women and things like that. We went to see him, after we stayed up all night discussing was it true or not true. When George started thinking it might be true, I thought well, it must be true; because if George started thinking it might be true, there must be something in it.

"So we went to see Maharishi, the whole gang of us, the next day, charged down to his hut, his bungalow, his very rich-looking bungalow in the mountains, and as usual, when the dirty work came, I was the spokesman—whenever the dirty work came, I actually had to be leader, wherever the scene was, when it came to the nitty gritty, I had to do the speaking—and I said 'We're leaving.'

'Why?' he asked, and all that shit and I said, 'Well, if you're so cosmic, you'll know why.' He was always intimating, and there were all these right-hand men always in-timating, that he did miracles. And I said, 'You know why,' and he said, 'I don't know

why, you must tell me,' and I just kept saying 'You ought to know' and he gave me a look like, 'I'll kill you, you bastard,' and he gave me such a look. I knew then. I had called his bluff and I was a bit rough to him."

Ono: *"You expected too much from him."*[150]

Yoko Ono was probably correct: We have perhaps had unreasonable expectation of gurus. And yet, when they or their followers declare themselves to be chaste and all-knowing, is it unreasonable to hold them to that?

"All You Need is Love (Krishna)"

—George Harrison

"If there is a God, we're all It."

—John Lennon, Rolling Stone, 1970

These issues were to be revived again the next fall when the Beatles met the man who started the Hare Krishna movement in the West, A.C. Bhaktivedanta Swami Prabhupada. He was also known as Swami Bhaktivedanta, and later, Srila Prabhupada.

In September of 1969, John Lennon and George Harrison, plus John's new paramour, Yoko Ono, met with Srila Prabhupada, who was then called Swami Bhaktivedanta. The Swami was the founder of the fledgling but rapidly expanding *Krishna Consciousness Movement*. In just a few years in America, Bhaktivedanta had already inspired a large following among the hippie communities in New York and the Bay area.

Two years earlier in January, 1967, the biggest bands on the San Francisco scene, including The Dead, Jefferson Airplane, Quicksilver, and Moby Grape played a concert to benefit the local Hare Krishna temple. Timothy Leary and the Acid chemist, Owsley Stanley II, were in attendance, as was Beat poet Allen Ginsberg who introduced the Hare Krishna Swami to the throng of thousands of hippies.

In his address to the crowd, Ginsberg, an "experienced" veteran of psychedelics, recommended that those coming down from LSD stop by the Krishna temple in order to help "stabilize their consciousness on reentry." By stating this, was Ginsberg subtly trying to rein in the wilder equestrian aspects of the psychedelic movement into a more "stable" channel of spiritual discipline?

I ask because around that time Prabhubpada had told Ginsberg that LSD was not necessary for the devotee of Krishna. The Swami's words:

"Krishna consciousness resolves everything, Nothing else is needed."

Not that Ginsberg didn't know this, or hadn't heard it before. His own early psychedelic experiences had been fraught with paradox and ambivalence. He had never really gotten back to the purity of his original cosmic revelation as he read Blake's *"Ah, Sunflower!"* way back in 1948. For years he sought to recapture this experience, as so many spiritual seekers do, myself included, but to no avail. Finally, in 1960, on a pilgrimage to India, he met with Swami Sivananda who counseled him:

"Your own heart is your guru."

Gradually Ginsberg underwent a conversion in which he realized that his approach to the spiritual life, including psychedelics, had been misguided.[151]

But not all hippies were willing to let go of the blessed sacrament of LSD so quickly. As one former hippie-turned-Hare Krishna recounts in the following fascinating interview excerpt:

Devotee: *Did you ask Srila Prabhupada if you could see Krishna?*

Kausalya: *Yes. I am embarrassed. I had been meditating and taking LSD. (Children, don't get any ideas.) Anyway, I said to Prabhupada, "When I take LSD, I see Krishna." And he said, "You see Krishna because Krishna loves you and wants to show favor to you—not because of LSD." Then he said, "Promise me that you won't take it anymore." And I said," I cannot do that right now. It is my sacrament." I am sure that for some of the older people here this is going to ring familiar. Anyway, I said, "I cannot do that right now." Then he said, "Well, will you come and stay here? I would like you to stay here, but..." Then he said, "But there are only two bedrooms, and one is mine, and Kartikeya is sleeping in the living room, and Govinda dasi and Gaurasundara have theirs. But please come back."*[152]

Had Prabhupada ever tried LSD himself? It appears that he had not. So how might he truly understand what was happening to his hippie devotees?

What if this devotee, Kausalya, had said to Prabhupada:

"Well, if Krishna wants to show favor to me, why can't he reveal himself to me without LSD, just through the Hare Krishna mantra or meditation? After all, Arjuna didn't have to take LSD to be granted a vision of Krishna in the famous 11th chapter of the Bhagavad Gita?"[iii]

Still, we must note well that Kausalya went on to become a leader of the Hare Krishna movement, meaning that, in his case, Krishna consciousness ultimately won out over LSD.

Turning again now to the historic meeting between Prabhupada and George Harrison, John Lennon, and Yoko Ono in 1969, we find this same tension. The difficulty here, however, was less about LSD, which was already on its way out of fashion, and more in reference to important questions of authority, power, and lineage.[153]

---

iii That said, I note how similar the "theophany" in Chapter 11 of the Gita is to psychedelic accounts, in addition to the author's own experience.

Without going into too much detail, during the course of Srila Prabhupada's opening discourse to the two Beatles and Yoko, he urges the assembled trio to "try to understand this Krishna Consciousness," which he notes is not a sectarian or religious movement.

"*Judge with your intellect,*" the swami suggests in his British accent at one point, "*and you will find it sublime.*" After his discourse, John and Yoko press him with questions and concerns, many of which are still relevant to this discussion.

One critical issue that John and Yoko bring up is the question of authority:

Yoko: *What is your answer to this question of authority? What is authority, and who has the authority?*

John: *Yes, we should go to a true master [you say], but how are we to tell one from the other?... That's what we're doing. We're going around. Actually, Yoko never met the Maharishi Mahesh Yogi. So, we're asking for advice about how to know what's real."*

Prabhupada's answer to them is "*sampradaya,*" meaning lineage: You have to have a teacher who is of a true lineage. Of course, to John and Yoko, that just begged the question of how one can tell one lineage from another, and which one to follow?

John: *Maharishi said he's doing the same thing, his mantra's coming from the Vedic [tradition]... seemingly with as much mythology as you, and he was probably right, so it's like having so many fruits...*

Prabhupada replies that the Hare Krishna mantra is the best mantra for this age, namely the Kali Yuga, the "dark age of materialism."

Yoko: *If it's the best one, why should we bother with anything else?... If the Hare Krishna mantra is such a powerful mantra, is there any reason to chant any other songs or mantras?*

John: *Isn't it a matter to the devotee. Isn't it like just a matter of taste... It's all the name of God, so it doesn't really make much difference, does it, which mantra you do?*

These are good questions. They didn't call Lennon the intellectual Beatle for nothing.

Meanwhile, George is characteristically quiet. What is he thinking? Is he silently fuming at John and Yoko for their intellectual mind games? Can't they see that this man, Prabhupada, is a true master and divine messenger?

And just what are John and Yoko thinking? Are they thinking that Srila Prabhupada has not given any satisfying answers to their most important questions?

Perhaps the answer can be found in George and John's subsequent song lyrics. In December of that year, George penned "My Sweet Lord." In the style of a Bhakti Yogi belting out a bhajan, Harrison expresses his intense desire to see and know and be with Krishna.

My sweet lord
Hm, my lord
Hm, my lord
I really want to see you
Really want to be with you
Really want to see you lord
But it takes so long, my lord

In December of the following year, 1970, John writes the song "*God*" in which he expresses, among other things:

I don't believe in Mantra
I don't believe in Gita
I don't believe in yoga
I just believe in me
Yoko and me
And that's reality
The dream is over
What can I say?
The dream is over
Yesterday
I was the dreamweaver
But now I'm reborn
I was the Walrus
But now I'm John
And so dear friends
You just have to carry on
The dream is over.

In other words, John Lennon and the Beatles may have been "bigger than Jesus," as Lennon famously told a reporter, but John never claimed to be Jesus or God. He was a simple human being like the rest of us who had to carry on and "carry that weight a long time." He seemed to finally understand that no matter how long and winding a spiritual seeker's road may be, we all have to go through whatever we need to learn in order to find and live our own truth.

Here is Rolling Stone editor, Jann Wenner, asking Lennon directly about he and Harrison's seemingly divergent paths in the now famous January, 1971 magazine interview,:

"It's strange that George comes out with his 'Hare Krishna' and you come out with the opposite, especially after that."

Lennon: *I can't imagine what George thinks. Well, I suppose he thinks I've lost the way or something like that. But to me, I'm like home. I'll never change much from this.*[154]

Note how Lennon's reply echoes the famous line from the Beatles song "Across the Universe," a line, of course, which can be read any number of ways: "*Nothing's gonna change my world.*"

Earlier that year, George had written the foreword to Prabhupada's book *Krishna: The Supreme Personality of the Godhead,* in which he proposes something that on the surface appears radically different from John's new direction:

"YOGA (a scientific method for GOD (SELF) realization) is the process by which we purify our consciousness, stop further pollution, and arrive at the state of Perfection, full KNOWLEDGE, full BLISS.

If there's a God, I want to see Him. It's pointless to believe in something without proof, and Krishna Consciousness and meditation are methods where you can actually obtain GOD perception. You can actually see God, and Hear Him, play with Him. It might sound crazy, but He is actually there, actually with you.

Swami Bhaktivedanta is as his title says, a Bhakti Yogi following the path of DEVOTION. By serving GOD through each thought, word, and DEED; and by chanting HIS Holy Names, the devotee quickly develops God-consciousness. By chanting:

Hare Krishna, Hare Krishna

Krishna Krishna, Hare Hare

Hare Rama, Hare Rama

I request that you take advantage of this book KRISHNA, and enter into its understanding. I also request that you make an appointment to meet your God now, through the self liberating process of YOGA (UNION) and GIVE PEACE A CHANCE."

ALL YOU NEED IS LOVE (Krishna) Hari Bol

—George Harrison

You'll note here that George has put his own spin on two of John's songs: "All You Need is Love" and "Give Peace a Chance." This is very telling. Although their approaches are quite different, the end goals of these two ex-Beatles, Love & Peace, are the same.

We might say that George is more of a *Bhakta,* a person who seeks God through love and devotion, and that John is a *Jnani,* or a person who seeks God through discriminating intellect: *neti neti*—"not this, not that." Or we could say that George is more Vishnu the Preserver, incarnating as Krishna to be the upholder of *Cosmic Order;* whereas John is Shiva the Destroyer, ingester of Soma, clearing the way to a thousand ego deaths. That said, it is best not to perceive this as a black and white, either/or issue. Both Beatles were complex individuals who embodied both *Bhakta* and *Jnani* streams in their lives and work, and in any case, *Bhakti* and *Jnana Yogas* are but two divergent rivers leading to the same Ocean of Love.

George Harrison remained aligned with Krishna Consciousness for the rest of his life. Like Gandhi, who uttered the name of Ram as he was shot by Nathuram Godse, so too did George utter "Hare Krishna" as he was being attacked by Michael Abram in his home only two years prior to his passing.

Interestingly, the other Beatles, including John Lennon, remained more or less in the Maharishi camp. Most particularly Paul McCartney who in recent years staged a concert in New York City to benefit the Transcendental Meditation movement, and honor the late guru of the Beatles.

I personally find this all very fascinating because I've experienced both sides of the equation: I've walked in George's shoes to some extent, and I've also, more recently, begun to see things more from the perspective of John and Yoko.

When I first got into Yoga in 1996, I felt like I had found *IT*! I was very open to the wisdom of the masters, and basically did what I was told to do. I was a lover, a *bhakta* singer/songwriter, and very naïve to the point of possibly even being dangerous.

At that point I would have seen Lennon as a lost, confused soul who couldn't see past his inflated ego. An ego which no doubt was the reason behind his initial break with the Maharishi. George might not have fared much better in my esteem. But at least he was on the right path, ostensibly willing to sacrifice his *little self* in service to something far greater.

But it wasn't long before I had serious doubts that weren't going away or being resolved. The spiritual experiences I had were enough to whet my appetite, but not enough to inspire me to spend my youth sitting all day long in meditation (which I actually did often enough early on). I desired more of an understanding of why I was doing what I was doing. I was also confused as to which teacher to follow, and why they sometimes seemed to be at odds with each other. I really wanted… I *needed*… answers that I just wasn't getting. I was told the Guru is supposed to be God, or at least like God, including being omniscient; but if that was so, why did I sense, like John Lennon did with Maharishi, that my beloved, revered teachers didn't really know me as well as I knew myself? I was also frightened of going deeper, and if I'm honest, maybe that was the real truth behind all my doubts…

Deepak Chopra—"Taking LSD Was Fantastic"

"Spell GURU: Gee You Are You."

—Deepak Chopra

Deepak Chopra is a postmodern "guru" who parted ways with his guru, the Maharishi, in 1991 after having an uncommonly close relationship with him. In recent years, "fallen guru" and founder of the now defunct "What Is Enlightenment?" magazine, Andrew Cohen, conducted an intimate interview with Chopra. In the course of the interview, Chopra goes into depth about his break with his teacher. He also mentions taking LSD in the Sixties, but doesn't go into detail, perhaps because Cohen is known to be very unsympathetic to psychedelics.

In other recent interviews, however, Chopra has gone into more depth on the subject of psychedelics, candidly talking about his drug use. Consider the following recent interview excerpt:

Interviewer: *What led you to try LSD?*

Deepak Chopra: *I was about 17 or 18 [mid-Sixties] and I was looking for "out of the box" experiences, and experimenting with LSD actually caused a shift in my consciousness. But addiction is such a serious disease because people are looking for the experience of ecstasy. When people have this experience for the first time through drugs, they think that if they keep taking drugs they will keep having the experience, but it doesn't happen that way. But because your brain has receptors to feel-good chemicals, you can induce ecstasy through your physical senses—for example, through sport or by achieving greatness: consider how Mandela felt when, through collective effort, an entire nation was liberated.*

Anyone with serious experience in psychedelics would strenuously object to some of what Chopra says here: Addiction? Does LSD create addiction? And does LSD merely provide access to ecstatic states? As wonderful as my own "runner's high" experience was, it cannot be compared with my psychedelic experiences, which are of a different, higher order. This is not to say that because my peak experiences weren't comparable, everyone else's aren't too. Maybe my peaks *were* profound and I just don't remember them!

While I *have* experienced profound highs in my past, at this point, I don't experience incredible highs except those that come under the influence of psychedelics. That said, it seems that psychedelics provide more of a "peek" into enlightenment rather than the "peak" of enlightenment, and thus they generally "pique" one's interest in walking the spiritual path.

I agree with Chopra that most psychedelic users do find that the more they use psychedelics, the more that the rule of "diminishing returns" comes into play. And, that these reduced returns are more common using laboratory synthesized drugs like LSD and MDMA then they are with plant medicines like Ayahuasca. However, that's not a good enough reason to not explore what these substances have to offer. Perhaps, because of this loss of effect over time, we should simply consider not doing these synthesized substances too frequently.[155]

In a more recent statement for the London press, obviously calculated to raise eyebrows, Chopra was a bit more enthusiastic about his LSD experiences:

"Taking LSD was fantastic. If I had not had that experience, I would not be where I am today."[156]

Of course, if *any of us* had not had almost any *particular life experience*, we would not be where we are today! This makes one wonder how serious Chopra was when he said this. And if he was serious, and not just aiming to get a rise out of people, then, coming from Deepak Chopra, this is quite a remarkable statement in support of LSD! But it would sure be nice to hear him expand on his thoughts on the matter a little bit...

Perhaps it would be useful at this point to hear about one of Chopra's two LSD trips:

Chopra to Andrew Cohen: *...I had tried LSD in medical school twice. One experience was with these American hippie medical students. We'd all taken LSD, and we were on a train from Delhi to Madras. We were looking at this poster of Mother Teresa, and we all started to cry. For that entire trip we wanted to be with Mother Teresa. So these were all very interesting experiences, but I never put them in the context of spirituality. But then when I started meditation, suddenly it clicked.*

Why wouldn't he have thought these were spiritual experiences? Perhaps he had not lived a spiritually–oriented life up until that time. But it still seems like he should have had some context for this first LSD experience, such as to think of this longing to be with Mother Teresa as a form of "Bhakti." Ultimately, according to Chopra in an interview with Andrew Cohen, meditation had a much more profound influence on Chopra than LSD:

Cohen: *What was the original reason you started to meditate?*

Chopra: *I was reading a lot about meditation itself, reading Muktananda's Play of Consciousness. I had always loved the theories of consciousness. I could tell you everything from Ludwig Wittgenstein to Schopenhauer to the Upanishads—I'd read it all by now. I just kept reading and reading voraciously. Then I started to read Vedanta and realized, "Oh, I've had these experiences." So when I finally took up transcendental meditation (TM), I really woke up. It was an amazing thing. I completely lost my desire for alcohol, for cigarettes, for meat, etc. It was transformative, absolutely. So when later I had the opportunity to meet Maharishi, or actually to see him in a lecture, I jumped at it. I was like a new convert. I started telling everybody why they should meditate."*

This sounds very familiar: in the Sixties, hippies were telling everybody why they should take LSD!

Chopra's recollection here is not unlike my own "conversion" to Yoga. Initially I wanted to shout about yoga from the peak of Mount Kailash. Many spiritual seekers will relate to Chopra's description of the effects of meditation:

Chopra: *I started feeling light. Started feeling bright. Started feeling joyful. Started feeling ecstatic. Started feeling that I loved everybody. Started feeling that I wanted to help everybody. I also started feeling that everybody in the world should meditate!*

Chopra became deeply involved with Transcendental Meditation, or TM, for the next two decades. During that time he became so close to the Maharishi that others in the movement resented him intensely.

By the 1990s, Chopra was as well known as the Maharishi himself. Chopra decided it was time to carve out his own niche. Here's an excerpt from how he described his parting from the Maharishi:

Chopra: *Then he [Maharish] said, "You don't realize"—he used this word—"we have an empire and it's yours." "Maharishi," I told him, "you don't understand. I don't want that empire. I want freedom. I want to think the way I think. I want to write the way I write. I want to speak the way I speak. I don't find that I can do that here." "You will be able to," he insisted. I replied, "No, I won't. It's a system, now, and it's a system that has created something that makes it impossible to work outside the system." He asked, "So what do you want to do?" And I told him, "I want to leave." These were his last words: "Then go. I will love you, but I will be indifferent to you, and you'll never hear from me again." And I said, "Okay. God bless." That was the last time I spoke to him.*

What is so striking here, and in other places in the Cohen interview, is the way the Maharishi sounds so completely human. Not an all-knowing being at all. Rather a mere man vulnerable to petty human jealous, much like Lennon had described him during the earlier Mia Farrow debacle that drove the Beatles away.

Were Lennon and Chopra simply egomaniacs beyond help? Men so large in their own eyes that they were unable to humble themselves to a (supposedly) divine being? And would I, myself, be willing to submit to this same human "deity"?

Let's leave that question for the moment and examine an anecdotal account of the Maharishi's personal activities with regards to LSD. The following story was originally posted on a Hare Krishna website:

Harikesa: …Once they gave the Maharishi four big pills of LSD.

Prabhupada: Who?

Harikesa: His disciples gave him, Maharishi, four big pills of LSD.

Pusta Krsna: Maharishi?

Harikesa: Yes. And he just stood there and said nothing happened. So everybody said, "This is proof that he's already there."

Prabhupada: Huh?

Harikesa: Because he just stood there and said, "Nothing is happening to me," everybody has figured that he is already there.

Prabhupada: "There" means where?

Harikesa: At the ultimate.

Prabhupada: Hell. (laughter)[157]

This tale is almost certainly apocryphal. The exact same story was famously told about Neem Karoli Baba, who was affectionately called "Maharajji," so it may be that here the "Maharajji" has mistakenly replaced the "Maharishi."

But the fact that this story exists at all is compelling because it demonstrates just exactly how negatively one Sixties era "Guru" might speak about another. Prabhupada's disparaging final remark about the Maharishi's spiritual location: "Hell" clearly demonstrates the kind of open warfare that existed between some "holy teachers" at that time. I myself have witnessed competitive animus between different "Gurus" on many other occasions. I say all this recognizing that the entire story could be complete fiction.

Coming Full Circle, Spiraling Upward

Psychedelics were a huge part of what made the latter part of the Sixties the fun, colorful and wild period it actually was—a fertile period in writing, film, dance, fashion, design and probably most amazing of all, in music. Yet by the end of the decade, there was a movement away from psychedelic use among the counter-culture, particularly LSD, whose decline as a mind-expanding spiritual tool began with it being made illegal, and therefore socially unacceptable within the broader society. And while legality was certainly an important factor in this decline, we must also recognize that psychedelic drug use was cautioned against by certain countercultural and spiritual leaders for more than just issues of legality. Consider these sobering words about the spiritual usefulness of LSD from Ram Dass, circa mid-1970s:

"So my conclusion about it now is: For those who don't know about other levels of reality, it [LSD] could, under proper conditions, if they are truly turned towards spiritual life, show them that possibility. It did so for me. Once they know of the possibility,

and they really want to get on with it, the game is not just to get high again, but to "be" and be includes high and low... I don't deem that for a being on the spiritual path the LSD experience is any longer necessary. It is very clearly not a full sadhana; it won't liberate you. Because there is a subtle way in which there is attachment, in the sense of feeding your unworthiness because you aren't it without it; and you have to look outside yourself to get hold of it. As a method, it also has the limitation that it over-rides stuff that you would best deal with. Grabbing at experiences and pushing aside old habit-patterns in order to get high is ultimately just delaying the process. Because ultimately you have to confront those habit-patterns and purify them.

"After you know of the possibility you get on with it and any time you're just after another experience you're just getting more hooked on experiences and experiences are all traps. The game is to use a method, and when you're finished with it, to let it go. This isn't a good and evil matter; it's just a question of honesty with yourself as to whether in fact you are using your opportunities in order to awaken as effectively as you can." (pp. 101-102)

Ram Dass brings up the crucial issues of attachment and honesty, getting down to looking at our ulterior motivations—why we do what we do. Today, the word "intention" indicates our inner motivation. In Sanskrit the word for intention is "*sankalpa*," and in the world of yoga, a *sankalpa* is made before any spiritual practice is undertaken. In the Sixties, there was not great clarity of intention and purpose in the use of "drugs." I use that term in quotes because though these substances do seem to have the power to *drug* us into a state of soporific senescence, they also have the potential, when used with a clear intention, to awaken and heal; let us thus now use the term "medicines" instead of "drugs."

As medicines, as opposed to drugs, we can see these substances as having medicinal value short of spiritual evolution. In other words, these *medicines* might not provide a "full sadhana," as Ram Dass cautions us, but as I look around, I don't find many people ready or willing to do a full yogic sadhana anyway. What I do see is many people who are open to the *remedial/medicinal* potentials of both yoga and psychedelics.

An ironic twist in Ram Dass' own story was that Dr. Andrew Weil, the father of Integrative Medicine, was the young student at Harvard who outed Leary and Alpert for giving psilocybin to undergraduates. The irony is that Dr. Weil went on to become a researcher and advocate of psychedelics himself, both for spiritual and medicinal purposes. You may have seen him on 60 Minutes telling the following story about how LSD cured him of a lifelong allergy to cats:

"I took LSD... I was in a wonderful outdoor setting. I felt terrific and, in the midst

of this, a cat came up to me and crawled into my lap. I did not have an allergic reaction to it and I never did since... That gave me the idea that [taking LSD] would be a great way to teach people to unlearn allergies... If the drugs were legal, I think I would recommend that some patients do it."

This is a remarkable, and possibly irresponsible statement by one of the world's most recognized and respected medical authorities. Of course, Dr. Weil was just being honest, choosing not to put up a false front to the world in fear of losing his professional reputation.

What we've seen in the cycle of psychedelics is a circular movement spiraling up from the cautious use of them for spiritual purposes, to misuse by people seeking thrills, to outright abuse and censure by law. But perhaps there is a more balanced approach we can take to "plant medicines," an approach where we perceive these substances not as a dead-end, but as an opportunity—an opportunity that defines the practice of Yoga in combination with psychedelics as a powerful tool for the spiritual seeker of enlightenment, a combination more useful than either one or the other alone. This is not to say that at some point the "tool," or as Ram Dass likes to put it, the "method" (*upaya* in Sanskrit), becomes superfluous; we are speaking here only of beginning stages, where most of us are at *now*.

From this vantage point, the most effective approach to using the yoga and psychedelic combination to seek enlightenment is to begin with *yoga, just yoga*. Then, after establishing a disciplined and solid yoga practice, the individual might well consider having a psychedelic experience. Using this approach and by building up one's yoga practice, the seeker takes the first steps to access spaces within oneself through yoga. Then, when he encounters these places during a psychedelic experience, they will already be familiar to him and he won't be as "rocked" by them.

I choose to close this chapter with a famous line from the end of one of the greatest rock songs of all time, Led Zeppelin's "Stairway to Heaven." Robert Plant later said he wrote the words of the song while meditating on "spiritual perfection" in front of the band's fireplace in the early Seventies. This particular line gets at how rock music and psychedelics can assist us in the spiritual process. We can see them as both cathartic and an aid in stilling the body and mind. That famous line is:

"To be a rock and not to roll."

9

Who I Am: Part 2

Autobiography of a "Gen-X" Yogi

The Wandering Jewish Minstrel

So if I could summarize the next 5 years of my life after that initial awakening experience, I would say that it was all about trying to understand what happened to me and to do whatever I could to bring back that lovin' feeling. Of course, I didn't completely lose the experience and at least I now knew that it was possible, so I did become somewhat less neurotic, yet at the end of the day I was still pretty crazy. Now that the floodgates of creativity had burst wide open, I started composing songs, even though I also felt that I would never write another song as deep and beautiful as the first one. I was most interested in the Singer-Songwriter genre that for me really started with Dylan, but perhaps had its heyday in the late '60s/early '70s. I really studied Dylan, and was also very inspired by a lesser-known songwriter of the '60s, Phil Ochs; I did my best to emulate, and in some regards, imitate both of them. I very deeply felt that music was all I really wanted to do with my life. It was what brought me the most joy of anything, and it helped me to stay connected with that deeper part of myself. So after college, without much of a vision or plan, I decided I was going to just go travel abroad, live like a gypsy and write songs.

Before I left that summer of '91, my mother and I had a garage sale to help fund my trip. During the sale, this freaky looking guy came up and started talking to me all about his guru from India. Seeing I played guitar, he went on about how he could have been a great guitarist himself, but he gave it all up for the spiritual life. At one point he told me I really needed to read a book called "Autobiography of a Yogi" by Yogananda, and I promised I would. Yes, even though this guy seemed like a whack job, there was something about him that made me listen to him and go get that book. I couldn't get into it though, because it all seemed too bizarre to me, and I was much more into this book on Dylan at the time. I did take Yogananda's book with me on my travels, thinking I would read it again at some point, but I never did—not in that whole five year period between 21 and 26, the age I recognized yoga to be my life's calling. When I finally did get into yoga, I completely plowed through the book in just a couple of weeks, it all made complete sense to me.

So back to being 21 and on the road... I went to London first, thinking I would get a job there for 6 months, live at a youth hostel, and work on breaking into the music business. Due to a recession that summer, though, I didn't have much success finding work, but I did quite a bit of "busking" (play music on the streets for money). I quickly realized that unless you were very good at busking, you couldn't make any kind of living at it (there was a probably apocryphal story going around that Paul McCartney once disguised himself and went to busk on the Tube, made next to nothing and gave it all away). It was definitely good practice, though. I also played at a local folk club where Dylan had played 3 decades before. My songs were obviously too far out for the owner of the place, an old folkie himself, because he never seemed to want me to play. I did get some nice responses from some other folkies there, but no one was exactly stepping forward to help me really get started. I was finding out how hard it is to really make it as a musician.

So, yet another bubble burst, after 2 months, I ended up going up to the Lake District, the country of the great romantic poets like Yeats and Keats, to work at Outward Bound. The golden nugget I took from the next six months, and perhaps what drew me there, was that I met a young woman at Outward Bound, very sensitive and very troubled, who befriended me. She claimed that she was a witch, had been persecuted horribly in a previous incarnation, and was determined to continue where she left off. She was the first person I was ever close to who had psychic gifts, and there was a part of me that put walls up around that. Yet at the same time I was certainly tuned into her pure heart and divine feminine energy, which I was beginning to understand was a theme in my life.

Otherwise, I kept writing songs and tried to figure out where on the planet I was going to go next... The Continent? Greece? (Heard the busking was better there...) Scotland? Ireland? Wales? Then one night when I was talking to my mother, she suggested I go to Israel and stay in Jerusalem with the rabbi who had done my bar mitzvah ceremony 8 years prior. My initial response was that Israel was the last place I wanted to go. I had no real interest in Judaism or exploring what being Jewish meant, had almost zero "Jewish identity," and was also hearing all of this stuff about Israel's mistreatment of the Palestinians... But finally, I relented, thinking I would just hang out there for a month or two, and then head up to Greece afterward.

I had no intention of staying there any longer really. Little did I know what a powerful hold Israel would have on me, and how many wandering young Jews just like myself had wandered right into a kind of reformation camp for the hapless Hippie Hebe. Before I left, my young wiccan friend told me I was going to become a rabbi…

Once You Go Black, You Never Go Back

This Conservative rabbi I was going to see was not what you would normally think a rabbi would be. He was not so "conservative" after all, more like a hipster rabbi. It was fascinating to get to know him now as a somewhat grown man, because I was seeing him much differently. One of the first nights I was at his little apartment, he had a couple young friends of his over, around my age, and I was surprised when he started passing a joint around. I didn't know what to do because I really wasn't into smoking pot, and had tried it only once before, just a few months prior at Outward Bound. I didn't get high then, but then again, I didn't really inhale deeply enough and hold it in my lungs. So I decided to go with the flow and try it again this time, but again I didn't really inhale deeply or hold it in. I was clearly not too interested in getting high that way, and potentially messing up my body. I guess it was like taking just a sip of champagne at a toast for social etiquette's sake.

My way of altering my consciousness was still running, something I had been doing almost every single day for years now. If I missed a day, I would run more the next day. It was hard to run in Jerusalem though, because I really wasn't finding places I could go that seemed safe and where I would find my way back. (Were Arab kids going to throw stones at me if I accidentally wandered into their neighborhood? I had no idea.) Good thing the rabbi actually had a treadmill in his apartment. He was a big runner, too, and later in my Israel sojourn he would be instrumental in my getting in with the Jerusalem running club and doing a bunch of races with them. One night he came in after I had done this intense workout on his treadmill, and I recall how sickened he was at how bad his place smelled and he had to open all of the windows to air it out. He was impressed though when he saw I had been running 6-minute miles at the highest incline setting possible on the thing. My endurance was clearly getting better and better.

While staying with the rabbi, I went out during the day and busked on Ben Yehuda Street, the big thoroughfare in the center of the new city. I can't tell you how many Israeli kids asked me to play "Hotel California," and I indulged them all and actually got pretty good at it. The shekels were flying into my guitar case, too, unlike London, though it was by no means a living wage. The rest of the time, I toured around town.

Soon the rabbi told me it was time to move on, find something to do in Israel. We considered my options together, but I think there was a part of the rabbi, who was basically an ex-Conservative rabbi who still worked as a *mohel* (he circumcised babies on the 8*th* day after birth), who wanted to see what would happen to this young hippie if he was thrown into an ultra-Orthodox, "black hat" yeshiva. That seemed like the best option to me, mainly because I was told it would be free, and I really had no money at that point. I was informed that I would meet a lot of young people there like me, and it would be a good learning experience. At that point in my life, I was definitely open to broadening my horizons, though again, just for a limited amount of time. I had no intention whatsoever of getting stuck at some yeshiva where my life would go nowhere.

And of course, that's essentially what happened. To make a long story quite short, I went through various stages of a "conversion" back to Judaism, what is called "Ba'al Teshuva." This all happened over a period of months. Slowly but surely, I was taken in by the wisdom of the rabbis and the brilliance of the ancient scriptures I was reading in-depth. I was finding so many similar truth seekers as myself, some of whom had already taken the leap of faith and with whom I had all these insightful arguments. I was not even close to being all the way there though, until I did a weekend program in the Old City of Jerusalem called "Discovery," put together by the organization Aish HaTorah. This program has one agenda and one agenda only, and that is to bring lost Jews back to Judaism, Orthodox Judaism. To that end, it provides every possible argument and marshals every possible strand of evidence that the Torah is the word of God, including the now famous "Torah Codes," to chip away at the skeptic's walls of defense. I personally came out of the program blown away, very much convinced that there was very good reason for me to become an observant Jew. I still wasn't ready to go whole hog on the bandwagon (there was still so much of it that I found unappealing), but I did begin wearing *tzitzit* (prayer shawl) and putting on *tefillin* (phylacteries, prayer boxes) after that weekend.

Then I went away to a kind of graduate program in Jewish Studies in a small town near the desert, Arad. It was there I learned Hebrew and a good deal about Jewish history, including much I did not know about Israel. When I returned to Jerusalem, I decided to enroll in another yeshiva, this one that was more "modern" where men and women actually learned together, and there weren't as many seemingly old world customs (like wearing black) that would make a modern person like myself bristle. I stayed there for two whole terms, about 8 months each. During that time, I was for all intents and purposes living the life of an Orthodox Jew, praying three times a day, celebrating all of the holy days, doing as many of the *mitzvot* (laws/commandments) as I could. And I was seeing that it all worked somehow, it was a very beautiful life, certainly. I even was able to do most of the things I liked to do, like outside reading, writing, music, running…

Running While High

I was at this time running with the Jerusalem Running Club I mentioned earlier, and we regularly traveled to different parts of Israel to run in races.

It was funny running with them, because whereas previously I had always been dead last running with the "recruits," now I found myself to be the star runner of the team. Partly that was due to the fact that my running had improved, particularly for the longer distances (you will recall my lack of fast twitch muscle fibers, but it was also because there just weren't that many elite runners on the team. I bring all of this up for one reason, and that is to go into the phenomenon of what is known as the "Runner's High," as I had one major experience of this during a marathon in Israel.

The race was along the side of the Sea of Galilee, or Kineret in Hebrew, which means "violin," so-called because it's shaped like a violin. But we didn't go all the way around, it was an "out and back" race, 13 miles out, 13 back. I still recall some of the more memorable moments: admiring my buff body in the hotel room the night before; going down early to pray the next morning, and half-listening to some born again Christians praying loudly and without ceasing in the next room; wondering whether to eat or not to eat, and then deciding to just have some egg yolks and a little juice; being, as always, tortured before the race about what I was about to do to myself. And what I was about to do to myself *was* torture, only this time around it turned out to be not so bad.

Well, for the first 12 miles or so it was a killer. I never drank during races, because I felt like it slowed me down, but for a marathon it's not really too wise. I may have paid for it this time, because even though I had gone out fast, like at 5:30 pace, towards 10 miles or so I began to die, and became very discouraged when many of the runners I had passed earlier now began to pass me. So I basically figured I'd had it. But then around the 12-mile mark, I suddenly felt this incredible surge of energy, from where I have no idea, yet I was fully getting what was meant by a "second wind." Not to play with words, but it really was like a wind was lifting me up and carrying me along (sounds almost biblical), and where just moments before I had been struggling physically and mentally, now the whole thing felt effortless. All I had to do was just go. It was very similar to when I had been in love—I was flying. And it lasted for the next 10 miles, all the way to the 22-mile mark or so when I suddenly "hit the wall" big time. I even became disoriented and began to slightly hallucinate. When I finally made it to the finish line, the officials were surprised to see me for some reason, and they thought I had cheated. Maybe they just weren't expecting me because I wasn't one of the elite runners and I ended up finishing 12th overall that day with a time of 1:37:42, almost 20 minutes faster than my previous best marathon time!

So what had happened there? On one level, we could say that my brain had flooded with chemicals—endorphins, dopamine, serotonin, epinephrine, and what have you—and that had produced a "high" feeling where life became effortless, much like it had felt for me when I had been in love. On a deeper level… we always need to go deeper, to the source of these issues, and in this case, ask why I had that experience and most of the other runners did not, or did so to a lesser extent. To tell the truth, I also had this experience in other races, but never that full of an expression of it. To me this means that I probably have a greater predisposition to having these kinds of "feel good" chemicals flooding my brain than most, because I tended to have a lot of "bliss out" type experiences in my early life. And again: But why? Why me? It's always the question, and it's something I'm still wanting an answer for… but let's go on because there's still much to unravel.

The Unraveling… I Go Back

Although only vaguely aware of it at the time, the real turning point in my spiritual journey in Israel was a debate about the authorship of the Bible that happened at the yeshiva. That said, looking at it now with the benefit of 20/20 vision, there were a lot of signs indicating that my days in Israel were numbered…

For one, the head of the yeshiva was floating the idea of adding a rabbinical program for the next year, and I thought the idea of receiving *semikha* (ordination as a rabbi) intriguing. I actually began to get really excited about being part of it, and then we were told the plan fell through, probably due to the challenges of implementing an Orthodox ordination at a yeshiva where men and women learned Torah together. Needless to say, the entire course of my life would probably have been far different had I become a rabbi.

I also applied for Graduate School at the Hebrew University of Jerusalem, another huge life decision that would have had me staying in Israel at least a couple more years. That, too, didn't happen as I wasn't accepted, perhaps because my Hebrew was not up to par. Nor was my Aramaic, when orally tested at the yeshiva right around that time—I decidedly underwhelmed my teachers with my knowledge of Talmud. Not to excuse myself, but Talmud really wasn't too exciting for me; I had a great respect for it, but much preferred pure Torah study.

One final sign that I will mention is that, interestingly enough, given his overall support for Israel as the Jewish homeland, my dad was very much against me staying in Israel, especially my going into the Israeli army, which I had been considering. The captain of the running team, a man named "Dudi," suggested that I could become a running and fitness coach in the army at this beautiful facility we had visited. I loved the idea and I assumed it meant that I would be in the army, but not have to go through the normal training and carry a gun. But, my dad talked me out of it, saying it was a totally crazy idea and that he himself would never live in Israel, let alone go into the army—and by the way, he said, don't fool yourself, you're going to have to go through training and carry a gun like everyone else. Similar to what he had told me years before about rather being Jewish than anything else, dad told me then that he would rather live in the USA than anywhere else on the planet. I argued with him, and yet deep down there was a knowing that he was probably right.

So the debate at the yeshiva only confirmed that inner knowing… All through my time in Israel I had struggled with a very basic of philosophical conundrums, that of epistemology (which I knew well from my philosophy studies in college). Epistemology asks: how do we know? In this case, how do we know the Torah (or the 5 Books of Moses, at least) is what it says it is, namely the word of God as dictated to Moses in the desert some 3+ millennia ago? As I've noted above, this question was largely settled for me when I had witnessed the brilliant exposition of the Torah Codes in the context of the "Discovery" program in the Old City of Jerusalem. That program had been instrumental in getting me to become a "Ba'al Teshuva," a returner to traditional Judaism, or as we gypsy hippie Jews joked in yeshiva, a "born again Jew." Yet I still had lingering doubts based on certain contradictions I was noting in my studies.

These doubts were confirmed in a most brilliant way by a professor from Tel Aviv University, an Orthodox Jew who also happened to not believe the Torah was actually dictated to Moses, and he was able to quote chapter and verse to make a most persuasive case. That wasn't the only clincher for me—what I saw was that the rabbis at my yeshiva, especially this one rabbi who it seemed had a ready answer for everything, were a little stumped by this guy. This whole episode kind of rocked the yeshiva, so much so that there was a "re-match" planned between that rabbi and the prof. I had already heard enough, though. My position was that the Torah was divinely inspired yet was not literally the word of God to Moses. I was (and still am) open to the possibility that being born Jewish in this lifetime means following the traditional Jewish path, yet I could not continue to entertain the literalist position. I actually remained Orthodox for another year or so, yet it was really only a matter of time before I, somewhat guiltily, let the whole thing go…

A Psychic in Jerusalem

All signs seemed to indicate it was time to go back to the States, and back I went. That summer ('94) proved to be another major turning point on my journey. Besides the culture shock of being back in the States again after so long a period away, and its attendant "deprogramming" effects, the most game-shifting development at that point was my reading the book *Many Lives, Many Masters*, by Dr. Brian L. Weiss.

This was the first book on the subject by a Harvard and Yale-trained psychiatrist who happened upon past-life regression therapy. Dr. Weiss has now written several books on this subject, and in the past 2 decades has gone on to be an internationally recognized figure in the field. For myself at the time, being but vaguely aware of New Age ideas and philosophies, this book was nothing short of a revelation. For me, it established beyond a reasonable doubt that there is life after death, and before birth; and that we, as the title suggests, live many lifetimes on our soul's journey back to Source. The fact that this book was given to me by my mother is to me now symbolic of how my mother has, at times against her conscious will, been an ally in my own spiritual journey, as I know that I am in hers'. I note this because, as we will see, the Nurturing Feminine archetype was to continue to be a prominent motif on my journey.

The impact that Dr. Weiss' book and the exploration of these new realms that the book catalyzed cannot be overstated. There had been a doubt in my mind about returning to Israel again to study at the yeshiva, and yet now I knew that to really fully immerse myself in these new avenues for self-understanding and growth, I needed to be back in the States. The doubt I had about staying or going was such that I had left a number of my belongings at the apartment where I was living in Jerusalem. I thus made plans to return for just 2 weeks to tie up loose ends, say my goodbyes, and gather my stuff. As for the latter, the fact that I either gave most of my things away or left them there for a later return trip that never happened (I have not set foot back in Israel since then), suggests that I probably went back this time primarily for the encounter I am about to relate to you…

So I had this friend at the yeshiva who did not appear to be the kind to go to see psychics, yet in a chance conversation with him early on that trip, he mentioned going to see this very gifted woman and highly recommended that I see her in the time before I returned. He was so enthusiastic about it, and I was now so open for the callings of spirit beyond the pale of traditional Judaism (the injunctions against witches, soothsayers, mediums, etc., in the Hebrew Bible are plain to see), that I immediately called the psychic up and made an appointment.

A few days later, I was sitting in her small apartment in Jerusalem for a two-hour journey into my soul. While I feel this whole experience deserves its own special, extended treatment (wait for the sequel), I will just touch upon the highlights here right now.

After holding my watch and going into what appeared to be a deep trance (she had difficulty opening her eyes), the psychic, Libba, began to relate the visions she was seeing in her mind's eye.

At first, I was pretty skeptical. What I saw was an overweight woman with a husky Philly accent who clearly spoke highly about who she was and what she did, while not offering me too much solid info that would appease my doubts about her authenticity. Part of the problem, of course, was that I had come in with too high expectations (something that has taken me years to learn to let go of!). She correctly pointed out that there was a side of me that was a huge problem/blockage, and this she labeled my "Judge." On the other side of this was a Don Quixote-like figure, tilting at windmills with all of these great romantic ideals about changing the world. In the middle of both of these, she saw in her visions (she was clairaudient and clairvoyant) this most remarkable, majestic Church organ playing the purest divine spiritual music. This, she said, was what I most need to focus on in my life, bringing the Judge and Don Quixote into harmony with this sublime vision of my life's mission.

In my mind at this point I was like "yeah yeah, this could apply to many people, how about telling me something that you couldn't possibly know!"

In my heart, I was still open, touched and amazed by the authority and authenticity with which she spoke, a power that emanated with a complete faith in who she was and what she was offering. (And yes, the Judge was very strong in me—I thought back to how angry I had gotten at the innocent El Al baggage claim official that trip when my bag had gone missing. Although I was in denial about it, anger was very strong in me back then.)

As I still was ostensibly Orthodox at that moment, she asked whether perhaps becoming a Cantor was the direction I was to go? She was completely down on organized religion, mind you, especially Orthodox Judaism (most Israelis are, actually), yet she was honoring the path I had, at least superficially, chosen. While I was a bit too shy to express myself (I was actually terribly shy, did I mention that?), deep down I already knew that the whole Jewish trip, at least up to this point, did not really get to the heart of my truth in this lifetime. So what I was feeling was that at some point, yes, I would finally bust it out and live my true love, which was musical expression, beyond any and all boundaries or forms.

Libba actually recognized this, too, and she more than a few times said things to me to seemingly try to snap me out of it:

"Spirituality is spirituality is spirituality... It doesn't matter what form it takes."

And: *"The world needs more rabbis like China needs more people... I don't see you as a rabbi, a cantor maybe..."*

But anyway, back to those gnawing doubts I had about this whole proceeding... There was still that part of me that was like, "Okay, she's a great reader of personalities and body language, and she's got me down," and the rest, I thought, was good "BS work," if you will. The mind needed more "proof" before it took all of this with more than a grain of salt, while the heart had already gone where the reason could not, and yet still...

And then, she dropped a bomb: "Who's Eddie?"

"That's my twin brother."

"Oh, at first I thought Eddie might be you, because you've been using your Hebrew name, Eliezer."

She then went on to say that she had done her fair share of research on birth order, and generally it's the younger of the two (which I am) who pushes the elder out and is his teacher. Needless to say, Libba was now definitely appealing to both my heart and my mind. I'll just note she did it again when she told me there was an "Albert" who had popped in, and what a very happy and grateful spirit he was. Another point for Libba: at that time I was saying "kaddish" (Jewish prayer for those recently deceased) daily for my Uncle Albert.

Let me stop there (for now) and wrap up this whole episode by relating how for years I wanted to share the CD of Libba's reading with Eddie, though I never did, as he was even more skeptical about all these things than I had been. Over time though, Ed began to open up—it started with a discussion of synchronicity. Once Ed became familiar with the concept, he began experiencing it everywhere. Then my bro started seeing "11:11" all the time, and that led him to do a major internet study of the phenomenon, the results of which he often shared with me over the phone. Finally, on our 40*th* birthday, for which we made a little pilgrimage to Joshua Tree National Park in SoCal, Ed gave me a birthday card with the touching and rather surprising words, *"I'm finally ready to walk with you on the spiritual path."* This seemed nothing less than a miracle. And it led to me finally playing the CD of Libba's reading, including the "Eddie" part, which certainly had its effect.

Not long after this, I lost the CD and my computer that had the audio file on iTunes was stolen. The audio of the reading had certainly served its purpose over that 15-year period. I had re-listened a number of times, each time gleaning new insights and having more respect for Libba and the great gift she had offered me that moment in time. She had helped me to truly tune in to my soul's purpose in this lifetime, and my gratitude is beyond words.

I will just note that my other psychic friend from England who had predicted I would become a rabbi was in a sense correct—I had certainly delved into Torah in a very deep way in Israel, and the rich spiritual teachings gleaned from this period I was to take with me and share, just not from a pulpit.

Into the Hippie Mystic, University-Style

Back stateside once more, I was now so very inspired to continue my study of everything mystical, spiritual, New Age, with special focus on life-after-death and the subject of reincarnation. I reasoned I could do this at least partly in the context of working towards a Masters degree back at my alma mater, the University of Pennsylvania, and I was right. Although my undergrad average at Penn (a B-) did not make me a too likely candidate to be accepted, my GRE scores were high (due in large part, I felt, by my really learning how to "read" through my Torah studies) and so that very fall I entered into the Masters of Liberal Arts, an inter-disciplinary program that essentially allowed me to create my own course of studies. I immediately proceeded to sign up for as many Religious Studies and Folklore classes as I could, even finding one in the latter department offered by a prof who essentially had spent his whole academic career studying such seemingly far-afield topics (for an Ivy League school) as extraterrestrial abduction, crop circles, and the Old Hag experience[iv], among other unexplained phenomena. Needless to say, my new, spirited foray "into the mystic" was well laid before me, and I laid into it all *con mucho gusto.*

This all led to my deciding to begin the PhD program in Religious Studies at Penn the following year (it took me only one year to complete the MA). I didn't know where I was going with it all, yet my passion for probing life's deepest mysteries through the lens of world religion and spirituality never wavered. At one point in my little office in the RS department, I had maybe 100 different titles on a wide-range of spiritually-oriented subjects, if that gives you any indication of my obsession with figuring out what on earth was going on.

With all the reading and writing I was doing, I also began to recognize the

---

iv Essentially, a cross-cultural phenomenon whereby a half-sleeping person feels as if an entity is on top of them pinning them down and paralyzing them. After taking the course, I had two experiences of this. Just recently, two friends also related having experienced this, without knowing quite what it was.

necessity for my own deeper engagement with all of this in an experiential as opposed to purely "armchair" way. As I've already noted, it's not like I hadn't had any genuine "mystic" experiences—the "Love" awakening experience some 7 years prior had been the true guiding light for me throughout—and yet… that was then, this was now! I had no real idea about meditation or other spiritual disciplines at this point and psychedelics did have their attraction as a way in…

That first semester, the book that really got me excited was Tom Wolfe's "Elektric Acid Kool-Aid Test," all about Ken Kesey and the Merry Prankster's wild LSD-fueled cross-country psychedelic bus trip to the New York World's Fair in 1964. Reading it got me "on the bus," as Kesey famously put it—definitively in the hippie camp. I was so enthralled by Kesey that I ended up sending him an email asking his opinion of my taking LSD? I was surprised to receive a relatively swift, if brief, reply back:

"Sure, go for it, just stay away from the hard stuff."

So there I had it, the blessing of the original Pied Piper of Psychedelia himself. Only problem was, I had no idea of where to, if I may use the 60's idiom, "score some acid."[v] The only person I could think to query was a seemingly crazy Chinese-American 60s-throwback named Kathy Change (originally "Chang") who could often be seen prancing around Penn's campus with her colorful, offbeat signs and slogans, protesting for radical social change. While at first I had thought her odd, if not really freaky, once I had become enamored with the counterculture movement, Kathy became a kind of heroine to me and I began to, discretely, follow her movements on campus.

One day as she was taking a respite from her usual mantic antics (a rare moment) in front of Penn's library, I got up the courage to ask her if she had any LSD. She replied, quite seriously, that she no longer did it at her advanced age (she was in her mid-'40s, the age of the author, I might add), something about how the prospect of going on like that for 8 hours was a little bit too much for her. I thought maybe she was just throwing me off the trail due to some paranoia as she often seemed like she was high on *something*, though it's true that when not "on stage," she was not such a flighty character, definitely more grounded and quite intelligent. Our little interaction ended with her saying she would ask around for me.

It was not to be, however. Not too long after this episode, I was shocked to learn one afternoon that Kathy had ended it all in one great final act of self-immolation,

---

v   I want to pause and note here that, as synchronicities would have it, I'm sitting typing away here in a small cabin on a tiny island in the Pacific watching a recent film on Netflix about Kesey's famous bus trip, "Magic Trip," and considering taking a tab of acid that was just recently gifted by a hippie chemist, an actual Doctor of Pharmacology. This will mark my first LSD experience ever. I'll let you know later (in the book) how it goes.

setting herself on fire in protest of the "System" at Penn's famous Peace sign that morning, right near our brief encounter just weeks before in front of the library.[vi] As her body went up in flames that day, a cop, the symbol of the system she railed against, ran over and risked his life to try to save her life. Some would say he was just interfering with her firm decision to martyr herself. I don't know. I personally had come to completely sympathize with Kathy Change's cause, if not her approach. I was by this point very down on the whole system myself, really upset and angry inside at what we were doing to the planet and future generations, and feeling helpless about being able to do anything about it. "We are the ones our parents warned us about," I laughed when I saw that once on a bumper sticker, referring to the counter-culturists. And yet really, it was true, I realized—I had become one of them, I had become one of the rainbow people, and that felt right.

Yoga OM-coming

Ah, Spring! That great symbol of rebirth, the herald and harbinger of new hope, love, transformation…

Anyone who has witnessed the change from the drab gray of winter to the fragrant bloom of the springtime months in Philadelphia knows just how wondrously magical that transformation is. And it just so happened that the Spring of '96, my 26*th* year, also marked the beginning of a radical shift in my consciousness, a love affair (if not honeymoon) with yoga that was to last until the time of this writing.

"He was born in the summer of his 27th year
Coming home to a place he'd never been before
He left yesterday behind, you might say he was born again
You might say he found the key to every door."

These lyrics from John Denver's classic "Rocky Mountain High," relating a rebirth on his coming to Colorado when he was 26, very much applied to me too, as they do to many of us during the time of "Saturn Return" (between the ages of 26-31).

Again, there are at least several books worth of material in all that was to happen that year and the years to follow, and yet a few highlights will suffice for now…

That Spring, a colleague in the RS department, a woman about a decade my senior named L, suddenly took it upon herself to mentor me in spiritual matters. She had been observing me and saw that I was "a seeker," as she termed it. While by day she was a professional Indologist-in-training, she was also the devotee of at

---

vi You can learn more about Kathy Change here: http://www.kathychange.org/ & http://en.wikipedia.org/wiki/Kathy_Change .

least several women mystics from India. So she encouraged me, giving me some of their books and suggesting that if I met some of them, a lot of my questions would be answered.

When I finally expressed more willingness, L began inviting me over to her apartment for meditation and to go see some of these women teachers on the weekends. During that time, there were four women mystics in particular who I took as my gurus: Ammachi, Shree Maa, Sri Anandi Ma, and Sri Karunamayi. Rather than give you a play-by-play, I feel it will be more helpful to share some of the most world-shaking ideas and understandings that were coming to me at this time so that you can get a better sense of why this all seemed so crucial to me.

First, there was simply the fact of meeting real authentic, *living* mystics, and learning that yes, they are out there (the X-Files motto kept coming back to me), and that magic, mystery, and miracles are still very much alive in the world. All that time I had spent in Israel, I hadn't delved at all into Kabbalah, nor really met any Kabbalists—well, maybe a few, but no one who really struck me as being on the level as someone like Ammachi (Mata Amritanandamayi), whom I met that summer in NYC and who is believed to be one of the few full avatars, or divine incarnations, on the planet. At the same time, I had developed a somewhat dim view of India and Eastern religions in general from my time in Israel. So it was really refreshing to see the idea that these were ignorant idolaters, based largely in cultural and religious prejudice. What I understood was that in every religious group you are going to find varying degrees of spiritual evolution, and we have a tendency to judge other traditions by the worst examples and not by the best.

The truth is that both Judaism and Hinduism are essentially based in the idea of Oneness, and all through history there have been saints, sages, and mystics who have pointed the way to this deep truth.[vii]

And this wasn't to be taken on faith alone! I loved that nothing seemed dogmatic in Yoga—in theory at least, it's all based in personal experimentation and direct experience. There are no intermediaries between you and the divine—you are your own mystic, shaman, and ultimately, guru. There *are* strong recommendations, however, such as developing a "practice," something you do every day, and a yogic *way of life* based in paths stretching back millennia that had been well-traveled by many a kindred spirit—paths that were suited for the various personality types: Bhakti Yoga for the devotional soul, Jnana for the philosophical, Karma for the more active in the world, Raja for meditative, etc.… Bhakti seemed my primary path, yet the others

vii All of what I was finding in yoga and India was also within Judaism, too, I was to later discover, yet it really hit "home" when I was exposed to yoga at that time, which to me means there was something deep and karmic going on there.

were strong in me too, and it eventually became about integrating and harmonizing all of these superficially distinct tendencies.

Another major teaching coming through then, and certainly a "corrective" to the counterculture ethos I had recently adopted, was simply the idea that charity begins at home. In other words, peace and harmony in the world had to start within myself. "You can't change the world, you can only change yourself" was an oft-recalled sentiment at this time. If I was angry and in protest at the world for doing something to me, or disturbed that the world was going down the pipes and needed to be "saved" (by me or anyone else), I really needed only to look within myself for the source of that anger, rather than think that projecting and expressing that anger "out there" was going to do anything but make things worse and create more *dis-ease* of mind and body. Meditation was hugely important in this regard, not only for showing me how much negativity and attachment I carried around with me, but also that I could step back from the mind and choose to act and think more consciously, rather than instinctively, impulsively, and impatiently. I could *respond* to life with love, rather than react to it through fear.

Conscious breathing also helped immensely in this regard, and especially breathing through the nose, not the mouth. "The mouth is made for eating, the nose is made for breathing," goes the Indian proverb. This was completely new to me and it took me months to teach myself how to breathe only through the nose. This alone was a huge shift! For all of my life until then, I had breathed only shallowly through my mouth and into the chest, and so teaching myself to breathe only through the nose and diaphragmatically really took some doing. This, in turn, put me more in touch with my mind and helped to calm it through changing my breathing pattern to slow and deep, rather than fast and shallow.

Living alone and according to the hippie world-view, I had also gotten quite far from the idea that "cleanliness is next to godliness." At that point I was showering maybe once every 5 days (on a mission to save water!) and my University apartment was pretty much a pig sty. To do the practices that I was now receiving from my teachers required me to take regular showers, put on clean clothes (often white), light a candle and maybe some incense (which I loved), and basically to purify my temple inside and out. When I did this, I realized how much of a weight it took off my mind and how good it felt.

The yogic concept of "*brahmacharya*" was also a refreshing perspective/corrective on something that had continued to be a source of confusion and guilt, namely sex in general, and *orgasm* in particular. As I understood *brahmacharya*, the idea is that there is nothing inherently wrong or dirty or shameful about sex in any form, and yet, there is wisdom in discernment and discrimination in how this great power is used and expressed. On this view, masturbation was not really recommended, not because it was "sinful," but only because it was often a wasteful expenditure of potent energy that could be put into the furtherance of one's spiritual development. The original meaning of sin was "missing the mark," so I could release the feeling of guilt and merely choose to not miss the mark by changing a habit that was not serving my highest interests. For me at that time, this meant getting off "beating the meat" cold turkey, which I basically did for the next 2 decades, though now I'm channeling it into the direction of actual relationships with real, live women—what a concept!

Speaking of turkey and beating meat, I had been vegetarian since I was 15 years old, coming to it not so much for ethical reasons as because I heard it would improve my running and overall health. Over time it became more about not causing suffering to other beings and conserving the earth's resources—yet until this point, I still ate fish, eggs, and dairy. I now felt inspired to completely give all of these up and become a vegan for the rest of my life. The result was definite feelings of lightness, clarity, and ease in the body, not to mention youthfulness and excellent health from then until now (not that becoming vegan was the sole factor in that, yet definitely a contributing factor). I will also mention that I have not, with a couple of rare and short-lived exceptions, taken any prescription medications in the past 3 decades.

Hatha Yoga was a whole new amazing world, yet I didn't get into it until about 9 months after all the other stuff. As I have seen with many men, it just didn't appeal to me that much from the one or two classes I had taken. I much preferred running, biking, swimming and weightlifting—manly-man cardio-muscular training which is how I generally worked out. Now suddenly, however, this yoga stuff made complete sense and I realized that it was really a lot more physically challenging than it looked! It was just that the class I had been in was gentle yoga and I was an athlete who needed to feel like I had actually done something.

I realized that the key was to practice yoga on my own and this I began doing religiously every day. Much of my early exploration of Hatha Yoga was just from this one little Sivananda Yoga book I had. After school I would go to my room, read the book and practice for hours, trying to imitate the people in the pictures. At first my goal really was to just be able to sit in the lotus pose and meditate. That didn't take but a few months, though, and the ego-mind is never satisfied, so it ultimately became about mastering every yoga pose in existence! While this never happened, I will say that *asanas* which I thought would take years if not lifetimes to accomplish came considerably sooner. After a few years, people began to ask me a question I've now been asked countless times: *Were you always that flexible?* My ultimate answer is: *Yes, we all are, we just don't know it yet.* I also mention to people how excruciatingly painful my early yoga practice was, almost like self-torture, and that if I just had some "before and after" pictures from then until now, showing how I became Uncle Gumby, my career would be made in the shade (ha!).[158]

Please keep in mind that I was convinced I had a powerful addiction to exercise due primarily to the endless running I had done since my early teens. It was to the point that if I missed even a day of running or other exercise, my body would actually begin to go through withdrawal symptoms that could be paralyzing. And light exercise wasn't enough; it generally had to be heavy duty to the point of exhaustion to do it for me (recently I discovered this is indicated in my natal chart).

From early on, I recognized that if only I could somehow eat less, I would not feel such a need to do so much exercise. I also realized that long distance running was probably not going to be so healthy for me over the long haul, especially competitive running, because I always felt I needed to be so "up" for races to get my vaulted PB (personal best), and that meant a whole lot of adrenaline and god knows what else constantly coursing through my system. The upshot was that I made a conscious decision to stop training and racing competitively and really focus on just Hatha Yoga as my main form of exercise. This meant that I slowly, slowly began to eat less, exercise less, and release quite a bit of self-imposed stress from my life. It also meant that I channeled the discipline and fitness from running into yoga, which is one reason I was able to achieve all the poses I did with no prior experience in dance, gymnastics, or even much stretching. That said, it also meant that I brought the same obsession, drive, and competitiveness from running to yoga, so that I took words like "achieve" and "accomplish," that we find in some of the yoga texts, in the same spirit. I say this all without judgment because it was, at the end of the day, still a movement toward greater clarity.

There was a part of me that was still conflicted about letting go of competitive running—maybe if I had just kept up the running, in another 12 years I probably would have gotten my times down and blossomed into a truly great runner… That was wishful thinking though. I had already been seeing my times diminish over the last few years and I knew I didn't really want to put such an immense effort into running anymore; it felt like a dead end.

Speaking of conflicted, let's get back to sex. This account would not be complete without mentioning what was definitely one of the most important developments of this period, namely my first relationship ever! Not just my first relationship, mind you, the first time I ever romantically kissed someone, let alone made love. Whoa.

Let's look at this: I was now 26 years old. I was handsome, healthy, and pretty much horny all the time. I had been in environments with a lot of potential mates for all of my teens and twenties. So what was up with that?

Well, it was a combination of waiting for Mrs. Right and really being too afraid of intimacy for various reasons ranging from guilt, to the time commitment, to being picky and prudish, to what have you. On one level, there was nothing that I wanted more than to be with a woman, a beautiful, sexy woman. On another level, there was nothing that I feared more, nor did I ever feel I could truly be in love as I was that first time. Interesting that it should happen right at this moment in my life—a time when I had finally realized that sexual moderation was wisdom and that I truly wanted to let go of my immoderation for good. I had actually stopped self-pleasuring for a good 7 months before fulfilling my lifelong fantasy of making love with a woman, giving birth to more inner turmoil. I was over masturbation, yet now I felt like I was succumbing to lust (I was), and if I could have just held on for a few years, I probably would have gone a lot further with my yoga practice.

On another level, I knew it was all what I needed at that moment in time and definitely a step in the right direction because I was becoming a less repressed, more liberated and sovereign being. Over time I was to feel that the way to not take sex (or anything) so seriously was to directly engage with it. That was one way, at least, the tantric way, the path of "getting through by going through," definitely a path for our time, as Osho and others so correctly saw.

One final area of my life needs addressing here before diving into the less personal material of this book, and that was the part of me that still wanted to be Bob Dylan, to be a famous musician. Well, I definitely had some talent, yet it became clear to me that it just wasn't going to happen and that I probably really didn't want that anyway. On one level I felt cocksure like, "Yeah, I could do that… if I wanted to," and on another, I sensed I needed a lot more work on myself to let go of all the stuff getting in the way of my writing and playing (namely myself!). In any case, I was pretty much on an enlightenment trip—the thought that this can all wait until I'm enlightened, then I'll come back to it, that I'm not going to make this the central focus of my life right now. So my musical abilities were put in the service of things like kirtan (communal, call-and-response songs & chants), a bhakti yoga practice just really beginning to take off at that time, a nearly mainstream phenomenon at the time of this writing.

Dark Night of the Moon / End of Spiritual Kindergarten

"Always look on the bright side of death."

—Monty Python

The bright side of the dark night of the soul is that you're no longer on the dark side of the moon, suffering under the insane illusion that you're getting somewhere special on your spiritual trip, or that there's somewhere special to get *to*…

The next 3 years constituted the "honeymoon" period of my love affair with yoga (or perhaps better put, yoga's "spiritual seduction" of me), a time when yoga was IT for me and could do no wrong. During this time I continued to practice and study for hours daily, went to see various teachers in the Tri-State area, traveled to India various times to visit my teacher at her ashram, and basically was a good, devoted yogi, or so I thought/hoped.

Throughout this period I had some amazing spiritual experiences: Kundalini and chakra openings, mind-blowing synchronicities, near out-of-body journeys, ecstatic bouts of laughing and crying, clairvoyance—not enough to completely remove that seed of doubt, yet definitely enough of a seductive carrot-stick thing to keep me in the game. Simultaneously, that subtle seed of doubt was being watered in various ways, such as beginning to become disillusioned with India, with my gurus and gurus in general (partly fueled by all the stuff that was coming out on the internet), with sex and being in a relationship (that first relationship was over in 3 years), with what was not forthcoming from my practice (what, no siddhis or enlightenment yet?!?), with the body, with Hatha Yoga… disillusionment with everything really.

And here I want to say that, from my perspective now, this is all just the way it is in this world, and most any kind of love we experience here, no matter how sublime, is generally ego-based and thus doomed to dissolve at some point or another. Every bubble will burst sooner or later. I've seen myself fall in love or get excited about the Next Big Thing enough times in this lifetime to know it's all a big ego trip/trap.

To recap, the NBT's (let's call them) for me, in this order, were: reading, writing, the trumpet, the guitar, sex, running, philosophy, romantic love, religion, spirituality, yoga, more sex (relationships), psychedelics, and ACIM. There was always a sense that the next big thing left the last big thing *in the dust*, and the truth might have been that the ego was just running away from getting in too deep.

So although I didn't fully realize it yet, what was happening was all in divine order because, according to my current understanding, once all the ego enticements and enhancements wear off, we are always left confronting those deep contractions that keep us holding onto life in the body, the feeling of separateness and special-ness, and in argument with God/Spirit. The path is then understood to be not at all about what you have accomplished, but what you can now let go of, recognizing that you are not the ego-mind/body complex, nor anything so impermanent. There's a sense in which for this to happen for some, the ego must be built up somewhat in order to be strong enough to submit to being dismantled and eventually dissolved. (Ram Dass: "You've got to be somebody before you can be nobody.") And I per-sonally didn't really, *really* get all of this, or begin to get all of this, until I had some psychedelic experiences, and even more recently, became a student of *A Course in Miracles*. These spiritual tools and guides effectively took me beyond yoga, or at least the whole yogi trip I was on, to undoing the ego (releasing fear) and seeing what still remained in the rubble of the aftermath. So rather than continue my "story" here, which I feel is really all of our story disguised as "mine," I will leave the rest for another time…

10

Neem Karoli Baba's Children

"Love is a stronger medicine than LSD"
—Neem Karoli Baba

*"You crave to be in as pure a relationship to the guru as the guru
is to God. There's a moment, like an initiation or an opening,
when the guru shows you who they are. Maharaj-ji opens his eyes,
and in an instant you see the universe. Then he closes his eyes,
and you're back. Or Krishna showing Arjuna his universal form.
It's like taking acid. As Maharaj-ji said of LSD, 'It allows you to
have the darshan of Christ.' It's the first thing that compelled all
of us to go on. But then you have to come back, do your work,
and go become it. The only way you can get that purity is to
let go of your impurities. It's a two-stage process: first the guru
shows you who he or she is (really, who you are reflected in the
guru), and then the guru sends you back to finish your work."*

—Ram Dass[159]

How could a book dealing with the topic of *yoga and psychedelics* not devote at least one chapter to the Indian guru Neem Karoli Baba and the Westerners he taught and influenced, including ex-Harvard Professor Dr. Richard Alpert? After traveling to India and meeting Neem Karoli Baba, Dr. Alpert took the name Ram Dass and is now one of the most respected commentators on both yoga and psychedelics on the planet. Ram Dass' work influenced many young people to go to India in search of enlightenment. We will meet some of them below.

Discovering Ram Dass

Ram Dass appeared on my horizon while I was researching my Master's thesis in 1995. His 1971 bestselling book *Be Here Now* seems to have marked the birth of the phenomenon now called the *New Age Movement*. Ram Dass was also instrumental in catalyzing fledgling "Age of Aquarius" groups. One source claimed that *Be Here Now* was second only to the Bible in readership—surely an exaggeration, but the book was certainly a bible of the counterculture. If so, I knew I needed to learn more about this seminal figure.

Dr. Richard Alpert first took psilocybin mushrooms with his Harvard Psychology Department colleague, Timothy Leary on March 6, 1961. After founding the Harvard Psilocybin Project, both men were accused of supplying undergraduates with psilocybin and dismissed from Harvard in May of 1963. Six years and literally hundreds of LSD trips later, Alpert traveled to India and met Neem Karoli Baba, whom he accepted as his guru. Ram Dass' time with his new teacher convinced him that Yoga might also bring him to enlightenment without the use of psychedelics. For Dr. Alpert, this was a revelation. Using his new spiritual name, Ram Dass, he wrote his groundbreaking book *Be Here Now*.

In *Be Here Now*, Ram Dass tells what is now a famous story about how he gave Neem Karoli Baba a very high dose of LSD and "nothing happened." What follows is largely about what happened after that:

• • •

At twenty-five I became fascinated by the Hippie movement of the Sixties and Seventies and started to educate myself all I could about this fertile and creative period. For the first time in my life, I was also open to trying LSD. Like millions of other people, I read Tom Wolfe's *Electric Kool-Aid Acid Test* about Ken Kesey and his Merry Pranksters. These psychedelic pioneers staged "Acid Tests," public experiences of music and coordinated visuals where all the participants "dropped" acid to participate and be "tested." Even though the sardonic Wolfe was critical of Kesey and his antics, I secretly wanted to escape back to that era and, in Kesey's famous phrase, get "on the bus" and go "Further" (or "Furthur"). I sense many other young people who have read that book have had that urge as well.

At that time, I sent Ken Kesey an email asking whether he still felt LSD could be helpful to my generation. I never expected a reply, but several weeks later I received a short message from the Chief Prankster in my inbox:

"Sure, go for it. Just stay away from the hard stuff" (meaning hard drugs).

Ken Kesey with his Magic Bus, "Further"

But I never did find a reliable source for LSD, and within a few months I was heavily involved with Yoga and was no longer considering psychedelics an option. Brad, from a Kundalini Yoga group, told me that in his younger days he had taken a lot of LSD, but had found that Kundalini Yoga was a more natural route to enlightenment, not to mention a more powerful and lasting one. He also claimed that by doing his Kundalini practice, he was able to stop his mind from hallucinating while on LSD.[160] I was very skeptical, especially as I was not getting much from Brad's Kundalini techniques. But after reading Ram Dass' *Be Here Now* and the story of Neem Karoli Baba's having no reaction to LSD, I began to think that perhaps there was more to Brad's claims about the power of Kundalini and yoga in general.

In 1967, the Beatles went to India to find out if meditation could create a natural and lasting high comparable to that produced by LSD. Dr. Richard Alpert was also there at the same time on a similar pilgrimage. Alpert had taken hundreds of LSD trips, always with the vain hope that he would find a way to stabilize his high and not come back down into his ego identity again. In a talk given in 1977, he noted how with psychedelics…

"I touched a part of my being that was full and complete as it was. But I 'came down' from that experience, as the terminology is used, and for six more years I tried every device I knew not to 'come down,' but I continued to 'go up' and 'come down.'" [161]

He further recalled how the failure of this approach to psychedelics led him to India, and ultimately to someone he felt could help him:

"In 1967 I realized fully the limitations of this method of trying to achieve a state of unity with the universe through psychedelics. That is, I just didn't know how to do it. I didn't know whether or not it could be done, but I knew we couldn't do it because nobody I knew could do it, and I was working with people like Aldous Huxley, Huston Smith, and many other very sophisticated people—priests, rabbis, ministers,

philosophers, musicians, and so on.

"However, in the course of those years, as I said, I had become aware that there was a body of Eastern literature concerning the nature of the experiences that we were having. So in 1967 I went to India, on to the East, hoping that I would make some connection. In fact, I was very fortunate and I did. I met a man who became my guru."[162]

That man was Neem Karoli Baba, one who has also been called a sadhu, yogi, saint, and even God. Those who have read *Be Here Now* know what happened next: Alpert gave Neem Karoli Baba a very high dose of LSD, which according to him and other eye witnesses, did not make the guru "trip out." Although this story has been told and listened to a thousand times in spiritual circles, here it is again:

"In 1967 when I first came to India, I brought with me a supply of LSD, hoping to find someone who might understand more about these substances than we did in the West. When I had met Maharajji (Neem Karoli Baba), after some days the thought had crossed my mind that he would be a perfect person to ask.

"The next day after having that thought, I was called to him and he asked me immediately, 'Do you have a question?'

"Of course, being before him was such a powerful experience that I had completely forgotten the question I had had in my mind the night before. So I looked stupid and said, 'No, Maharajji, I have no question.'

"He appeared irritated and said, 'Where is the medicine?'

"I was confused but Bhagavan Dass suggested, 'Maybe he means the LSD.' I asked and Maharajji nodded. The bottle of LSD was in the car and I was sent to fetch it.

"When I returned I emptied the vial of pills into my hand.

"In addition to the LSD, there were a number of other pills for this and that—diarrhea, fever, a sleeping pill, and so forth. He asked about each of these. He asked if they gave powers. I didn't understand at the time and thought that by 'powers' perhaps he meant physical strength. I said, 'No.' Later, of course, I came to understand that the word he had used, "siddhis," means psychic powers.

"Then he held out his hand for the LSD. I put one pill on his palm.

"Each of these pills was about three hundred micrograms of very pure LSD—a solid dose for an adult. He beckoned for more, so I put a second pill in his hand—six hundred micrograms. Again he beckoned and I added yet another, making the total dosage 900 micrograms—certainly not a dose for beginners. Then he threw all the pills into his mouth. My reaction was one of shock mixed with fascination of a social scientist eager to see what would happen. He allowed me to stay for an hour—and nothing happened.

"Nothing whatsoever.

"He just laughed at me."[163]

Now, when I first read this story, I mostly believed that it was true. Partly my belief was based on having met other saints and gurus who, like Neem Karoli Baba, seemed to be at such a high state that almost anything was possible for them. Once again, though, the skeptic in me wanted tangible evidence of miraculous powers, and my experience up to that point had been that such evidence was not usually very forthcoming. As I mentioned, I had always seemed to just miss being in the room when the guru materialized something from their hands or feet, or when some miraculous healing took place. The one time that I did witness a materialization right in front of me, I thought it might be sleight-of-hand. After all, magicians do such things all the time and it looks completely real. The difference, of course, is that a spiritual teacher is not supposed to lie or trick people for personal gain. So I was in a bit of a quandary: I wasn't going to fully believe 100% until I felt I had incontrovertible proof; yet, I was also in the process of learning that "believing is seeing." In other words, perhaps I would see these things only after truly surrendering to their improbable possibility...?

Would you trust this man? Neem Karoli Baba ("Maharajji")

Terence McKenna, as noted earlier, was in India right around this time, and he also had his doubts about materializations and other demonstrations of spiritual power. Neem Karoli Baba, McKenna maintained, most likely palmed the LSD, fooling Ram Dass (and eyewitnesses like Bhagavan Das[164]) into thinking he took it.[165] McKenna had apparently seen enough fake holy men in India to awaken the skeptic in him. For myself, I had only heard about them second-hand, in books like Gita Mehta's *Karma Cola,* and in shocking stories making the rounds about Sai Baba and other controversial gurus.

Ram Dass no doubt heard the sleight-of-hand objection many times after *Be Here Now* was published, and it seems to have bothered him. After a subsequent trip to India a few years later, he began to tell a follow-up story to his original one, and it went like this:

The whole thing had happened very fast and unexpectedly. When I returned to the United States in 1968, I told many people about this acid feat. But there had remained in me a gnawing doubt that perhaps he had been putting me on and had thrown the pills over his shoulder or palmed them, because I hadn't actually seen them go into his mouth.

Three years later, when I was back in India, he asked me one day, "Did you give me medicine when you were in India last time?"

"Yes."

"Did I take it?" he asked. (Ah, there was my doubt made manifest!)

"I think you did."

"What happened?

"Nothing."

"Oh! Jao!" and he sent me off for the evening.

The next morning, I was called over to the porch in front of his room, where he sat in the mornings on a tucket. He asked, "Have you got any more of that medicine?"

It just so happened that I was carrying a small supply of LSD for "just in case," and this was obviously it. "Yes."

"Get it," he said. So I did. In the bottle were five pills of three hundred micrograms each. One of the pills was broken. I placed them on my palm and held them out to him. He took the four unbroken pills. Then, one by one, very obviously and very deliberately, he placed each one in his mouth and swallowed it—another unspoken thought of mine now answered.

As soon as he had swallowed the last one, he asked, "Can I take water?"

"Yes."

"Hot or cold?"

"It doesn't matter."

He started yelling for water and drank a cup when it was brought.

The he asked, "How long will it take to act?"

"Anywhere from twenty minutes to an hour."

He called for an older man, a long-time devotee who had a watch, and Maharajji held the man's wrist, often pulling it up to him to peer at the watch.

Then he asked, "Will it make me crazy?"

That seemed so bizarre to me that I could only go along with what seemed to be a gag. So I said, "Probably." And then we waited.

After some time, he pulled the blanket over his face, and when he came out after a moment his eyes were rolling and his mouth was ajar and he looked totally mad. I got upset. What was happening?

Had I misjudged his powers? After all, he was an old man, though how old I had no idea, and I had let him take twelve hundred micrograms of LSD! Maybe last time he had thrown them away and then he read my mind and was trying to prove to me he could do it, not realizing how strong the "medicine" really was.

Guilt and anxiety poured through me. But when I looked at him again he was perfectly normal and looking at the watch. At the end of an hour it was obvious nothing had happened. His reactions had been a total put-on.

And then he asked,

"Have you got anything stronger?" I didn't. Then he said, "These medicines were used in Kulu Valley long ago. But yogis have lost that knowledge. They were used with fasting [elsewhere Ram Dass says "Hatha Yoga"]. Nobody knows now. To take them with no effect, your mind must be firmly fixed on God. Others would be afraid to take. Many saints would not take this." And he left it at that.

When I asked him if I should take LSD again, he said,

"It should not be taken in a hot climate. If you are in a place that is cool and peaceful, and you are alone and your mind is turned toward God, [then you may take the yogi medicine."] then it could be useful. It would allow you to come into the room and pranam to Christ." (Meaning, you could come into the presence of Spirit.) "But you can only stay two hours," he said, "and then you have to leave again. It would be better to become Christ than just to pranam to him, but your medicine won't do that for you. It's not the ultimate samadhi."[166]

At the time I read these stories about Neem Karoli Baba , I still felt they might be true. It didn't occur to me that Neem Karoli Baba's asking for LSD again after 3 years might seem unusual to some, but it did seem strange that upon ingesting the LSD, the guru would look crazed one moment and completely composed the next. Then again, Neem Karoli Baba was known as a trickster guru, with inexplicable behavior and radical teachings. He certainly fit the archetype of the "crazy wisdom" teacher.[167] So perhaps Ram Dass' tales of Neem Karoli Baba aren't so far-fetched.

Needless to say, there's been considerable debate about these alleged incidents. Seeking more information, I wrote to a man who lived in India as an initiate into the Naga Babas for three decades, Baba Rampuri. Rampuri had known Neem Karoli Baba around the same time as Ram Dass so I wrote to him asking how he felt about Ram Dass' story. He replied simply, "This is in the genre of miracle stories, and there are better ones." Rampuri added that Ram Dass and the other Westerners didn't know any Hindi, and Neem Karoli Baba didn't know any English, so an accurate account of what the guru said was highly unlikely.[168]

Others agree that Ram Dass' Neem Karoli Baba tales are at best an embellishment, and at worst, completely made-up. You can see how this might be if you consider the following: Before becoming Ram Dass, Alpert claimed he took hundreds of psychedelic trips, trying every possible permutation of *set and setting* in an effort to never come down from the high. Finding no success with LSD, he eventually journeyed to India to see what the yogis there could teach him about drugs and their relationship to yoga. Then he met Neem Karoli Baba, a being who was always high! So what better way to bring this point home to the hippies on the home front than to create a myth around Neem Karoli Baba's power over LSD that would demonstrate the power of yogic discipline over psychedelic exploration?

Granted, this, my sense is that Ram Dass, always the consummate raconteur, most likely embellished the actual incident, but that the story itself is no mere tall tale. There was too much riding on *Be Here Now* for him to have completely fabricated a key story within it. And there were other witnesses, such as Bhagavan Das and Lama Surya Das (see below), who have corroborated Ram Dass' version of events.[169]

The question then, again, becomes: Did Neem Karoli Baba really take the LSD Ram Dass gave him? We'll never really know, but I feel there's a strong likelihood that he did. Many Westerners who have tried LSD would be amazed that a corpulent old Indian man could remain unaffected after ingesting a high dose of LSD. But if we look at the charismatic personage of Neem Karoli Baba, and the powerful influence and effect he had on so many seekers of that generation and onward, it seems far less incredible. Here was clearly a being of high spiritual capacity—even other spiritual teachers of his day recognized him to be a radically awakened being, a perfected master (*siddha*), a saint, or even an Avatar, God incarnate.

Such a one was Mikhail "Omraam" Aivanhov, the great Bulgarian Magus. Aivanhov traveled to India from France in the late '50s where he met with many of the great Indian saints and sages of the time. Among them was Neem Karoli Baba, who bestowed upon Aivanhov the name "Omraam." From then on, Aivanhov was "Omraam Mikhail Aivanhov" until his passing. I find the relationship between Omraam Mikhail Aivanhov and Neem Karoli Baba to be especially telling because I have been a student of Aivanhov's spiritual teachings for the past decade, and know him to be a remarkable spiritual teacher in his own right.[170] So for me, Aivanhov's connection to Neem Karoli Baba certainly adds more weight to Ram Dass' stories about his guru.

• • •

Reading Ram Dass opened the door for me to this whole issue of *yoga and psychedelics,* and once I had walked through that door, I naturally wanted to learn more about how *yoga and psychedelics* played out in the lives of other Neem Karoli Baba devotees. But before I relate to you what I discovered, let's consider the words of another Indian teacher, Swami Kaivalyananda, speaking in the late Sixties/early Seventies, and making a similar point to that made by both Meher Baba and Neem Karoli Baba about psychedelics:

"Drugs have been used in ancient times also. It is not a modern phenomenon. They have got some value, but the value is psychic value. They can give some psychic powers and some psychic insights, so they do have some meaning. But we cannot use drugs for the revealing of spiritual truths. Here the method is discipline… Drugs will help those people who believe that the sensory organs are the only instruments of experience and knowledge. At least we will know there are psychic perceptions also, not only the material world and sense world… LSD could be useful to Americans who are attached to the worship of material attractions. These people could begin to see life with a different view. So drugs can open doors for those with very limited and narrow perceptions."[171]

No one likes to hear the "D" word, but there it is: Discipline. And once again, the suggestion is that psychedelics do not give access to the "ultimate Samadhi." And yet, Swami Kaivalyananda suggests these things still might be of value to us in the West, who have been born and bred in a materialistic environment. Interestingly, the Swami makes no mention of the fact that many yogis in India still use these "drugs" themselves, and his contention that they do not reveal "spiritual truths" is one we will continue to wrestle with here.

Bhagavan Das: 1st Yogi of the Psychedelic Era (Who Nearly Missed It)

Despite being a decade his junior, Bhagavan Das (born Kermit Michael Riggs) was Dr. Alpert's guide in India, and it was he who actually introduced Alpert to Neem Karoli Baba. In *Be Here Now*, Ram Dass paints such a glowing portrait of his young mentor, he nearly mythologizes him to the point of apotheosis. We get the sense that Bhagavan Das is already "there," that Bhagavan Das can do no wrong. In fact, the book's title comes from Bhagavan Das: In response to Alpert's neurotic behavior throughout their journey, Bhagavan Das often reminds Alpert to "just be here now." Though Western born, Ram Dass leads us to believe that Bhagavan Das is in fact a great yogi who has heroically found his way back to his Mother India. It was as if Alexander the Great, instead of conquering the Far East, had stayed in India and lived among the yogis. Here is Ram Dass in *Be Here Now*:

I met this guy and there was no doubt in my mind that he "knew." It was just like meeting a rock. It was just solid, all the way through. Everywhere I pressed, there he was! [172]

Personally, I found Ram Dass' depiction of Bhagavan Das in *Be Here Now* so endearing and compelling that I just had to find out everything I could about him. So I purchased old cassette recordings of Bhagavan Das from Ram Dass' Hanuman Foundation. Not long after that, I was amazed to discover that Bhagavan Das was actually teaching in the Philadelphia area where I was living at the time.

Soon after, I was with Bhagavan Das at a local yoga studio. Then, as if in answer to my call, Bhagavan Das's spiritual autobiography, "*It's Here Now (Are You?)*" was published. I devoured it hungrily, and came to feel that Ram Dass' mythological spin on his young mentor hadn't stretched the truth all that much. I felt certain that Bhagavan Das was a genuine mystic yogi who had truly accessed some deep places through his yoga practice.

Bhagavan Das had explored psychedelics as well, though unlike Ram Dass, he had come to them after having attained yogic discipline-induced revelations with no substances involved. I can certainly relate to this path as I too, was a yogi who did traditional *sadhana* (spiritual practice) for years before exploring psychedelics.

Perhaps like Bhagavan Das, even after having had some chemical-free mystical experiences, I too was still curious to find out what effect psychedelics might have on my consciousness. I wanted to find out what the difference was, if there was a difference, between my previous yoga-induced highlights and those that could be produced by psychoactive substances. I also was curious to see if psychedelics could take me places that my own intense spiritual practice had not previously taken me.

Bhagavan Das' book reveals that psychedelics did open new vistas for the young twenty-something yogi in India. It's particularly interesting how Bhagavan Das plays down Ram Dass' deification of him in *Be Here Now*, saying essentially that as much as Ram Dass needed him as a guide, Bhagavan Das needed Ram Dass for a simpler reason: he knew Dass had the "yogi medicine" from America, LSD, and he wanted it!

The portrait Bhagavan Das paints of the Jewish-born Dr. Richard Alpert is something of a neurotic mess: a Woody Allen-esque figure seeking enlightenment. Bhagavan Das implies that he would not have led Alpert to Neem Karoli Baba had it not been for the LSD.

Bhagavan Das exaggerates to make a point: he was he more immature, confused and searching than Ram Dass let on. Even after having had numerous spiritual experiences via yoga alone, Bhagavan Das still wanted to see for himself what LSD was all about. Having left the States for India in 1963 after JFK's assassination, he never had a chance to partake of the acid craze that had rocked his generation not long after; he had missed that boat, and here was his chance to swim in its wake.

Bhagavan Das finally got a chance to experiment with LSD not long after meeting Ram Dass. In his autobiography, he vividly recalls his first experience:

"I stared into the sun, both eyes wide open, from ten that morning until the sun set in the early evening. I traveled with the sun all the way across the sky. I heard this extremely powerful 'Ommmmmmmmmmm!' coming out of the sun and I plunged deeper into the sound. I slipped through the sun into a huge black hole and realized suddenly and completely that God lives behind the sun. The sun is his door."[173]

From the way he recounts experiences like this, it's clear that Bhagavan Das's psychedelic revelations were quite meaningful and helpful to him. It's also clear from his memoir that he continued his exploration of psychedelics (particularly plant medicine) for quite a long time after, both while he was in India, and the years subsequent to his arrival back in the US.

Along the way, he relates some very interesting anecdotes from a rich life, among them how he was heavily involved in Native American plant medicine ceremonies under the guidance of Little Joe Gomez, and how he partied hard with the controversial Tibetan Buddhist and founder of the Naropa Institute, the "crazy wisdom" teacher, Chogyam Trungpa.

A decade later, in the Eighties, Bhagavan Das had a revelation of Jesus and disavowed himself of all drugs and things Eastern, getting heavily involved in the Evangelical Christian movement. Since the early Nineties, however, partly through the influence of the Hindu teacher Mata Amritanandamayi (Ammachi, the "Hugging Saint"), Bhagavan Das was very much back in the Eastern/Indian fold. Though he does not say in his memoir whether he still uses psychedelics, one suspects he does, even if only occasionally. One gets the sense that Bhagavan Das was an equal opportunity mystic seeker who would take a transformative mystical experience any place he could find it.

Bhagavan Das, from around the Time of *Be Here Now*

It wasn't until the late '90s that Bhagavan Das, with the help of a ghost writer, wrote his spiritual memoir. Mind you, this was quite a long time after many of the events he depicts. Still, because of who he is, and the fact that he managed to bridge Eastern and Western spiritual cultures as few others have, I take his cautionary words about drugs very seriously:

"I want to be honest about the part drugs played in my spiritual development, but I also want to make a serious point: drugs are a very dangerous path. You definitely have to have protection. The way you protect yourself is with the love you have for your guru—the guru watches out for you. If you don't have divine guidance and protection,

drugs can kill you.

"This is why the essence of spiritual life is truly the guru. It's not a popular position in the West anymore since we've had so many guru scandals, but it hasn't for one moment stopped being true. If you want to learn Ayurveda, you have to have a guru. If you want to learn to meditate, you need the guru.

"If you have a real guru, a Satguru, then you're protected. If you don't—if you try to go the direct route without a guide—then you don't ingest the drug, the drug ingests you. Drugs are Shakti. By definition, the guru is a person who, like Shiva can hold the Shakti. You can get addicted or overdose if you're not using drugs worshipfully. I had some very good experiences with drugs, but I don't recommend them to others because most people in the West want the poison—they don't want Shiva. And they don't have elders to show them how to use poison in a sacred matter... there are many safer ways to raise your consciousness than experimenting with drugs, and most gurus in India prefer more conservative routes. Doing your meditation, japa, and hatha-yoga is a slower path, but the effects are more lasting, and you run less risk of frying your nervous system. Without a doubt, self-discipline pays for itself in the end."[174]

Interesting that Bhagavan Das should basically quote the party line here, rather than saying something to the effect that, "I, Bhagavan Das, will now recognize that as I am now an elder (if not a guru), I can assist others in doing what I did, *both* traditional yogic sadhana and drugs?"

Obviously drugs worked wonders for Bhagavan Das, even though he already had come under the wing of a recognized spiritual master, Neem Karoli Baba, and had also been doing serious *sadhana* for years prior to his initial forays with LSD. And, he declares, in no uncertain terms, that his LSD experiences went beyond any previous mystical high in those years of his intense austerity in India. When Ram Dass and his group asked Bhagavan Das what his first LSD session was like, he notes in his memoir that,

"I admitted to them that it was the most incredible thing I'd ever experienced in my life. It was amazing to go that deep that fast. Within a few hours I'd reached a deep Samadhi (psychic absorption) and still had psychic energy going. I must have done one hundred thousand mantras or more on that trip... three days of constant repetition. It was very powerful."

I felt the exact same way after I took San Pedro cactus the first time, and even more so after using Ayahuasca. Those experiences led me to believe that only a very small percentage of people could ever access such experiences without the aid of a psychedelic medicine... *regardless of how much yoga they practice.*

It took me many years to realize all of this for myself, namely, that yogic spiritual practice might not be enough to reach and retain enlightenment. So currently I am following Bhagavan Das' lead and exploring just how yoga and psychedelics might complement and support each other in the spiritual quest.

• • •

Bhagavan Das's autobiography is fascinating, and everyone I've given it to seems to share that fascination. Although Bhagavan Das' downplays this idea somewhat, what his book recounts is a living spiritual mythology, something most Westerners have no real conception or understanding of, let alone experience. And if this memoir is true, or mostly true, and I feel that it is, then what Bhagavan Das says about psychedelics should carry weight for all of us.

But by his own admission, Bhagavan Das does not have all the answers, nor has he attained the stature of his guru, Neem Karoli Baba. Therefore, we must look elsewhere for a guide to the "ultimate Samadhi" with or without the help of a psychedelic sacrament.[175]

Postscript: I recently watched "Karmageddon," the somewhat damning documentary about Bhagavan Das, with my yoga students, most of them women. Then I went to Bhakti Fest in Joshua Tree, California and did not see Bhagavan Das there. Hmmm. To be continued…

Baba Hari Dass: The Silent Yogi

Perhaps it would be wise to pay attention to what one of Neem Karoli Baba's foremost Indian disciples has said about LSD, and by implication, other psychedelics.

Baba Hari Dass was with Neem Karoli Baba for a long time before Ram Dass and Bhagavan Dass came on the scene. For much of his life he lived the life of a simple monk, having taken a vow of silence in 1952 at the tender age of 29. The only way he communicated with others was by writing brief messages on a small chalkboard. When Ram Dass met him, Baba Hari Dass was giving silent spiritual chalkboard lessons to Neem Karoli Baba's Western devotees. Ram Dass was so impressed with these lessons, that Baba Hari Dass figured prominently in Ram Dass' *Be Here Now,* and thus another spiritual star was born![176]

However, newfound fame and international recognition did not go to Baba Hari Dass' head—he continued his vow of silence and has done so to this day. Even when Ram Dass brought him to the US to teach and give satsang in the early Seventies, he taught in the same silent manner. Baba Hari Dass's teachings from that period are available in a beautiful little book entitled, *Silence Speaks: From the Chalkboard of Baba Hari Dass.* It was from this book that I got a sense of this silent yogi's perspective on Western spiritual seekers' interest in psychedelics.

I wasn't surprised by what I found: Baba Hari Dass was not too positive about such drugs. To the young Westerners who plied him with questions, he wrote adamantly on his chalkboard:

"Hallucinatory drugs are not good for Yoga sadhana. To get out of illusion, one needs a pure mind free from all delusion. If one takes a drug and makes more delusions, then how can he get out of illusion?…

"I don't think LSD is good for sadhana. It accelerates the change of Elements inside the body a hundred times more than usual, which causes visions of different kinds of geometrical patterns and different kinds of colors, light, and so on. LSD can harm any nerve in the brain permanently…

"It's a general feeling among older people that all those who are in Yoga are drug people. It's a wrong idea. Drugs and Yoga can't go together. No one sits on the dirt while he is wearing clean pants."[177]

Baba Hari Dass

When a young seeker asked him, "Can we reach the same level of awareness alone, as with ganja and other drugs?" Baba Hari Dass replied:

"By Yoga you can attain much higher levels. Drugs merely excite the energy centers (chakras) and can give you a glimpse of what it looks like… When one takes LSD he sees the patterns [of the chakras, etc.], but can't fix upon one Element. Concentration

cannot be maintained and so one doesn't get the power of the patterns he sees."

Echoing his guru Neem Karoli Baba, Baba Hari Dass is clearly stating that while one may reach certain higher levels of awareness via psychedelics, they are not the highest levels and your visit cannot be sustained. He does acknowledge that they can provide a "glimpse" of what heightened states of awareness look like, but beyond that, LSD is not helpful and may even be harmful. His words carry added weight in that he seems to speak from personal experience with LSD.

Another question put to Baba Hari Dass was: Why do extensive yoga practices in order to raise one's Kundalini if one could do it quickly and directly via the use of psychedelics?

"If a person takes a drug he can be trapped—energy goes up and comes down hard. If one really tries to get energy excited, he can do it, but the method should be right. Only by Sadhana [yoga practice] can one move the energy up with permanent benefits."

Baba Hari Dass is of the traditionalist school, preaching what I always heard: Don't dabble in drugs, stick to Yoga—it's slower, but it's surer, safer, and the results are more enduring. Still, a young yogi in the crowd around this gentle silent figure wonders, "Can't drugs be helpful at all in gaining knowledge of the Self?"

Baba Hari Dass smiles as he writes his reply on his chalkboard:

Then all here would be enlightened!

And everyone shares a good laugh.

But he didn't really answer the question…

Lama Surya Das: What Would Buddha Do? Or, Just Say "Maybe"

These days Ram Dass likes to call him "LSD," by his initials, and he laughs merrily; but there were many years when Lama Surya Das would have inwardly bristled at the association.[178] Richard Miller was a young seeker in India in the early Seventies when he, too, came into the orbit of Neem Karoli Baba, who gave him his spiritual name "Surya Das," which means "Servant of the Sun." As with nearly all of the Western devotees of Neem Karoli Baba, Miller had experimented with psychedelics. Like Ram Dass and many others, psychedelics had partially inspired him to seek the wisdom of the East. What distinguishes Miller from the others is that he was drawn to the Tibetan Buddhist path, eventually becoming a Lama. These days he generally discourages the use of psychedelics publicly.

In his 1997 book, *Awakening the Buddha Within: Tibetan Wisdom for the Western World*, Lama Surya Das has some choice words to say about those heady days of the late Sixties and early Seventies:

"We were young; many threw caution to the winds and played with their heads. It was simply what was happening back then. In the intervening years, we've become more sophisticated and wise; we've seen too many examples of bright men and women who left too many brain cells behind in the name of mysticism. Now I personally don't use drugs, and I don't recommend drugs."[179]

Surya Das has an interesting point here: It is certainly true that we in the West have become much more "sophisticated and wise" with regard to psychedelics. At one time a significant number of Baby Boomers believed psychedelics might be a kind of cure-all for society's ills, a golden road to Enlightenment. But as young spiritual seekers like Dr. Richard Alpert, Richard Miller, and many others discovered, nothing is that simple. The Hindu and Buddhist teachers that they encountered, for the most part, had very little good to say about psychedelics. This was surely a surprise since so many of the top Western "gurus" of the time: Aldous Huxley, Ken Kesey, Carlos Castenada, Timothy Leary, Gary Snyder, and Alan Watts, had mostly only praise for them. Certainly Ram Dass' conversion from LSD-guru to yogi-disciple was a reflection of that shift in consciousness away from that extremist position.

As an example of how the Eastern teachers reacted to the "hallucinogens," Lama Surya Das recounts what happened when he tried to explain a transformational psychedelic experience he had experienced to one of his Tibetan teachers, Lama Yeshe:

"Back in the early 1970s, I remember trying to discuss drugs with Lama Yeshe. I described to him in colorful detail my cosmic mystical experiences during a one-week solitary trek through Nepal. I spent two days meditating at a Himalayan hot spring, under the influence of hallucinogenic mushrooms. I had hoped and even expected Lama to explain these things and even help me understand. Instead, he laughed loudly and exclaimed, "Western boy's dream!" He would say no more. He just kept laughing."[180]

Lama Yeshe was quite a character himself, having "dropped out" before receiving a full Geshe degree from Sera Monastery, even though he had studied for it for many years. He used to joke that he was a "Tibetan hippie." With this perspective of him in mind, it is very interesting that Lama Yeshe would not condone the use of psychedelics. Did he fully understand the impact the magic mushrooms obviously had on the young Surya Das? Why didn't Lama Yeshe say more or give a full explanation of his view to this sincere young man? Had he ever ingested a magic mushroom or other psychedelic himself? Lama Surya Das, however, took Lama Geshe's mocking laughter to heart:

"I intensely longed to become one with the infinite awareness of luminous presence I had experienced on that trek in the mountains. I wanted to be that, not just visit that through a drug-induced state. I knew that my vision quest deserved further

development. Lama Yeshe generously taught me how to be closer to these realities through the practice of Tibetan meditation and breathing exercises; he wanted to show me the difference between chimerical dreams and the realistically achievable, imma- nent reality of clear light within each of us."[181]

We seem to keep coming back at Neem Karoli Baba's admonition to Ram Dass: "*It would be better to become Christ than just to pranam to him, but your medi- cine won't do that for you. It's not the ultimate samadhi.*"

As Huston Smith has likewise cautioned, the truly religious and spiritual life aims not at "altered states," but "altered traits;" not at "religious experiences," but "religious lives."[182] Recall how Ram Dass took LSD hundreds of times in a futile attempt to never "come down" from the "high." The message is that the true quester after enlightenment will ultimately never be satisfied with a drug-induced state, however cosmic or revelatory. He or she will eventually realize the necessity of a radical transformation via the disciplined path of spiritual practice and compas- sionate living, moment to moment.

Reading Surya Das' book, I wondered whether he was guilty of throwing the proverbial "baby out with the bath water" by not fully acknowledging the catalyzing influence that psychedelics had on his *own* life's journey. Perhaps he would not have been open to seeking a higher state of spiritual awareness in life had he not had his initial mystical experiences brought on by psychedelics like LSD and mushrooms? Speaking more broadly, perhaps psychedelics were the perfect prescription for a generation emerging from the repressive and materialistic 1950s? Even today, per- haps some in the West could still benefit from a psychedelic experience to awaken them to the possibility of other realms beyond their gray, mundane existences?[183]

Lama Surya Das

It is noteworthy that at just the moment *Awakening the Buddha Within* was being published, psychedelic use saw a resurgence. The Buddhist journal *Tricycle*, responding to this cultural shift, featured a round-table discussion on psychedelics and Buddhism.[184]

Some of the most respected scholars in the Buddhist world submitted essays on psychedelics and Buddhism. Among this group were Jack Kornfield, Joan Halifax, Joan Hogetsu, Michelle McDonald-Smith, Rick Fields, and Rick Strassman. The conclusions reached by this diverse group, were, as one might suppose, mixed. Some came out pro, some con, and some, like yours truly, sat in the Lotus position on the fence.

At the time, Jack Kornfield had this to say on the subject of psychedelics:

" *Any tool or practice that can open the heart and show that we are not separate, that touches the realms of universal loving-kindness and universal compassion, can be valuable. For some people psychedelics can open the mind and reveal that consciousness creates the world, that physical reality is created out of consciousness and not the opposite. They can show that reality can be filled with light and humor. They can show that there are realms of tremendous transcendent understanding and realms of many different scales of time, eternally slow or eternally rapid. They can also open us to hell realms where there is extraordinary pain and seemingly no way out…*

Kornfield went on to make the following radical suggestion:

" *I see psychedelics as one of the most promising areas of modern consciousness research. I would not be surprised if at some point there comes to be a useful marriage between some of these sacred materials and a systematic training or practice that I have described. That marriage will have to be based on an understanding and respect for the ancient laws of karma, grounded in compassion, virtue, an open heart and a trained mind, and the laws of liberation. Given those, there might be some very fruitful combination.*"[185]

Kornfield's sentiments echo those of another *Tricycle* contributor, Rick Strassman, whose ideas we considered in our Soma chapter. Strassman went even farther than Kornfield, suggesting that:

"*…Dedicated Buddhist practitioners with little success in their meditation, but well along in more intellectual development, might benefit from a carefully timed, prepared, supervised, and followed-up psychedelic session to accelerate their practice. Psychedelics, if anything, provide a view. And a view, to one so inclined, can inspire the long hard work to make that view a living reality… This type of work also may help develop a more broad-minded and universal approach to the spiritual.*"[186]

Kornfield then tempered his view somewhat by adding the following note of caution:

"I see psychedelics as having been enormously useful as an initial opening for people, and at certain stages it may be possible to use them again wisely, but with the constraints of "shila"[i.e., the Buddha's teaching against intoxicating the mind.] But they can be easily abused if one is not careful about the set and setting..."[187]

Those remarks notwithstanding, Kornfield echoes the essence of Neem Karoli Baba's message to Ram Dass when he says:

"Whatever leads to opening the heart and mind and letting go is beneficial..."[188]

Is it impossible that a similar sentiment might have been shared by the highly experimental and explorative Gautama Buddha himself?

Perhaps it was this open dialogue with other Buddhist colleagues and friends that led Surya Das to temper his early view in *Awakening the Buddha Within* in an expanded essay he wrote for Allan Hunt Badiner's 2002 spin-off of the *Tricycle* article, *Zig Zag Zen: Buddhism and Psychedelics.*

In his essay for that book, "The Zen Commandments," Surya Das weighed in on the issue of psychedelics and spirituality while demonstrating more of the humor and lightheartedness for which he is known. After making clear that he has chosen the Buddha's Middle Way and does not want to be seen as a "cheerleader for drugs," he does lay out important points about psychedelics, and the pros and cons of their use for spiritual seekers. On the one hand:

◎ *Psychedelics were a big impetus for him and many of his generation to devote their lives to Dharma, or Spirituality.*

◎ *Psychedelics can, at least temporarily, remove the ego barriers and give one a glimpse of expanded awareness (Emptiness, Holiness, God, etc.).*

◎ *Psychedelics opened his "cosmic sense of absurdity" and showed Surya Das why and how not to take himself, or life, too seriously.*

◎ *The experience induced by psychedelics is real, not unreal.*

◎ *These substances have been used over the millennia by mystics, yogis, shamans, other spiritual seekers, and even recognized masters... Lama Surya Das' own last Dzogchen master, Nyoshul Khen Rinpoche, after hearing the reports of Western Buddhist practitioners regarding psychedelics, asked if he could get some, but he left his body before this happened.*

Then again, on the other hand:

◎ *Drugs can be dangerous, particularly to the immature and unstable; and psychedelics in particular can make us addicted to spiritual thrill-seeking which "creates a karmic conditioning that limits our infinite conscious potential."*

◎ *It can crack the ego-shell, but it can also, when it's all over, serve to reinforce the ego because the ego works even harder to "protect its domain."*

◎ *It can lead to psychosis, and even death, as was the case with some of Surya Das' friends.*

◎ *"Drugs are a means, not an end in themselves… Consciousness-altering drugs are not a religion." In other words, if you use them at all, use them to get a glimpse of what being free of the ego is like, but then walk the middle path and don't become a "chemical burnout" or "psychedelic relic."*

◎ *The drug culture and societal context are more complicated today than they were in the Sixties, with an "atmosphere of risk, guilt and paranoia that we did not suffer to such an extent" in the Sixties.*

◎ *"It's easier to get enlightened than to stay enlightened." It's easier to have a drug-induced theophany than to cultivate an authentic spiritual life. But one can, over time, develop the ability to have the same experiences without the aid of drugs. In this regard, Surya Das cleverly advises us to beware the "premature immaculation," thinking that you have become fully enlightened from a drug experience.*

Even though Lama Surya Das often claims "Just Say No," with all of the above precautions in mind, at the end of the day, he is clearly telling us that psychedelic exploration may be consonant with spiritual practice:

"It is a Buddhist precept to refrain from intoxicants that cause heedlessness. If we are heedless, we may cause harm to others and to ourselves. However, I think taking certain drugs in a conscious, mindful manner—as a spiritual experiment, in a safe container, with a guide or loved one—can be an important part of spiritual experience." [189]

But perhaps Lama Surya Das's most telling words are these:

"…Now when I am asked about the use of drugs for spiritual purposes, especially by young people in public, I usually just say no, or just say maybe. Meanwhile I'm thinking: read between the lines. Just notice my initials, Lama Surya Das. What can I say? I "just said no" for decades. Yet there remains within me an inner smile, like the Cheshire cat's shit-eating grin."

In other words, just say yes… maybe? …no?

And the Laughing Neem Karoli Buddha Baba smiled.

Krishna Das: Chant Master of the Heart

A common thread in the accounts we have provided thus far is how psychedelics were the "way in" for many of the Sixties spiritual seekers. (And as we shall see in a later chapter, how they continue to be for young people today). Krishna Das was born Jeffrey Kagel in 1947 and has been dubbed the "Chant Master of America." His music has touched the lives of millions, but might not have were it not for his early experimentation with psychedelics. His journey offers us yet another potent reminder of just how influential psychedelic substances were for his generation.

In his recent memoir, *Chants of a Lifetime*, Krishna Das reveals that his first truly eye-opening spiritual experience happened under the influence of peyote:

"I don't know if I was in fact crazy, but I'd always been searching for a way out of my life as it had been going so far. I had my first powerful experience of a way out in the summer before my senior year in high school, when a friend and I took peyote together. As the drug began to take effect, I looked around and thought, Oh My God. Now I understand. This is the way it is. *Everything became perfectly clear; and I saw that my closed-up, hard, cranky, neurotic, depressed state was totally unnecessary, totally wrong. I was filled with bliss. Of course, I was also driving around with 'one hand waving free' and my head in the sky and almost drove into the pond by the library! Although the lights went out again at the end of the trip, I'd seen something that I could never forget. The problem then became:* How can I get back there?" [190]

Here is an essential point regarding spiritual experiences, whether they be plant-induced or internally-generated: once a higher state of consciousness has been reached, call it enlightenment, there is almost always the overwhelming desire to return to that state of blissful, loving awareness, to return "Home."

Many spiritual seekers become seekers in the first place because they don't feel at home in the universe. They KNOW there's more to life than what they're experiencing. Then they are graced with some kind of experience that confirms this: yes, there is more to life!

Once the experience is over, however, a new kind of seeking begins—how to "get back there," as Krishna Das puts it.

In Jeffrey Kagel's case, getting back there came partly through 10 tabs of acid that he scored at the beginning of his sophomore year of college:

"Who 'I' was began to change. When I took that first tab of acid, I was in college and going to classes. I had a job and played on the basketball team. By the time I took the tenth tab, I was living alone in the mountains of Pennsylvania, taking care of a broken-down farm with two dogs, a cat, two goats, and a horse, with no human beings in sight." [191]

It seems that LSD had the effect of leading the young seeker to choose the solitary life of the yogi, a more nature-based, hermetic existence. He had read a lot about yoga and yogis in books—books such the highly mystical and influential *Autobiography of a Yogi*—but it wasn't real for Jeffrey Kagel until he actually met a real yogi in the flesh: Ram Dass.

Krishna Das with Ram Dass in Maui, 2010

"...I walked up the stairs and into the room where Ram Dass was sitting on a mattress on the floor. He was dressed in a long white robe and was wearing lots of beads. The moment I walked into the room, something happened inside of me. Immediately, instantly, without a word being spoken, I knew that whatever it was I was looking for—and I didn't know what it was—was absolutely real. In every molecule of my being, I knew that it existed in the world and that it could be found. I didn't know if I could find it, but this moment changed my life."[192]

Of course, the young seeker was only to find what he was looking for, just as Ram Dass had, in Neem Karoli Baba. Not long after meeting Ram Dass, Kagel went to India and received from Neem Karoli Baba the name for which he is now internationally recognized, Krishna Das. At that time, Neem Karoli Baba also asked his young devotee to promise him to give up smoking hash, saying:

"If you can't do a little thing like this, how will you ever find God?"

Krishna Das did give up smoking, but after Neem Karoli Baba passed, he went through a deep depression and became addicted to crack cocaine. Meanwhile the band that a young Jeffery Kagel had fronted in the early 1970s called "Soft White Underbelly" went on to international stardom as "Blue Öyster Cult." Perhaps you've heard of them?[193]

"Burn out the day / Burn out the night / I can't see a reason to put up a fight / I'm living for giving the devil his due / And I'm burning, I'm burning, I'm burning for you."

Yes, it appears Blue Öyster Cult's rock classic *Burnin' for You* could have been the soundtrack to those years. Or they could also be the message of Maharajji, or Christ… or even Krishna Das.

Jai Uttal: Moving Through Stage Fright

I began listening to Jai Uttal's music in the late Nineties, just as kirtan or *sacred chant* music from India, was reaching a greater world-wide cultural recognition. The first CD I had of Jai's was his 4th offering, Shiva Station; and while I thoroughly enjoyed it, I also was a bit uneasy about his combining kirtan and world music. My sense at that time was that Jai's music wasn't sufficiently traditional or devotional. But I got over that and have since found a deep appreciation for his music, playing it regularly in my yoga classes. As it turns out, Jai was just way ahead of the kirtan musical curve. My ears and sensibility just weren't ready for it yet.

Unlike most of the other devotees in this chapter, Jai hasn't yet published a spiritual memoir beyond blog posts so I sought him out for an interview. Surprisingly, he readily agreed to it, even though he'd only met me once and quite briefly. Here's how it happened:

The first time I had the opportunity to hear Jai perform live was when I went to his "Return to Shiva Station" kirtan music event on Maui in April of 2014. His recently released CD of the same name was a re-envisioning of his unconventional kirtan music of the Nineties, so things had come full circle. I didn't know what to expect, but Jai seemingly easily took each song from stately majestic to lively ecstatic and then back again in just fifteen minutes. Much of the crowd of some 2-300 people were on their feet singing and dancing, swept up in the bhakti. Ram Dass, who has lived on Maui for a decade, was in the audience that night, and at one point Jai touchingly thanked him for bringing Neem Karoli Baba's message to so many people.

By the end, I was inspired. As a musician and kirtan wallah myself, I was deeply appreciative of what Jai pulled off, seemingly effortlessly to my eyes. So after the concert I approached the stage, shook Jai's hand, and then mentioned this book and asked him for an interview. I was a surprised when he gave me his email on the spot, and not long after we were conversing by phone.

Which brings me to the focus of this particular segment. I am not concerned here specifically with what Jai and I discussed, or even yoga and psychedelics *per se*, so much as I am the basic human psychological underpinnings of life, music, and the spiritual quest. Something that both yoga and psychedelics have personally helped me with.

From checking out some of Jai's interviews prior to ours, what struck me the most was how this Grammy-nominated kirtan artist has deeply struggled with shyness and being his own worst critic. You wouldn't know this about Jai from his music or his performance unless he intimated it to you. For what I witnessed on stage that night on Maui was a consummate artist and a master of his craft. Even when Jai fumbled a guitar chord at the outset of a song he had just introduced to us, without missing a beat he quipped: "If I ever learn to play it [the song]." It was classic.

There's a lot of ego in the world of music, perhaps more so than in other fields and of expression. But ego cuts both ways. On one side of the coin, heads, ego takes the form of self-aggrandizement and competition. Perhaps most clearly expressed in the realm of hip hop where freestyle putdowns are *de rigeuer*. On the flip side of the coin, tails, is the feeling that "I'm not worthy," or "How could I ever compete with *that*? These two sides reflect, to use Freud's coinage, *superiority* and *inferiority complexes* that we all tend to shift back and forth between, though generally tending more towards one than the other. I have, like Jai, tended toward feelings of inferiority, resulting in a paralyzing shyness in my younger days that essentially kept me locked in a closet of my own making for years.

The first and only gig I ever played with a band in college, I was in a trio composed of just me and a very talented bass player and drummer in a tiny night club off-campus. We were slotted for just a 15 minute set, which was fine by us as that's all we had prepared. We had vigorously rehearsed an instrumental version of Led Zeppelin's "The Song Remains the Same" and it rocked, so we kicked off with that.

Well, the drummer and the bassist kicked off… me? I was… I was sure *trying* to join in… But I was so nervous that I couldn't actually move my fingers! Not surprisingly, after several tortuous minutes, club personnel asked us to get off the stage.

Afterwards, guys I sort of knew from the music circles around campus were congratulating the bassist and the drummer on their incredible playing,, conspicuously avoiding me. Very embarrassed, I just kind of slunk out of there with my head down. The experience that night had a debilitating effect on my self-esteem. It was years before I was to play onstage with a band again.

When I eventually got into yoga some 5 years later, one of the first and most essential things that yoga addressed for me was that intense nervousness. It manifested itself in certain yoga poses like the Navasana, Boat Pose during which my entire body would shake uncontrollably. But I persevered in my practice, and after four years of disciplined work, I began finally teaching yoga. Because I had practiced the asanas so much, I thought it would be an easy transition from student to teacher. But it turned out to be another embarrassing situation when I once again couldn't keep my hands from visibly shaking. It was a deep personal disappointment and I wondered if I would ever get any relief from this affliction. But there was an upside: my intense focus on asana and the eight limbs of yoga resulted from my intense desire to get control over that shakiness. Twenty years later, most of that nervous energy and painful shyness is gone, though very occasionally it does still rear its head.

I'm about the same age now, forty-four, as Jai was when he embraced becoming a kirtan artist and singer. This late start came nearly two decades after Neem Karoli Baba left his body. Jai told me that from his early teens in New York he had gotten heavily into yoga and meditation, reading all the spiritual literature available at the time. While in New York he also smoked pot and took LSD, but virtually stopped completely after moving to the West Coast. There he took up residence in a little ashram in Berkeley where he studied music with Ali Akhbar Khan. He was just 19 years old.

One day Ram Dass showed up in Berkeley and Jai heard him speak. Very impressed and inspired to travel to India, Jai went, though he was going to see a different guru, not Neem Karoli Baba. As destiny would have it, that guru was not available and a week later Jai found himself at Neem Karoli Baba's ashram. He settled in and stayed for the better part four months.

From the start, Jai felt attracted to Neem Karoli Baba"s magnetic and charismatic being, receiving many profound teachings in his dreams. Jai told me there was always a sound track of kirtan playing around Maharajji. Most of this music was led by traditional Indian singers, but a fair amount was also done by young Western devotees like Jai and Krishna Das.

This was no ordinary kirtan however, it went deeper than mere singing and chanting of mantras and bhajans (spiritual songs). Jai shared with me that by the end of those four months, Maharajji had transformed his music into the deepest, most heartfelt spiritual "desperate longing" that he could imagine. Jai's life was completely transformed, and he had the "incredible realization that Maharajji had been his protector and savior for lifetimes and he was finally back in his grace." Though there were times over the years when Jai felt disconnected from his guru, that initial realization and his commitment to his guru never wavered. Jai even mused that perhaps his occasional feelings of disconnection were simply his guru being playful, a form of leela or divine play.

Let's pause for a moment and note this familiar dynamic for the spiritual seeker: Even with the intensity of an initial encounter with the mystical, whether it be via a psychedelic, a meditation practice, or a teacher or guru's insights, the nearly universal experience is that the magic wears off and we find ourselves seemingly back where we started, but now with a remembrance that *it exists and is possible to reach.*

For Jai, his struggle began when he returned to the States after that magical period in India. The adjustment was truly difficult and he had a hard sense of displacement. He hadn't done drugs in India, but he now found himself using pot again to transport himself beyond this world for temporary relief. Sometimes he and his friends would smoke marijuana and go out onto the streets of Berkeley to sing kirtan. But after a while, using marijuana felt less and less comfortable, and gradually Jai began using harder drugs to "chill out, calm down, and soothe anxieties."

Jai told me he really dug himself into a hole with all of that, living that way for years. But even during this dark time, Jai maintained a constant and complete knowing that Maharajji was his protector. He told me explicitly that the "guru saves us from the final fall."

Eventually, with Maharajji's help, he pulled himself out of the darkness. Jai credits and thanks Neem Karoli Baba for keeping him from dying by his own hand. He also credits his guru's grace for his current global success as a kirtan artist.

Like many of his era, psychedelics opened Jai up to other realms of spiritual possibility. He told me psychedelics had a lot of value for him because they transported him from normal consciousness into a paranormal one. This was especially useful to him in his younger years when he was struggling to find his way in life.

Ultimately, Jai's current spiritual practice is to surrender to God and whatever experience God has for him, whether comfortable or not. So any use of substances to change his consciousness feels like a distraction from his basic intention to surrender and deal with what is presented to him, rather than try to escape it.

Jai also stated that spirituality is not all simply about reaching altered states. The "essence [of spirituality] is not in those states," says Jai, but rather in what we do: "compassion, service to others, humility." This reminds me of one of Maharajji's most famous sayings: "Love all, Serve all, Feed all," which sometimes is shortened to just "Feed People."

Jai also mentioned Maharajji's telling Ram Dass that LSD was used by yogis in ancient times and that it allows one to "enter into the room with Christ," but not to *become* Christ. When I brought up the famous story of Maharajji's taking the LSD and it having no effect, Jai noted that "The level of altered consciousness that LSD or any substance brings you to is like a mosquito compared to the giant consciousness Maharajji has… We're not like that!"

These days the only substance that Jai uses is a good strong cup of coffee to start his day, he told me with a laugh. Even though his wife is Brazilian and he has been offered, even begged, to join in Ayahuasca ceremonies many times, he has always declined the invitations, never having felt any attraction to do it. He agreed with me when I suggested that Ayahuasca may be the LSD of Generation-X. He also told me he knows many people, including close friends, who have had extremely positive experiences with Ayahuasca. And so he recognizes that there are many different paths up the mountain, but he has still always politely declined.

For myself, getting back to the issue of letting go of "fear," an umbrella terms that includes states of anxiety, nervousness, angst, worry, paranoia, dread, profound sadness, etc… Ayahuasca was the perfect prescription to wipe away a lot of those layers of fear. Ayahuasca gave me tools to cope with my fears that yoga alone had not revealed to me. Before experiencing Ayahuasca, I was extremely nervous and self-conscious around people. This was especially true when it came to performing music or speaking in front of an audience. This is no longer the case.

Ayahuasca didn't just bring me to a new heightened state of awareness, a state I had never reached by my own efforts, it also inspired me to make subtle adjustments in my attitude and actions. In short, it helped me clean up my act and be a better, more humble and kind human being. And as I relate in the final chapter of this book, it brought me to a spiritual teaching that has further helped me in integrating and passing on the teachings I received from the "medicine."

Steve Jobs: "Steva DOS"

> *"Taking LSD was a profound experience, one of the most important things in my life. LSD shows you that there's another side to the coin, and you can't remember it when it wears off, but you know it. It reinforced my sense of what was important—creating great things instead of making money, putting things back into the stream of history and of human consciousness as much as I could."*

> —Steve Jobs

"Dear Mr. Steve Jobs,

Hello from Albert Hofmannn. I understand from media accounts that you feel LSD helped you creatively in your development of Apple Computers and your personal spiritual quest. I'm interested in learning more about how LSD was useful to you…

I hope you will help in the transformation of my problem child [LSD] into a wonder child.

Sincerely,
Albert Hofmann"

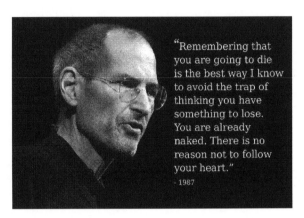

"Remembering that you are going to die is the best way I know to avoid the trap of thinking you have something to lose. You are already naked. There is no reason not to follow your heart."
- 1987

Some might protest, including Steve Jobs, in this esteemed spiritual company, but my point is to show how incredibly pervasive an influence both LSD and Neem Karoli Baba have had on our culture. Would Jobs' Apple have been the innovative, cutting-edge, break-all-the-rules, out-of-the-box company it was had it not been for the tech guru's use of LSD and his encounter with Ram Das' *Be Here Now* in the early '70s?

And what if Jobs had been successful in meeting Neem Karoli in India in '73 instead of just barely missing him due to the master's passing?

To my knowledge, no essay has ever been researched and written on the extent to which Jobs' use of psychedelics inspired or influenced his creative ideas, but it's definitely a subject that would seem to deserve treatment… As I type away on my MacBook Pro whilst millions of other spiritual seekers research and are inspired by nearly instant information from their iPhones, laptops, or other Apple products.

It is in this sense that *all of us alive now,* whether we know it or not, are Neem Karoli Baba's spiritual children. Can we separate what birthed within the Sixties counter-culture—racial equal rights, woman's liberation, gay liberation, environmental awareness, etc.—from what has developed and come to pass in the greater culture since? From computing to art to music, everywhere we look in our current culture we see the influence of psychedelics. This is because the counter-culture *became* the culture and brought along with it the lessons of Neem Karoli Baba. Granted, a true mystic or yogi might say that one can simply bypass this information-intoxicated age, knowing that everything that truly needs to be known can only be truly known on that inner-most motherboard. Yet this is a book for the rest of us...

Shyamdas (1953-2013): *"Stay in the Bhav"*

> *"All forms of Yoga lead us to bhava—the enlightened, inspired state of pure being. Bhava creates in us a direct experience of the unity of all things. This journey of kirtan (sacred chant) introduces the subtle relationship between non-dual vision and loving devotion as the foundation for the yoga experience."*
>
> —Shyamdas

Unlike most of the Neem Karoli Baba "children" above, I had not even heard about Shyamdas until around 2008 when I first saw the yoga documentary "Enlighten Up!." In the film, Shyamdas plays himself as a spiritual guide and supporting actor to young Nick Rosen as Nick journeys through North India. Once Shyamdas got on my radar, he of course began showing up all over the place...

When I was in Nosara, Costa Rica, a Canadian yoga teacher there told me that Shyamdas had recently visited and she gave me some of his kirtan music. Then a local yoga studio in Florida invited Shyamdas to be their guide for an India trip. When my twin brother and I celebrated our 40*th* birthday in Joshua Tree, I learned about the widely popular Bhakti Fest, which Shyamdas was instrumental in bringing to life. But for all of this, it somehow still didn't click in my mind that Shyamdas had also been a devotee of Neem Karoli Baba. Perhaps because Shyamdas seemed to be a Krishna devotee who hung out a lot in Vrindavan, and he never mentioned his connection to Neem Karoli Baba in "Enlighten Up!".

I messaged Shyamdas not too long before his passing about setting up an interview for this book and he was very open to it, but I simply waited too long to follow up.

Like a number of young spiritual seekers in the late Sixties and early Seventies, Shyamdas was inspired by Ram Dass to go to India to meet Neem Karoli Baba. But unlike many seekers of that era, he *stayed* in India, learned the languages and even translated scriptures. Shymadas got heavily into both Bhakti Yoga and Advaita Vedanta, taking initiation into the Vallabh Sampradaya lineage whose ultimate view of reality is that *"the world is true and is the ultimate manifestation of the Supreme Godhead, Krishna. Everything is Krishna and nothing but Krishna."*[194] This differs from the Advaita Vedanta of Shankacharya, which holds that the world is a manifestation of *maya*, the cosmic illusion.

So Shyamdas was both a pure bhakta or devotee, and also a learned scholar or *pandit*, from which we get the word "pundit." My sense is that one isn't drawn to spiritual things without some previous deep experience, perhaps both in this lifetime and in previous incarnations. In the difference between the Vallabh Vedanta and Shankarcharya just mentioned, before I used psychedelics I wondered, *"Wow, how did these guys ever even figure this out?"* The metaphysics, that is. Myself, I had an intellectual and faith-based belief in the fundamental unity of things, but this wasn't grounded in experience. But after psychedelics, my perception of an enlightened state became real and tangible. Although I could not sustain such a state, I now knew it existed and this kept me in pursuit of this ego-less state.

Prior to meeting Ram Dass and going to India to find Neem Karoli Baba, Shyamdas experimented with LSD. That was the way in those days, whereas for my generation it's been generally the other way around, India then psychedelics. And that's a good thing for us, because we got the grounding in yoga first, giving us the tools to anchor our psychedelic experiences in a way that is not overwhelming or harmful to ourselves or others. And with elders like Shyamdas reminding us to "stay in the *bhav*," in the feeling, the "one love" heart-space, we are more likely to find a merging of yoga and psychedelics that works for us.

Like those listed above, Shyamdas is definitely one of Neem Karoli Baba's "children."

Shyamdas in the "Bhav"

Reviewing this diverse group, one can't but feel more and more respect and appreciation for the influence that Ram Dass and Neem Karoli Baba have had on the world of yoga. Both teachers have brought much needed *bhakti* to the sweaty, huddled yoga masses yearning to breathe free.

11

On Psychedelics: The Gurus Weigh In

"In all sacred traditions, God, the Absolute Reality, is One. And to be steadfast in living a righteous life is one. To faithfully live by these truths is the highest self-discipline. But there is nothing higher than the Guru—no reality, no teaching, higher than the Guru."

—The Guru Gita

Is the Guru Dead?

For the last couple of decades the West has seen a "Stripping of the Gurus" trend, with numerous scandals and exposés putting into question the legitimacy of the spiritual guide. This downtrend, interestingly enough, has been concurrent to the mainstream fascination with Yoga. I would suggest there is a connection between these two developments, and that Yoga has had to shed its "cultish" image somewhat in order to reach the mass audience it has.

Instrumental to this downtrend was the rise of cult-watch sites on the internet. Sites such as Rick Ross', where cyberspace denunciations of the behavior of Sai Baba and other gurus went viral. That and the fact that a number of gurus who rose to fame in the 60s and 70s (Muktananda, Osho, Swami Rama, Krishnamacharya, etc.) took their *mahasamadhi* or died in the 1980s and the 1990s. Once they were gone, postmortem "recriminations and revelations" from unhappy former devotees popped up in the mass media and online not long after.

Now, by no means have gurus fallen completely out of favor. Some, like Amrit Desai, who was forced to leave the Kripalu Institute in the mid-90s due to a sex scandal, have even come back into favor. And today there is a new kind of guru, teachers such as Eckhart Tolle, Deepak Chopra, Gangaji and Adyashanti, who have taken the role in a less of a top-down model that the mainstream spiritual seeker finds more acceptable.

We have also seen a trend of more female gurus taking the lead. Figures such as Mata Amritanandamayi, affectionately known as "Ammachi," and "The Hugging Saint," Sri Karunamayi, Sri Anandi Ma, Shree Maa, Sai Ma and Gurumayi. I should mention once again, that most of my own gurus have been women. Due to the controversy surrounding the male gurus, seeking female teachers was a conscious choice on my part, although by now the women gurus have seen just as much scandal as the men.[195]

Theoretical issues aside, it is important we establish exactly what a guru is, and why the figure of the guru has been so central to the Yoga tradition. Connected to this is the age-old issue of whether a spiritual seeker needs a guru to reach enlightenment, or can one "go it alone."

Who, or What, is a Guru?

The Sanskrit word "*guru*" literally means "weighty," or "one who has or carries weight." In English, the noun "heavy" sometimes refers to a person who has a certain degree of knowledge and experience, earned either through lineage (*sampradaya*), and/or spiritual practice (*sadhana),* and sometimes by birth. Thus the guru's thoughts and opinions are "weighty"and reliable—they hold water. So in this sense, a guru is a "heavy" or a "heavyweight," and their presence commands respect. They possess *gravitas*.

There is a more familiar "folk" etymology of guru, however, and that is that "ru" means "darkness," and "gu" means "the one who dispels," and thus a "guru" is one who illuminates the darkness. The guru sheds light on the illusions and delusions of the spiritual seeker groping in the dark, ignorant of their true nature. To this end, the guru traditionally uses any means necessary to help dissolve the barriers of his or her disciple's ego. In this sense, some of the "gurus" presented below are not strictly gurus in that they don't take on disciples and actively guide them on the spiritual path. They are more like wise counselors who have important insights to share with us.[196]

One final, more contemporary understanding of guru, comes from speaking each letter of the word "guru" out loud:

"GEE, YOU ARE YOU!" TM[197]

Even though this sounds like an advertising slogan, it does carry a deeper message: The guru is within in you, and any external guide can only give you guidelines to help you find that inner teacher. Ultimately you have to sing your own song, dance your own dance, and beat your own drum, however offbeat it may be. The lesson of all gurus is to not try and be someone or something that we are not. Judy Garland put it well: "Better to be a first rate version of yourself than a second rate of someone else." For some people, being oneself might entail using psychedelics, or living as a celibate yogi, or to go wherever your path leads you. But your unique path is uniquely yours and won't work for others.

Many Lives, Many Gurus

One of my beloved gurus once sat me down and shared with me the following thoughts on the true significance of the guru, which I paraphrase here:

There is really only one Guru, and that is God, or the One who takes form as the Many. That Great Guru, the True Self, is not embodied, except in the sense that we all embody It—It is both within all of us and *without* us simultaneously. All other Gurus are really only "*upa*" *gurus*, or subsidiary gurus. They can help you dispel some of your spiritual ignorance and perhaps point you in the right direction—to the moon, to the sun, to the elixir vitae/Soma—but they won't, they can't, make you drink.

You may have a "*moola Guru*," a root, or *primary* guru or *Satguru* who guides you throughout your entire lifetime. But most Gurus will only be temporary supports until you can stand on your own two feet. Until you, recognize that "Gee, You Are You"—the guru is within you.

A related teaching also found in the Yoga tradition is that *everything* is our Guru—every tree, flower, insect, person, and moment in time. There is music in all things, the poet said, if we only had ears to hear it. We can connect all the dots to complete the Big Picture if we but had the eyes to see it. We could learn the language of all things and see the guiding hand of spirit everywhere in our lives. This sounds whimsical, perhaps, but for a few it may be a reality.[198]

Can a Plant Be a Guru?

Over the course of my exploration of psychedelics, the question has arisen time and again: Is there any way these substances might be considered "gurus"? Could psychedelics serve as a substitute or subsidiary for a living teacher? Might they be more effective than any human guru, however divine or enlightened, as some have recently argued ?

To answer this question, it seems reasonable to take a hard look at both sides of the equation; namely, both into the lives and teachings of human gurus, and also into the immense potential of the "plant teachers."

This section will attempt to explore both gurus and plant medicine with the caveat that if one truly seeks greater understanding in this area, it's important to go directly to the Source; i.e. a living guru, or a plant teacher. Please also keep in mind that, I can only give so much contextual background, having sacrificed depth for breadth. If you are interested in probing more deeply, there are books and online resources provided in the endnotes.

Osho

> *"…So do not mistake [an LSD experience of Samadhi] for samadhi and do not cling to such experiences, otherwise they will be obstructions in meditation. You have felt so much in LSD dreams that, when you go in real meditation it is faint. It is not so vital that the feeling is not of such a great upsurge. Compared to your dream experiences meditation will look faint. This will create a depressive mood. You will feel something is being lost. You have known something and this something is not coming through meditation. Then the mind will say, "LSD is better." And if you go on taking LSD your mind will become less and less meditative. And meditation and its experiences will go on becoming fainter and fainter. So don't take LSD again."*
>
> —Acharya Rajneesh (Osho), 1970[199]

An entire study of Osho's views on psychedelics over the course of his teaching ministry would be in order, but I am simply presenting just one quote from an earlier satsang when he was still using the name "Rajneesh." Here Osho echoes what just about every guru, swami, or acharya of that era was saying: "Don't do drugs. Meditate." If Osho were alive today, perhaps his thoughts on the use of psychedelics might have been different. I leave that for a future study.

Swami Satchidananda

> *"The problem with drugs is that while they elevate you, they immediately drop you back down again… Yoga gives you a natural high."*

> *"You want organic food, right? Why not organic Samadhi?"*

Yoga's "natural high" is still chemically based, though the chemicals are endogenous, meaning they are produced internally. And for most of us, yoga's natural high is also not a permanent state. After several hours, or a day, or a week, the effects wear off, leaving the devotee needing to repeat the process. But whether one works with plant medicine, or with meditation alone, slowly but surely through repeated application, the spiritual seeker becomes stabilized in what might be called a permanent high: A state of awareness better described as a state of *equanimous balance*. The seeker is no longer riding the roller coaster of emotions and settles firmly in a fixed state of *loving presence*. So rather than label either meditation or plant medicine as innately "better" than the other, we see that both methods have the potential to bring one into a state of yoga, or union with universe: Enlightenment.

Swami Satchidananda's analogy about organic food and organic Samadhi could also work the other way: Just as most of us are not ready to go "breatharian" and live on oxygen alone, psychedelics may help the spiritual seeker prepare the way for his or her enlightenment by providing them with the tools to operate once they arrive in this heightened state.

Swami Kaivalyananda

> *"Drugs have been used in ancient times also. It is not a modern phenomenon. They have got some value, but the value is psychic value. They can give some psychic powers and some psychic insights, so they do have some meaning. But we cannot use drugs for the revealing of spiritual truths. Here the method is discipline… Drugs will help those people who believe that the sensory organs are the only instruments of experience and knowledge. At least we will know there are psychic perceptions also, not only the material world and sense world… LSD could be useful to Americans who are attached to the worship of material attractions. These people could begin to see life with a different view. So drugs can open doors for those with very limited and narrow perceptions."[200]*

Again, one reason I have been using the term "psychedelic" as opposed to "entheogen" here is precisely because some spiritual teachers deny that the substances in question actually provide access to the world of Spirit. This is an interesting question, but beyond the scope of this book, yet one I hope to return to in future offerings. My own personal sense is that, indeed, I have seen the manifestations of the mind in all its glory, but Spirit or spirits?

Alan Watts

"The idea of mystical experiences resulting from drug use is not readily accepted in Western societies. Western culture has, historically, a particular fascination with the value and virtue of man as an individual, self-determining, responsible ego, controlling himself and his world by the power of his conscious effort and will. Nothing, then, could be more repugnant to this cultural tradition than the notion of spiritual or

psychological growth through the use of drugs...

"[W]hen I was first invited to test the mystical qualities of LSD-25 by Keith Ditman of the Neuropsychiatric Clinic at UCLA Medical School, I was unwilling to believe that any mere chemical could induce a genuine mystical experience. I thought it might at most bring about a state of spiritual insight analogous to swimming with water wings. Indeed, my first experiment with LSD-25 was not mystical. It was an intensely interesting aesthetic and intellectual experience which challenged my powers of analysis and careful description to the utmost.

"Some months later, in 1959, I tried LSD-25 again with Drs. Sterling Bunnell and Michael Agron... In the course of two experiments I was amazed and somewhat embarrassed to find myself going through states of consciousness which corresponded precisely with every description of major mystical experiences I had ever read. Furthermore, they exceeded both in depth and in a peculiar quality of unexpectedness the three 'natural and spontaneous' experiences of this kind which I had had in previous years.

"Through subsequent experimentation with LSD-25 and the other chemicals named above (with the exception of DMT, which I find amusing but relatively uninteresting), I found I could move with ease into the state of 'cosmic consciousness,' and in due course became less and less dependent on the chemicals themselves for 'tuning in' to this particular wavelength of experience. Of the five psychedelics tried [LSD-25, mescaline, psilocybin, DMT, and cannabis], I found that LSD-25 and cannabis suited my purposes best. Of these two, the latter, which I had to use abroad in countries where it is not outlawed, proved to be the better. It does not induce bizarre alterations of sensory perception, and medical studies indicate that it may not, save in great excess, have the dangerous side effects of LSD, such as psychotic episodes...

"There are two specific objections to use of psychedelic drugs. First, use of these drugs may be dangerous. However, every worthwhile exploration is dangerous: climbing mountains, testing aircraft, rocketing into outer space, skin diving, or collecting botanical species in jungles. But if you value knowledge and the actual delight of exploration more than mere duration of uneventful life, you are willing to take the risks. It is not really healthy for monks to practice fasting, and it was hardly hygienic for Jesus to get himself crucified, but these are risks taken in the course of spiritual adventures. Today the adventurous young are taking risks in exploring the psyche, testing their mettle at the task just as, in times past, they have tested it—more violently—in hunting, dueling, hot-rod racing, and playing football. What they need is not prohibitions and policemen, but the most intelligent encouragement and advice that can be found.

"Second, drug use may be criticized as an escape from reality. However, this criticism

assumes unjustly that the mystical experiences themselves are escapist or unreal. LSD, in particular, is by no means a soft and cushy escape from reality. It can easily be an experience in which you have to test your soul against all the devils in hell."[201]

Watts, like Huxley, was one of the great *agent provocateurs* of the Baby Boomer generation. His work had a profound influence on the burgeoning hippie counter-cultural movements, catalyzing the quest to explore both psychedelics *and* Eastern Mysticism. How many young people were inspired to make a pilgrimage to the East after reading Watts' work is beyond estimate. His writings and lectures were, and still are, portals into the worlds of which we speak.

Most interesting here is Watt's amazement and embarrassment to find that LSD could provide *even deeper* mystical experiences than those that had come to him spontaneously. Coming from a person as brilliant as Watts, we would be wise to take pause at his responses to the objections to the use of psychedelics. Yes, they are dangerous and risky, yet every worthwhile endeavor is, he explains. And yes, they do seem to provide a quick and convenient escape, a task that takes years of discipline for the ascetic yogi to achieve; but with psychedelics there's a sense that one is jumping off a cliff into the complete unknown, while with yogic discipline it is more like following a trail up a mountain. Which path is the greater challenge, and which more worthy of the final goal? And does it matter?

Meher Baba

"The state of ecstasy brought about by music or some extraneous influence like drugs does not mean spirituality. It is a state in which the mind overpowers itself, and is a weakness to be guarded against. Instead of running wild, the mind should be self-composed. This comes through control.

"Tell those that are (taking drugs) that if drugs could make one realize God, then God is not worthy of being God. No drugs.

"Many people in India smoke hashish and ganja. They see colors and forms and lights, and it makes them elated. But this elation is only temporary. It is a false experience. It gives only experience of illusion, and serves to take one farther away from reality...

"Tell those who indulge in these drugs (LSD, etc.) that it is harmful physically, mentally and spiritually, and that they should stop taking these drugs. Your duty is to tell them, regardless of whether they accept what you say—or if they ridicule you or humiliate you, to boldly and bravely face these things. Leave the results to me. I will help you in my work...

"You are to bring my message to those ensnared in the drug-net of illusion, that

they should abstain, that the drugs will bring more harm than good, I send my love to them.

"Now in India, since ages, there are those who have been used to drugs—they are drug addicts. They are the ones who take ganja, then they take charas, and bhang— and they feel uplifted when they take these drugs. And they see colors and signs, and they feel, through their hallucinations, that they have reached the goal.

"And that false experience is also not continuous. There is a break in their experience. And that is the reason why it is not real. Those who take ganja and drugs, they get uplifted through the drugs, and then, in the end, they go crazy-mad…

"Now we come to those persons who have experiences through drugs. They feel that they have realized God because they get certain experiences. But… the guideline is that their experience is not continuous. Even though that is hallucination, even that is not continuous. And that is the sign that it is not true experience… Such experiences are harmful physically, mentally and spiritually.

"It is absolutely essential for a spiritual aspirant who genuinely longs for union with God, the reality, to shun false practices of yogic postures and exercises, meditation on other than God the beloved, experiments with certain drugs, and fad for types of food. These things do not uplift the aspirant, nor do they draw him out of the rut of illusion. Experiences born of these practices wear off no sooner than the aspirant withdraws from, or is thrown out of, the orbit of the effects produced by the technique employed."[202]

Recently I spoke with a man who had been a Sufi from a young age. He had gone to Meher Baba's headquarters in Virginia Beach in the mid-1970s when he was about 25. Initially he had a fairly strong dislike of the "Baba Lovers," who seemed controlling, holier-than-thou and cultish. Then he had an open-eyed vision of Meher Baba telling him that he was his guru. He stopped taking drugs and became a follower. This lasted about 15 years. At that point he allowed himself to begin smoking pot again, which led to the use of other substances. Today, he's still a devotee, but not in the same way he had been.

I've heard stories like this about Meher Baba's "appearances" enough times now to wonder if Meher Baba truly was the "Avatar of the Age," as he claimed, or perhaps something else… Certainly his message about not doing yoga postures and drinking kombucha would put millions of people today in the land of the lost and I would be one of them.

Ram Dass and Neem Karoli Baba

Neem Karoli Baba (to Ram Dass): "*These medicines were used in Kulu Valley long ago. But yogis have lost that knowledge. They were used with fasting. Nobody knows now. To take them with no effect, your mind must be firmly fixed on God. Others would be afraid to take. Many saints would not take this.*" And he left it at that.

When I asked [Ram Dass] if I should take LSD again, he said, "*It should not be taken in a hot climate. If you are in a place that is cool and peaceful, and you are alone and your mind is turned toward God, then you may take the yogi medicine.*"[203]

Ram Dass: "*…First off, I want to say that I would never recommend to anyone that they use psychedelics as a means to alter their consciousness. But if someone comes to me and says, "I'm going to take this," then I say to them, "I think you should study and understand something about the method you're about to use, so you can enter it in the spirit of it being a Yoga for you, a path toward union… Listen carefully to your own heart; if you feel that using psychedelics seems to be part of your practice, then use them, but use them very consciously.*"[204]

Neem Karoli Baba's saying that even "many saints" would not take LSD, with the implication that this is due to fear, is important for us to consider. The "fear factor" involved in taking a psychedelic cannot be underestimated, nor should we downplay the fear that comes into play in their marginalization by mainstream society. Fear leads us to condemn as we project onto "others" our insecurities and hidden self-hatred. But for those with the courage to ingest such substances as a spiritual practice, the result can only be the lessening of fear. This is because under the influence of a psychedelic, one often finds oneself, willy-nilly, living through one's greatest fears. I take both Maharajji and Ram Dass' words to essentially be a "license to pill"—if the set and setting is optimal.

Baba Rampuri

Baba Rampuri is an American-born initiate of the Naga Babas and author of *Baba: Autobiography of a Blue-Eyed Yogi*. I was so impressed with Rampuri's book, I initially sent him a list of 18 questions based on my reading. Rampuri graciously replied in great detail to each question, and a wonderful email correspondence was born. This is a brief excerpt of that correspondence.

Author: One thing that I am feeling needs to be addressed more in the yoga community, and one which you addressed at the recent World Psychedelic Forum, is the sacramental use of entheogens. How might plant medicine fit into a yoga program of expanding one's consciousness? And what is the role of psychedelics in a world where the old order is dying out, and a new one is being birthed?

For now, my main query is whether you are suggesting that spiritual seekers should immerse themselves in Yoga in order to understand the similarities and differences between chemically-induced altered states, and altered states reached through meditation or yogic discipline?

Rampuri: *Om namo narayan!*

Perhaps what you call "altered states" we can include in "the extraordinary world," and we might say that those who explore altered states are scientists or academics, but those who live in the extraordinary world are yogis.

I think Ayahuasca is a very wonderful healing and knowledge-giving plant Goddess, whose power is most manifested when She is given proper respect, which is usually the work of a true shaman. We made a ceremony recently in Switzerland.

There is a big difference between the scientist and the shaman (read: yogi), which is one between the ordinary and extraordinary worlds.

AL: Do the Naga Babas use any psychoactive "aids?" I recently read about the Deeksha Movement using an ayurvedic compound (leyham?) as one such aid.

Rampuri: *Babas have been using psychoactive substances from the beginning of time. In the arati to Shiva, His devotees all through India sing, "Bhanga Datura ka Bhojana." "For his meals He eats cannabis and dhatura."*

AL: Can the Guru system work for us today? Or could entheogens [psychedelics] serve as a teacher in lieu of a physical guru? Or perhaps plant medicine could function as a supplement or complement to teachings that are derived from a variety of spiritual sources such as books, teachers like yourself, meditation practice, etc.?

Rampuri: *I don't know exactly what you mean by the "guru system." The guru system today seems to be based on marketing, internet, and faith, and if its that you are referring to, then, anything goes. If you refer to discipleship, lineage, and oral tradition, then there can be no substitute. Chemicals, bio or otherwise, are not teachers. Just because they use wine in the mass doesn't mean that you drink a bottle of wine and achieve Christ-consciousness (whatever that may be). You cannot include Nancy Reagan and her "just say no" policy in consciousness exploration.*

Author: Ram Dass said in the early Seventies that although LSD apparently had no effect on Neem Karoli Baba, the guru did say to him that LSD could be usefully used in a sacramental way. He added that LSD didn't provide the "highest Samadhi" (or "true Samadhi"); that it could give you the vision of Christ, but it couldn't make you Christ…

Rampuri: *I don't believe that Ram Dass mythology, personally. Just because you are high doesn't mean that sugar doesn't taste sweet. Taking LSD is inviting a spirit to possess you to some degree for some period of time. What happens next… Well, it's different for different people.*

Author: So you don't believe that Neem Karoli Baba took a massive dose of LSD and it had no effect on him?

Rampuri: *I see that statement as hyperbole, as a means of saying "He's so high that when he takes acid, nothing happens!" I don't know what Neem Karoli Baba took and what he didn't take, but this is in the genre of miracle stories and there are better ones. I also visited Neem Karoli Baba (who I found very cool) from time to time, and I can tell you that neither Ram Das nor any of his followers spoke any Hindi during baba's life and baba didn't speak any English.*

Author: Could you say a bit more about gurus?… In the late 90s I went to India for the first time and was very disturbed when I found out there was a fierce rivalry between two women gurus, both of whom I deeply respected.

Rampuri: *These are businesses. What tastes better, Coke or Pepsi? Who will protect you best, John Kerry or George Bush? What is the most nutritious breakfast granola? As long as you are a good shopper, the best you can come up with is a "good deal." But the competitor will match the good deal next week or month. Consumerism, whether diet beverages or gurus, it's the same!*

Break the consumption paradigm and you will see a whole different world out there. That part of the reason for your fascination with psychedelics: for a short while you are not a consumer, you're too stoned to choose!

I hope this is helpful for you. Most important is to start asking the question, "How do I know things?"

Goddess Bless You!

What I found really interesting is that someone who is such a lineage holder of the yoga tradition would be willing to deconstruct it like this. I don't necessarily agree with Rampuri's view that the Neem Karoli Baba LSD story was a fabrication, a "Holy Lie." As I get older, I do see how money does talk, even when it comes to spirituality, and I have also witnessed ego and competition amongst spiritual teachers, and also within myself—it's all one. I would say that psychedelics do help to see these things clearer, yet they can also possibly lead to throwing the guru baby out with the plant medicine bath water. If everything is ego, everything illusion, then nihilism and suicide are not far away. That said, I do take to heart Rampuri's position that there can be "no substitute" for lineage, discipleship, and oral tradition. The next excerpt from Bhagavan Das also affirms this position.

Bhagavan Das

"*I want to be honest about the part drugs played in my spiritual development, but I also want to make a serious point: drugs are a very dangerous path. You definitely have to have protection. The way you protect yourself is with the love you have for your guru—the guru watches out for you. If you don't have divine guidance and protection, drugs can kill you.*

"*This is why the essence of spiritual life is truly the guru. It's not a popular position in the West anymore since we've had so many guru scandals, but it hasn't for one moment stopped being true. If you want to learn Ayurveda, you have to have a guru. If you want to learn to meditate, you need the guru.*

"*If you have a real guru, a Satguru, then you're protected. If you don't—if you try to go the direct route without a guide—then you don't ingest the drug, the drug ingests you. Drugs are Shakti. By definition, the guru is a person who, like Shiva can hold the Shakti. You can get addicted or overdose if you're not using drugs worshipfully. I had some very good experiences with drugs, but I don't recommend them to others because most people in the West want the poison—they don't want Shiva. And they don't have elders to show them how to use poison in a sacred manner... there are many safer ways to raise your consciousness than experimenting with drugs, and most gurus in India prefer more conservative routes. Doing your meditation, japa, and hatha-yoga is a slower path, but the effects are more lasting, and you run less risk of frying your nervous system. Without a doubt, self-discipline pays for itself in the end.*"[205]

In most circles I have been a part of, the plant medicines are ingested in a "sacramental" way where there is a calling in of guidance and protection from angels, masters, spirits, etc. I cannot say that some people have not been psychically damaged using psychedelics. A world-renowned astrologer told me in no uncertain terms that I had dimmed my aura through their use, and he counseled me against writing this book.

But I will leave this an open question, and simply suggest again that a good deal of research and preparation is a wise idea before partaking of any psychedelic substance. For a yogi like Bhagavan Das, who had years of yogic discipline behind him before first trying LSD, his maiden voyage on acid was perhaps made that much more potent, stable, and useful. Yet it is important to note that the frying of one's nervous system is a potential hazard whether one is working with a psychedelic, or with Kundalini Yoga. It's possible to "overdose" on both.

Perhaps the best rule of thumb is that if one has any concerns or fears about ingesting, whatever substance or practice it is, it's probably wise to consider whether the timing is right.

Ralph Metzner, with Ram Dass

RM: *I think many people in the psychedelic drug "movement," to judge by some of the internet self-reports, seem to... think that just taking a drug is in itself a spiritual practice. And it isn't.*

RD: *I don't know that it isn't. We very rarely ritualized it to make it a sacrament.*

RM: *Yes, but isn't that the point? It has to be taken with that kind of intention and preparation. The way the shamans in the Amazon do with ayahuasca and the Native American Church folks do with peyote. And just taking the pill without that preparation and intention doesn't do that. The Charles Manson story really brought that point home to me. Here he was, taking LSD and using it to brainwash his followers to be sex slaves and killers. That really brought home the truth of the set and setting principle. After my ten-year experience in the Agni Yoga meditation school, I always have integrated psychedelics with spiritual energy-work. I wouldn't ever take them either, except with a sacramental attitude. But at the time of course, none of us knew any better. We just winged it as best we could, with the limited knowledge and experience at our disposal.*[206]

Metzner's observation on Internet self-reports about psychedelic experiences is only part true: Now, as in the Sixties, there are many spiritual circles where these substances are approached in a sacramental way. I myself have now participated in at least 15 Ayahuasca "ceremonies." At all of them, intention and ritual and respect for tradition were very much in play. This respect for ritual and ceremony includes many in the yoga community today who are now exploring plant medicines in a yogic way. And Metzner's work has much to do with this. His recent books on Ayahuasca and magic mushrooms were extremely helpful to me in my own early explorations. We owe so much to the work of Metzer, Leary, Alpert and many others who paved the way for a more balanced approach to psychedelics in contemporary western culture.

Timothy Leary

"If you are serious about your religion, if you really wish to commit yourself to the spiritual quest, you must learn how to use psychochemicals. Drugs are the religion of the twenty-first century. Pursuing the religious life today without using psychedelic drugs is like studying astronomy with the naked eye because that's how they did it in the first century A.D., and besides telescopes are unnatural.

"A psychedelic experience is a journey to new realms of consciousness. The scope and content of the experience is limitless, but its characteristic features are the transcendence of verbal concepts, of space-time dimensions, and of the ego or identity. Such experiences of enlarged consciousness can occur in a variety of ways: sensory deprivation, yoga exercises, disciplined meditation, religious or aesthetic ecstasies, or spontaneously. Most recently they have become available to anyone through the ingestion of psychedelic drugs such as LSD, psilocybin, mescaline, DMT, etc. Of course, the drug does not produce the transcendent experience. It merely acts as a chemical key—it opens the mind, frees the nervous system of its ordinary patterns and structures.

"We always have urged people: Don't take LSD unless you are very well prepared, unless you are specifically prepared to go out of your mind. Don't take it unless you have someone that's very experienced with you to guide you through it. And don't take it unless you are ready to have your perspective on yourself and your life radically changed, because you're gonna be a different person, and you should be ready to face this possibility."[207]

Leary was a *rascal* guru, a radical rapscallion ring leader if there ever was one, and he consciously played the part to a "T," leading to his crucifixion in various ways over the course of his lifetime. Perhaps he did have an overinflated view of his own usefulness to the human race, but his genius and his legacy speak for themselves.

There's a sense in which we can see Leary as a modern day Socrates, an elder "gadfly" accused of leading the youth astray, and just as thoroughly misunderstood and unjustly punished. It wasn't until I read his memoir, *Flashbacks*, that I first got a sense of who Leary truly was, namely a sincere seeker after truth in his own unique way. I realize his detractors would say the book is full of outright lies and distortions. Possibly so: He certainly was the master of re-invention and revisionary history. Yet don't we all do this?

Leary's view that psychedelic drugs are the religion of the 21st century is an idea that merits exploration, as is his idea that psychedelics level the playing floor, dismantling all the hierarchical structures of organized religion. Terence McKenna, who Leary once dubbed "the real Timothy Leary," said essentially the same thing. Were both these men simply far ahead of their time? Or were they too invested in their "image" to open to higher truths?

Swami Muktananda

Q: What do you feel about the use of drugs for attaining Self-awareness?

SW: Self-awareness does not depend on anything, but if you take drugs in the name of attaining Self-awareness, you will become dependent on the drugs. Kabir Sahib said, "Never have the hope that you will attain the Self while taking intoxicants." The Self has its own effulgence. The intoxication of drugs is derived from the light of the Self. When this is the case, how can drugs make the light of the Self reveal itself?

A person becomes addicted to drugs and then to keep himself from admitting this mistake, he says that they give him Self-awareness. When your mind turns within, when you become very, very pure and subtle, the Self reveals itself to you. Every day we chant and meditate and observe good conduct. We do not do these practices to attain the Self because we have already attained the Self; we do them to make our mind purer and subtler so that we can perceive the Light of the Self. The Self is very subtle, and our mind and intellect must become extremely refined in order to experience it.

If the mind becomes intoxicated and too excited, it becomes rajasic [over-stimulated] and impure. That is why a person who is addicted to outer intoxicants will find it difficult to experience the intoxication of the inner Self. Meditation affects extremely refined sensory nerves for which drugs are much too strong—these nerves cannot even bear strong coffee. That's why drugs are forbidden by the scriptures.

You should become intoxicated only on God's love. A saint said that person whose mind has been completely cleansed and whose heart has become completely pure becomes intoxicated only on God's love. And it is the best intoxication. When you get drunk on the intoxication of love for God, all outer drugs will seem insipid by comparison.

Even if you get high on marijuana, you don't get very high, and when the effect wears off, you come down—perhaps even lower than before. To get high again you have to use more marijuana, otherwise you might not be able to bear your own company. But as you get higher and higher on the intoxicants of the Self, you will reach a state from which you will never come down. So if you want to get high, get high on God's love. You cannot experience this intoxication through drugs.

Meditation is far more potent than marijuana, but before you can get meditation, you first have to give up drugs completely. There are no "downs" in meditation; there are only "ups" because the high of meditation will never desert you. It keeps getting stronger and stronger, so powerful is the inner intoxicant. No drug, however potent, can influence a real meditator. It is said that Mira was given poison to drink, yet it caused her no harm because she was under the influence of a far mightier "poison"—the ecstasy and nectar of her love of Krishna. I am not speaking of any miracle or siddhi; this happens naturally to one who is divinely intoxicated.

Therefore, meditate with love and interest. Don't seek the aid of drugs; they will dull the refined sensory nerves in your brain. Those who meditate with the aid of drugs always remain insecure and dissatisfied.[208]

It is useful to keep in mind that Ram Dass was instrumental in bringing Swami Muktananda to the West, partly at the behest of his own guru, Neem Karoli Baba. Please also recall that Stanislav Grof and his wife Christina were once devotees of Muktananda. Muktananda told Grof that Soma was concocted from a creeper and is still being used by the priests in India to this day. Muktananda also may have had something different to say about the value of Ayahuasca, as we'll see later in this chapter.

I would first ask in regard to what Muktananda says here: In which scriptures does it say not to take intoxicants? I don't doubt there are such scriptures (certainly there are Buddhist texts), it is just that I am not aware of them.

A seeker's rationalizing a "spiritual reason" for taking drugs is an important point as it gets directly into the psychology of guilt and cover up that sometimes comes into play here. But we can also reverse this argument and ask whether the guru, in this case Muktananda, feels threatened by his or her students' use of psychedelics?

The snake says to Adam and Eve, "The Big Man doesn't want you to eat that, because if you do, you'll become like him." So they bite, and they get banished. Whether this was "good" or "bad" is an open question. Perhaps all paths to enlightenment are good and value judgments are useless. Or perhaps some are simply more expedient than others. These questions would all be a moot point if Muktananda's lineage was not without scandal.

Muktananda's point about drugs dulling the sensory nerves is also well taken. My own experience suggests that a much more subtle refinement of the senses is possible through the deliberate path of meditation. Once again, let us consider that the fable of the tortoise and the hare contains universal wisdom: Slow and steady wins the race.

Yogi Bhajan

"Drugs and Kundalini Yoga don't mix."

"The term 'pothead' derives from a state of mind peculiar to those who use marijuana. This state of mind is said to be caused by blockage of spinal fluid and acupressure meridians at the base of the neck."[209]

"If you have to be addicted to something, be addicted to doing sadhana daily. Otherwise, addiction is not a source of freedom. And you are not free by taking drugs. The neurons of the brain will become feeble. You will lose your nostril pituitary sensitivity. You can never smell the subtlety of life. You'll always be dragging your life."[210]

"Many people who stick to sadhana have been found to be totally clear of the abnormalities created by the use of drugs."

"When you lose a part of you, folks, you are gone. One part that you are losing these days with drugs is called Impactuous Sensitivity. This generation, the Sixties generation, has lost it. Drugs may do good to you for a while, it's your money. I'm not asking you not to use them, but you shall never be you again."

"That's why I started Kundalini Yoga. I wasn't interested in gaining my leadership or membership. I saw the tragedy of mankind. I saw how damaged they were. We picked up young bodies left on trails, eaten by animals, unrecognizable, and sometimes their identification led us to their homes. You can't believe it."[211]

Peter Tosh's song "Get Up, Stand Up," made famous worldwide by Bob Marley, has the lyric, "half the story has never been told."

This book attempts to tell the *whole* story in a nonjudgmental, and objective way that also makes clear that the hippie trail has its share of dead on the wayside.

Here is more of that tale: People seem to love or hate Yogi Bhajan. I've talked to people in both camps and feel the truth, as always, probably lies somewhere in between.

A personal story: I was once on a flight reading a yoga book when I sensed the passenger sitting to my left looking over my shoulder at it. Finally he asked me about what I was reading. A conversation ensued revealing that he had lived at Yogi Bhajan's ashram in New Mexico from the early Seventies to the early Eighties. While my plane mate appreciated the practice of Kundalini Yoga, he eventually had a major falling out with Yogi Bhajan. And he wasn't alone: about half the residents of Yogi Bhajan's ashram left en masse with him at that time. The man went on to tell me had been very high up in the Bhajan organization and over dinner one night he revealed to the master his intentions to leave. Yogi Bhajan apparently responded with some very ugly things to him, including threatening his son's life. The implication was that his life would be cursed if he left the organization…

I believed this man's story as it was then ancient history and he had no personal stake in it anymore. I've heard similar stories from others, including Tom Law's report in Chapter One.

We can and should ask: Does this detract from what Yogi Bhajan taught, or his legacy? Perhaps not, but it should give us pause before we deify or give our power over to any such person. And if we can question one thing a "master" says, what should keep us from questioning everything they say? It is my understanding that a genuine guru would not have felt so threatened by the departure of a disciple.

Martin Ball

Q: *On the subject of gurus, I've been a student of Yoga for years now, so I'm very interested in your saying that the plant medicines are far better than any human guru in terms of what they can teach us. But some disagree. Those who followed Neem Karoli Baba do not support the use of plant medicines. Ram Dass being the prime example, of course, but many of Neem Karoli Baba's Western devotees basically stopped taking entheogens once having come in contact with his teachings. Any comments?*

MB: *Gurus are pretty funny about entheogens. They talk about how they are "false awakenings" and how you "have to do it on you own." According to whom? In my understanding, God created the medicines so we could commune with God. Anyone who would tell you different is pushing some ego-created agenda on you about how you should be or who you should be. I simply don't buy it. And besides, if God didn't want us to use DMT for example, God wouldn't have filled our bodies with it, put it on our nerve endings, or made it so readily available in nature. People who claim that it is not a path to genuine spiritual experience are trying to impose human ego-creations on God. It's silly, when you think about it.*

I'm not sure if Neem Karoli Baba, for example, said that LSD produced a "false awakening" or "false Samadhi," or whether he said it wasn't "the highest Samadhi." This is because Ram Dass' stories say different things in different places. But there is a difference. LSD can help the spiritual seeker attain a high mystical state of consciousness, but as Neem Karoli Baba counseled Ram Dass, you can *pranam* or bow to Christ on psychedelics, but you cannot *become* Christ.

As far as gurus saying that one has to do it on one's own, I would suggest that whether the method is meditation or medication, one still must be able to take what was revealed on the mountaintop back into the world. Back into embodied "love thy neighbor as thyself" living reality. In this sense, yes, everyone must do it on one's own.

The argument of "why would God create plant medicines if he didn't want us to use them" begs the question of who is God? And does God act in our world? The metaphysics of *A Course in Miracles,* for example, is that God is perfect Oneness and therefore cannot recognize any ego-created separation between God and us. Even if we were to open to the possibility that God did create DMT as a way of waking some of us up from illusion, and I for one am very open to this, how could we know if it was God and not the ego that had created it?

Ganesh Baba

"ΨΔ : Once a Psychedelic [psychonaut], always a Psychedelic"

"The world will divide between the alpha-betas and psi-deltas (alcoholic beefeaters and psychedelics), you will see."

"We psychedelics must become more familiar with the essence and structure of consciousness, because it is out of consciousness we come and to consciousness we return."

"Ganja is gyana [jnana] yoga—it is an abstraction; you are a little bit abstracted from sensory experience. It gives you room to move your psyche about."

"Live high and die high!"
—an often repeated Ganeshian aphorism

"Since time immemorial we have used plant substances to help us recognize the higher frequencies of knowledge." [212]

Ganesh Baba speaks as an heir of the time-honored Shaivite tradition of using psychoactive substances sacramentally to "live high and die high." I have now been around enough Shiva people to see this in action and respect their way of life. I have also witnessed teachers who can transmit very high experiences through their mere *darshan,* a Sanskrit word referring to the blessing conferred by the touch, gaze, or mere presence of an enlightened being. I say this without value judgment: both have their pros, and both can also be traps.

Recently I met an Indian man who claims he can tell people what their Hindu deity "archetype" is, meaning the archetype that most resonates with them. This is a man with an advanced academic degree from the West and who is clearly very well-versed in Hindu mythology and the symbolism of the various Hindu gods and goddesses. After only speaking together for several minutes, the man told me my archetype is Shiva. Without going into detail as to why I feel he is correct, I will just say this makes perfect sense to me. It also accords well with the fact that I found psychedelics to be well worth exploring, enough to devote years of my life and this book to the subject!

Eckhart Tolle

Please note that what follows is an excerpt from. Here Oprah asks Eckhart how his LSD experience compared with his awakening experience:

Eckhart: *It's not quite the same thing because what I experienced [in his awakening experience] was much more subtle and beautiful. The acid I experienced has almost a violent thing where violently the perceptions—sense perceptions—become so magnified that there was no room for thinking anymore. But I could see why people say, for some people it's a glimpse of what it means to perceive the world without this continuous interference of mental noise.*

Oprah: *Yeah, but your trip without acid was better.*

Eckhart: *Much better.*[213]

While I am sympathetic to what is expressed above, and have likewise said that my own "trip without acid" was "better," in the sense of more fulfilling, this is not true for everyone. Some will not come to spiritual practice without first taking a psychoactive substance. Compassion means meeting people where they are and giving them the tools to lighten their journeys, free of value judgments.

Gangaji

"Similarly, with psychedelics, I once took acid and it felt polluted and horrible. My experience was terrible. Then there was a moment of 'Okay, let it be what it is! Just surrender and let go.' Instantly it was blissful and peaceful."

This is a common experience with both meditation and psychedelics—the more you fight the mind, the more it fights back. It's like the thousand-headed Hydra of Greek mythology that cut off one demonic head and ten more grow in its place. Ignore it and it will starve to death, leaving you to experience the pure bliss of enlightenment rooted in the now. This is true for everything else we experience in life: If we feed the negative tendencies of the mind, we create a hellish consciousness for ourselves; but if we focus on our divine nature, we create heaven. Both heaven and hell are only a thought away. With psychedelics this choice is dramatically magnified so we are suddenly able to witness this truth that much more clearly.

Rabbi Zalman M. Schacter-Shalomi

"Since the time of this first trip, I had several more experiences under hard and soft psychedelics. I have had some bad trip experiences and some very ecstatic ones. I hope I have learned from them. It has certainly had a profound effect on me and in many ways has restructured my life. For the better'? Who can say? There are times when I am not so sure. Some of the old games I played with an unsophisticated "sincerity," I can no longer play that way. I am not satisfied with my own unconscious deceits. I know myself better, and at times this hurts. I knew more before. I used to think I had more answers. Now I have more questions. I cannot lead others with such great self-assurance as I had. In theology, where before I would spend time arguing for a precise formulation, I now see the other point of view as clearly as my own, and I can no longer invest my views with the same vehement assertiveness. Alan Watts expresses my views on myth and a dynamic meta-theology far more closely than Maimonides, who is static....

"While I can share what has happened to me and help in some measure in the planning of experiences in order to avoid some of the bad trip pitfalls, I am no longer sure that soft or hard psychedelics are a panacea. I don't think that I should promote the use of psychedelics any more than mysticism or religion. I do think I should make my insights and experiences available to those who feel that they wish to have such information in order to plan their own experiences, or after they have had them, to make sense of them. Before taking anyone with me, I have found that it is wise to ask the I Ching or an equivalent oracle. Personally, I am glad that I am alive at this time and am able to enter the heaven-hell realm at chemical notice. On the other hand, it makes no real difference, since the one who can take it and the very same one who cannot are one and the same. The experience teaches that there is no ultimate advantage to be had. Yet at the same time, it teaches that you don't have to play bad games if you don't want to...

"Does LSD turn plain folks into saints? Does a revelation at Mount Sinai turn plain folks into saints? Only forty days after seeing God face to face, the people worshiped a golden calf. So it is clear, is it not, that only moral effort is rewarded by sainthood? But then what about grace? And if you say grace works by predestination, what about free will? And so it goes... ad infinitum.

"I am sure that when you have it all figured out, you yourself will provide the next question that starts another round of games. While we exist, what else are we going to do? We exist forever in the NOW."[214]

In the mid-'90s, after traveling to Israel, but before I got into yoga, I talked briefly to Reb Zalman about the possibility of studying under him for rabbinic ordination, but was disappointed to hear that he was no longer offering that. I include Reb Zalman here because he also is a guru and has a unique perspective coming from the Jewish fold, journeying through the Holocaust to religious Orthodoxy to the psychedelic Sixties and beyond. I take from what he says here that he was as much in a quandary about all of this as I am. I see him as doing very similar work as Ram Dass within the context of Judaism.

Krishnamurti

Q: I think it is possible under certain drugs to know myself with analysis—there is no conflict.

K: *If one takes LSD or various forms of drugs, that helps a great deal, because in that there is not conflict at all. So you please take drugs. Does it really, does any drug, LSD, marijuana, any of them—does it really expose the totality of the content of consciousness, or does it bring about chemically a certain state of mind which is totally different from the understanding of oneself? These drugs—I have never taken them—they have taken them in India a great deal—I watched many people there. I have also watched students in universities in America, and many, many other people who have been taking various forms of drugs, LSD, marijuana, you know I don't know what all the other names are—psychedelic drugs. If you have observed, these drugs do affect the mind, the brain cells themselves. They destroy the brain. If you have talked to one or many of those who have taken drugs, they can't reason, they can't pursue a logical sequence of thought—and the doctors and the scientists are beginning to say it does destroy the very structure of the brain cells. Not only LSD but marijuana, which is much more dangerous than LSD because that leaves a toxic condition in the brain cells and is more difficult to get rid of. In India they have taken drugs for millions, for thousands of years and they are the most ignorant people who have taken drugs. And all the so-called intellectuals in India have denied it, said don't do it, touch it. I am not asking you not to take it, it's up to you, but when you see the effect of it, on people— they have no sense of responsibility, they think they can do anything they like, many, many hospitals are full of these people who mentally are unbalanced through drugs…*

Q: I find your sequence of thought illogical. And also I cannot see how you can argue against drugs if you have not any experience of taking drugs.

K: *Ah wait. How can you argue against drugs if you have not taken drugs yourself? Must you go through various forms of experience; must you get drunk in order to understand sobriety? Must you get angry in order to find out what it is not to be angry? Must you overeat in order—and so on and so on. Can't one observe without going through all the human mischief?*[215]

Yes, you can know *for yourself* whether something is for you or not by observing others or based on reports and reasoning, but to make a general statement *against them* from a position of influence and authority might also be labeled "mischief."

Sri Brahmarishi Narad

"The fact that entheogenic drugs induce a greater sensitivity to subtle spiritual and psychic energies, and speed up the influx of impressions from deeper levels of consciousness, raise the immediate question of how these energies can be properly understood and handled. Obviously, if these energies are not guided, they can do more harm than good. The application of traditional Yoga meditation techniques while under psychedelic experiences, provides a constructive solution to this problem."[216]

This links to Ram Dass' quote above, that he would never counsel someone to take a psychedelic, but if they were dead set on doing it then there are preparations and guidelines that should to be taken into account. The book before you is providing not just a way to think clearly and critically about psychedelics, particularly in relation to yoga but also how to think clearly and critically about *anything*. It is also providing ideas for how yogic philosophy and techniques might be of assistance for those who choose to embark on a psychedelic journey.

Jack Kornfield

"I see psychedelics as having been enormously useful as an initial opening for people, and at certain stages it may be possible to use them again wisely, but with the constraints of "shila" [Buddhist proscriptions]. But they can be easily abused if one is not careful about the set and setting... Whatever leads to opening the heart and mind and letting go is beneficial..."[217]

Although I have discussed this highly regarded Buddhist teacher's view of psychedelics elsewhere in this book, I include his perspective here for balance to some of the other views expressed. From a space of *metta*, loving-kindness, how can we not see that for most people who use them, meditators included, psychedelics do open the heart and mind? Even if only a little bit and for a little while? To paraphrase Sheryl Crow, if it makes you feel good, can it be that bad? And if it opens one's eyes to new possibilities that might never have been glimpsed? Insights that could be life-changing? Can we really "just say no" and leave it at that?

Ramana Maharishi

"I do admit that drugs have some beneficial effect. A certain drug can make the whole body melt and flow like a milky ocean. One man told me that when he was given chloroform before an operation, he experienced a nectarous bliss and longed for that state again. The Chinese look like skeletons, but when they take opium, they feel like giants and do any amount of difficult work. These drugs, however, must be taken in limited amounts and secretly. Otherwise all will demand them. Moreover, after some time, the drug habit will become a great fetter and obstacle to jnana (the yogic path of Self-inquiry). Its addicts will not flinch from any crime to satisfy their cravings. So, it is best to remain desire-less. Having seen the effects of all these drugs, I have decided that to be as we are is best. To strive for knowing one's real nature through self-inquiry, though it is a little difficult, is the only safe path."

While the substances in discussion here are not physically addictive, they may be psychically so. This is a more subtle and thus a deeper addiction. I have been personally addicted to spiritual experiences. And if "addiction" is too strong a word, let's just say I've craved experiences, whether a repeat of ones I had in the past, or a longing for others of which I had only heard. "Addiction" to spiritualized ego is another aspect of this, which again may be a subtle tendency to think: "I'm better because I've had this or that experience."

Of course, we can see addiction within all "seeking," whether it involves seeking through psychedelics, mystical experience, or sex. And there are risks with everything in life. Yet if the ego is the only thing that truly dies, then what is there to be afraid of? Of dying before reaching enlightenment? What if we even gave up on seeking enlightenment?

Maharishi Mahesh Yogi

"We could accept that there could be some drugs which could influence the nervous system to reflect real transcendental consciousness. It could be possible… the possibility exists. Only we say that from the effect that we hear—from these mescalines and such things as are known today—they don't seem to meet the requirement… Otherwise there could be medicines which could set up the nervous system to that level… And when that consciousness is achieved, it would be real transcendental consciousness which will transform the life of a man, as is done through meditation…

"…there could be that gradual application of the medicine, so that as the mind keeps on retiring from the gross and becoming more subtle and more subtle, naturally all those intermediary steps are naturally fulfilled… The use of that could also be to that value. There could be that manner of taking that drug could such like that like that

like that... So if it is done in this way, then we could accept the possibility of transcendental consciousness through drugs."

Question: "Could that drug be the nectar of the Gods?"

"Then that might be Soma Rasa."[218]

The Maharishi was speaking at a time prior to the widespread use of Ayahuasca. By this point I have heard from enough sources, even shamans who themselves follow a guru, that Ayahuasca is the original Soma, or at least is of the same plant family. This may explain the growing interest in Ayahuasca in spiritual circles, particularly yoga circles. It may also explain why people feel the need to continue to "apply" the "medicine" again and still again. I myself have used Ayahuasca approximately 25 times, and while there is much that is repetitive in these "journeys," there also is a clear sense of a refinement occurring.

Dr. Robert Svoboda

"Personally, I am very fond of Ayawaska [Ayahuasca], me personally. And I think it is a very fine thing, except of course like anything else it can be misused... Many of the shamans in South America do nothing all day long except protect themselves from other shamans or attack other shamans, what is the benefit there?...

"People used to ask Vimalananada [his Tantric guru]: Where can we find the Soma that's mentioned in the Veda?" And he used to say that Soma you're never going to find, because you have only located it if you are already immortal. Because it's immortal already. So forget it. What you can do, though, is you can find a nididrabya, which means something that is not Soma but will have a similar effect inside you. And then you can use that. It will not transform you the way that Soma does, so completely and totally, but if you work with that it will progressively transform you as much as you can be transformed. For him he used Whiskey, Scotch Whiskey, for me I like very much Ayawaska, taken with some other things to alter the effect slightly. Different people have different things that they use. Some people will use cannabis; some people will use other substances. Even arsenic trisulfide is a very fine potential Rasayana, but of course it's very poisonous. Mercury is a very good Rasayana, it's also very poisonous. You have to be very careful when you start using things that are very strong and very poisonous so that you only get the good effect and not the bad effect. But it has to be a personalized thing, because the real Soma, you and I—as human beings, we are not going to locate it."

As an Ayurvedic physician, Dr. Svoboda understands the idea that each individual has a specific constitution, and that some substances will be suitable for some and not for others. It is the same for practices, or teachers, etc. Some are suitable for some and not for others. This point is very simple, yet can be missed in a book that deals with generalities and abstractions. Ayahuasca works well with *my* particular constitution, so well that every time I use it I wonder what I ever did without it.

Following up on the words of the Maharishi, Dr. Svoboda suggests that substances like Ayahuasca, while not Soma, can be applied in a progressive way to bring about a transformation of consciousness. And that this *is* a legitimate yoga practice.

The Beatles

"It [LSD] opened my eyes... We only use one-tenth of our brain. Just think of what we could accomplish if we could tap that hidden part! It would mean a whole new world if the politicians would take LSD. There wouldn't be any more war or poverty or famine... It made me a better, more honest, more tolerant member of society."[219]

—Paul McCartney

"[When I first took LSD] I felt in love, not with anything or anybody in particular but with everything."[220]

"Acid is not the answer... It's enabled people to see a bit more, but when you really get hip, you don't need it."[221]

—George Harrison

"I hope the fans will take up meditation instead of drugs."

—Ringo Starr, 1967

"I got the message that I should destroy my ego, and I did, you know. I was slowly putting myself together round about Maharishi time. Bit by bit over a two-year period, I had destroyed me ego. I didn't believe I could do anything. I just was nothing. I was shit. Then Derek [Taylor, Apple press officer] tripped me out at his house after he got back from L.A. He sort of said, 'You're all right,' and pointed out which songs I had written: 'You wrote this,' and 'You said this,' and 'You are intelligent, don't be frightened.' ... I've always needed a drug to survive. The others, too, but I always had more, more pills, more of everything because I'm more crazy probably... [LSD] was only another mirror. It wasn't a miracle. It was more of a visual thing and a therapy, looking at yourself a bit. It did all that. You know, I don't quite remember. But it didn't write the music. I write the music in the circumstances in which I'm in, whether it's on acid or in the water."

—John Lennon

It definitely was and is a powerful message to all of us that the Fab Four ultimately saw the limitations of LSD. They were among the first to recognize the greater potential of other, slower and steadier spiritual tools, such as meditation and chanting. Nevertheless, it seems that a psychedelic period was a necessary stage in their own individual and collective (r)evolution and involution. Perhaps many of that era would never have realized the necessity of spiritual seeking without first "breaking through to the other side" through psychedelics.

Lennon's LSD experience is particularly resonant for me as I had a very similar experience with Ayahuasca (see the Epilogue). During that experience, I felt that everything I had ever done was done from ego, and my whole life seemed to me to be just one big sham. I was left with the deadening sense of being damned, doomed unto eternity, and that I might as well hang it all up and go home. But a good friend kept reminding me I was a "good person" who had done many good things. Still, I was totally ready to commit myself to an ashram, a monastery, or a hermitage for the rest of my life—to save the world from myself, if not to somehow be saved from this vision of myself as a demon.

But Imagine what would have happened in John Lennon's case if he had sealed himself up and never blessed the world with his wonderfully poignant swan song, "Imagine"? And what if I, too, had faltered before the gloom of ultimate futility and never attempted to write the book you are reading?

I sense that the experience of "ego death" is a prerequisite for the artist before he can create a great work of art. Such an experience puts one in touch with what is truly essential *to be and to share with others.* Yet the ego death experience alone is not enough, clearly, as it still requires interpretation and integration to sow the seeds for "rebirth." That is where other forms of spiritual practice, like yoga, come in to play.

Ken Wilber

" I'm sort of well-known as not having a whole lot of experience with psychedelics. And I've written about what I believe, what I think was one very large LSD trip in college that I wasn't particularly fond of. But I never really did any psychedelics at all, not even sort of experimentally. Not because I didn't want to or anything, it just really wasn't sort of in the cards for me…

"My sense is that the people I know that have done it responsibly have gained a lot from using psychedelics to open up a certain space. But there are downsides. Particularly in this movement, you find there are two general approaches to consciousness studies. One is the druggies, and one is the meditators.

"And the druggies are into altered states, and the meditators are into stages. And

the meditators believe that you have to actually discipline and work and it's four years, ten years, fifteen years, to reach a stable realization of these higher states and stages. And the psychedelic or drug side is much more into altered states, ayahuasca, LSD, any sort of number of altered states, and they don't tend to get into permanent realizations based on these things.

"*I happen to believe that both of these models—I use states and stages—I believe both of them are required. But there's kind of an acrimony between these two groups. There are very few people that do drugs and are serious meditators. And the people that only do drugs, I think eventually it kind of tends to catch up in away. I don't see permanent realization coming from these things, I don't see permanent access to some of these higher states, and I think at some point the simple neurological noise of the ingredients starts to almost outshine the luminosity that was there, perhaps, at the beginning.*

"*And so the people I know that I've watched over thirty years that have done only drugs have become increasingly, frankly, unpleasant people, and disillusioned, and sad, in certain ways. It's not to say that meditators do all that much better, but there is at least a chance with meditators that you can have a permanent realization that is enduring and not merely a transitory state.*

"*I think people do better if they either have a judicious combination of the two, or if they do mostly meditation. And my recommendation is don't just do drugs, because people tend to get into trouble, and the theories I see coming out of people that just do drugs are frankly pretty wacky theories. They don't take enough evidence into account, they are not inclusive enough, they don't include other types of data and evidence and I think they are very partial.*"[222]

Despite what I might have implied elsewhere in this book, Wilber's view presented here is one of the most balanced and grounded ones on our subject. Those who use psychedelics often discount or avoid meditation because it is generally more subtle, slow, and often frustrating. Plus, it does not provide access to the mind-blowing fireworks that often accompany psychedelic experiences. I often wonder now if one can even meditate effectively after having danced with psychedelics? Clearly some people can. But others seem to lose the ability to focus and become reliant on external substances. Whether this is good, bad, or indifferent is still an open question…

Sri Nisargadatta

"*No doubt, a drug that can affect your brain can also affect your mind, and give you all the strange experiences promised. But what are all the drugs compared to the drug that gave you this most unusual experience of being born and living in sorrow and fear, in search of happiness, which does not come, or does not last. You should enquire into the nature of this drug and find an antidote... Birth, life, death—they are one. Find out what has caused them. Before you were born, you were already drugged. What kind of drug was it? You may cure yourself of all diseases, but if you are still under the influence of the primordial drug, of what use are the superficial cures?...*

"*...all a Guru can tell you is: 'My dear Sir, you are quite mistaken about your-self. You are not the person you think yourself to be.' Trust nobody, not even yourself. Search, find out, remove and reject every assumption till you reach the living waters and the rock of truth. Until you are free of the drug, all your religions and sciences, prayers and Yogas are of no use to you, for based on a mistake, they strengthen it. But if you stay with the idea that you are not the body nor the mind, not even their witness, but altogether beyond, your mind will grow in clarity, your desires—in purity, your actions—in charity and that inner distillation will take you to another world, a world of truth and fearless love. Resist your old habits of feeling and thinking; keep on telling yourself: 'No, not so, it cannot be so; I am not like this, I do not need it, I do not want it' and a day will surely come when the entire structure of error and despair will collapse and the ground will be free for a new life.*"

This is indeed a powerful message that gets right down to the root of the issue. An issue which lies beyond questions of whether to ingest or not to ingest plant medicines. For indeed, we will be lost if we do not come to terms with the one Drug that has created this vast illusion and which we perceive to be so real.

Presently I will share more about *A Course in Miracles*, a text which has con-firmed for me that the world we see is an illusion created by the ego. For now, I will merely affirm that the Advaitic truth that Sri Nisargadatta shares here is also aligned with that understanding, AND for the sincere spiritual seeker, the psychedelic ex-perience can help clarify what this powerful "drug" is, though it is also true that psychedelics are also not essential to this realization.

Adyashanti

"...the state of consciousness that a great majority of humanity is in is not natural. It's altered. We do not need to go looking for altered states of consciousness; humanity is already in an altered state of consciousness. It's called separation. Separation is the ultimate altered state of consciousness... Contrary to a popular misunderstanding, enlightenment has nothing to do with an altered state of consciousness. Enlightenment is an unaltered state of consciousness. It is pure consciousness as it actually is, before it is turned into something, before it is altered in any way."

This is similar to Nisargadatta's point. Yes, fear, guilt, and separation are all altered states based in ego, but this still begs the question: Can mind-altering substances be used to help us to see our illusory state more clearly? For myself, I will say that plant medicines have indeed helped in this regard, and more and more spiritual seekers today are finding this to be true.

Adyashanti's own awakening satori experience was apparently at least partly occasioned by his Zen training, and even he still had layers to work through to make it full and permanent. Similarly, while psychedelics can show us what it feels like to be in non-dual awareness, it would then be up to us to deepen this awareness through the day to day work of looking at our mental patternings.

Srila Prabhupada, Founder of ISKON, Hare Krishna

"We attended the next meeting Wednesday night. It followed the same format as the first. After the last kirtana, I went up to Srila Prabhupada and began to question him. "Have you ever heard of LSD?" I asked.

"No," he said.

"It's a psychedelic drug that comes like a pill, and if you take it you can get religious ecstasies. Do you think that that can help my spiritual life?"

"You don't need to take anything for your spiritual life," he told me. "Your spiritual life is already here."

I agreed with him immediately, although I would have never agreed with anyone else who would have said such a thing. I agreed mainly because he seemed so absolutely positive that there was no question of not agreeing. "Yes, my spiritual life is here," I thought to myself. I knew that he was in a state of exalted consciousness, and I was hoping that somehow he could teach the process to me."[223]

"Your spiritual life is already here" is quite a profound statement. After many years of seeking, I, too, have come to understand that we already have all the resources we need to navigate this illusionary reality. And we already have all we need inside ourselves, too, to find our way back home. We can do this by simply tapping into our own core essence; a place in us that is already home and *knows* it.

So if we already have IT and know IT, why do we need anything outside of ourselves to show us this? In this sense, psychedelics can heap more illusion on the illusion that the power does not lie within ourselves.

That said, Srila Prabhupada's exalted state was not something many have attained; a revelatory which I doubt that I myself would ever have even glimpsed without the aid of plant medicine. We simply cannot discount the incredible value of direct experience of these altered states *for ourselves*, as opposed to getting the insights they produce secondhand. No matter how brilliant a teacher or teaching may be, as Terence McKenna famously said: "It happened to me."

Terence McKenna

"I had traveled India in search of the miraculous. I had visited its temples and ashrams, its jungles and mountain retreats. But Yoga, a lifetime calling, the obsession of a disciplined and ascetic few, was not sufficient to carry me to the inner landscapes that I sought.

" I learned in India that religion, in all times and places where the luminous flame of the spirit had guttered low, is not more than a hustle. Religion in India stares from world-weary eyes familiar with four millennia of priest-craft. Modern Hindu India to me was both an antithesis and a fitting prelude to the nearly archaic shamanism that I found in the lower Rio Putomayo of Colombia when I arrived there to begin studying the shamanic use of hallucinogenic plants.[224]

"[Psychedelics] are democratic. They work for Joe Ordinary. And I am Joe Ordinary. I can't go and sweep up around the ashram for eighteen years or some rigmarole like that.[225]

"LSD burst over the dreary domain of the constipated bourgeoisie like the angelic herald of a new psychedelic millennium. We have never been the same since, nor will we ever be, for LSD demonstrated, even to skeptics, that the mansions of heaven and gardens of paradise lie within each and all of us.

"A lot of people pass through the thinking I'm a guru and take enough trips to understand that no, I was just a witness. I was just a witness."[226]

While I do not subscribe to all of McKenna's statements above, I do appreciate his defense of psychedelics on behalf of the common person, the "Everyman" spiritual seeker. I have already noted the "remedial" benefits of both yoga and psychedelics, and it is mainly for these seekers that this book is written. Most of us will never attain to the spiritual heights of Yogananda, Ramakrishna, Ramana Maharishi, Anandamayi Ma, or any great mystic past or present. Nor will many of us succeed in going very deep in our meditation practice. So we must recognize that for some spiritual seekers there are other tools available to make this inward journey and they have a right to use them. It really is that simple, until we complicate it.

Swami Satyananda Saraswati (Bihar School)

"Many years ago, I smoked so much ganja that I had a problem with my lungs, but I am not an addict. I took it because I though it was necessary for spiritual life. Certainly I believe that hashish, opium, LSD, or any chemical or narcotic can be useful at some point in spiritual life. Extracts from the hemp plant are used to treat schizophrenics and other mental patients. The same substance, when smoked by a healthy man, can turn him into a mental case...

"We only see one aspect of drugs like opium, marijuana, LSD, etc. We do not see the other side. We also do not try to know how they come into our lives. You can't reject them by restricting them. You can only reject them by accepting them. Whether it is ganja, alcohol or something else, it will not lose its attraction as long as you censure it."[227]

Here is more support for the "remedial" or *medicinal* usage of psychoactive plants, and this is from a contemporary yoga master whose school has influenced millions of spiritual seekers worldwide. Perhaps what we need is less legal restriction in the usage of these substances and more wise guidance either from a guru, a shaman, or eventually even a healthcare professional. In the Sixties when many of these substances were made illegal, there were not many "gurus" who could perform such a function. And nowadays there most certainly are.

Swami Satyananda Saraswati (Shree Maa)

"There are seven levels of consciousness defined by scripture. Each of these has innumerable possibilities for expressions, but primarily we can strive for awareness of these levels. They have been described in our book entitled Tattva Jnana.

"Once we understand the nature of the various levels of consciousness, and we are sincere in our desire for that experience, then there is no other need of external stimulation in order to attain that experience. Once we have proved that existence, then all that is required is the will to enter into that state of awareness and the knowledge of how to shift our consciousness. No physical substance will take us there...

"You cannot have recreational samadhi. The word itself means to transcend all changes and modifications of the mind—to become completely still within. Sa means all. Ma is the measurement. Dhi is the mind. All is the measurement of mind: unlimited, infinite, Satchidananda—True existence, Infinite Consciousness, Pure Bliss!

"An external substance creates a dependency. Sadhana promotes freedom; freedom through discipline—not freedom from discipline.

"I do not take nor promote the use of psychedelics. Sadhu means efficient—someone who has become so efficient at doing whatever he or she does, that they need not repeat the experience again."

Swamiji is one of the most inspirational people I have ever met. He was also a major catalyst for my initial foray into yoga. I sensed his responses to my email interview questions, however, were more rooted in the psychedelic culture of the Sixties and Seventies, rather than where we are right now. Back then there was much more undisciplined *recreational* use of psychedelics. But there were also small groups of people using it sacramentally in the context of a spiritual practice. There were also people like Leary, Metzner, and Alpert who were studying psychedelics from a scientific perspective.

The current use of Ayahuasca within the circles I've participated in has been deeply respectful, disciplined, and accompanied by a sincere and spiritually focused intention. Within these medicine circles it has been my observation that no matter how efficient one is in one's spiritual practice, repeated applications of the plant medicine are generally desirable or even necessary to receive the most benefits. This is why ceremonial use of plant medicines often becomes a ritualized and repetitive behavior.

As my original Ayahuasca shaman guru put it to me, we are seeking the undying Self amidst the ever-changing flux of the mind during the Ayahuasca session. This generally does not happen all at once, and it will not happen for everyone, but it can with time and practice. The goal is to get to the point where one is established in the Self and thus no longer needs an external substance to assist in the process. As the saying goes: Once the boat takes you across the river, you no longer need the boat.

Paul Brunton

"The drug way of coming to this consciousness belongs originally to a distant era, when spiritism, of which ancestor worship was then also a part, was the most widespread religion on both sides of the Pacific Ocean. For primitive people, descendant of Lemurian and later Atlantean races, it was as far as they could develop at the time. A minority of the higher teachings followed, drew beyond the herd and prepared the way for higher teachings yet to come. The astral, or psychic, centres were sufficiently alive to need only a little prompting by the tribal leaders or priests—usually a group affair at certain festivals It was then that their drugs obtained from nature were used or, in the case of followers of the darker side, misused, even abused, resulting in sorcery, sex,

orgies, and black magic. In the more moral use of drugs, although the higher kinds of religious and mystical experience were not attained, the idea of survival was firmly implanted, along with respect for traditional codes, teachings and ways. The development of intellect dimmed the astral centres. The use of drugs is an attempt to revive what is no longer proper for modern man...

"Young persons are easily deceived by the sham uplift which drugs may confer. It is an astral plane experience, not a Buddhic plane one, as it seems to be.

"What the drug taker gets is imagined reality, no real reality. Consciousness assumes the experience of knowing Truth, gives him the most vivid idea that this is IT. The end-effect is not to bring him nearer to the goal, as he wrongly believes, but farther from it. Such are the tricks the mind can play on self.

"The drug experience, however exalted it is, never really gets beyond being an astral plane copy, a pseudo-contact with a pseudo-god. It is illegitimate for modern man to break Nature's safety barrier in this way. He may pay a penalty with health, sanity, or self-deception...

"...The glimpse brings him to himself, but no drug can do that. The drug brings him before a vivid mental picture which he lives; it is still only a picture—sometimes horrible like a nightmare, sometimes sublime like a mystical ecstasy. But never in these experiences does he enter his true self, always he is looking at and living with a picture."

Despite Brunton's disparagement of Meher Baba in his book *A Search in Secret India*, his and the self-proclaimed Avatar's views on "drugs" are strikingly similar. And they are also both very much worth reflecting upon. Yes, after all of my own searching in "secret India" and beyond, I do feel both men deserve our respect and consideration. However much their statements feel like ghosts from a bygone era when *primitive* peoples and their practices were looked down upon as less evolved. There is still a little part of me that wonders: Well, what about the "sham" in "shaman"?

I don't know. But I do know enough to be still and know that I don't know. Yet I still do know that, well, you know...

Ganga White

"Even seasoned psychonauts and neuronauts have sometimes opined that while it may be possible to have a spiritual experience, philosophical insight, or religious experience, you have to come back and do it on the natch. They may say that such experiences are analogs of true (genuine authentic), religious experience. We need to ask what, or who, is the arbiter of true religious experience? Furthermore, is spiritual experience measurable at all? The arguments leveled against the validity of entheogens can equally be aimed in the other direction. We could also question whether the experiences obtained by prayer, rosary, mantra repetition, or years of trying to stop the mind, are more valid and "natural" or if they are merely mechanical repetition and hypnotic self projection?

"Who or what can dictate the authenticity of religious experience and is it measurable? If there is an acceptable measure, it is usually centered around how that experience later expresses itself in daily life with compassion, love, kindness and care. With that metric so many who have been touched by psychedelic awakening report, or have friends and family reporting, obvious and significant transformation and opening of these essential, evolved human attributes.

"Psychotropic substances are powerful tools, and like all tools, they can cut both ways—helping or harming. Paracelsus offered a great guiding principle when he pointed out that the difference between a medicine and a poison is dosage, usage. There are many examples of great opening, creativity, insight and positive transformation from entheogenic experiences, but unfortunately, we've also seen the opposite. We must acknowledge that the same is true in the arena of traditional religion. In these epochal times of religious fervor and extremism, East and West, sometimes it seems riskier to experiment with religion than with drugs. With religion you can end up trapped for a life time in the confines of one myth, or worse, living your whole life for the promise and reward of one erroneous idea of what lies beyond that ultimate mystery we call death.

"I mainly want to suggest that many of the arguments against psychedelics have as much validity, or the lack thereof, when aimed back toward organized religion. I heard a Zen master once lecture that if psychedelics provided true awakening or spiritual experience, one would not ever have to approach them again. This is a common point of view. I would ask why the same isn't said of the Zen cushion or approaching the Zen master or guru? Is wisdom and realization a destination we arrive at, or a constant journey in ever unfolding, changing possibility? If it is an ongoing process, a journey of constant vigilance, awakening and reawakening, then tune ups, from life, from teachers or plant friends are welcome along the way.

"Due to the current level of drug hysteria that tries to demonize and marginalize those who work with psychedelics, many yogis and yoga teachers are hesitant to speak publicly of their experiences. However, I've had the opportunity to have many scholars, teachers and leaders talk with me in depth about the benefits they've received through their use of entheogens and sacred plants. Some point out there are two different ways to use these allies—using psychonautical tools for the experience they offer in and of themselves, and also the use of these tools to open, enhance and deepen the dimensions of traditional practices. In other words, when potentiating the practice of meditation, *pranayama, asana, dance, massage, Thai Chi or other modalities with psychotropics, whole new worlds, depths, and perspectives can (open up) be made possible.*

"Once on a pilgrimage deep in the Amazon, I was invited to a Tea ceremony with a few elder maestros. At the peak of the session, galaxies (or jeweled visions) swirling around me, I was asked why, after years of meditation, self study, and yoga would I be interested in, or bother with, this strange brew. I replied that if a hundred people spent many years in yoga, prayer, chanting and meditation, there may be a few who have a profound mystical experience of oneness, the connection of all things, the immensity of life, the immeasurable. But on the other hand, if the same people, with good guidance and attitude, participated in some ayahuasca sessions there may be a few who don't have such a visionary experience. I added that after observing hundreds of people partaking of this sacrament, I witnessed only positive effects. Ayahuasca seems to have a beneficent guiding and forgiving wise presence...

"...Anyone intent and serious about exploring life, consciousness, and his or her own mind would want to be open to all the avenues available. The disciplines of yoga and meditation offer powerful pathways. Entheogens contribute some of the most potent means we have and offer the possibility to open the deepest levels of human consciousness. Visionary realms, internal microcosms, external macrospheres, and other realities or dimensions can be accessible. Whether the plant potions are a medicine or poison depends on personal discernment, intelligent and careful use, set and setting, and wise counsel." [228]

This passage is from an addendum to Ganga White's book, *Yoga Beyond Belief*, a book that has been very well received in the yoga world, not to mention by all of my students who have read it. The phrase *"beyond belief"* from the title is a direct translation of the Greek word "paradox." Initiation into deeper dimensions of spiritual life occurs in recognition of the paradoxical nature of all things. It is the understanding that every mere belief is limiting insofar as it stems from purely rational, linear, and fear-based thinking, as opposed to intuitive, experiential, holographic knowledge, or "gnosis." Gnosis is another Greek term and it is symbolized by the *ouroborus*, the image of the snake eating its own tail, as well as by the infinity symbol.

Even before ever ingesting any psychedelic, I had already begun to resonate deeply with the pathless path of paradox. There was actually a moment I can point to when I recognized that any thought that arose in my mind could be limiting, particularly if I clung to it. Reading Ganga White's *Yoga Beyond Belief*, meant a great deal to me. I looked to the author as an elder of the previous generation who was putting his reputation on the line to make a powerful statement on behalf of plant medicines. I see him very much in the tradition of Terence McKenna, who clearly was unafraid to speak his mind to the spiritual establishment.

Still, our open question returns: Which came first, divine revelation via fasting, prayer, and meditation, like Moses on Mt. Sinai; or did it come first through the ingestion of Soma, Manna, mushrooms, or any other of the myriad psychoactive flora that avail themselves in every region of the planet? And if one was the true and original method, is it correct to see the other as inferior or a degradation of the first?

There's another possibility to consider, too: Perhaps these seemingly dichotomous "paths" to the divine were both "mutually arising?" Meaning that they came into being and were discovered at the same time, with the purpose of serving different individuals with unique spiritual needs, just as they are doing today.

Whatever the answer to these profound questions is, it is clear from Ganga White's words that the use of plant sacraments is meant not as a replacement for traditional practices of posture, breathwork, and meditation, but as a very useful *complement* to them.

Gordon Sumner (Sting)

"I have never had a genuine religious experience. I say this with some regret. I have paid lip service to the idea, certainly, but a devastating, ego-destroying, ontological epiphany I simply have not had. More devout souls than I may have visited this realm through prayer, meditation, fasting, or from undergoing a near-death experience. Religious literature is full of such visionary claims, and while I've no reason to doubt their veracity, I would venture to say that such experiences are rare. For every St. Teresa, Ezekiel, or William Blake, there are millions like me with no direct experience of the transcendent, of the eternal, of the fathomless mystery at the root of all religious thought. But the ayahuasca has brought me close to something, something fearful and profound and deadly serious…

"…I may be out of my gourd, but I seem to be perceiving the world on a molecular level, where the normal barriers that separate 'me' from everything else have been removed, as if every leaf, every blade of grass, every nodding flower is reaching out, every insect calling to me, every star in the clear sky sending a direct beam of light to the top of my head. This sensation of connectedness is overwhelming. It's like floating in a buoyant limitless ocean of feeling that I can't really begin to describe unless I evoke the word love. Before this experience I would have used the word to separate what I love from everything I don't love—us not them, heroes from villains, friend from foe, everything in life separated and distinct like walled cities or hilltop fortresses jealously guarding their hoard of separateness. Now all is swamped in this tidal wave of energy which grounds the skies to the earth so that every particle of matter in and

around me is vibrant with significance. Everything around me seems in a state of grace and eternal. And strangest of all is that such grandiose philosophizing seems perfectly appropriate in this context, as if the spectacular visions have opened a doorway to another world of frankly cosmic possibilities."[229]

Sting is a musical genius, and his persona and music has served as a kind of teacher or "guru" for many over the past nearly 4 decades. From the moment the prepubescent me saw the video for the Police's "Don't Stand So Close to Me" in the early Eighties, I was in love with his music, and my respect for his genius has only grown over the years.

Sting's interest in yoga began just prior to mine, but his rock-star status had more impact on yoga's entré into mainstream culture. Particularly when, in the early 1990s, he stated that yoga enabled him to make love for eight hours straight!

The excerpts above are from Sting's recent book, *Broken Music: A Memoir*, and shed light on the profound effect that plant medicines like Ayahuasca can have, even on those who already have a spiritual orientation. Surely Sting's solo work from the Nineties onward must in part reflect his Ayahuasca experience and thus has subtly influenced many of us who were coming of age in the current Age of Ayahuasca:

"If you love someone, set them free…"

Danny Paradise

Question: "You consistently emphasize that it's unimportant to follow a guru. What are the reasons, why do yogis call for gurus anyway?"

Danny: "Having a 'Guru' may be from another age. Anyway one definition of 'Guru' is someone who lights your candle… but you hold it yourself!

This is the age of personal responsibility and personal reality leading to understanding of 'Universal Responsibility'. The teachings of Ashtanga Yoga are self-correcting and self-teaching once a person has taken a certain number of classes. Good teachers are looking to create total independence, freedom and Universality. If someone wants to have a group of disciples or followers then they are missing the point of the teachings of true Spiritual traditions and all Shamanic practices. Rather than creating independence they are trying to create dependence!

"Of course, we need teachers to help inspire us and pass on the details of ancient wisdom traditions and techniques safely and carefully. The original Yogis were anarchists, freedom thinkers, outside the regular order of life… and advisors to the Kings. Only later when the priest classes rose up did the idea appear that you needed a medium to connect to the Spirit and the Great Soul.

"In fact, the message of Yoga is "there's as many roads as there's soul's of men!" Each

individual creates their own way of communication with their soul and the Great Soul.

"Some people however, love to be followers and constantly be told what to do, think and feel. This is not the understanding I have of Yoga or the essence of true Spiritual teachings. A true teacher is not on a power or control trip but rather is looking to create as many masters as possible! Those that appear at their steps are led to a door and encouraged to enter!

Ultimately we are all teachers and students at the same time. We're all leaders in this age! Everyone has a responsibility to use their voice to create a better world!"

Danny Paradise is one of the world's most well-regarded yoga teachers and also a public advocate of shamanism and plant medicines. His words reflect the sentiment in certain yoga circles today that the time of the guru-disciple relationship is passing, or has passed. Of course, there are still gurus on the planet with thousands and perhaps even millions of followers, and this may go on unabated for a long time to come.

To take Mata Amritanandamayi, or Ammachi, "The Hugging Saint" as one example: Ammachi, who has millions of devotees, was largely responsible for my being attracted to yoga back in the mid-Nineties. Even when I began to have doubts about other teachers, I knew that I could still rely on Ammachi, who I felt was an avatar on the level of Jesus and Buddha. In recent years, I have followed major attempts to bring Ammachi down with fascination, and particularly that of ex-disciple Gail Tredwell's exposé, *Holy Hell*. But I also know that such claims will not affect the masses of people who follow her.

Speaking with some of Ammachi's devotees recently, I was told that she has been advising her followers not to do Ayahuasca. This accords with what I know about Ammachi as she also has tried to keep her flock from going to see certain other teachers. The essential message is to stick to one path, and one path only. If you want to reach water, dig just one deep well, not many shallow pits. It takes a great deal of faith in a teacher who gives this message, because of the possibility that they are afraid of losing their devotees.

David Swenson

Ashtanga Yoga teacher David Swenson on himself and his older brother Doug doing yoga in Texas in the early Seventies:

"We used to practice yoga out in a park... There were no yoga studios, there were no yoga clothes, there were very few yoga books... What yoga gave me was an inner strength that I don't know I would have had otherwise... there were a lot of drugs in the late Sixties and early Seventies... but until this day I've never done drugs in my life,

I've never had a drink—and I don't have anything against those things because those were the people I hung out with, they were the funnest people. But the yoga gave me something... we used to joke, we used to say that yoga gets me high."[230]

In 2000, I took a forty-hour Ashtanga Yoga course with David Swenson and found him to be a Master Teacher, a "guru" on the level of Dharma Mittra. Little by little, I was able to piece together Swenson's spiritual journey: Starting with his discovery of Ashtanga from David Williams, to his break with Pattabhi Jois to become, of all things, a Hare Krishna for a while! (He memorized the entire Bhagavad Gita!) Ultimately, after many years of practice, he reached his current status as one of the celebrities or "titans" of yoga. David is extremely disciplined about his practice. He told us that for years he practiced Ashtanga A, B, & C series! This wasn't just talk: His yoga demonstrations are clear evidence of this great discipline.

His words shed light on another element of his discipline, namely his determination not to drink or take drugs for his entire life. One could look at his life and say that maybe, just maybe, he had the best of both worlds—he was able to have a lot of fun and actually accomplish something that many aspire to accomplish.

Dennis McKenna, Ph.D.

"Plants and fungi make a large variety of so-called secondary molecules. There's an enormous chemical diversity of these secondary compounds, and they're not essential for life because they don't occur in all species. But in the species that do make them, they serve a function—and the function that they serve is basically a messenger function. In a sense, the secondary compounds are a language for the plants. It's the way that plants communicate with other organisms in their environments and maintain their relationships. In some cases the communication is quite simple. It can be something like a repellent, or a defensive compound. But when you're interacting with organisms that have complex nervous systems, it gets a little more interesting, a little more complicated, and I think that bottom line on the evolutionary scale is that these plants are teachers.

"This isn't really a scientific theory. It's more a personal belief, I suppose—but it's one that is verifiable to an extent. These plants are trying to teach our species about nature, and about how we fit into that. In some ways, you could say it's essentially a conduit to a community of species' mind. Or, if you subscribe to the idea that all of the species on the planet are organized into something like a conscious being, like Gaia, then these are the tools that let us communicate directly with Gaia, directly with that consciousness... Gaia, if you will, through these plants, through these substances that seem so close to our neural chemistry, is trying to tell us to wake up, to realize the

context in which we inhabit this ecology, and reorder our thinking accordingly. The message is that we're part of nature, and that we have to nurture nature. We have to be humble, and, as a species, we're not particularly humble. And we have to understand that we don't own nature, and nature is not there for us to exploit, deplete, and destroy. We have to rediscover a different attitude toward nature, a different way of looking at nature, and living in nature." [231]

Here's a view of plants not as spiritual teachers, per se, but as chemical messengers helping to insure the survival of all species on the planet. There is also a spiritual component to this, however, as McKenna is suggesting that plants can inspire an awareness of the web of life, the connectedness of all things.

Many who have ingested Ayahuasca in a group setting know the feeling of unity that occurs, the sense that there's only one being present in the circle. And in this context,, certain psychic abilities, or *siddhis*, do sometimes manifest themselves, telepathy being a primary one. This is how the shamans in the Amazon have communicated for ages, and it is why the scientific name for Ayahuasca is "telepathine."

Jerry Garcia

"In my life, all kinds of drugs have been useful to me, and they have also been a hindrance to me. As far as I'm concerned, the results are not in."

As fitting a summation of the whole shebang as any, I would say. That and: what a long, strange, and quite possibly enlightening trip it's been…

• • •

So, dear reader, where do you personally stand on the issues mentioned? What do you make of using plant medicines as a spiritual path, or for greater spiritual insight? If you side with those who say that psychedelics should never be used, then why? If you side with those who recommend their use, again, why? Or are you on the fence? Do you think it necessary to actually use a psychedelic substance to make a decision about whether it is helpful? Or is it wiser to rely on the wisdom of "gurus" who give clear counsel that enlightenment can only be permanently attained through the discipline of long-term yogic practice?

Postscript

Sai Baba Inspires a Devotee to Become an Ayahuasquero

A noteworthy synchronicity occurred during the writing of this book. I had been considering how to approach my students regarding the issue of gurus and their fall from grace in some segments of the American public's eye. Sathya Sai Baba came up, who at that time was arguably the most controversial spiritual figure alive (he died soon after). With an estimated ten to fifty million devotees worldwide, the South Indian teacher was either loved and adored as the greatest living Avatar on earth, or despised as the biggest fraud ever exposed on YouTube.

Before any of the allegations came out against him in the late 1990s, I had already read several books authored by Sai Baba devotees and was impressed by their accounts of him. The writing was thoughtful and the stories about this self-proclaimed incarnation of God (avatar) were mind-blowing.[232] Because my own avatar guru, the acclaimed Karunamayi, was from around the same region in South India, I could better appreciate Sai Baba's cultural context. It also helped to have visited both Karaunamayi and Sai Baba's ashrams, which helped me to note the similarities between them and understand the cultural context better.

Not long after my introduction to Sai Baba, the internet was abuzz with reports of sorcery, pedophilia, black magic, and faked materializations, all of which led many, including myself and even longtime Baba devotees, to have major doubts about this acclaimed "Godman."[233] For me, this precipitated a long period of deep questioning and soul-searching. "Perhaps he is a dark, demonic force seeking to delude the innocent?" I wondered. "Maybe all of these gurus are!" How could I truly know unless I got some outward sign, or inward confirmation, that Sai Baba is truly as he claims to be? Lacking that proof, I inevitably lapsed back into an agnostic, fatalistic position of, "Well, if the truth is meant to reveal itself to me regarding Sai Baba, it will."

Which brings us to the intense present moment of this writing, wherein I still don't claim to have any kind of answer, except to relate the following development: Recently while doing research for an image of a lotus, a link caught my eye. Clicking it, I was led to a tribute website created by a Sai Baba devotee. Presented in succinct form it is the best Sai Baba tribute I have ever seen. After reading it, I sent it on via email to my yoga teacher training students, asking them for their feedback. Here is the text of that email:

Hi Everyone,: I just came across a website I want to share with you, and the reason is because next month we will be reading "Autobiography of a Yogi," and a lot of the questions and issues that will come up with that book are to be found surrounding Sai Baba. Some say he is a fraud, others say he is the greatest Avatar (incarnation of God) alive today. In about 2000 I visited his ashram outside of Bangalore and stood in line for a good long time just to see him from afar. I really don't know what to make of all of this. I would love to hear your impressions...
http://www.saibaba-aclearview.com/

Not long after, I heard from my Peruvian friend, Liza. She described to me an incredible Ayahuasca ceremony with a trained Peruvian shaman she had recently participated in, saying I absolutely had to come to the next ceremony. She told me that this shaman is also very attached to the yoga tradition. And the shaman's newly married wife's guru lineage was the Swami Nityananda-Muktananda-Gurumayi lineage, the latter guru featured in the popular book and movie, "Eat, Pray, Love."

This was a double whammy for me. Muktananda received bad press after he died in 1982, kicked off by an exposé entitled "The Secret Life of Swami Muktananda,"[234] Scandal has also followed Muktananda's successor, Swami Chidvilasananda, known more popularly as Gurumayi. Even Ram Dass in his new book, *Be Love Now*, subtly criticizes the "spiritual materialism" of Muktananda and his lineage, writing,

"I felt there was an element of personal desire and a misuse of power."[235]

This is interesting because in his 1974 dharma talks at the Naropa Institute, Ram Dass had noted the display of wealth by Muktananda, but downplayed it by saying he understood it meant "nothing" to him.[236]

Clearly public opinion of Muktananda and SYDA Yoga has soured among segments of the yoga community. It's worth mentioning, too, that from early on, as open as I was to paths and teachers, I felt no attraction to the SYDA Yoga path and I took an agnostic stance in regard to Sai Baba.

My Peruvian friend Liza ended up organizing a ceremony for the Winter Solstice, Dec. 21st, 2010. And so there I was, suddenly having to confront my feelings head on regarding these gurus, and what it means to drink Ayahuasca with ceremonial offerings, mantras and prayers being made to them, just as I had done my own gurus so many years ago.

After imbibing my share of the first round of the brew, I felt no noticeable effect. I simply enjoyed just sitting in the lotus position listening and meditating to the beautiful *icaros,* or songs of the shaman, which he chanted in a rich, soothing baritone.

Because there were a few newcomers to our group, which often means a lighter dose is distributed, I half-expected the second round to again be mild. So I was somewhat surprised to find that upon downing the dark viscous liquid contained in a small shot glass size cup things really started to open up in my head.

Unfortunately, I can't say I was "pleasantly surprised," because the Ayahuasca experience for me is not exactly pleasurable. The words "awe-full," "terrifying," and "shocking" are more apt. I often refer to the Ayahuasca process as one of "shock and awe" and being "scared straight," in the sense that the brew often reveals grotesque, nightmarish scenarios, seemingly based on my current psycho-physical state. The brew seems to ask me: *"So... is this what you really want? Can you die with things where they stand right now?"* And the answer, for me at least, is always "No." I always feel as if I have unfinished business and invariably leave the Ayahuasca experience with a keener awareness of my "inner demons," even if I am not yet ready to vanquish them. I sense, though, as I did that night, that were I able to take the brew on a more consistent, intensive basis, I would make far greater progress in altering, or perhaps better, *forgiving*, certain unserviceable personal habits, and perhaps then my experience would not be quite so challenging.

After the closing of the ceremony, I spoke with the shaman with Liza translating into Español: The shaman actually spoke to this very issue, telling us how *madrecita*, the mother vine, or Ayahuasca, reveals something new each time, and it is never the same lesson. You can take it a thousand times, and he said he has, and still you will encounter fresh insights and revelations. He also said that true shamans, like true gurus, can be numbered on one's fingers (I recall once reading that Sai Baba said his true devotees could be counted on his fingers). I couldn't help but feel love and empathy towards this man. He was clearly a gentle, compassionate person, very down to earth and approachable. So, based on my nascent understanding of teachers, this man has impressed me as being a true shaman.

After awhile, I finally sensed it would be okay to ask this shaman how he became a Sai Baba devotee. He replied that many years ago he had gone to India to see Sai Baba and was granted an interview with him, a favor not easy to procure. Apparently, Sai Baba helped him get his life together and led him to the path of Ayahuasca Shamanism. He didn't elaborate further, and I didn't press him, though it seems doubtful that Sai Baba would have directly told him to take Ayahuasca. It most likely happened through synchronistic events.

As for the sensed synchronicity that informed the writing of this piece, perhaps you're wondering if I also feel that Sai Baba was somehow behind it? Well, if Sai Baba truly is a full incarnation of God, a Purna Avatar, then yes... otherwise, no.

I could write a volume on all the synchronicities I've noted over the years, with an entire chapter devoted to those connected with the writing of this book alone. These uncanny events never fail to impress me, but nor do I have any fixed beliefs as to what they truly mean.

But back to the main thread: So how did I feel about being part of a sacred ceremony where Sai Baba and Muktananda were worshiped? I really didn't mind as I remained open to the possibility that these gurus were truly legitimate. I also felt a great deal of respect for the husband and wife shamans, who may not be fully aware of all of this debate about what they do, and would be clearly unaffected by it, even if they knew. They've been touched and inspired by their teachers, and that's what is important, that they feel that their life has been improved from having that sacred connection.

As for the question, "Is the Guru Dead?" Clearly, from this one example, and many others I could proffer, the answer is emphatically "No." And a definitive "No" would also be the correct response to the question of whether psychedelics died with the Sixties. They obviously have not. Rather, it seems to be the case that these things go in cycles, with each new generation discovering one or the other, or both, anew again. We are approaching a time when there will again be greater respect and acceptance for these psychoactive substances, and along with that, driving it forward, will also be deeper understanding and wisdom regarding how to use them in a more enlightened and enlightening way…

• • •

This shaman's experience is interesting in that he was led *to* psychedelics as opposed to *away* from them like many of his generation. There are many current Sai Baba devotees who will attest that he inspired them to give up drugs of any kind. A good example is Maynard Ferguson, the jazz trumpeter, who was at Millbrook with Leary and Dr. Alpert in the Sixties, including the first day they all took LSD together. Subsequently Maynard Ferguson became a life-long devotee of Sai Baba.[237] Another example is Isaac Tigrett, founder of the Hard Rock Café who came to Sai Baba in the Sixties after years of hard drinking and drugs.[238]

A final and most notable example is the British academician and ex-Sai devotee, Robert Priddy and his acknowledged use of psychedelic drugs. Before leaving the Sai Baba organization, Priddy had posted several documents on the Web in which he spoke cautiously in favor of at least the initial insight into the mind and consciousness that substances like LSD can provide. Here is one relevant excerpt:

"Despite my involvement in a wide variety of practical jobs or activities before taking university education, my mind had continued increasingly to process everything according to mental attitudes and approaches gradually adopted from childhood

onwards. This became a 'mental burden,' something from which many who go through our over-conceptualized education suffer unknowingly. The mind was largely pre-programmed and often functioned as a reducing valve or advance filter, pre-forming and so distorting experience even before it had sunk in. 'It' did this even before the fullness of a perception had time to register properly, translating raw sensory facts into ideas so fast that I had lost sight of the gaps between ideas—or perhaps of the true links between percept and concept. In this way it is possible for the mind to become like a prison, working too independently of consciousness with a quasi-life of its own. Anyhow, I had come to construe the natural world of things and people too easily and was often unable to get directly involved with them.

"I discovered some of this ailment in myself by using the psychedelic agents cannabis and later, in a shockingly convincing and exhaustive way, with the chemical mind-altering (or mind-suspending) substance LSD-25, which showed me that there was a gap between perception and thought, and that re-opening it led to wonderful experiences of a much higher consciousness than anything previously encountered by me. A proper training in meditation might possibly have done the same more smoothly and securely, though doubtless only after many years of constant practice.[239]

Priddy goes on to describe a bit of that initial experience with LSD-25:

"For some few yet limitless hours I knew that a true, undying perfection and purity is within and that it is supra-personal. That it was covered over by the habitual activities of the mind was a certain insight of which I never really lost sight afterwards. In that living presence, that expansive present moment of translucency without beginning or end, I could not doubt that we all essentially are that pure awareness. Only temporarily are we alienated from our authentic nature, good and whole (even 'holy'), while lost to ourselves in the vast and bewildering realm of matter and mind, space and time.

"I hope that I shall never again have to undergo the intensity of sadness and inner pain that came when I had to return to the worldly sphere, sinking slowly down layer by layer into increasing forgetfulness of that immanent all-encompassing joyfulness! It was in a sense a rebirth, back to bodily constrictions and the material world, back to its old problems and to very much my same old self too. Still, there were marked differences, for a new basic trust and hope was engendered; a case of believing through seeing. Indeed, I think I appreciate how much more fortunate or talented they must be who can believe sufficiently to discipline their activities towards such realization without having had such proofs."[240]

Yet over time, Priddy began to see the limits and potential pitfalls of psychedelics like LSD-25:

"After some years I did occasionally try various strong bio-chemicals and also

LSD-25 again with varying results, both hellish and heavenly. I did not become ad-dicted, the experience being so powerful as to have a most subtle, long-term draining effect on my spirits. There was also the growing realization that the results were less inspiring as time went on and progress towards making such awareness permanent was not noticeable.

"On one occasion the effect of LSD-25 on me was extremely unpleasant in-deed for the larger part of the 8 hours. Instead of finding any clarification of per-ception, I was plunged into a whirlpool of eternal repetition from which all things seemed infinitely hopeless and without rhyme or reason of any sort. There seemed to be no hope of escape, a very terrible condition indeed! This lasted "for ever"... ex-cept that I recovered and found that about six hours had passed. For anyone who is trapped in that sort of sphere (definitely qualifying as one of the hells that make up the lower spheres of existence in Eastern spiritual pantheons) I must say that sui-cide must sooner or later become attractive. Fortunately, the episode ended well..."
Priddy's final word on the subject seems to be one of very cautious support:

"Though this particular biochemical eventually gave many people such glimpses or 'trips' into the realm behind the cosmic illusion known as maya in Vedantic thought, its effect most evidently differs in clarity and scope (depending on the person and many variable circumstances) and is always short-term. After eight to twelve hours one was 'back to normal reality,' however much one disbelieved in its ultimacy or remembered that it is but a troubled dream of impermanent nature.

"There were also those who were unfortunate and spent their time only in an inner hell and often failed to return to reality for some time. Seldom that this was, some very few persons found themselves in mental wards and a handful of them never came to themselves again, while in a few others it reportedly released states of psychosis, depression and intense paranoia during which some even committed suicide. On the other hand, most reliable reports from most highly-reputable clinics document many wonderful cures from the most ingrained and otherwise incurable obsessions and paranoias..."

"Because physically-induced expansion of consciousness can only be temporary and can often lead to an unbalanced life in disturbing the step-by-step progress of per-sonal development and spiritual growth, it is neither advocated by most psychologists nor spiritual teachers. Such expansions of awareness can only eventually be consolidat-ed through gradual evolution of the psyche by controlled moral and mental discipline in living. Results cannot be expected without long and sustained efforts that always require the greatest patience. The use of bio-chemicals like LSD-25 to alter conscious-ness is like reaching for 'plastic grapes.' They do not allay one's hunger. They can also

create an illusion of knowledge and power and that can be harmful...

"That striving for the experience of higher consciousness by both artificial and 'natural' means is well illumined in Indian religious lore. Even the attempt to attain such super-consciousness and the powers inherent in them is fraught with real dangers unless one has a perfectly-realized master who has trodden all the ways in advance. It is also advised against as being a selfish aim; putting one's own liberated happiness before that of the world, which inevitably also eventually works against oneself.

"However one may classify the type of consciousness that arises, and by whatever means or techniques it is reached, it can not be more than a preview of what can be fully attained only by living a pure, devoted life. Though bio-chemicals did not give a short-cut onto the heavenly highway, they did sometimes allow a brief crossing of that highway. My egoism was not removed nor my soul purified, yet I certainly was torn out of the cloud of self-oriented unknowing that afflicted me before."

This is fascinating on a number of levels: A highly trained academician who found the use of LSD-25 very useful in understanding his own mind, and going beyond it to the place of "pure awareness." But his continued explorations led him to the realization that there was a limit to what could be received from such substances, and a dark disturbing underbelly to the experiences they engendered.

Such considerations eventually led Priddy to the "perfectly-realized master," Sai Baba. Priddy no doubt felt Sai Baba would lead him to those same profound states of consciousness he had attained via LSD-25, but in a much more gradual way, much as Ram Dass did Neem Karoli Baba. But ultimately, after two decades of devotion to Sai Baba, Dr. Priddy parted ways with him, turning into one of his fiercest critics.

Which all leads me to wonder if Priddy's view of psychedelics has subsequently changed. Does he still feel that psychedelics cannot themselves lead one to enlightenment? And does he still avow that only a true master can lead a spiritual seeker to enlightenment?

Is the Ayahuasca experience different than that produced by LSD? Did Sai Baba really lead our Peruvian shaman to the jungle brew? If so, could this be a clue to its widening use in spiritual circles?

One other rising world spiritual teacher is worth mentioning here: Sri Prem Baba. Sri Prem Baba, whose followers believe him to be an enlightened master, used Ayahuasca in the Santo Daime church in his homeland of Brazil. He has also overseen Ayahuasca ceremonies for his followers on his teaching tours across the globe. Most interesting for us, Sri Prem Baba's own spiritual path brought him into deep connection with Sathya Sai Baba, who became a guide and inspiration on his path.[241]

• • •

Things became even more interesting when I returned for my second Ayahuasca ceremony with the husband and wife shaman team. Before the ceremony began, the shaman's wife told me that in a ceremony the previous night Baba Muktananda had come to her in a vision and whispered in her ear this succinct message:

"*Ayahuasca has the same properties as Soma.*"

Admittedly, she knew I was writing the book in your hands, which raises that as a question, but she told me she was not thinking about that at all. Well, I certainly have had many visions with Ayahuasca that come completely unbidden from God knows where, so it's not that unlikely that her vision could have occurred. On the other hand, if Ayahuasca visions well up from our unconscious as they do in the dream state, then they can be influenced by other information we store there, such as events, impressions, and wishes from waking life. The shaman's wife, who clearly had some investment in Ayahuasca being a part of the yoga tradition, might have wished that vision into being.

The ceremony that night was considerably easier than the first. I felt an even stronger bond to this beautiful husband and wife team. This was reinforced after the ceremony when the husband, beaming, sat down in front of me to help me with my "*libro.*" He proceeded to tell me, in Español with another participant translating, that there were many very interesting characteristics about "*Somalata,*" which is Soma's full Vedic appellation.

Among the things this Shaman told me were:

◎ That *Somalata* and Ayahuasca are plant "cousins."

◎ That the knowledge of Soma has been lost in India, and is now solely to be found in the Amazon region.

◎ That Soma was used in Atlantis and Lemuria and was an important part of the spiritual culture of those ancient advanced civilizations.

The overall message I got from these shamans was that the use of Ayahuasca is a legitimate yoga practice with a long ancestry and the blessing of some of the most influential gurus of our time.

Still, though I felt much love for these shamans, and I felt that love returned, I still had lingering doubts about the use of psychedelics within yoga practice. Maybe I now simply knew too much about the other side of the debate to believe what they were saying with 100% faith.

12

Contemporary Guidance for the Perplexed

Yoga, Psychedelics and Global Healing

Liana's Iboga Report: "Love Holds the Universe Together"

In 2010, a close friend connected me with an Iboga Shaman from Gabon, West Africa. Iboga is the time-honored plant medicine originating from Africa. It is illegal to use in the United States, but legal in Canada and South America, where it has proven very effective in breaking addictions to hard drugs such as heroin, as well as pharmaceuticals.

Initially, my friend was enthralled by this shaman. She even traveled to Costa Rica to take Iboga journeys with him for her insomnia. Later she brought him to Florida to speak to our local tribe about his spiritual work. Some of my yoga students, including Liana, were present at that meeting. All were charmed by the shaman, including me. So when I was offered the opportunity to return with him to Costa Rica and experience a traditional Iboga healing ceremony, I was all in.

My iboga experience was fascinating and I am grateful for the opportunity to have had it. But I also felt that what I experienced was not as advertised. Without going into detail here, I was under the impression that during the journey I would enter the "spirit world," meet my ancestors and be able to speak with them and ask questions. This did not happen. What did happen, and quite fascinatingly so, was that I did see pictures of my immediate family, including my maternal grandmother, flashing on a kind of internal silver movie screen. This was only after I went through a *cartoon clown world* in which I received the darshan of Ronald McDonald and Michael Jackson!

But perhaps the most remarkable and telling event that night was that in the midst of giving me more Iboga wood to assist me in purging, the shaman suddenly asked me how this experience compared with Ayahuasca. I sensed he felt threatened by the Amazonian plant medicine, which he had never tried and I sensed never would due to his allegiance to Iboga, but still I told him my truth: I felt I had gotten more from my Ayahuasca journeys.

From that moment on, our relationship was never the same. And I was not too surprised when, not too long after this, a vendetta against this shaman started for sex-related indiscretions, and my friend was very much a part of the attempt to bring him down. Her initial near deification of this shaman had now turned to intense dislike, partly because he had also propositioned her in the midst of her own healing retreat.

My point is not to disparage this shaman. I have come to realize that we are all on our own healing journey, including myself. Jesus's words continually ring true for me: Let him who is without sin should cast the first stone.

But we do need to realize that in the spiritual community there are self-styled gurus, teachers, masters and shamans of all kinds teaching their own path to enlightenment, perhaps often without being fully enlightened themselves. Because of this there will always be fallings in and fallings out between teachers and students due to their perceived failings.

Ultimately, as we will see from Liana's story, it may be that the plants themselves and our own intuition may well be the best teachers. So without further ado, here is Liana's remarkable story of the healing power of plant medicine:

When my Yoga teacher told me about a plant that was helping people with addictions, my heart leapt. Would I finally be able to get off the prescribed medications that I had been on for 20 years? I had a physical injury in my late teens and was in chronic, unrelenting pain at 20. After a month of this new awful sensation, I sobbed before I got out of the car in my driveway and wondered how people could live like this. I was in my second year of college studying mysticism and psychology. One day I went for a walk on the beach and my left arm went completely numb as the pain in my shoulder and arm increased. I began the long search to find relief. I saw a Chiropractor who seemed to help only a bit. Months into his treatment, he told me I was a discouraging patient because I never got better! Why couldn't I "get better" like other people? And I was too young to be so disabled!

After college, I had to give up an art and teaching career, though I had an amazing opportunity dropped in my lap. I found some relief with a different chiropractor, rolfing and the cozy warmth of marriage and having babies. I had to hire a housekeeper and could not carry my own children. I cuddled and nursed, lying down and on the floor and taught them to climb on me carefully. I could not lift a grocery bag, scrub pots and pans and even the slightest wrong movement could increase the pain for hours. I prided myself on how I was able to remain a positive person in spite of my left shoulder and did get better for a few years. I tried to give my children and husband my all, but remained compromised.

During a stressful divorce, the pain returned with a vengeance and I could not sleep due to the intense physical pain. My last awareness at night and my first in the morning was the pain in my shoulder.

When my second child weaned herself, my doctor put me on Amlitriptaline and I remained on it for several years before being switched to Klonipin, Carasoprodal and Trazadone—a cocktail of pills every night to guarantee dead, dreamless sleep. As a single mother in a heart breaking post-divorce situation, pharmaceuticals seemed the only way I could function. I studied many forms of physical, psychological and spiritual healing with many improvements mentally but not physically. It was embarrassing to be an herbalist immersed in the natural world, holistic health and organic farming, who couldn't figure out how to sleep. I tried cutting down the dosages but that left me sleepless, exhausted and in more pain than ever.

The remarkable plant that made it possible for me to become free of long-term prescription drug use is called Iboga. I learned that heroin addicts, alcoholics and prescription drug users alike have all had encouraging results from this little known psychotropic plant. Iboga is illegal in the States but used successfully in Canada, South America and Europe. As a young woman during the 70's the intensity of my life led me to part ways with my friends who were regularly tripping on LSD and mushrooms. However, taking a plant medicine 40 years later for a dependence on drugs made perfect sense to me.

I met the West African Shaman in Florida and decided to fly to Costa Rica for treatment. It was to be 2 weeks at The Retreat House taking the plant medicine twice. The Shaman said that the Iboga soothes the receptor cells that are "addicted" to a substance and makes withdrawal easier with no shakes or DDT's. I had been unsuccessful in titrating off of the medications for years and this seemed to be an extreme but possibly life changing experience. I had high hopes this would do the trick. The second night one other woman and I were to do the Iboga Ceremony while about 10 other people and the Shaman supported, sang and meditated with us. There was a staff of 3-4 helpers who were to check on us and administer to our every need during the Ceremony and the rest of the night and next day.

The drums and singing began, the Shaman performed invocations in his native West African language and gave us our first spoonful of powdered Iboga. It tasted like powdered wood with chunks of charcoal. It was so dry, I had to drink some of the Iboga tea just to swallow it. As I chewed, it numbed my mouth. I heard my late *father's sarcastic voice, "Well, only you would find a Shaman in some exotic place, trav-el thousands of miles, spend a heap of money, to give you a dirty, foul tasting root to help you do something completely unnecessary in the first place: after all these were perfectly reasonable prescriptions to manage a real medical problem." But I knew that my recurring nightmares were exacerbated by the pills, and that the dull, heavy feeling that I awoke with each morning was continued avoidance of the root causes of my problems. For twenty long years, I lived with chronic physical pain, trauma, PMS and suicidal ideology. Knocking myself out with a handful of muscle relaxants, antispas-modics and sleep inducing anti-depressants each night was only a partial solution. Now I was on a quest to discover how to soothe and perhaps even heal both my fraz-zled nervous system and shoulder/neck injury.*

As I chewed the second teaspoon, which took 10 minutes I remembered one of the most important life skills I've ever learned, continuous connected breathing. I began conscious, full inhalations. Hidden terror peaked out of the corners and stood next to the great courage it had taken to be there. The breath practice helped calm me and laid the groundwork to have a remarkable and astounding "journey" all night long and into the next day. After vomiting a bit into a handy pail brought exactly at the right moment I was put on a bed with blankets and the pictures began. The Shaman came around and tried guiding me but I knew better what I needed. Years of psychotherapy and eco-spirituality studies paid off tremendously that night. I meant no offense to the well-meaning Shaman in my wordless state but took off on my own for an adventure of a lifetime.

Every sense was magnified and I felt as though my awareness was penetrating deep inside my being like never before. I was lifted up into an infinite sky and saw in great detail an enormous web of life. Plants, animals, people, countries, forests, oceans, centuries of teeming life, young, old, every human accomplishment and contradiction possible and my own death moment, were all in a Technicolor experience of motion, sensing and vision. An unshakable certainty of the existence of God came over me. There was no question, no nagging doubt about the nature of reality. All the spiritual books and teachings I'd immersed myself in for decades were true! There is no way I can describe the sense of peace and joy that flooded me at that moment. There was no such thing as a fearful idea or experience. Even my own death, revisited several times during the night was smooth, matter of fact, easy and natural.

An endless river of incarnating consciousness flowed all around me. I saw many of my own lifetimes and the lifetimes of other's whom I've known in this life. It was utterly fascinating as the visceral sensation of flying though time and space magically showed me a vast, multi-dimensional cornucopia of form and spirit.

Love really was what held the whole Universe together! It was almost overwhelming, but in this grand movie there was only room for deep understanding, wisdom and knowledge. I was being held gently by an invisible, benevolent force while I witnessed the sheer volume and beauty of life in the Cosmos. Sometime in the evening, minutes or hours later, I was brought to my own bed and the journey continued for the rest of the night. Michael and Luna took great care of me, checking me to see if I wanted water or needed to get up and pee.

A marvelous feeling of pure happiness filled me as the dawn broke over the mountains the next day. When I decided to get up and try to walk the Shaman was surprised. Everyone was watching and smiling when I told them of the wonders I'd experienced. I could see that my state was energizing others around me. Great conversations and walks under the Carob Trees followed for the rest of the days even though the Shaman's shortcomings caused me to leave the Retreat a week early, but that is another story. Suffice it to say I was in a clear and new place internally that enabled me to learn how to sleep naturally again. I could actually feel the cells of my body vibrating in a different way and that first day off of the medications I took a nap in the hammock in broad daylight, which for me was unheard of. I was reveling in a profound sense of safety and relaxation. The vestiges of traumatic past events were somehow soothed with a comforting, non-physical balm of unknown origin.

Though I met many challenges when I returned to my life in Massachusetts, I was changed fundamentally. Never again did that all too familiar hysteria rear its frightening head and threaten my entire existence. I felt myself sinking at times but never all the way to what I called my bottomless pit of despair. I remembered my Iboga Journey many, many times over the course of the next few years. And the most surprising thing was that I wasn't in more pain without the prescription drugs, and emotionally I could handle my broad range of emotions with a newfound grace. I could sleep sometimes 6 to 8 hrs at a time. When I awoke in the night I did Yoga and could fall back asleep. This was nothing short of a miracle and the freedom I felt was glorious. I was able to bear meditating, full breathing and exploring my inner nature for the first time on a regular basis. I had a tangible sense that I was connected to everybody and everything, and that I mattered. The Iboga experience had powerfully affirmed my hope that love in all its wondrous expressions is our ultimate reality and purpose. Extraordinary healing and fundamental personal change was not only attainable, but lasting. I feel great gratitude for all the healing plants of the World and what they do for humanity.

Amazing, right? What is most remarkable about Liana's experience is that not only did her plant medicine experience help her to finally sleep, but that the effects and impact of her experience were *long-lasting*. It is also pertinent to note how *deep breathing*, just as we practice in *yoga*, was such an important aid in the safe and comfortable navigation of her Iboga journey. Clearly this experience was crucial in Liana's healing journey, helping to restore her connection to the divine, affirming for her the knowing that Love is behind it all.

Mushroom Medicine: The Story of Elena

During the summer of 2002, a student at the University of Florida went inner-tubing down a river with some of her friends just north of Gainesville. Somehow the current carried the young woman far beyond her companions, and getting concerned, she jumped out of the rushing current to look for the path to take her back. Instead of the trail, she found herself beside a cow pasture enclosed by a fence. On impulse, she jumped the fence to discover the pasture was covered with brownish-beige mushrooms. These appeared to be the psilocybin mushrooms that she had heard people say grew in that area. She had been told to look for a dark spore print underneath the mushrooms and upon identifying it, she decided to try one right then and there. This even though she had never eaten a magic mushroom before. After tasting one, she looked for something to carry a bunch back to her friends, and finding an old piece of plastic bag, she filled it, and made it back to the group.

Back again with her group, she handed out the magic edibles to friends and strangers alike. Everyone was appreciative. In the car on the way back to Gainesville, the mushrooms started to kick in, but they didn't really get going until Elena got back. Mushrooms can take up to two hours to take effect. Elena had eaten 3 fresh mushrooms of various sizes, which is a sizable dosage for a first time user, and over the next several hours a few memorable things that happened:

First there were the moving walls and the colors around people, which Elena took to be their auras. Next, Elena noticed that she felt a greater empathy towards people, and felt like she could understand the feelings of others as if they were her own. For example, there was another young woman, an acquaintance from school, who had not taken the mushrooms. Elena saw that she was crying about someone, another young woman, and to verify this was so she asked her, "Why are you crying?" The only thing was, though, the girl wasn't crying, and she wondered what Elena was talking about. As they shared, it came out that Elena's feeling was correct: The young woman had been in turmoil about her sister. Even though she wasn't crying, that was how she was feeling.

The reader should understand that this is not something that Elena would normally say to someone, particularly because she typically felt more inhibited.

Towards the end of her first mushroom experience, Elena locked herself in the bathroom for at least an hour, gazing in the mirror. As she tells it now, she was having an identity crisis. Although this was strange for her at the time, she ultimately took it as a positive development.

After the effects of the mushrooms wore off, Elena felt cleansed. She had been on the Benzodiazepene, Librium, for a year prescribed to her by her psychiatrist who was helping her deal with the suicide of her boyfriend. Now she felt that all of the drugs she had been taking had been a "waste of time," and she had lost years of her life. She remembers thinking very clearly at that point, "This [the mushrooms] is the only medicine I need, and this is the only thing that's helping me." She concluded that they were "lots more effective and less dangerous" than the pharmaceuticals.

And there were other beneficial side effects, too: The mushrooms permanently changed her eating habits from a meat to a largely raw food diet, which she feels has made her healthier. Elena also feels that, far from killing brain cells, mushrooms increase her brain function and learning capacity. She regularly takes them as an "herbal supplement" to help study for her exams. And she is saying this from the experienced perspective of having taken mushrooms up to one hundred times. Even a "bad trip, Elena was able to view in a positive light.

Still, she didn't go off her prescription meds right away or stop seeing the doctor, because at the tender age of 19, these were still more available to her than mushrooms.

Elena had gotten into chemistry prior to her mushroom excursion. Her boyfriend who committed suicide had a Ph.D. in Chemistry and had been a mentor to her. When he died, she had stayed away from chemistry because of the association. But now her interest was re-awakened and she returned to it, specializing in botany, entomology and mycology. Also, whereas before Elena's inclination and training had been towards the scientific and skeptical, after her mushroom experience she became much more open to the spiritual. As she told me:

"They did open a lot of doors. I had been very scientific before. I would say, 'There is no God, how can there be?' There's still a little bit of that in my thinking, but after taking these things, I do feel that there is a soul."

And while Elena had been interested in Yoga before, she could now more deeply appreciate the spiritual and therapeutic value of Yoga, seeing it as providing many of the same benefits as psychedelics, but on a lower level. She also notes how the psychedelic experience can be made even more powerful through using yogic techniques such as chanting. She finds that while on mushrooms, her body is more supple and naturally wants to move and do yoga postures. In Elena's experience, then, the two disciplines, yoga and plant medicine, complement and reinforce each other.

So this was Elena's story, as she reported it to me. I first had the pleasure of meeting Elena in the fall of 2007 when she showed up in my yoga class one evening at a local Wellness center. I immediately could sense her eagerness to engage with yoga more deeply, especially when I mentioned that I was about to start a Yoga Training Program. Elena ultimately joined the program, though making no mention of any of the above until a year into the Yoga Teacher Training.

Once I heard her story, I recognized that Elena's tale is reflective of the resurgence of interest in psychedelics that's happening currently. It's also a prime example of the remedial, "self-medicating" function that both *yoga and psychedelics* are playing in contemporary Western culture. Elena and Liana's stories of healing will resonate with many. They demonstrate that while psychedelics may not be the "be all and end all" of spirituality, they are capable, at the very least, of providing temporary relief and insight on the journey of life.

Ayahuasca Yoga: Padmani's Experience

Again, Elena's story is not so uncommon these days; some version of it is happening all over the globe, to young and old, men and women, and perhaps with more and more frequency. This is due in large part to the Internet, of course, yet also because there are those in spiritual sub-cultures, like the yoga community, who have begun to take deep interest in psychedelic substances as a result of their yoga practice and commitment to inner exploration.

To see this at work, let's look at another story, this one of a 30-something yogini, Padmani, a lawyer and yoga professional based in Toronto, who, unlike Elena but very much like myself, was initially quite reluctant to try a psychedelic because of understandable concern for her well-being and her yoga practice. In an essay that was originally published on Daniel Pinchbeck's Reality Sandwich website, Padmani revealed the following:

As a longtime proponent of the whole yogic lifestyle thing (no meat, alcohol, caffeine, or late nights for me, thank you) I was initially reluctant to participate in the ayahuasca ceremony, despite the Amazonian tea's reputation as a sacred plant medicine of the highest order. Like many, I had heard horror stories about violent Ayahuasca-induced purges, and on a practical level, I wondered how I would do my morning yoga practice if the all-night affair left me nauseated, weak, and sore. I also had lingering concerns that the psychoactive brew could somehow undo years of disciplined practice and virtuous living, destabilizing my physical and energetic bodies, not to mention what it might do to my calm mind.

Hello yoga people—is this you? I can certainly relate to Padmani's words. A lot of us who were attracted to yoga in the first place were pulled in by the "clean living" lifestyle, which has been heavily promoted at least since Swami Satchidananda told the flower children in the Sixties that yoga could give them a "natural high." Personally, I never wanted to do anything that would harm my body in any way, and it was that conservative concern (some would say "obsession") which enabled me to achieve a certain degree of proficiency in the postures and ability to sit quietly in meditation. Like Padmani, though, I was ultimately drawn in both by curiosity and desire for deeper experience. As Padmani goes on to relate,

"Though curious, I waited almost five years before I agreed to experience ayahuasca for the first time. The change of heart came after a meeting with an internationally-renowned yoga teacher who drew a strong parallel between ayahuasca and the mythical ritual drink Soma, which is described in the Rigveda as nothing less than the nectar of immortality: 'We have drunk Soma and become immortal; we have attained the light, the Gods discovered' (8.48.3, as translated by R.T.H. Griffith). 'Well,' I thought, 'if it's good enough for the Gods, enlightened beings and celebrity yoga teachers..."[242]

Unlike Elena, then, Padmani came to plant medicine via yoga, not the other way around. I, too, would have never dreamed of doing what Elena did prior to becoming better grounded in yoga practice. I don't know if I was truly ready for psychedelics when I was in my twenties (and early thirties); even though the desire had been there, the drugs had not been, leading me to think that the Universe and my guiding angels or whatever were watching out for me, making sure I didn't do anything that would not be in my highest interest. Perhaps the way that happened was through the egoic defense of fear/anxiety about my body; certainly I prized being "in control" at all times, and to mess with my brain unnecessarily was a very scary proposition, so those fears had to be allayed—in both my and Padmani's case, it was through it being commended to us by someone we respected (in my case, Ganga White; in Padmani's, I was to later surmise, Danny Paradise). As with most fears, giving up our fear led to some incredibly enriching and healing experiences.

I wonder if Elena's case is more the exception than the rule these days—whether most contemporary yoga people get into psychedelics after being involved with yoga, as opposed to the other way around as it was in the Sixties (Ram Dass is a prime example). My sense is the former, but this would have to be studied. Clearly this book is primarily an offering to those who have explored yoga and would like to go deeper, but it is also certainly for those who have experimented with psychedelics and would like to know how yoga practice (or related disciplines) can assist and support the psychedelic experience.

Certainly Padmani's yoga background was important both for navigating her ayahuasca experiences, and also for understanding some of the deeper lessons she was being shown. In her Reality Sandwich essay, she goes into some detail about these experiences, beginning with an almost unbelievable story about how she learned a lesson from a praying mantis! As Padmani relates:

The praying mantis yoga lesson was the first of many yogic teachings that have come to me in ceremony. Sometimes the ayahuasca makes me move around, mostly wild inversions and heart-blossoming backbends, and sometimes it puts me into deep states of meditation where my breath all but disappears into the stillness of my being. Even the dreaded purges feel good and cleansing in a way, not so different from the seemingly strange purification practices prescribed in the ancient yoga manual, the Hatha Yoga Pradipika ["Light on Hatha Yoga," a text from the 14th Century, attributed to Yogi Swatmarama ~ author's note].

Most significantly, I was initiated into the practice of Nada Yoga (the yoga of sound) during a ceremony. It happened when I began to perceive what yogis call the inner music, the primal sound signified by OM, which came at first in a dazzling symphony of clanging bells, snare drums, and cosmic sitars. During that same night, the hinge joint of my jaw popped wide open and music and poetry flowed unstoppably from my mouth for several hours. The telepathic message I received (this time from a cheering chorus of insects and amphibians) was that, as a yogi, I have an obligation to literally open my mouth wider and speak out on behalf of those who can't."

As I said, having a heritage like yoga to help make some sense of the psychedelic experience can be very helpful, not to mention comforting, for one feels grounded in and connected to an ancient technology of transformation, and can draw upon the insights of the tradition. It's very interesting to note that in addition to the purification practices Padmani experienced, the "Nada Yoga" into which she was initiated also seems very similar to what is described in the *Hatha Yoga Pradipika*, a classic treatise on the subject. Could it be that Padmani was re-discovering things she had learned in a previous lifetime? Drawing on a point by Rajneesh (Osho) from a previous chapter, it seems important to point out that these experiences could to some degree be the result of one's psychological set going into the experience, whether conscious or subconscious.

Whatever the case may be, it's clear that Padmani's Yoga background not only helped provide a comforting context for her "Nada Yoga" experience, but it also provided her with "tools" in the form of asanas to help move the energy that was coursing through her. In turn, ayahuasca shed light on the *asanas* themselves, showing Padmani how the original yogis learned directly from nature.

"Ayahuasca took my yoga off the mat and made my practice practical. At one time, I did poses such as locust, scorpion, cobra, dog, and tree without thinking too much

about their correlates in the natural world; they were little more than exercises with fanciful names. Now it seems obvious that before there were yoga studios, designer yoga-wear lines and sticky mats, the yogis took their teachings from nature. The first yoga teachers were the plants and animals—and yes, the insects, too. They say the practice of yoga is directly informed by nature. Now I finally get on a cellular level why yogis have such a close friendship with the earth: because we're not separate from her."

Indeed. And I would ask (rhetorically): Isn't an experiential insight like this invaluable? Especially for the yogi/ni who is interested in a radical search for the roots of things, who feels a passionate calling to explore the nature of reality and consciousness…?

I would take Padmani's insight a bit further and suggest that it's not just that the yogis were great observers of the natural world, yet further, that through their ability to achieve oneness with nature, they were able to tap into the cosmic energy that made a cobra a cobra, a dog a dog, etc., and through that BECOME THAT. In other words, in deep states of meditation (or through the use of psychedelics), they would actually become the animal itself, thus truly learning how it felt to be that creature.

However it all happened, we might at least just take pause and wonder that both Elena and Padmani reported that the energy of the plant ingested moved/inspired them to perform yoga postures, and that this was felt to be of benefit to their bodies and their yoga practice. This is not uncommon. I myself have experienced this and also witnessed it on numerous occasions in the context of sacred plant ceremony. Another of my contacts, Krystle, has also experienced something similar with psychedelics; not yoga postures per se, but *mudras* (hand gestures) and *mantras* (toning of sacred sounds). Let's consider her story next.

Krystle Cole : Empathic Entheogenic Guide

I first "met" Krystle by way of her YouTube "" videos. I had been researching MDMA in preparation for my first experience and found her video on the subject to be very helpful. I appreciated Krystle's openness and realness, and over the course of this past year I've watched all of her many videos dealing with different aspects of the entheogenic experience.

More recently, I became a member on her NeuroSoup website www.neurosoup. com, which gave me access to her book "Lysergic," dealing in large part with her adventures with psychedelic renegade Todd Skinner, who was ultimately incarcerated for producing vast amounts of LSD in an abandoned grain silo in Kansas. It's a fascinating first person account of romance, intrigue, the effects of various kinds of psychedelics, and how their use can lead to antinomian behavior.

There were several things in particular that I wanted to hear Krystle elaborate upon. For one, she mentioned how on some psychedelics she would begin chanting mantras and performing mudras that she had never consciously learned (see also Yogi Zen's story in the chapter on Kundalini). This was something I had first witnessed in the context of the Kundalini Yoga group I had been in and was also amazed to discover that psychedelics could produce similar effects. I was also interested to learn more about how Krystle had discovered how to initiate a psychedelic experience without actually taking anything.

Krystle graciously granted me an email interview, and what follows is our correspondence, complete and unedited…

Author: Have you made any kind of formal study of Yoga since getting into all this? Or, have you read any books in particular on the subject? If so, which ones? What have you gleaned from them that has been especially useful to you? I ask this in particular because you've written of how you've done mudras while under the influence, as well as the power of mantra/chanting.

KC: *I have not had any formal yoga training other than taking a few yoga exercise classes. I have read a few books about mantras, mudras, etc. I have also done my research on the subject. To be honest, most of what I know about it is what I have learned through my experiences. There's very little written on the subject and that is why I feel as if I should speak about my experiences with it.*

When I read about the ayahuasqueros and how they would sing ayahuasca songs during their experiences it meant a lot to me. I especially took to heart the experiences I read about where they learned songs that the plants taught to them. The songs, to the outside observer, would seem like they were from another language or the person that was singing would sound like they were speaking in tongues. This is exactly what happened to me. We have discussed this topic at length on the NeuroSoup forum. [Krystle then quoted a long piece she had posted on the NS forum, which you can read either there or on my website.]

I was also very interested to hear more about Krystle's perspective on gurus, as I noted she seemed to feel they were unnecessary. I had always heard the party line that "you need a guru, you need a guide on the spiritual path, don't try to go it alone, it's too dangerous." Yet more recently I was feeling that not only are there exceptions for every rule, but perhaps this particular rule was also another trap to keep one in fear, guilt, and lifelong servitude.

Author: Are there any spiritual teachers who you are especially fond of, or from whom you have learned something? Who are they? Todd wrote to you, "Be careful of Guru systems." Have you found any Gurus appealing to you? Why or why not?

KC: *I don't believe that people need spiritual teachers. I believe that we can learn anything that we need to through self-exploration. If you are a god, then why do you need someone else to show you what god is?*

First off, I would like to explain that I believe that I have felt what death is like during many of my entheogenic journeys. Death is a transition, nothing more and nothing less. When we die, we go back to the one mind that we all share and we no longer perceive the self unto which we currently cling. Death can be sad because you say must goodbye to many of the sensations and feelings of this life. At the same time, death can be happy because you are no longer trapped by the senses. You are free and most of all you are timelessly and infinitely whole once again.

Wise words. I've noted that some of the old timers (like Alex Grey), as well as a number of the new researchers of plant medicines, like Krystle (and Martin Ball, below) prefer the term "entheogen" to "psychedelic," so I asked Krystle about her word choice…

Author: Do you like the term "psychedelics"? Or, why do you prefer the term "entheogens" more? Is there an even better word to describe what these substances are and do, or are all labels too limiting?

KC: *I prefer the term "entheogens" because of its spiritual connotation.*

While there are moments when I am in total agreement with this sentiment, from a research and philosophical standpoint I do feel it's begging the question to say that these substances show us God, or give us access to Spirit. Terence McKenna wouldn't go that far, remember. And Meher Baba held that LSD, contrary to popular opinion, had no spiritual saving grace whatsoever. At the most, I would suggest they can show what it feels like to be free of ego for a while. But they also could take some further from Truth and deeper into illusion by having them believe that what they are experiencing is God or from God. Maybe it is, maybe not…

I do very much appreciate Krystle's work, and certainly resonate with her final words about her mission in this life:

"Helping others be able to get more out of the psychedelic experience is the main purpose of my life. That is why I have put together the NeuroSoup website and that is why I do the YouTube videos. The way I look at it, an incredible gift was bestowed upon me. I have been able to experience numerous entheogens and remember my experiences about the entheogens that I have taken in ways that many others have not. Because of this, I feel as if it is my karmic duty to be a positive force in the world. I believe it is my purpose and my path in life to continue to spread knowledge about the spiritual use of entheogens."

Sam & Nick Powell: On Psychedelics and Yogic Practice

Nick and Sam Powell are identical twin brothers who grew up in Santa Monica, California. I first connected with Nick via correspondence regarding an essay of mine on the subject of yoga and psychedelics that Reality Sandwich had featured on their site. Nick was just one of many who commented on the piece, but I found his to be particularly thoughtful and intelligent.

Contacting Nick via email, I was surprised to discover he was only 18. I asked him if he might be interested in a phone interview for this book, to which he unhesitatingly agreed and that was the start of an ongoing relationship with both Nick and Sam that has lasted 6 years.

Over the course of that time, I met with Nick and Sam in California on several different occasions. On one, Nick and I got up at 3 in the morning to do a somewhat intense Kundalini Yoga practice together. On another, Nick and Sam came with some friends out to Joshua Tree National Park to visit with my fraternal twin brother, Ed and me who were there celebrating our 40*th* birthday. I also shot some footage of the twin brothers talking about their life and relationship to yoga, psychedelics, and the spiritual quest—footage which I have yet to do anything with.

Getting close to the publication of this book, I realized that I just had to include the brothers here, so I requested that they both write an essay bringing things all up to date, 6 years later. As you will see, they both wrote very insightful pieces on their take on things right now. What might not be so readily apparent is that while the both boys clearly experienced some amazing things together on their early psychedelic journeys from the young age of fourteen on, as time passed Nick began to find yoga, particularly 3HO Kundalini Yoga (of Yogi Bhajan) to be of particular help to him, to the point where he essentially stopped using any substances. Sam, on the other hand, also found yoga helpful, just not to the point of giving up all substances. I sensed an uneasy tension between the twins on this point, and so was actually a bit relieved in a way to read that Nick has found what I perceive to be a healthy middle ground, as you will see.

Nick Powell

As a fourteen-year-old living in Los Angeles, I'd exhausted the margin of joy my psychological disposition had to offer. Six years of growing up under the Bush administration with two more to go, a stressful family life (my divorced parents could never reach a consensus on how best to raise me and my twin brother Sam, leaving us feeling a bit like ping-pong balls shooting back and forth between houses and sets of rules), and a school environment seemingly designed to suppress my natural inclinations to learn, had me in knots of frustration that could only find expression in the ironic and transgressive. When I wasn't off seeing punk bands with names like "Cheap Sex" and "The Adicts (they intentionally misspelled it)," I was watching early John Waters films or playing violent video games like "Grand Theft Auto." It was all fun on the surface, but beneath it was a bleak, anxious feeling. Even the budding empathy that had prompted me to become a vegetarian and identify closely with radical anti-war politics felt like futile sentiment against the backdrop of doomed world.

When Sam and I, together, started smoking pot around the end of eighth grade, we'd inadvertently gifted ourselves some desperately needed breathing room. I'd already stopped doing my schoolwork by then, partly from the general boredom and burn-out, but largely due to a deeply felt need to pay closer attention to the spaces between my prescribed schedule. Marijuana both validated and magnified those spaces, and throughout the next six months, Sam and I were introduced to drugs that did so even more: MDMA, psilocybin, and LSD. It was my first LSD trip in particular that validated my imagination to the extent that dropping out of high school the next day seemed like a no-brainer. I still maintain that this decision—which, off the cuff, might be a parent's worst nightmare—was crucial to my psychological development, and in ways well beyond the initial catharsis.

Leaving school meant moving in with my dad full-time. Sam, seeing no fair scenario in which he had to go to school and I didn't, quickly joined me. With our dad gone a lot, we became weekend ravers with very little structure in between. Sure, we checked in with a home-studies program twice a week for about an hour (we later got our "equivalency certificates"), but for the most part, life was an unconstrained creative canvas that reflected our mental dynamics back for us to absorb with profoundly new sensitivity.

For me, it was two-fold. On the one hand, I'd engineered an environment that perfectly suited a deep exploration of the subtler realms of mind. Between the psychedelics and ecstasy I would do almost every weekend—in addition to my penchant to be stoned whenever possible—I was in a near-constant visionary space, immersed in elaborate cartoon scenarios superimposed upon the mundane landscape of my San Fernando Valley neighborhood, and prismatic, abstract intelligence when I closed my eyes. What became apparent before long, however, was that this whole trip was bound within the orbit of certain bad habits I'd developed.

Cocaine and prescription-grade opiate use ran concurrent to my psychedelic experimentation. In contrast, they were consciousness reducing drugs—ones that a child-hood rife with binge levels of sugar, TV, and over-stimulating digital media had primed my synaptic pathways for. When I began turning to these substances to numb *my more difficult emotions, I knew there was a fork in the road. I could either stare the unsavory, un-pleasurable aspects of life directly in the face, or destroy myself running from them.*

By some miracle, I chose to quit all non-psychedelic drugs (though I consider marijuana a psychedelic, I stopped using it, too). I was guided to pick up a book on Zen Buddhism I noticed through the corner of my eye at a local bookstore, and I started to silently meditate for a brief period each day. I also began reading books by Terence McKenna and Daniel Pinchbeck that articulated the astral sensibility already obvious in my day to day experience.

It was about six months into this detoxification of sorts that the idea of yoga as a means of self-mastery became intriguing. I'd gravitated towards the "2012 meme," which was an episode of apocalyptic excitement that buzzed within the psychedelic community for a while. The focus ranged from new-age glitter to downright paranoia, but in more lucid moments, touched on some crucial insights that emphasized how our industrial-age tendencies towards greed and insecure self-interest are at a wall, and now threaten our survival as a species if not for a more empathetic and ethereal transformation of values, and a practical reform of our social systems. I took to calling what I saw as the end-all of this process "the fifth dimension," and I rambled and wrote about it obsessively. The basic asanas I'd begun doing out of a book on hatha yoga seemed to be preparing my body and mind for it. I was also dropping acid twice a week for good measure.

Perhaps that can explain the nonchalant way in which I strolled into my first Kundalini yoga class in July of 2008. As sure as I may have been that I was already set on my path, I perked up unexpectedly when the teacher, Guru Singh, sat down and announced that our species was "entering the fifth dimension." For the rest of his lecture and the subsequent yoga set and meditation, I was convinced he was reading my mind. Much like with psychedelics, I'd discovered an answer that I only subconsciously knew I was looking for.

I came back to Guru Singh's classes as often as I could, as well as attending classes taught by other established teachers. The practice of Kundalini yoga made me feel more awake and engaged—mentally, emotionally, physically, and beyond—than my most informative psychedelic trips led to believe was even possible. I bought a manual on developing a personal daily practice, which allowed me to earnestly explore the vast archive of yoga sets and meditations taught by the late Yogi Bhajan, who I learned was behind this system of teachings. The more that I looked into, the more I marveled at the synchronicity. Yogi Bhajan was said to have come to America in the late Sixties out of a deep sense of obligation to assist the many psychedelic experimenters in cultivating and grounding their spiritual awareness to collectively serve what he felt was a coming era of conscious civilization.

Since I shared this aim so concertedly, it took a while for me to object to anything in the teachings, short of wearing a turban. As an orthodox Sikh—as bearded and turban-clad as could be—Yogi Bhajan also flatly recommended a strict abstinence from drugs of all kinds for his students. Given the powerful yoga sets, chants, and meditations I was practicing, I'd spontaneously halted my intake of substances in general (even caffeine!), so this was no problem. I was also enjoying the wave of relief that came from not having to worry about draconian legal penalties, simply for altering my state of mind. After a few years, though, when my daily practice (about an hour of Kundalini yoga, followed by an hour of chanting in the ancient language of Gurumukhi) had become a deeply established habit, I found myself routinely Googling things like "yoga and psychedelics," looking for an external authority—some hip yogi, perhaps—to validate my revived interest.

This time around, I felt that should I choose to use psychedelics, I owed it to myself to be as disciplined as possible. While of course, I couldn't buy the over-simplified, seemingly puritanical opposition to them that Yogi Bhajan and the majority of Indian and Buddhist teachers voiced, my mind had slowed down enough to see that I got a bit carried away with my earlier use, probably biting off more than I could chew. It left some psychic scabs, so to speak, in the form of an inflated notion of myself and my place in the cosmic scheme. I feared compromising the clarity and balance that I felt I'd gained since. Plus, I was alarmed to have seen some friends over the years have schizophrenic episodes through downright reckless intake. All in all, I questioned whether my inclination to do them again was out of a genuine desire to grow, or simply an impulse to retreat from the purifying potential of embracing the mundane non-intoxicated realms, where all the obstacles of my impatience, my sense of entitlement, my stored bodily tension, etc., would emerge front and center.

In spite of these reservations, I ended up smoking pot again, here and there. I also undertook a few DMT and mushroom trips. My conviction, that I've stuck by, was to always do yoga and meditate sober, beforehand. This is a crucial tenet of what I see as "moderation" in its truest sense. In occasionally using psychedelic substances this way, I'm able to better set my intention and process their impact, both during and after the intoxication. As long as my meditation practice is consistent, independently of them, they seem to inform and support it—anything from a mist of cognitive amiability, to a "deep-issue massage," depending on the substance and dose—and often, they highlight their own superfluousness. While some might view that as a sign to "hang up the phone," as Alan Watts famously said, I trust that if I couldn't benefit from them, *my desire to do them would be gone; and I do draw a distinction between desire and impulse, though a bit of Dionysian revelry can be healthy once in a while, too.*

I think that the tendency certain spiritual practitioners have to shame psychedelics as "bad" and unnatural, stems from a kind of institutionalized self-preservation mechanism on the part of most yogic traditions, but for the more ancient, shamanic ones. I do understand how such thinking can help an ashram run smoothly. Daily chores would certainly be disrupted by the monks erupting in involuntary laugh-fits, or ripping their clothes off to dance in ecstatic revelation. I can also see why some argue that the same applies to conventional life in Western society (I've certainly seen a few incompetent therapists that have—no offense to the good ones!). If that's true, though, I think it's fantastic. We live in a time when we desperately need the type of radical creativity and insight that psychedelics provide. While I'm not so daft as to exclude possible exceptions, it's very difficult for me to imagine receiving the initial reality check I was gifted through my first LSD experience without the LSD. Perhaps I would have eventually found my way to a yogic practice that would have, alone, served the same purpose, but I don't want to second-guess it.

In our contemporary society, where yogic practices are the stuff of booming industry, and psychedelic usage is at its highest on record since the 60's, it makes a lot of sense to wisely combine the two, freed from trappings of the ancient traditions they derived from, to assist us in the unique new challenges we face. While psychedelics offer us an initiation ceremony for the secular age, yoga and meditation are tools to carry us through, as conscious spiritual beings with physical and psychological flexibility.

Sam Powell

When I think about how I was introduced to psychedelics, I often think of how little skepticism I actually had in my teenage years about exploring what is often observed and believed by many to be a relatively unexplored realm of human experience, and one that can provide reliable access to some very powerful frequencies of consciousness. As with most people who've encountered what they might only care to describe as a mystical or spiritual experience as a result of taking a psychedelic, I never really considered that I could possibly have an experience that would be either of those things. I definitely never guessed that they would do anything to make me feel as though I'd awakened some kind dormant force within myself that would proceed to expand my entire world-view and bring all my self concepts into a much deeper spectrum of awareness over the next 7 years, nor that they would emphasize and bring to light some of the very specific patterns and observations that they did, and come to serve as one of the main catalysts and tools to assist me in my own spiritual growth and personal awakening thus far.

When I first tried LSD, the word "consciousness" wasn't exactly a staple in the list of words I would commonly use to describe anything I had to ponder about my life at that point. Also not yet on that list were words like "ego death," "transcendental experience," "subjectivity," etc.

My twin brother Nick and I were both in a place where we started to feel very bored and disenchanted by our high school and all it expected of us coupled with the narrow focus of what we were learning. So we started to develop the idea on some level that only the most far out and unexplored territory within the scope of available experiences would be likely to contain any content of true value to us, at least as far as being able to give us the kind of intellectual satisfaction or further understanding of life in general that we were looking for.

LSD became a natural consequence of the type of rave culture we were immersed in on weekends at this time. We would go to parties thrown in renegade locations like warehouses and industrial complexes as well as bigger raves at licensed venues, all with a circle of people through which a multitude of psychedelic experiences were readily available. The most popular drug as is common at raves was MDMA, which at first induced in me what felt like a complete emotional breakthrough equivalent to what one might experience through years of therapy, but it gradually lost its appeal. After my first several times trying it, I got the impression that the peak positive effects had already happened, and it was then where my focus as far as psychedelics started to shift more towards tryptamines like LSD and psilocybin.

I was amazed by the profoundly different effects this particular class of drug had in not only altering my mood and the way I felt, but in creating a temporary yet powerful shift within the perception of both my inner and outer worlds. They would invoke what felt like an ascending thought form within my mind that allowed me to see beyond the superficiality of things in a number of interesting ways, and enabled me to recognize profoundly deeper and subtler patterns within the construct of life, as well as express those observations clearly. There was some initial confusion for me at first as is common with psychedelics, but I always felt (and still feel) that there are no inherent dangers in taking them, as long as one is able to learn from and integrate the lessons and information being presented in the trip, in addition to researching things like proper dosage and making sure that they're taken in a safe environment.

As I continued taking psychedelics over time, I started to feel for the first time ever like I was operating on a level that was providing me with direct access to a seemingly infinite number of insights into my own ways of thinking and personal patterns of behavior, as well as the very real sense of a certain universal energy and collective *consciousness to which I was becoming attuned. I started to become cognizant of many ways in which I was able to change my life and improve my own well being, just by finding better and more responsible ways to navigate through my own mind and thought forms. This did a lot to stimulate my analytical mind as well as creativity, and I would often catch the slightest glimpse of a force that felt extremely intelligent while at the same time other worldly.*

It wasn't until my first "breakthrough" experience with DMT or dimethyltryptamine, (one of the main active components in ayahuasca) that my notions of a possibly higher, or at the very least fully immersive and hyper-real hallucinatory dimension were boldly confirmed, just as the late Terence McKenna predicted they would be, complete with fully operational and autonomous spirits or entities. After that I couldn't really help but view my own consciousness as a kind of inter-dimensional vehicle for spiritual experience, and as is a common side effect of this type of consciousness expansion—the need for various anchors became apparent. Nick and I had been practicing zazen meditation for a while before we were introduced to Kundalini yoga by a friend, which Nick started doing daily and I continue to use at a different rate that works for me. Yoga and mediation have both been extremely instrumental in helping me find and sustain a harmonious balance between the vastness of the internal self and the vastness of the external world."

From Left: My twin, Nick, friend, me, and Sam

Martin Ball: Entheogenic Evolutionary

Not long after submitting my first piece to Reality Sandwich in 2008 (the one on the Yoga Sutras), I received an Amazon gift card for my birthday and decided to add to my steadily growing library of psychedelia. One book that I ordered was *"Mushroom Wisdom: How Shamans Cultivate Spiritual Consciousness,"* by Martin W. Ball, Ph.D. When it arrived in the mail, I was impressed with it enough to decide to contact Martin and request to ask him some questions. Somewhat to my surprise, Martin seemed happy to oblige, and the answers I promptly received from him were very full and carefully thought out. After getting such quick responses to my first two questions, I figured that we would just go on corresponding like this indefinitely. So I sent a third question… but received nothing from Martin for a solid week. I wondered what was happening.

In fact, what was happening was that Martin had been experiencing a breakthrough on his journey with entheogens, something I was not aware of because I had not been listening to Martin's most recent "Entheogenic Evolution" podcasts.[243] When I did finally tune in and listen, I was rather amazed to discover the following:

One day in late February, Martin was smoking salvia divinorum, but much to his surprise, it felt just like 5-MeO-DMT (Martin has described 5-MeO-DMT as an immediate launch into the heart of God, which is experientially very different than most salvia experiences). A little shaken by the experience, he went to take a shower after it was all over, came back later, and in the process of putting his ceremonial instruments away, found that a feather he had been using started to seem to move about in his hand, as though it were being moved by energy currents. Martin immediately recognized that it was the same energy that he feels during his other entheogenic experiences where his arms would move in symmetrical patterns. However, salvia being short acting, he was no longer under the influence of the plant and in a "normal" state of consciousness. Somehow, the energy that he had previously only been able to consistently perceive and feel while in an entheogenic state was suddenly immediately present and accessible. He began to experiment with the feather, and realized that the feather was teaching him how to work with energy, and he also found that the feather could answer "yes" or "no" to questions put to it. After exploring that for a few days, Martin realized that he could do energetic re-balancings with people, with very positive results. Apparently some of the people he worked with had entheogenic-type experiences themselves simply from the feathering without ingesting any substance.

Martin also realized that he could now enter into an entheogenic state (particularly the 5-MeO-DMT state) without actually taking an entheogen. In other words, he no longer needs the "medicines." What was more, he quickly found that his ability to enter into deep energetic states was rapidly producing a cascade of conclusions about the fundamental nature of reality. In a short period of time, Martin found himself in the curious position of being able to explain the nature of reality from an entheogenic (God within) perspective. In sum, he suddenly found that he had consistent and comprehensive answers to some of the most fundamental questions of existence. Answers to these questions (such as the nature of God, questions about life after death, alternate realities, the nature of consciousness, etc.) became immediately obvious and clear. To his great surprise, the answers to these questions were at odds with virtually every religion or metaphysical system previously formulated. Energized by the startling revelations, Martin decided to share these conclusions with his podcast-listening audience. In doing so, he has been uncompromising in sharing his conclusions on the nature of reality, something that has ruffled quite a few feathers.

As I said, I found this all pretty fascinating, though not quite sure what to make of it. It was 2am and I went to bed because I had to get up early the next morning to teach a yoga class on the beach. When I got up I was still processing Martin's podcast. The yoga class was fairly uneventful, except for one little thing… When I went to collect my belongings at the end of our session, there was a feather stuck between two strings of my guitar, almost as if someone had stuck it there for me. I looked around and asked all of the students if anyone had given me a feather (why they would, I have no idea), but everyone said they hadn't. Strange. Here it was just 9 hours or so later after listening to Martin talking about his magic feather, and the universe is giving me a feather. I took it as a sign of some sort…

Later that day, I emailed Martin and told him the story about finding the feather, adding that I sensed a connection to him, noting that we had met in cyberspace right around the time of his breakthrough, maybe just a week or so before. Sensing that all the synchronicities were nudging me in the direction of continuing our relationship, I asked Martin if I could write about what was happening with him. A few days later, Martin emailed back saying that it would actually be most ideal if I would come meet with him first, but if not, I could do an email interview with him, especially because so many people had been writing him with questions. What follows are just a few questions and answers from our email correspondence.

Before reading it, though, I want to just mention again that Martin received a good deal of flak for certain podcasts in which he freely dispensed his views on God and the nature of reality (what Martin humorously has referred to as his "ontological onslaught"). I myself was somewhat taken aback by some of Martin's monologue, such as his saying that he didn't need to be open-minded (as one podcast commentator suggested he be), but I figured that after all, it *is* Martin's podcast and he is free to express his views. And considering that Martin has spent much of his life engaging with existential issues, that he does have a Ph.D., and that he's certainly explored entheogens far more than I have at this point, it might be worth my while to listen and deeply consider his perspective. Perhaps you will feel the same. So with that, I will leave you to a few selections from our email interview…

Author: Would you relate for the readers how you got onto the path of entheogens, and what were some of your earliest experiences with the medicines? Did you decide right away that you were going to devote your life to this, or did it happen over time?

MB: *My first experience with entheogens was with psilocybin mushrooms. It was the summer after my first year of college and I went to the "Gathering of the Vibes" festival in Northern California with some friends at the beginning of the summer. While we were in our vehicle in line to get into the festival area, a fellow walked by saying "shrooms… shrooms" and our driver bought some. I had never tried mushrooms before and didn't know what to expect or how much to take or anything. That night we split up the bag and headed out to enjoy the show. I got separated from my friends and as the mushrooms came on, I quickly realized that I had no idea who I was. It was very disconcerting and I felt lost and afraid. I finally found my friends and relaxed, but overall, I wasn't impressed. I felt, "well, that was strange. I don't know if I need to do that again."*

I tried mushrooms a few more times, but quickly started to develop what might be called "flashbacks," though I don't think that was accurate. I found that I could spontaneously slip into mushroom-like states of consciousness just by looking at trees or blades of grass or any other sufficiently complex patterning. It really worried me as I felt out of control, so I stayed away from mushrooms for a couple years after that.

I eventually went back to mushrooms after I got involved in "shamanic drumming," where you play a drum rapidly and go on "journeys" with your eyes closed in the dark. I was never too impressed with that methodology—it always felt somewhat contrived to me—but on my last "journey," I found myself watching a golden eagle fly down to the ground in front of me. Where it landed, a collection of mushrooms sprang up and it bent down and ate them all. The eagle then transformed into a rainbow light version of myself and said, "If you want to visit with the eagle, eat the mushrooms." So that was the last time I did that kind of "shamanic drumming" work and the very next time I ate mushrooms, I had a life-changing initiation into the world of the mushrooms. What I learned from that one journey became the basis for my book, Mushroom Wisdom.

Author: When I read that the first time, I noted how similar your initiation experience with mushrooms was to my own initial experience using the ayahuasca analogue "Jurema" (Mimosa Hostilis and Syrian Rue). As with yours, it felt like an initiation, there was a life review, it was extremely beautiful and profound, and it was life-changing. After that experience I decided that I was going to devote my life to better understand these plant teachers.

I guess one basic question I would ask you based upon what you wrote is: What do you think it was that changed in your life that led you to have such a profound experience later when in those earlier encounters you did not receive "initiation" from the mushrooms? Was it just that you weren't ready for it when you were younger? Was it a different strain of psilocybin? A bigger dose? Set and setting? All of the above? You basically answer this in *Mushroom Wisdom*, but since now you're in a different space, perhaps you will have a new perspective…

MB: *When I first tried mushrooms I had very little idea of what was meant by the phrase "spiritual experience," so really I was just getting started opening up that area of my life. In retrospect, I can see that the mushrooms basically opened me up right away, which is why I started having spontaneous experiences early on. It was a bit much for me, however, so I struggled with it and had to learn how to better control myself and deal with the fear of losing control. Zen meditation helped a lot with that. When I later went back to mushrooms, I had done a great deal more reading about psychedelics and what an "entheogenic" experience is about.*

I'd also want to express that "big experiences" are important because they can really shift our perspective on reality, but I'm not a big proponent of the idea that we can suddenly become awakened and then that's it. Many spiritual traditions treat the "enlightenment" moment as some final end point or liberation or whatever. I've progressed through so many different levels of mystical and awakening experiences that it has to be understood as an ongoing process and not a final achievement.

Author: What I find interesting is that we seem to have had somewhat similar experiences: I had no real religious faith as a young person but from early on had many questions. I started off studying Philosophy, but ultimately realized that there aren't any real satisfying answers in the Western academic study of Philosophy, and later switched to Religious Studies. That didn't do it either, but out of that came a deep encounter with India and Yoga that did answer a lot of my questions. But that, too, was ultimately not enough, though I recently found my way to plant teachers for further guidance. When I did, an "initiation" experience inspired me to devote my life to exploring these things.

What is the purpose of the entheogens? Why would you recommend that we use them? Why do you say that they are the best teachers, better than any human teacher or guru? Do you have any human teachers from whom you still gain insight or inspiration?

MB: *To put it as simply as I can, my understanding is that entheogens and vision-ary medicines affect us the way they do because that is how God, the Divine Being, intended it. They are our direct line of access to interfacing with the Divine Being with-out any intermediaries. This is incredibly significant as, in my understanding, basically all our spiritual systems are defective or illusory in one way or another. Most people have a hard time with my saying that, but it is not difficult to see how priests, gurus, and other spiritual leaders can lead people astray with their basically fantasy-based systems of spiritual growth and purification, once you understand what the problem is and how ego has infected all of our religious and spiritual systems. It's complicated to explain this in brief as really each religious or spiritual system needs to be addressed in-dividually. There are some jewels hidden away in the rubble, but for the most part, I've concluded that most religious systems are more illusory than not. The best way to avoid this problem is to go directly to the source for yourself, and that is what the medicines do. We all come into this world with the capacity to interface with the Divine directly without anyone else telling us what to do or think or believe. My suggestion is that we take advantage of that fact and explore our divine natures for ourselves.*

Personally, I've never worked with a spiritual mentor or guru. I've been initiated by several Mescalero Apache medicine people, but even there, their primary teaching to me was, "This is how we do it, but you'll have to find your own way. That's the way medicine works. Discover it for yourself." I've really taken that to heart and would have to agree with it. For me, the clearest way for us to discover ourselves is to work with the medicines. That's what they do. That's why they work the way they do. They're gifts and we should use them.

Author: So here's a question I've been meaning to ask you for a while, and for-give my playing devil's advocate here: Isn't it a bit of an assumption to say that these substances are from God and reveal our Divine nature to us? I'm sure there are plen-ty of people out there who look on these things (drugs, they call them) as leading people astray, away from God and into narcissism. Even to use the term "entheogen" is misleading, they say, because whether these things truly reveal God to us is an open question (Terence McKenna voiced this sentiment). Others have said that at best these things give us deep insight into the psyche, but not into the true nature of the Divine…

MB: *I'd say that people who think that way are making judgments not only of others, but also of God's work through evolution. In my view, the Divine Being lives through nature and through us as living beings. The fact that we have DMT in our brains, lungs, spinal fluid, blood, and on our nerve endings isn't an accident. The fact* that substances like DMT are readily available in nature is also not an accident. DMT is one of the primary means that the Divine uses to communicate with us. It is the very medium through which divine energy expresses itself through us. If people genuinely believe in God or a Divine Being and also believe that the physical world we live in was in some sense created or evolved by this being, then how can they rationally say that something like DMT is a drug and is bad for us in some way when we are living, breathing, walking and talking DMT beings?

I also find the narcissism argument rather odd as well. While of course people can get carried away by how they choose to interpret their visionary experiences (which is why I always advise people to consider their experiences as lessons and not as literally true—it is very easy for egos to grasp onto fantasy and stories), I don't think that entheogens can be criticized for leading to narcissism any more than any other spiritual or religious practice. Most religions have a sense of collective narcissism on a widespread scale and have really confused ideas about the nature of the divine or the nature of reality. People cling to these ideas and create all kinds of fantasy worlds for themselves and in the process, often become judgmental of people who don't buy into their fantasy. That, to me, is collective narcissism. There are so many "one true paths" out there that it's absurd.

The flip side of the "one true path" narcissism is the wildly wishy-washy "it's all true" version of "spirituality" that promotes sloppy thinking, lack of discernment, and a feel-good vibe that we're just going to accept anything that people say simply because they say it's "spiritual." We tend to value this these days and call it having an "open mind" or being "tolerant" or even "enlightened." In my view, people get sucked into a great deal of fantasy and down right silly thought here too. It's narcissistic in the sense that people use this mode of thought to consider themselves as "spiritually awakened" or "ascended," but that's just another ego trap.

The reason why entheogens are so effective is because they force you to face yourself. For the discerning traveler, these can be very illuminating experiences and the potential for growth and self-discovery is greater than through any other methodology. But if they let their egos get attached to their visions or their personal interpretations of their visions, then they can become just as lost as anyone else. That's why in traditional societies that use entheogens, the medicines are integrated into culture and into the community so people can work through these experiences together and collectively.

In the end, I think the strongest argument for entheogen use is that they open us up to direct energetic experiences. Energy is real. Visions aren't. Visions are great and they can give us many insights, but the real work is working with the energy. I rely on energy, and energy cannot lie. It's actually impossible, if you think about it.

Author: You gave the impression in your podcast that you no longer feel it necessary to take entheogens, but that you will do so if you feel called to do so (or directed by the feather). Is that correct? Are you still having 5-MeO-DMT experiences without actually taking it?

MB: *It's funny, but my ego is actually a little disappointed in this. I really enjoy working with the medicines and find them infinitely fascinating. But no, I no longer need them. For lack of a better word, I've made a transition and I no longer need the medicines. Given that the medicines are there to help us discover ourselves, once we make that discovery, the mirror is wiped clean, so to speak. In this transition what has occurred is that my ego or normal sense of self hasn't evaporated or anything, but it has loosened up. I can now freely slip into profoundly psychedelic states of consciousness without ingesting any medicine at all. The most powerful of these experiences are immediately comparable to my experiences with 5-MeO-DMT, which is by far the most profound of all the medicines that I've had the honor of working with. At the beginning of this transition, I was a bit concerned that "Martin" was going to evaporate and I was going to walk around with this strange voice all the time and move more like an energy being than a normal person, but I've found that I only go into deep states when it is necessary and most of the time I can just be "normal," so to speak, and don't have to worry about it.*

I should perhaps clarify a little bit of what I'm talking about here. For the past year and a half I had been going through a very intense personal exploration into my relationship with the divine, working regularly with ayahuasca at the local Santo Daime church and also working with 5-MeO-DMT at a local entheogenic temple along with occasional sessions with mushrooms and salvia divinorum. This was quite a challenging process for me and I write about it in my book, The Entheogenic Evolution. Basically, I underwent a profound process of energetic opening and clearing in the quest to discover myself and my relationship to the Divine, or God. The end result is that I am extraordinary clear on what that relationship is and the medicines have done their work. For example, after having made this transition to not needing the medicines, I took a large dose of 5-MeO-DMT, and though this is a metaphor, in the experience all I saw was "myself" in the "mirror." I've processed through what I needed to process through in order to understand myself, the nature of reality, and the nature of the Divine Being. Now that I've reached that point, there really isn't a reason for me to take the medicines.

An exception to that might be in working with others, but even there, it isn't necessary. I can feel and work with the same energy in a non-altered state that I used to need the medicines to perceive and work with. I'm also happy to work with others in their use of entheogens. For example, recently I've been doing energy work for people while they are using salvia divinorum. It's quite amazing. Even though I'm not using the medicine, I can easily tell what they are experiencing at an energetic level and can even communicate with them without having to speak out loud. It's the kind of thing I never would have believed if I weren't doing it myself and getting confirmation from others in the room that I wasn't speaking out loud but the person I was "speaking" to can repeat back to me what I "said" to them. It's hard to believe.

Author: At the outset of *Mushroom Wisdom*, you touched on the idea that entheogens are a "great equalizer," leveling the spiritual playing field, so to speak. I'm wondering if you would expand on that a bit, and maybe connect it to the debate about whether/why the "Guru" is dead for us these days, and whether the entheogens can perform the same essential role, as well as the issue of whether we need to use these things under the guidance of an experienced shaman/guru?

MB: *"Entheogens are a great spiritual equalizer because they make profoundly spiritual states of consciousness available to anyone willing to learn to work with them. While this is true of other spiritual modalities such as meditation, yoga, prayer, fasting, drumming, etc., entheogens stand out for their effectiveness in engendering such states when used in a responsible manner. For most people, I speculate that it would be more likely for them to have deep and profoundly transformative experiences with entheogens than through virtually any other means. However, I also feel that entheogen use is most productive and beneficial when paired with other forms of spiritual practice, especially meditation and energy work (such as through martial arts, yoga, dance, body work, etc.).*

Entheogenic spirituality is not easy, so it is important to understand that to advocate entheogens as a tool for spiritual development is not to advocate what could be described as an "easy" path. There is some judgment that because entheogens make spiritual experiences so readily accessible, it is taking an "easy" path, as opposed to years of dedicated meditation and prayer to reach such profound levels of consciousness. While entheogens do make deeply profound states more accessible, there is nothing "easy" about working with these profound plant teachers. Entheogens can be more demanding than any spiritual teacher or system of practice and they require deep dedication to working with them for personal spiritual development and growth. But with that said, it is also true that they do make profound experiences more accessible to more people than any other means of cultivating spiritual consciousness.

It is highly significant that the entheogens themselves are the teachers in the context of entheogenic spirituality. In traditional societies, shamans create the context for new initiates to encounter the sacred medicines, but shamans tend not to be "gurus." The role of the guru is to personally guide the spiritual seeker along the path to enlightenment and is the ultimate judge of the seeker's progress. With entheogenic spirituality, the shamans are the technicians of the sacred and hold the knowledge of how to use the medicines as tools. Their role is to teach the initiate how to use the medicines and access their wisdom, but the source of the real teachings is the medicines themselves.

Entheogenic spirituality therefore places a great deal of responsibility on the individual. It is in largely private, subjective experience (even if done in a group setting) that the individual encounters the power of the medicines. The lessons that unfold are unique for each person and no two sessions with a visionary medicine are the same, even if there are similar characteristics. When done with the proper intent, preparation, and dedication, lessons build on each other over time and the initiate can progress through infinite levels of spiritual awakening and evolution.

An encounter with a visionary medicine is always an encounter with the self—with all levels of the self from the ego to the "higher self" to one's divine nature as an embodiment of Source. Because of this, the medicines always "know" exactly who you are, where you are at, and what lessons you need to continue on your path of spiritual development. The truth is right there, but the choice is always yours. How will you respond to the lesson? What will you choose?

One needs neither a shaman nor a guru to have such lessons through entheogen use. Yet having a trusted guide or teacher can be very important for helping the spiritual seeker through difficult passages in the entheogenic journey. Our modern Western society is lacking in models who are experienced with entheogenic spirituality; shamans, gurus, or otherwise. Most "mainstream" spiritual practitioners have little to no knowledge of entheogens or their potential, and even the most "enlightened" spiritual leaders can be highly judgmental of entheogenic spirituality.

Therefore, finding a good guide can be exceedingly difficult. Much Western use of entheogens is overtly "recreational" and while spontaneous spiritual experiences can develop in such contexts, their regularity and depth can be greatly increased and enhanced by guided ceremonial use. It is for this reason that many Westerners are drawn to work with indigenous healers and shamans or participate in religious use of entheogens such as through the Native American Church, the União do Vegetal, or Santo Daime.

As entheogenic spirituality becomes more popular, the need for experienced teachers and models will grow. Ideally, centers could be opened where those who choose could be initiated into the Mysteries. Initiates could be taught how to dedicate themselves to the experience, how to center their thoughts and focus their minds and how to let go of fear and judgment as they turn within and let the experience unfold. With the right *contexts, deeply transformative spiritual experiences could be made available to more and more people, giving them a direct experience of divine realities and transcendent states of consciousness. Even if only encountered once, an entheogenic experience can be life-transforming. And for those who are called to do the rigorous work of evolving themselves at the guidance of the plant teachers, they could be given a context in which to do their practice in a safe and supportive way."*

Author: I have a few questions about this, touching on the issue of whether using entheogens is "cheating" or "the easy way."

Of course, they're not easy at all. It can be quite a rigorous and terrifying path, as we know—Awe-inspiring in the face of the Mysterium Tremendum. Ego-death… never a fun thing (for the ego). On the other hand, having been connected with the Yoga of asceticism (*tapasya*), I also know that it is also not an easy path, and perhaps it is more gradual, slower, but also ultimately more lasting…

I'm thinking of one of my teachers in particular, Swami Satyananda Saraswati, who did years of intense tapas in India (including 40-day fasts, chanting in icy rivers and lakes, 3 years chanting into the fire) and can now seemingly enter into samadhi at will… My sense is that he would be one of those teachers who would say, "How can you compare my hard-earned Samadhi with your little drug trip?" And the answer is: I really can't because I've never experienced Samadhi except possibly via plant medicine.

My personal experience was that ayahuasca gave me the initiation that I never received from my gurus. With only one teacher did I even have any kind of mystical experience, and that I believe was due to a Kundalini Shaktipat initiation I received. Very blissful, yes, and very subtle compared to the plant teachers. Still, my question to you is whether the "slow and steady path," like in the Tortoise and Hare story, might be ultimately the choicest (long lasting) in the long run?

MB: "*Because entheogens can produce radical states of spiritual consciousness rather reliably and consistently, they can be seen as an accelerated path of spiritual development. This is not to say that it is "easy," just more accelerated. However, an accelerated path is not necessarily a stable path, especially for a spiritual seeker who is ungrounded or easily carried away by imaginal or fantasy-like thought. It is therefore important to recognize that entheogenic spirituality does hold the potential to destabilize certain personality types if undertaken recklessly or without proper precautions and spiritual discipline. Like any powerful tool, entheogens must be used responsibly and with care in order to actually maximize their potential benefits.*

Ideally, someone following entheogenic spirituality should have some kind of grounding in spiritual practice outside of entheogen use. Meditation, yoga, energy work, all of these are good for clearing the mind, centering, tapping in to the energies of consciousness and the body, and staying focused. Furthermore, such practices contribute greatly to a person's ability to stay focused and remain "on task" when working with entheogens.

How long the effects of spiritual awakening last ultimately depends on the dedication and focus of the individual. Some people only need one powerful spiritual experience with entheogens and this experience can last them for their whole life. Others might have a powerful experience but then not be transformed because they haven't focused themselves on bringing that into their life in a grounded way. It all comes down to the individual.

I don't think that there is any inherent difference between spiritual experiences that are achieved through individual effort through a spiritual practice and those achieved with the aid of entheogens. They are just different methods and use different tools. Whether the realizations "stick" or not is up to the individual and his or her personal dedication to spiritual growth and awakening."

Author: Could you give us a sense of some of the criticisms you have been hearing, and what you would say in response. Has anyone said anything to you that has given you pause? Has anyone given you a critique that has in any way inspired you to modify what you've said?

MB: *This will sound pretty closed minded to some, but no, no one has given me pause. Basically, I'm articulating a rather unique perspective on reality and I'm confident in what I'm saying. It comes directly out of my experience of working with energy, and as I am now fond of saying, energy doesn't lie. Some people don't like that I'm dismissing ideas of astral planes or reincarnation or life after death, etc., and they feel that I'm not respecting their beliefs or even their experiences. I've been criticized for being closed-minded and full of myself and my ideas. My basic response is that I'm presenting a radically consistent and coherent picture of the nature of reality that starts from a very basic proposition: God is an energetic being that permeates itself through fractal patterns. This is what I've learned directly from my entheogenic experiences. All of my other conclusions basically follow from this initial starting point and my working with the energy. So, I'm more than happy to listen to other perspectives on reality, but in order to be really taken into consideration, they would have to deal with my starting point. Otherwise, we're talking about apples and oranges or quibbling over details without getting to the fundamental theory or position beneath it.*

For example, let's take Buddhism. Buddha said that there is no God. Well, I fundamentally disagree because I have thoroughly explored my self and my nature and have found that the source of my being is a living energetic being that is the source of all existence. I can't think of a better word for that than God. So, I have a fundamental disagreement with Buddhism. Buddhism also says that the whole point is to reach nirvana and free ourselves from the wheel of reincarnation. Well, I think that is fundamentally flawed.

Someone might say I'm not respecting their religion because of this, but I don't see the point of "respecting" something that is flawed or erroneous. Keep in mind I'm a professor and I have to grade papers and exams all the time. Students are mistaken about what they say and write all the time. If I were grading papers based on the criteria that I not offend someone for not respecting their beliefs, I'd never be able to give students grades. You either get the answer right or you don't. You've either thought out your argument or you haven't. And when it comes to reality, something either does or does not exist. And energy doesn't lie. I don't care if you're Buddhist, Hindu, Christian or whatever. Believe whatever in the world you want. Reality is still real and if you put your hand on an electric socket, it will shock you because energy is real and it cannot lie or deceive you. Belief isn't a question here. So we can talk about respecting beliefs all we want, but that doesn't help us understand reality. I'm interested in reality. I'm not interested in beliefs.

• • •

So there you have it. I hope you will understand now, you who have thoughtfully listened and considered what has been discussed here, why I find what is happening with Martin so fascinating and helpful, even though as of this writing I am not in complete agreement with him. You will note that not only has Martin's story and words shed light on most if not all of the questions this book has dealt with, but they've also provided insight into other issues, too.

Of course, what I feel, and what Yoga really boils down to is the idea that only what one deeply experiences and Knows (in the Gnostic sense) is true. So even though I feel attracted to Martin's work and am very interested in what he has to say, (particularly as we both are coming from a similar background in regard to our search for God) what it will comes down to me is actually having a 5-MeO-DMT experience myself.

Drew Hempel: Spiritual Translator

Of all of the commentators on the pieces that Reality Sandwich featured on their site (the ones on the Yoga Sutras and Yoga & Shamanism included in this book), there was one who stood out for me as someone that I wanted to connect with as what he was writing was done with so much conviction and intelligence, not to mention being pretty far out there (a plus for me). This was Drew Hempel. Drew and I are about the same age and come from the same socio-economic background, share common interests, and have had pretty similar life trajectories. As with myself, Drew did not explore psychedelics before first delving deeply into Eastern religion, in his case not yoga but Qigong. What's interesting is that both of us not only began to deeply explore spiritual phenomena in the mid-Nineties, but we also first tried psychedelics in almost the same year, too, and ended up doing an analogue of ayahuasca called "Jurema" at around the same time. Here's an excerpt from an email interview in which Drew related a bit about his spiritual journey:

Drem Hempel: *I began researching paranormal phenomenon after I had attended a chi-emitting lecture by qigong master Effie P. Chow in 1995. I visited my best high school friend, James T. Hong, in San Francisco to further research qigong in 1996. I attended a Tibetan monk lecture in 1997 and in 1998 I began practicing Yan Xin qigong. In 1999 I met qigong master Chunyi Lin.*

Since I had researched qigong masters, I knew right away that Chunyi Lin was the real deal. I sat up right near him when he did a chi-emitting lecture for my graduate class… Chunyi Lin demonstrated his abilities to me by first shooting chi at me with his fingers, without touching me. I was standing up doing a simple exercise he teaches, he walked by and I could hear this flicking sound of his fingers. I immediately saw this bright light and my body filled with bliss, better than what I experienced with the stunning girlfriend I had at the time. Chunyi Lin later said, in Level 2, that he could say what percentage an organ was functioning. I went up to him and asked about my right kidney since I could feel heat there. He looked at my right kidney from the front of my body and immediately I felt this laser-heat with great bliss, only on my right kidney. He then said: "oh about 70%." When Chunyi Lin enters the room for class you can feel the whole room fill with this magnetic bliss and I could see this bright light around his head. Later I saw his spirit bodies leaving him as they went around the room to heal people. He stated that once in deep full-lotus meditation in the mountains, Chunyi Lin levitated up 9 feet, spiraling next to a pine tree. Once he turned wine into water during a drinking contest with the town drunk. Chunyi Lin has many amazing stories and from my experience with him he is completely professional.

Chunyi Lin showed us x-rays from people he had healed and one female was in the class who was still bald from cancer treatment but he had healed her as well. He said when he first did a healing in Minnesota it was on a cat that was deaf—he just put his hands on the cat's ears. By the time his friend had changed clothes to play basketball his friend's cat could hear! Then this Mexican lady had a rare lung disease and didn't want a transplant. Her son took her to Chunyi Lin's small tai-chi class and after a few classes she no longer needed her oxygen tank. She had been a patient at the Mayo Clinic so soon word got around and then the local newscaster who did the story on Chunyi Lin actually quit his job so he could go work for Chunyi Lin…

I later dropped out of graduate school due to the corruption and censorship I had undergone. I re-entered only to finish my degree by taking classes from qigong master Chunyi Lin. Six months later I had spent 8 days on only half a glass of water and during that time I experienced the highest level of healing energy. I saw dead spirits who regularly attend Chunyi Lin's chi-emitting lectures. I healed my mom of a serious case of "smoker's legs" so she no longer needed surgical stockings. I accidentally pulled this old lady's spirit out of the top of her skull—without even touching her. I had pre-cognition, telepathy and telekinesis on a regular basis. I had transcended death and when I sat in full-lotus the room would spin around me in a space-time vortex…

This was all about 10 years ago and I met Chunyi Lin when he still was not well known outside of the Twin Cities. I took classes from him for a few years off and on and then he moved his healing center out into a far suburb. I don't have a car and just work a part-time nonprofit entry—level job, so I haven't continued classes with him since 2005. I do sit in full-lotus as much as possible and I continue to shoot electromagnetic energy out of my pineal gland while I suck in electrochemical energy from other people.

Basically I've read one book a day on average since I finished my intensive qigong training back around 2001. The energy level I had obtained was dangerous in mainstream society unless I practiced professionally. So instead I've focused on translating the experience back into western science terms. I'm still working on my diet and have yet to integrate doing full-lotus healing while functioning in mainstream society.

So Drew, like myself, had been a disciple of a living yoga master, had developed certain paranormal abilities (or *siddhis*—I was not as advanced as Drew), and then spent time re-integrating into the mundane world, becoming a translator, or bridge for those seeking interpretation of the teachings and insights into conventional parlance. It was from that place of having re-integrated into society that both of us began our exploration of the plants, wanting to know what new insight they might offer in the nature of reality. I asked Drew about his early psychedelic experiences…

DH: *I first took salvia in 2006 or so. I first took it as an herb and it was just like really strong pot—time slowed down. I was in public when I took it but then went to* a friend's place to wait for the salvia to wear off. Then I next took it at home while in full-lotus and I realized the salvia caused internal climaxes while in full-lotus. The secret of having internal climaxes is what enables a person to sit in full-lotus for as long as they want. So salvia is a catalyst for healing and activating the parasympathetic nervous system. Before I took salvia I had researched it online and even though I had a full quid—as much as possible that I could chew—I experienced no visions.

So then I bought some concentrated smoke but it wasn't standardized and wasn't as strong or about the same as the herb. So then I got standardized 10x but it still wasn't as strong. I then got 17x and this time, while in full-lotus, the internal climaxes were so powerful that almost immediately my pineal gland opened up and my sense of space-time became deeply warped. I didn't have any visions but I ended up hitting level 6 [note: Drew told me that his references to levels is the extent the third eye is open], blacking out, and when I came to I could hear my family or discarnate beings that I knew watching over me. I had the distinct sense that not only was taking salvia not real but that my whole life had not been real and that my sense of place on earth was also not real. It was a very deep cleansing of my chakras—I remember not being able to think of names or places. I tried to think about what salvia was and I distinctly asked myself: "What is Mexico?" I couldn't not figure out what "Mexico" meant…

"At that point, from sharing my experiences to friends and online, I realized that I still hadn't had any visions. My experience of my life as not being real and physical reality as not real was still a drug-induced hallucination for me. In other words, soon after it happened even though the experience was very real, I also knew why it happened. The information I received was profound yet I could easily analyze it psychologically. I probably did have some form of spirit communication with my family and friends as a meshing of my deep subconscious and also their subconscious. Still I had not seen any other spirits nor had any other hallucinations besides the sensation that the room and my brain together had collapsed into pure consciousness.

Not too long after I got 21x salvia and now I easily hit Level 6 every time I smoked it. I would come out of Level 6 blackout not knowing how long I had been blacked out. I was still in full-lotus though and before I blacked out I also had several internal climaxes. So I started recording what time I would take deep inhales and then when I woke up I would record how long it had been. I did this a few times and finally I woke up while still maintaining awareness of what had happened. Normally I'd wake up having forgotten I had smoked salvia, having forgotten I had existed or the world existed, etc. This time when I woke up from blacking out I heard myself saying very loudly: "I think I opened my third eye."

The experience that Drew mentions of this whole existence not being real, including our individual life, is one that I have also had numerous times now with psychedelics. It's the basic experience that underlies metaphysics, and it was lacking this that I wondered how I could accept the essence of Vedanta, let alone teach it, for example. It's rather challenging to return to "business-as-usual" after having such experiences, and it generally leads to a greater ability to love and empathize than might have been possible otherwise. I was wondering what his plant explorations meant for Drew in the grand scheme of life and what he knew to be true at that point. Another excerpt from our email interview:

Author: What is your overall view of the value of psychedelics/entheogens right now, putting it in perspective with all else that you know and have experienced? What do you know about these things that others need to be aware of? How can they be of assistance to someone on the spiritual path, or in one's life? Would you say they are more harmful than beneficial for most people, or vice versa?

DH: *"The problem with psychedelics is that it's still too cerebral. Again, if a person can sit in full-lotus then the body is being transformed. For example I think it was Andrew Weil who describes being able to do a yoga posture while on LSD but then as soon as the drug wore off he could no longer do the posture. He was inspired by his LSD experience to know it was now possible to do the yoga posture but he still needs to do the yoga training. Yoga training is difficult in modern society because sex sells and so modern males are usually addicted to ejaculation. We are taught that celibacy means less sex when in fact celibacy means more sex and also reveals the secret connection between sex and love. Unfortunately the psychedelic scene is still based on cerebral patriarchal males who do not know how to control their lower bodies and therefore still are controlled by the anger-fear dynamic of the kidney-liver energy."*

Drew speaks to the challenging work of embodying the experiences one has, and this generally requires a daily practice, a discipline. It also requires *brahmacharya* for the male, something we both discovered for ourselves along the way.

I was getting the sense that Drew was leaning toward the view that one requires a guru or teacher, as he had in Chunyi Lin, I was just curious of his views on whether psychedelics could work alone, without a teacher…

Author: Some in the psychedelic movement, such as Martin Ball, are very outspoken in their view that entheogens are better than any human teacher or guru, and that a guru or master isn't even necessary. How do you feel about that? Do entheogens "level the playing field"? What can masters or gurus teach us that drugs can't and vice versa?

DH: *If we study DMT traditionally, it's the same as yoga training. In other words, a strict healer relying on plants has to not eat any sugar (fruit), not eat any salt, and* then go into isolation away from females—for months. So again the power is from ionization of the body's electrochemical energy without losing the energy through the de-conversion of the electromagnetic energy back into physical ejaculation. Once the third eye is open, then there is a "free energy" circuit so that females are healed while at the same time healing males through the love energy. The source of the love is pure consciousness beyond any physical tool. This is why songs are used to guide the shamanic plant healing—when we listen to the source of sound we resonate with pure consciousness which then creates holographic reality...

The healing with plants is first used for diagnosis, so a real plant healer can see inside the body just like a real yoga master. Then the plants are taken to heal the ill body. This is very similar to yoga healing, only that with the yoga energy master the healing is done directly through "laser-love" energy. So the diagnosis of the illness and the healing take place at the same time, because in order to see inside the body you all take into your own body the other person's illness. It's the pure consciousness that does the healing through the principles of complementary opposites. The plants on their own are only electrochemical energy and so to build up the opening of the third eye there must also be a special diet and also isolation from females and also control of the male lower body. The full-lotus body position does this without needing isolation from females, without needing any psychedelic plants.

Author: What was your overall feeling about the Martin Ball podcast and interview I sent?

DH: The electromagnetic awareness of Martin Ball is still stuck in the lower chakras. Gurdjieff's book (by Ouspensky), "In Search of the Miraculous" has the best translation of Taoist Yoga back into Western psychology. So I'm able to read a person's "essence" or their electromagnetic awareness. A Number 3 person is someone who focuses their conceptual awareness so strongly that the third eye starts to open up. A Number 4 person has the third eye permanently magnetized. It takes a lot of work to get to Number 5 which would be an energy master, someone who can completely heal their own body. Gurdjieff's system is based on Mahayana yoga's level of consciousness. So I would say Martin Ball has had some level 8 consciousness experiences from taking psychedelics but he still needs to do meditation transformation to permanently transform the electrochemical emotional energy of the lower organs into the laser-love energy of the pineal gland. The electromagnetic fields need to build up quite strong so that telekinesis, telepathy and precognition become repeatable abilities. As Master Nan, Huai-chin explains in the best Mahayana Buddhism books in modern times, most people "fall back into worldliness" before the third eye is fully opened. This is what happened with me as well—when the paranormal powers develop, the full-lotus *becomes easier and easier, but as the powers are used, the ego gets attached and then the chakras get blocked up again.*

So the easy test for paranormal abilities is the full-lotus. A true healer can open up the body channels because that's the source of the healing energy.

Author: Please also talk a little bit about your experimentation over the years, especially with Salvia and Ayahuasca. (In your RS comments, you referred to Ayahuasca as the "top psychedelic"… Is that according to you, or does that seem to be the consensus?) Also, have you ever used 5-MeO-DMT? I have not, but from what I have read and heard, it seems to be the most powerful psychedelic, even more so than Ayahuasca.

DH: *My coworker wanted to try DMT and I decided to do the same experiment [as with salvia] by testing it against the full-lotus qigong.*

When I brewed up the ayahuasca analog of mimosa and syrian rue, I tested it as a sip and immediately felt this full-body internal climax sensation. I knew this was much stronger than salvia, yet had the same power to open up the electrochemical Kundalini energy. I then slugged down the whole amount, maybe 15 grams of mimosa and 3 grams of syrian rue. I was sitting in full-lotus and the internal climaxes kicked in but unlike the salvia, the internal climaxes kept getting stronger and deeper and more blissful. I then heard this high-pitched buzzing and space-time collapsed as the Kundalini electrochemical energy built up so strong that my pineal gland exploded with light.

I woke up after hitting my head on the corner of this wall, while I was still in full-lotus, but the impact actually cracked open the chakra on my forehead. It sounded like a gun shot and then I heard more gun shots as I continued in full-lotus and the energy channels in my brain opened up. Then I saw rainbows and more rainbows, as this space-time vortex. I could maintain my intentional left-brain awareness but then it would get sucked back into this rainbow vortex.

Deep energy blockages in my body opened up and the bliss was so enormous that later I described it as being "fucked by God." I could feel my tailbone splitting open with this deep orgasmic bliss. The rainbows were inside my body as much as warping space-time. When my intentional thought pondered a question, the answer would be provided by a holographic experience stored in my body—a release of an energy blockage. Space-time continued to get sucked in a rainbow vortex back into pure consciousness and now I had to just submit to the vortex.

I had to accept that I was beyond death and that everything was a holograph—my body and external reality was all one and everything I experienced externally was also stored in my body. Deep memories as energy blockages were revealed as I felt my body being healed with the rainbow light. I found myself being stuck in this rainbow vortex and I had to continually die, I had to continually accept the healing whether I wanted to or not. As I posed questions, the answer was always that it's another illusion of this rainbow vortex which then emptied out into pure consciousness, formless awareness, and then the formless awareness would recreate the rainbow vortex which would then be experienced as three dimensional form. Even the qigong masters were stuck in this rainbow vortex which was the secret astral realm of immortality—in this vortex everything was a joke. I was listening to the Bushman trance healing music and they too were laughing along with the secret of the universe—the rainbow vortex of pure consciousness which regenerated physical form while at the same time grounding up any illusion of our intentional ego.

The fundamental truth is that we do not exist—that only this cosmic rainbow snake or vortex created by formless awareness is real. Even the planets and the physical universe are a holographic illusion. Everything we experience is interrelated as energy blockages that get constantly undone and then knotted up, constantly sucked back into the rainbow vortex.

I realized that my DMT vision was the same as the Level 4 Rainbow meditation of the qigong training. This is the level that heals the deepest illness of HIV positive and bone marrow cancer, etc. I really felt I was in this rainbow body astral realm and then I heard this sound coming from my heart chakra. I was not making the sound—the sound was making me. It was the OHM that creates the universe. Then I heard a higher pitch version of the same sound coming from the center of my brain.

Soon after, I threw up and passed out. I desperately wanted to end the DMT trip and I even tried to jerk off since I thought that might stop the drug. My intention to do so was sucked back into the rainbow vortex and then I lost control of my arms before I could even get my hands in my crotch. My hands and arms were automatically going into healing mudras and I was going through the ending exercise when coming out of deep qigong meditation—rubbing the kidneys, rubbing the head and covering the eyes, massaging the ears, massaging the feet and the toes. The energy was making me do this automatically. I felt like I was with qigong master Chunyi Lin and his assistant qigong master Jim Nance in the rainbow vortex of reality, along with the Bushmen healers, all of us having transcended death.

I desperately wanted to drink some water but I didn't have the physical control to reach out to the water glass just a few feet from me. Finally I fell asleep while the drug slowly wore off. When I woke up five hours had passed, I had a severe headache and my body was totally relaxed yet felt completely spent.

Towards the end of our interview, I asked Drew what written sources and/or researchers he has found to be most helpful, seeing that he is both a mystic and a scholar and has clearly read widely.

DH: *Qigong master Chunyi Lin is of such ability that it's next to impossible to find someone who can do his level of healing. He can read past lives, do long distance healing, and has telepathy, precognition and telekinesis. When you take classes from Chunyi Lin, the experience is so profound that I've spent 8 years just reading a book a day to translate the learning back into Western concepts. That was already after I finished my Masters degree. So there's a fundamental difference between Western left-brain dominant reality and right-brain dominant shamanic reality. For me the connection between the two is nonwestern music. To even write about spiritual experiences which are very healing and powerful actually threatens the holistic integrity of their truth. In other words, the spirits get mad—there is a certain karmic balance—what the Mahayana Buddhists call "merit." Language is based on left-brain dominance so the experience of listening is also logically inferring the source of the I-thought. Otherwise we humans are cut off from the source of reality which creates all energy healing. No one can teach us this since we have to always question who is experiencing any type of energy or space-time transformation. The ego is such a powerful illusion that the more science attempts to discover the truth, the more humans destroy the foundation for our physical existence. This is why Vivekananda called science "the external path." I would say that Vivekananda's books on yoga are probably the best texts covering the integration of Western philosophy with nonwestern paranormal spiritual powers...*

My favorite book on the subject [of energy healing and spiritual transformation] is "Taoist Yoga: alchemy and Immortality" trans. by Charles Luk. The book is too inaccessible for most so I recommend Mantak Chia's first book, "Awakening the Healing Energy of the Tao" which has the reports of beginning Taoist Yoga practitioners...

Probably my favorite meditation yoga book is Yogananda's "Autobiography of a Yogi." His lineage is the same as the Taoist yoga teachings which rely on the "small universe" or microcosmic orbit as the foundation of the practice, then leading to the full-lotus or padmasana posture (the pyramid vortex energy).

I'm still processing all that Drew shared with me, though I will say that he definitely has a great ability to translate these really challenging non-verbal experiences and insights into language that we in the West can more readily understand, and he has done so prolifically on the Internet for years now. One tentative conclusion I take from all of this is Drew's recommendation to learn from a living master and have some kind of practice to fully embody whatever mystical experiences one has, whether through meditation, psychedelics, or otherwise.

Alan Lowenschuss: From Great Fear to Love

I first learned about Alan through some pieces he had put out on the Internet detailing his experiences. Intrigued by the parallels with the subject matter of this book, I emailed him to see if he would agree to a phone interview. He reluctantly agreed, saying that he would have to okay the manuscript before it went to press, to which I readily agreed. What follows is the complete, unedited interview…

Author: You've written some detailed first person journey reports of your psychedelic explorations that were fascinating to read, not to mention very helpful. Would you mind summarizing not only how you came to the use of plant medicines, but also what you specifically learned from them?

Alan: *I will put it very simply: As a beginning student of yoga, I was always seeking for mystical experiences that would give me some inspiration and encouragement that I was on the right path. I did have quite a few experiences in my first several years that did keep me going, yet these became fewer and further between as the years went on. Partly due to this, I began to seriously struggle with both self-doubt and doubt about my Indian teachers and the path I was on, which led me to ultimately take a major step back from it all. Perhaps I became more honest with myself about where I was at. And where I was at was that I wanted to experience the world more, become "someone" in the world and prove that I was okay. Not to mention have more hot sex!*

Author: Come again?

Well, isn't that what everyone secretly wants, when they're honest with themselves?

If they're misidentifying themselves with their ego, yes.

Right! Well that goes without saying. Anywho, what effectively happened is that being in the world for a while just led to a whole bunch more layers that needed to be peeled away. And now I had all this guilt and fear about "falling" from the yoga path, of not being a true yogi and deserting my lineages. I had always felt like, "Oh, I can go back to that anytime, let me just experience the world a little more…" Yet it wasn't that easy to go back. Psychedelics in a sense brought me back, but it was a painful process.

How so?

Just to work through all that guilt, shame, fear, misidentification with the body, the personality, the life story. Every time I've partaken of a plant sacrament it's been like that, though it's definitely become less challenging over time.

Can you give us a few highlights from your psychonautical expeditions?

Sure. My first several journeys were by myself at home with stuff I ordered over the Internet, San Pedro cactus and Jurema (an ayahuasca analogue). The San Pedro produced some of the most amazing sacred geometrical stuff, and I also recall listening to music and how "in" the music I became.

The Jurema was my first experience of a "bad trip" in the sense that I didn't think I was going to come back from it (and at one point felt I was stuck in this weird time loop) and it also resulted in an ego-death experience in which I felt I had been dismembered. It was so traumatic that I vowed never to do it again, yet there I was back at it in not too long—not because I was addicted, mind you, but because I needed to know. The next time I did it, I experienced this intense and horrifying loneliness, a sense of being completely cut off from others, God, love, everything. I thought of my mother and really felt her pain and cried deeply, and I very seldom cry.

Would you say that the Jurema opened your heart?

Yes, more so than it was. It made me painfully aware of how lonely and separate the ego really is, and again, how horrifying that is if we really look at it or can feel it in that way. My next experience with Jurema was my last. All I can remember is what seemed like hours of witnessing the most ugly, distorted faces, and feeling that I was a false guru who had been coming back lifetime after lifetime to lead people astray and be punished. That was the first time I really purged with the stuff and it was bad, coming out both ends, and shit.

Ooh, ugh. So what else?

Then I started to do the traditional ayahuasca brew with different shamans. What I began to recognize was that once all of the initial layers were out of the way on these journeys, I felt like I had in the first year of yoga—in my bliss body. I experienced that with mushrooms, too. It was always like a taste of enlightenment, a coming home to my true self, or Self. The work then became how to be in the world and still maintain that state, to be in the world but not of the world. It's been a process, yet I do feel the journeys help immensely. They've helped me to see areas that still call for attention."

You've noted that in this sense the plants effectively do something similar to that of a traditional guru?

Right. They show you where you're out of alignment, which means where you're still living from fear, which includes guilt, shame, lust, anger, etc. Initially, the medicines apparently needed to use "shock and awe" tactics to wake me up out of all of the illusion I was still asleep in. I sometimes say they "scared me straight." The thing is, the less fear you have going in, and/or the greater your ability to release the fear when it arises, the easier will the journey be, and that's so simple, yet not so easy! Especially when in the throes of a full-on psychedelic experience.

Wow, that sounds so similar to my own experiences! You've written about how you feel Ayahuasca brought you to *A Course in Miracles* and how helpful that's been to you on your journey, could you say a little about…

Definitely. ACIM mainly just confirmed and shed light on many of the realizations

I was having, and it also contained some things I had never seen anywhere else, particularly its metaphysics. Simply put, psychedelics, particularly ayahuasca, had enabled me to release much fear, which in ACIM is no different than ego, and the ego is essentially an attack on God (or Source, Spirit, True Love). When we feel fear about anything, it goes back to the one great Fear which is the fear of God, the fear of death of the ego (small self). It was probably just fear that kept me from psychedelics for so long, nothing more. So although I had those additional layers of illusion in my mid-thirties that I mentioned, I would say I was further along when I began to explore psychedelics for the very reason that I was open and ready to receive their teachings.

So where are you now with it all?

Well, I would say that life in general doesn't hold very much for me anymore, there's not too much that excites me or drives me like there used to be, including sex. I've also seen how even though there might be a twinge of regret, or the slight arising of anger, or that bit of lustful feeling still there, I can quite easily witness and let those things go these days. I guess I see these as some signs of progress, that I've been able to let go of a shitload of fear and can now look people in the eyes, see them as me, as a soul and not a body, and be present without having to know or do or be anything else. See, I wouldn't have even been able to say "shitload" before because of the societal taboo around "bad" words and my own going for years without saying them. Yet, to quote Shakespeare, "there's nothing good nor bad but thinking makes it so," and we can choose to see everything with love and as Love, if we wish.

Hmmm… I'm kind of going through that myself at this point and want to ask for your advice. You know, I'm about to publish this book and am a little bit concerned about the reaction from the worldwide yoga community…

Well, first of all, are you sure anyone's actually going to even read your beloved book? And even if they do get it and look at it, who will really fully engage with the material and in an open-minded way? Let's put it simply and clearly: People who judge you or the book harshly: 1) Probably haven't really read the whole book, or if they did, they saw only what they wanted to see; and 2) Probably could use some psychedelics themselves. So tell them to take 2 tabs and call you in the morning, then you'll talk [stoned laughter all around]. And if they can't do that, tell them to do what veteran yogi Norman Allen told Nick in that popular yoga movie "Enlighten Up": Go fuck themselves [even more profound stoned laughter]. In any case, here's my understanding now: It's all about letting go of fear, which means letting go of agendas because all agendas are fear-based. If you end up taking a psychedelic, you were meant to, no regrets. And if you end up publishing your book, you were meant to, too. Haven't people been reading some of it and telling you it's worth publishing?

For sure.

So what's the problem, you ain't ever gonna please everyone. But if you ask me, for someone who has done a certain amount of work on their self—or rather, been dissolving their ego—your book is really superfluous because they've learned to rely on inner guidance to help decide these matters. This is all too heady.

Point well taken. Did you read the manuscript I sent you [of this book]? What did you think?

Let's just say that the thing I like most about your book is that it exists, period.

Ha, nice, good to hear. I'll take that as a compliment, I guess…

Yeah, I just wish there was a bit more humor in it.

Hmmm… So anyway, just for the record, how do you pronounce your name and if you don't mind me asking, it's an unusual name, what are its origins?

I would go into it, but it's a kinda a long story and not a very interesting one at that. Pronounce it any way you like, I don't care. "Love by any other name is still Love."

13

Who I Am: Part 3

Autobiography of a "Gen-X" Yogi

Yoga, Ayahuasca & A Course In Miracles
Long Reads & Short Roads Home

> *"Everything in your life is there as a vehicle*
> *for your transformation. Use it!"*
>
> —Ram Dass

> *"Rise, awaken, seek the wise and realize. The path is difficult to*
> *cross like the sharpened edge of the razor, so say the wise."*
>
> —Katha Upanishad

> *"Fear binds the world. Forgiveness sets it free."*
>
> —-A Course in Miracles

> *"Love is the strongest medicine."*
>
> —Neem Karoli Baba

[Please Note: all participant names in the following true story have been left out due to the sensitive nature of this subject. If you are aware of the identities of those involved, please honor the author's request for discretion. Thank you.]

"You are not a true master, and you will NEVER be a true master!"

Harsh as they sounded and crushing as they were to his ego, the words seemed inevitable and eerily familiar. They also felt completely appropriate for that moment. And in that moment, surely he was demonstrating their truth by his laying face down on the ground outside of the ceremony space, sputtering, unable to sit up, barely even able to focus his mind for more than a few brief seconds at a time before it was once again hurled back into a horrifying vision of himself as a demon who was being cursed by the Divine Mother.

The woman's fury continued, for a moment a little less fiercely, realizing perhaps that she had gone too far:

"At least… you will NEVER be on the level of the Shaman!"

Yes, he knew, it was true. This was happening because he had not known his true place in the universe—he was suffering under the illusion that he was somehow on par with the shaman, or even in competition with him. This now was happening and HAD to happen as he needed to be tested and asked to submit to the teacher and the medicine, ayahuasca.

This process had been set in motion during his first session with the Shaman some 6 months prior. After that ceremony, he had written a long, detailed account of his journey, part of which related a competition he sensed developing between the Shaman and himself.

Here is a small portion from his journal:

"[I sensed a] power struggle between myself and the shaman. Serious questions began to arise in my mind: Where is the shaman taking us? Who are we truly serving here? How do I know what the shaman's true intent really is, if he even is even truly aware of what it is? Or maybe he is truly of the purest intentions, but maybe the aya-huasca and the traditions are not of the highest vibration. In which case, I really can't rely on him or the brew, I better start directing this experience toward the highest. I actually did sense that I/we were kind of stuck in some high astral spheres and could go higher. When the shaman chanted in Quechua, too, it sounded very cool, but also somewhat demonic.

"Now please don't misunderstand me here—I'm just relating to you things that were coming up for me and don't want you to think I'm passing judgment in any way. In fact, all of this got pretty much resolved anyway by beginning to think along the following lines:

"I do feel that Shaman is doing the best he can here, just as I am doing the best I can, though we are both still human. If I judge him, I judge myself. If anything, he is more humble in that he long ago joined with a time-honored practice that goes way beyond him, for which he is but the instrument. He is not the teacher here, the ayahuasca is the teacher, and he is just speaking/singing on its behalf. In fact, I later felt that actually he IS the ayahuasca. And here I am who is captaining my own ship without compass, very much asleep at the wheel, not fully connected to anything truly ancient, very much distracted by all of our society's many distractions, living in mental disarray. If I doubt anyone here, it should be my own egoic-demonic nature, which is

leading me to have such doubts in the first place!

"*I think the final resolution came when the Shaman stopped singing, lay back on one arm, and said: 'You see now the inner battle taking place. Ayahuasca forces you to choose which side you are on...' Or something to that effect. That was it! Who are you serving? Is it truth or falseness, purity or impurity, awakeness or asleepness? Looked at from that perspective, this is a choice that we all have to make, moment to moment. It's an ongoing process. Fall asleep, and you risk opening yourself to energies that are not fully awake. So the task is to be very vigilant—don't miss a beat, don't have a second thought! That became one of my mantras for the night: "No second thought!" Later, towards the end, the Shaman began singing a song in Spanish that had the line "no otra pensa," and that just confirmed what the ayahuasca was teaching (and again, he was the ayahuasca, or so I felt.)*

"*Another mantra for the night was "don't back down," and it was a bit of an epiphany when I suddenly realized why keeping one's back straight is so important—it's literally not letting your back down!*

"*This was all in the first couple of hours.*"

[Note: This was his first experience with a shaman using the traditional brew. He did have previous solo experiences with the Mimosa-Syrian Rue analogue, which is similar, yet also quite unique.]

Now, on this subsequent night, his sophomore trial with the Shaman, it felt like he was being shown that if he were to continue on this path, he needed to release all of his doubts once and for all and surrender to the medicine, as well as its divinely appointed administrator, the Shaman. This was an initiation. He also had a sense that this whole ceremony was there precisely for him to receive this very lesson. In any case, he seemed to have not much choice but to witness the undoing of what he had mistaken as his identity—the egoic, false self. Sometime later in the evening, the fallen yogi was rudely awakened once again by Kali:

"Do you now see that all of your yoga practice means nothing, it's worthless! All of the yoga you've ever done has been completely useless!"

Strange as it might sound, he did not try to defend himself a bit in response to this new, seemingly over-the-top attack and respond something along the lines of, "Well, now, let's just hold on one little second here and be fair... Worthless? Useless? You mean none of it's ever been of any value? Well, I beg to differ..." As if he could! No, not even a whisper of objection came out of his half-open mouth. Even if his brain and lips could have even begun to form such a coherent line of reasoning, and even though there was a small part of him that was shocked in disbelief at the piercing words spewing from the mouth of this apparent channeler of Kali Ma, he was down for the count and there was a much deeper and greater part of him that knew that it was all true, that he needed to just take it lying down, as it were. So he found himself merely assenting: "*Yes*" was all that squeaked out as he struggled to raise himself.

"Well, sit up and focus your mind!!!"

Yes, it was all about the mind in the end, wasn't it? Not so much about the body. He had obsessively practiced and prided himself on these amazing contortions and tricks with his body, yet that was all just the preliminary, tip-of-the-iceberg work of yoga, and did not by any means signify "mastery." Mastering yoga, mastering the mind, would require a much greater work and discipline than he had even dimly imagined was necessary. In fact, in the past decade or so of his yoga journey, he had slipped into a kind of mental complacency in regard to his practice, a comfortable numbness, if you will, feeling that he had somehow made it on some level because he was no longer so perturbed by certain external events.

Yet this night was showing him painfully and exquisitely pointedly how much work there was to really do as he proceeded down the rabbit hole into deeper layers of his being, and that his journey was really only just now beginning…

Now, that was all just on one level, a secondary level of interpretation. On another, more primal level, again, he felt himself as the rankest demon imaginable, completely cursed and doomed to lifetimes of torment due to having abruptly left his teachers years before and debased the yoga tradition with his phony, watered-down teachings that were guided not by a truly divine inspiration, but rather his own fear-based financial concerns (fears), the desire to have an easy life, etc., all due to having fallen away from the true path of yoga. In essence, he had missed the point, missed the mark, and this was not just a "mistake," this was his Doom, his Damnation. Perhaps what especially killed him (the ego) was the feeling that he was exposed, and that everyone, all of his students, really could see through his whole charade and were just playing along with the façade on the surface of things. (He saw it as no coincidence that all of this happened on the same day that he graduated 12 students from his Yoga Teacher Training program with, to all appearances, a very beautiful ceremony, enjoyed by all.)

Here is another piece of what he wrote after that first session that might help paint a fuller picture:

"One of the first things that came up was that I really don't have it together as a teacher. I was seeing all of the things that aren't completely kosher about what I do, especially in light of what I could be (and I was being shown that, too, particularly later) and in light of the night's facilitator, our Shaman, and I was just seeing how much I

am currently missing the mark, all the little things I need to do to clean up my act and be 'crystal clear.' I don't think the ayahuasca is asking for anything less than that. In which case, we all are falling short of the mark. And I understood that, too, and I also recognized that as much as I was in awe of the shaman, he, too, is going through his own process of evolution.

"I also saw that our 'human condition' is what it is insofar as we have allowed our egoist-demonic nature to get the better of our higher impulses to evolve beyond selfishness. And I saw all-too-clearly how much ego I truly have, how much I think of 'me' over and above 'we,' how many times my immediate, unconscious thought is not for the upliftment of others, but for the aggrandizement of myself. As I said, it wasn't too pretty.

"Again, though, I realized that we've all made this luciferous rebellion again God, it happened long ago. We chose to be separate, to want to live apart from God, to go our own way. But it hasn't truly served us, nor the highest good of all. So now the task is just to correct course and consciously choose to expand our consciousness beyond our egoistic prison.

"That said, I was feeling this all very much being applied to me personally, and I actually felt exposed. I felt as if now the students who had come to be taught yoga were all seeing me for who I really am, which is a fraud, phony, half-baked yoga dilettante. I felt the shaman was seeing all of this, too. What added fuel to this was the fact that the energy began to move me into 'kriyas,' or automatic bodily postures and movements.

"For example, I suddenly realized I had my arms raised in the air. Just a little later I discovered my upper body was being circled around like I do at the outset of most of my yoga classes. It's not that these didn't feel good, they did. And these were the kinds of experiences I had always wanted to have 10 years ago when I had been in a Kundalini yoga shaktipat group but never did. Now I was forced to acknowledge that although these were 'fun,' they also were the result of unconsciousness, of my own asleepness. I again had a feeling of slight embarrassment that people were seeing me, particularly my students, and realizing I didn't really have it all together. (This was all somewhat confirmed later when one of the sitters told me that at one point I looked like one of the asuras/demons who do yoga poses as a way to gain favor of Lord Shiva—something from a Hindu comic book she read.)"

Again, note that was from his first night's experience with the Shaman months before, one in which the Shaman had used less potent medicine. This night's journey had taken things to their absurd conclusion: Not only was his life and teaching a complete farce, which would have been bad enough as it was, but he was also cursed forever for his phony "practice," plunged into the deepest and darkest hell to shake and tremble and be humbled at the feet of the "true" yoga masters, among whom the Shaman was also numbered. He was being made a laughingstock of the universe—an example of what NOT to do, or else be damned for eternity. He was the Cosmic Fool, the Jokerman, the Buffoon. And he couldn't get up for falling down. God knows he was trying.

Keep in mind that this was a VERY powerful brew that the participants had been given that evening, the most potent that the Shaman had ever administered. In fact, the Shaman was originally going to offer 2 nights of ceremonies, then at the last minute decided that with this particularly potent brew only one would be necessary. (Later the yogi was told that he wasn't even the worst off that night. Apparently there was a woman who kept pleading "Please God help me!" over and over again, to the point that some of the other participants were considering calling 911. As with the yogi, she was eventually taken outside and plunged under a cold shower, ultimately coming through the other side of her own nightmarish ordeal still alive to process it all.)

To begin at the beginning…

The medicine had taken effect almost immediately that evening, and it was very soon that he found himself writhing on the ground like a snake, actually very much enjoying the feeling of it, yet also remembering that they had all been asked to sit up and sit still during the ceremony. Still, having no consciousness of time at that moment, but sensing that he was actually getting away with this behavior for a while, the thought occurred that maybe this was permitted…?

The thought also arose of some kind of special dispensation due to the very unique way the medicine was moving him—him, and only him. These passing, half-conscious thought-bubbles were quickly burst when the shaman came over and informed him, firmly yet gently, that he needed to sit up. This was part of the Shaman's tradition of using the ayahuasca, not just to have a cool psychedelic journey, but as a meditative, yogic practice to master the mind. Apparently true mastery means complete stillness. Some moments later he was back in his body enough to say, "I'm really trying to…" and he did actually manage this for a moment, only to collapse back down again unconscious a moment later.

Not too long after the Shaman came over, he was forcibly removed by sister Kali, or so it felt in that fragile, suggestible state, where the littlest word or gesture can be magnified to cosmic proportions.

Indeed, later he was to reflect on how quickly the whole journey went south, given the sudden roughness with which he was being treated. If he had just taken the brew on his own, he thought, maybe he would have just writhed on the ground the whole time and the entire experience would have been as heavenly as it felt in that moment of writhing. He would have continued, perhaps, to have a view of himself as this highly advanced being with a special connection to the medicine, evidenced by his blissful, serpentine movements.

As it turned out, as soon as his very suggestible/susceptible ayahuasca-flooded body-mind was given the idea that there was something wrong with him, the whole experience in an instant became hellishly tormenting. Suddenly he began to see how clearly every thought he had ever had, and hence every action he had ever performed, had come from a place of selfishness. As you might guess, this was unbearable to see. He later recalled clearly expressing at this moment something to the effect of, "So much ego… it's all ego." This was within earshot of Kali and it appeared she just knowingly and triumphantly harrumphed.

Then began the ordeal—the being put under the cold shower (by another sitter, who also handled him roughly, he felt), left out on the ground outside the yurt, the verbal humiliation of "the great yogi," and the continued negative energy thrown at him… all of which ultimately resulted in him lying unconscious face down on the ground for the duration… until the Shaman finally came out and did a whole healing ceremony over the completely devastated, humbled one.

Not long after this, as the Mrtyunjaya Mantra was being chanted, he was led, by a considerably more subdued Kali (also coming down from the experience), back into the hall to be with the others once again. Only now he was in a state that could only best be described as a "blank slate." For the moment, at least, every illusion, every selfish or arrogant conceit had been removed from his awareness. He was in a place of complete submission and had to be actually led by the hand, like a little child, back to his place among the gathered. Only he wouldn't sit in his assigned seat, he would only sit down to the left of the Shaman. This was not conscious, mind you, it was told to him later. Also not apparent to him was how much his physiognomy had changed within the space of the last 4 hours (which felt more like an eternity). He did not look like himself, he was told by his close friend who was also present there (though not allowed to leave the yurt to help him), he appeared completely other. It was scary, she said.

He recalls sitting there motionless, in another world, only half-hearing, as if from afar, the closing words of the Shaman. One piece of the discourse that did make it through to his awareness and stick: *"When we first begin working with ayahuasca, we start to see how much inner work there is to be done."* Indeed, the night's events seemed to have proven this to him without a shadow of a doubt. But what to do when you've seen that your whole life is a lie, a complete and total sham? It all seemed futile. There was a part of him that wanted to do nothing but leave every-thing he was doing and join the Shaman in the Peruvian jungle to continue with this process. Or perhaps to just meditate for the rest of his days unto death…

Yet that was not an option at this point, and the waking nightmare continued. In the coming days, it felt as if his heart was breaking, or maybe just broken was his will to live. For about a whole month he had difficulty just looking people in the eye after what he had seen about himself. Some close friends tried to convince him that he was being too hard on himself, that he was "a good person," that everyone really loved him, etc. He wasn't completely buying it, after what he had seen. And yet, slowly, slowly, a healthier, more balanced ego-perception began to be born and assert itself. And through this process of ego re-assertion, a thought came to full flowering that had been there in seed form all along:

"I didn't deserve that treatment from them."

So he wrote a letter to his persecutors, as well as the Shaman. At this point, in a still somewhat paranoid state, perhaps, he really felt that the whole ordeal had been orchestrated by the Shaman, and that the two others had conspired in it with him. However, he was certainly clearheaded enough not to accuse the Shaman of this, yet to make it clear to him and to the "sitters" involved that he felt that they had acted inappropriately. Indeed, as he was to learn only later, according to the rules for sitters laid down by the Shaman himself, sitters are to speak very little, if at all, to the participants, and certainly not to speak negatively or harshly to them in that very vulnerable state. Yet he did not need this information to feel that he had been mistreated.

So he wrote his letters.

The letters to the sitters tried their best to refrain from accusatory or judgmental language, just to express that he felt what had happened was inappropriate and he was seeking some kind of acknowledgment and resolution with them. From the sister sitter who had held his head under the shower, he received a response that essentially took to say,

"Join the club, we've all had our asses kicked by the medicine, deal with it."

There was no further response after he wrote a follow-up in which he said that what happened left him feeling abused, even raped. (He had perhaps gone too far with that one.)

The letter to the Kali sitter sister received even less of an acknowledgment, just the maddeningly brief text:

"Peace to all Beings."

The Shaman's email response was disappointingly sparse and non-committal.

His words were cordial, encouraging even, yet said nothing about what was done, only that everything really was fine, and that the yogi was doing good work and should keep on doing what he was doing—that things would get much better for him, he'd see. The Shaman also suggested coming down to Peru at some point for a *dieta* (a more extended retreat working with the medicine). Again there was a follow-up, and again no response. So he was left to wonder and stew a bit more in all of this…

Until a few months later. It was the end of July and the Day Out of Time gathering brought him once again back to the site of his humbling at the yurt. Only this time things all seemed to be turned around. In the morning, he offered a well-received yoga session in the yurt to the assembled, followed by an equally well-received series of sound healings with didgeridoo in the main house. (Interestingly, while this was happening in the main house, a team of workers dismantled the yurt—a last act of revenge by the woman of the house whose partner, still owner of the property but not often there, had gotten physically violent with her and then gone off with another woman. The thought occurred to him that this sudden turn of events in this relationship was at least partly due to the immensely powerful energy of the ceremony and the medicine from that tumultuous night months prior, and complemented the poetic full-circle closure to the whole affair that was to come…)

At this time, the yogi also met a woman from Peru who he was to develop a close friendship, and who just happened to come all the way from the other coast with another Peruvian woman. At the end of the day he and the second Peruvian got to talking and it suddenly dawned on both of them that they knew each other from the first retreat with the Shaman! Yes, this was none other than the Shaman's wife or lover (he was never quite clear on this point) just that at that moment the two had agreed to be apart, yet she was still helping the Shaman to organize his gatherings.

He asked her if he could tell her something in private, and she agreed. They went for a walk during which he shared the events of the night at the yurt a few months before, a gathering at which she had not been present. Much to his surprise, she noted that the Shaman was already thinking that it would not be wise to continue to work with the woman whom he felt had acted inappropriately at the ceremony as they had received similar reports, and he was asked if he knew of anyone else who might be in the liaison position for the next gathering in the area? To shorten what could be another longish tale, what ended up happening is that through some mysterious process he became the organizer for the next ceremony! And that ceremony turned out to be a very blessed experience for all involved, and the Shaman himself noted that it was one of his best yet (and he had done many).

To Recap this Turn of Events

We saw the yogi's complete humiliation/devastation at the yurt, a major ego-death experience that left him in a very vulnerable state, deeply questioning his very existence, feeling that his whole life was one big lie. Also, there was the feeling that he had been abused by the Shaman and his assistants. Then, just a few months later, there was a redemption of sorts during a Day Out of Time, a day when the whole thing got turned on its head, and the felt sense of a conspiracy against him seemed proven to be all in his head. He ended up interviewing the Shaman for a book he is writing on the subject of yoga and plant medicines

Of course, the yogi in this story is me. I decided to write the story in the third person for various reasons, including seeing it more objectively, not getting too caught up in the "I" of it all.

I did not write it in third person to hide behind a literary disguise. I completely own the story and have retold it to the best of my ability with no alterations. I choose now to write from the first person again to bring my journey up to date—and there is quite a bit of updating to be done, for where I am now is a decidedly new space of understanding of all of this.

Three years, three relationships, three publishers, several other ayahuasca Shamans, and a whole host of new experiences and thinking on this whole subject later, I feel that I am in a better position to share about yoga, truth, illusion, ego, spirit… and psychedelics.

Some of the High and Low-lights of My Journey

◎ Having 2-3 well-known publishers interested in this work, and at the last moment, just when IT was about to happen, the deal was about to be made, being turned down, and in the process reviving those deep down feelings of unworthiness, of not having it all together.

◎ Definitely connected to that: Getting into three relationships during this period where what felt so right at the start, ended so quickly back in shadow-land once again. I seemed to be getting the message not to fool around with being in relationships, at least not until I work through these deep blockages, particularly around finances. One seeming sign: At the climactic close of one of them, my laptop was stolen and I had not backed up the latest version of this book, which I had in any case put off for months as I pursued the path of true love. In the subsequent aftermath, on a mushroom journey together, that particular romantic partner later reopened that same Mother Wound from the ceremony (and from other, past relationships, including with my birth mother). Suffice it to say, next to ayahuasca, these relationships have revealed the deepest truths about my inner barriers to real love.

◎ Meeting with a world-renowned astrologer who just happened to have been a Meher Baba devotee for the last 4 decades. Recall that in the early Sixties, the Indian guru Meher Baba had a pamphlet published in America, *"God in a Pill?"* through which he wanted to warn the hippie youth of the dangers of the use of LSD and other similar psychedelic compounds. Among other things, this small book declaimed that, contrary to popular countercultural opinion, these and similar drugs were NOT in the least doorways to the spiritual. The self-proclaimed "Avatar of the Age," Meher Baba's writings on this subject were enough to prompt the former Harvard Psychology professor Dr. Richard Alpert to write to him for counsel. The master replied that LSD only served to bring Alpert and those who were truly ready, to Him. Not long after, Alpert went to India and found his guru, another Baba, Neem Karoli Baba, and the rest is history.

Getting back to the story at hand, although the astrologer in question did not explicitly say it, I gathered that the catalyst for his becoming a devotee of Meher Baba was an LSD trip in the early '70s during which the MB appeared to him and told him he was his teacher, which would make sense as he had essentially informed Ram Dass that the only redeeming value of LSD was to possibly bring to the Avatar those who were ready for Him.

Interestingly, more recently, another world-renowned astrologer told me about an LSD trip of his in late 1969 during which he saw a face in the clouds that looked like Zeus with the sun shining through his eyes. On returning to his apartment, he turned on the radio and the first thing he heard was the news of Meher Baba's passing. He realized then that it was Meher Baba's face that he had seen in the clouds. Note that he was not a MB devotee then nor since.

In any case, the astrologer who is a Meher Baba devotee counseled me strongly against writing this book. He also stated that I had severely damaged my aura through the use of psychedelics. While there is a part of me that feels there is truth to what he shared, another part truly doubts it; I want Meher Baba himself to tell me that my aura is damaged, while I'm on LSD! In any case, I was impressed with Meher Baba's teachings and do take *them* to heart.

And then there was that other Ayahuasca shaman and his wife with whom I did several medicine journeys. He was not native Peruvian, but had trained in Peru and was also interestingly a follower of yet another Baba, the controversial South Indian self-proclaimed avatar, Sai Baba (Sai Baba had not yet passed when I first met this shaman.) Like the other Peruvian-trained shaman I had worked with, his ceremonies included the traditional *icaros* from the Amazon, as well as Sanskrit mantras, and even some specific to Sai Baba. When I told him of this book, he took great interest and promised to help me with it. At one point, he even sat me down and gave me a whole beautiful dissertation in Spanish on the subject with a translator. The main point I gathered from it was his very confident assertion that ayahuasca is none other than Soma, the psychoactive brew of the ancient Vedas, or at least a sister of it. Where he got this information I did not ask, though I understood that it was from the medicine itself, as well as from other trusted sources. It's interesting to note, too, that his beloved partner, a follower of Swami Muktananda and Gurumayi, excitedly shared with me that Muktananda told her during one of her medicine journeys that ayahuasca is no different than Soma. Perhaps you can see how confusing this can be as to who and what to believe when one guru says one thing and another strongly maintains something else. (I will also note that at this moment in time, I had serious doubts about the spirituality of both Sai Baba and the Muktananda/Gurumayi lineage, and also questioned whether these teachers would ever condone the use of ayahuasca as a spiritual tool.)

On that note, I recently met yet another Baba, Prem Baba, believed to be an enlightened being, who currently presides at an ashram in Rishikesh, India, yet who is from Brazil and grew up heavily immersed in ayahuasca shamanism, later training extensively in psychotherapy. The particularly interesting thing about this teacher is that he openly uses all three layers in his teaching: the traditional yogic layer, the psychotherapeutic layer, and the medicine layer, skillfully weaving them together into a teaching that he calls "The Path of the Heart." That said, in recent years he has moved away from offering ayahuasca sessions in certain parts of the world like the US, partly due to the illegality, and also apparently because he wants to place more focus on silence and meditation. It appears his worldwide following is growing rapidly.

• • •

What Ayahuasca Has and Hasn't Done for Me

Clearly Ayahuasca hasn't made me enlightened, if there truly is such a thing, though it has done the work of a traditional guru and illuminated the darkness within (Jung's "Shadow"), which has allowed me to be more aware of and correct/prevent self-serving, fear-based thoughts, words and actions.

It also hasn't made me completely free of fear, though through it's use I feel so much more free of the grosser manifestations of fear than I did 5 years ago before I began on this journey, something which I attribute to directly facing and living through my deepest sources of suffering with the medicine.

It hasn't yet completely unblocked my heart and throat centers, which perhaps have been closed at least since 11-years-old when my parents went through a very painful separation and then divorce, partly which I blamed on myself. Yet it has helped me to be much more aware of those blockages, based in deep-seated feelings of guilt and self-loathing, and to be seeking tools with which to release them.

It hasn't brought me financial abundance or even much greater day-to-day joy in living; yet again, it has made me so much more conscious of self-sabotaging thoughts and actions (such as how the ego sabotaged the publication of this book), so that slowly, slowly, I am emerging from the shadow world based in fear and self-serving and preserving impulses into living a life based in love, loving others as myself.

Finally, and perhaps most amazingly, I do feel that I've been guided by the spirit of ayahuasca this whole time to the different places I've lived, the people I've encountered, and the lessons I've learned along the way. I also feel that it has brought me to a deeper understanding of the human psyche, which in turn has prepared me for the next huge revelation on my journey, the most recent and the last that I will share here…

• • •

A Course in Miracles

"This world you seem to live in is not home to you. And somewhere in your mind you know that this is true."

—A Course in Miracles

I had known about this particular book since I had first moved to Florida 10 years ago to teach yoga. It had always been just on the periphery of my awareness, and there had been the thought: "Hmmm, that might be a really worthwhile read at some point…" The author occasionally showed up in little local spiritual publications I picked up occasionally and I was generally impressed by what he was saying, feeling he was tapped into something. Several years later, after opening a yoga school, something prompted me to purchase a deck of inspirational cards based on the author's book which I would occasionally give to my students, only to discover after a while that the cards seemed a little off, not completely the New Age thought system that has more often than not become what we think of as mainstream "spiritual" thinking. After a while, I didn't feel so comfortable using the cards anymore, so I stopped giving them out.

In more recent years, someone gave me the particular book in question, Gary Renard's *Disappearance of the Universe (2003)*, and I carried it around with me for a good long while before finally actually reading it this past March while putting on a yoga retreat in Bali. At first, I just read it on the fly and skipped around in it, thinking I could just extract nuggets from different parts of the thick text that seemed interesting, as I often do with books these days (you?). Until I realized that to really receive the full impact and import of the book, I would have to read it start to finish. I ended up going through most of it on Nyepi, the day of silence in Bali where no one goes out or uses electricity, which allowed for just the right environment to devote to one of the most fascinating and catalyzing books I've ever read.

Essentially, Renard's *Disappearance* is a primer for *A Course in Miracles (ACIM)*, though on the surface it's disguised as something else. That perhaps is a draw for someone like me. If it had clearly been about ACIM from the start, I might not have ever picked it up, for the same reason I never got into the Course itself (too big, biblical, Christian, etc.), though it too was ever on the periphery of my awareness. Renard himself says that if it hadn't been for what happened to him to cause him to get into ACIM, he would probably never have understood the Course, as it's just too inaccessible to the lay-reader. It is a fact that Renard's book has brought many lapsed ACIM students back to the Course, and also inspired many more, like me, to pick it up and begin to understand its message. What is still controversial is how Renard's book came to be written…

As Renard tells it, it all began back in 1993 when he was living with his wife in Connecticut and going through a rather rough period in his life. Then one day, out of the blue, he was visited by these two Ascended Masters in his living room who appeared just as real to him as any other two people sitting on his sofa. Thus began a series of 18 talks between Renard and the Ascended Masters, Arten and Pursah, that was to become the basis of "*Disappearance.*" Renard claims he actually recorded most of these talks and transcribed them, but then later threw away the tapes. (This reminds me of Krishnamacharya and Pattabhi Jois claiming that they created Ashtanga Yoga from an ancient yogic scripture written on palm leaf, the Yoga Korunta, which they said was not too longer after eaten by ants.) While reading *Disappearance*, I kept debating with myself as to whether or not Renard actually could have come up with all of this on his own. On the one hand, it's quite brilliant and there's so much in there that would have been challenging to pull off by himself. On the other hand, he had 10 years to write it and he's clearly a really smart guy. It really could go either way, and in any case, the secret is well-kept with Renard.

Whatever the truth may be, the fact is that while there is minority Course contingents who seem out to get Renard for being a fraud, there seems to be a majority of insiders in the Course community who have found Renard's book to be helpful and clarifying, whether he is the sole author or not. While there is still a part of me that wants to leave this whole question open, it is enough for me to know that Renard's book has earned the respect of longtime Course students, not to mention that I myself found it helpful. So without further ado about nothing, what's so important about all of this that I feel called to share about how it helped my own process?

First of all, the Course (and this is very much about the Course, not Renard's book, which was just the inspiration to pick it up) is for the most part very much in keeping with the deepest teachings of yoga as found in Advaita Vedanta, as well as with Eastern mystical thought in general. Bill Thetford, who dictated the Course for his colleague, Helen Shuchman, the channel for the material, once called ACIM a "Christian Vedanta." That's a nice way of concisely summing it up, yet it's really not Christian in the conventional sense (though it claims to have been dictated to Shuchman by Jesus); and it's not really Vedantic either, considering that it has certain emphases, such as the practice of forgiveness, which we don't find explicitly in the Vedantic texts. It actually presents more of the Gnostic/Mystic teachings of Jesus, such as what we find in the Gospel of Thomas, and which Renard's books have brought to the fore.

For the sake of brevity, I will list what I feel are the essential points of *A Course In Miracles:*

1. *Only what is truly permanent is Real, all else is illusion.*

2. *The world, and even what we think of as the Universe, is impermanent and thus illusionary (the Sanskrit term is "Maya.")*

3. *The only thing that we can really say to be Real is Love, and Love is synonymous with God (or call It what you wish: Source, Self, the Absolute, Oneness, etc.).*

4. *Everything else that is not Love was created by the ego in primal fear of God's retribution. The ego lives and thrives on separation, and it created the entire Universe to hide from God.*

5. *There is only one Ego appearing as many. The ego's horrific fear of God/Love is deeply buried in each of our subconscious minds, and all the little fears we feel in our life go back to this one primal fear. The irony is that even though one of the ego's greatest fears is of being alone in the universe, cut off from others and Source, that's its whole game—to create separation, division, and thus, in a word, Fear. It is this Fear that keeps creating new bodies over and over and over again, thus perpetuating the illusion of separation.*

6. *Through specific mental disciplines using our discriminative capacity (essentially a kind of Jnana Yoga), particularly that of Forgiveness, we make the journey back to God/Source.*

7. *True forgiveness, as the Course teaches, is not just to forgive someone even though you still feel they wronged you, but rather, to recognize that there really is only one Ego appearing as many. We have never truly been separate from God, and thus there is truly Nothing to forgive! Yet we do need to forgive, as it is through the practice of forgiveness that we remind ourselves of the truth of what we are, and we restore the mind to its original wholeness, the Christ Consciousness.*

8. *As we do these practices, we are not fixing anything, but rather correcting the ego's deranged thought system. We are essentially removing the blockages to Love within ourselves, and waking ourselves up out of the dream/illusion of separation that the ego created. The Course says (like it not, believe it or not), this whole process of forgiveness and awakening to our true Self is what we're really here for, what we all REALLY want, nothing else. Deep down, we know*

that this is not our true home, and yet we've played along with the illusion out of fear of God, and yet ultimately God is Love, which has no opposite.

So applying all of this to my own journey… What I discovered, first with meditation, and later with ayahuasca, is actually how profound, primal, and deeply embedded my own suffering truly is. I was most painfully aware of this as a teenager, yet covered it over with things like distance running which provided merely a temporary Band-Aid for that core existential angst. So on the surface, I could be relatively free of that pain, yet it still existed within me on a deep level, and was the true source of my feelings of unworthiness, guilt, shame, self-loathing and anger to the point of rage at all life.

I used to feel I was unique in this, and that was both a source of pride *and* disempowerment, which I was continually cycling back and forth between—inferiority, then superiority, and back around again. What has taken a long time to dawn in my awareness is the idea that what I thought was unique to me is really a human (or rather, Cosmic) problem that I mistakenly took personally. Or rather, we *think* it's a problem. Our suffering seems so real, and yet ultimately, say the great wisdom teachings (Buddhism, Vedanta, the Course, etc.), it's not truly real, and at the heart of things we have always been safe at home—and in our heart of hearts, we know this.

So with these medicine journeys, I could stop at a certain level of interpretation and say: Wow, I didn't realize how really fucked up I am, I really still have so much shit to work on!!! And in a relative sense, yes, that's true. On a still deeper level, if I do that, I also get sucked into making the whole thing more real that it is, rather than merely witnessing it, releasing the judgment and forgiving the thought that there is anything other than perfection, that there is anything that can truly affect Spirit, that behind all of this is Unconditional Love.

The only problem with this approach is that it's very challenging to do that and not feel guilty and in fear of the judgment of others, not to mention the sense that one is escaping the "real world" and one's "true" feelings. One teacher friend on Maui has been trying to get me to first feel my inner rage, particularly at my father, saying that I'm in denial, numb, and the only way out is in and through. That seems to me to be but one method, one path. Another, though, and more in line with the Course, is to recognize that the deck has been stacked against us all—perhaps through millions of years and thousands of incarnations of thinking we're a body-mind-ego—and perhaps the best we can do is, yes, to acknowledge those feelings, yet also release them with forgiveness—forgiveness of everything, with the acknowledgment that, to quote that Leonard Cohen song, there is a crack in everything (and everyone) in this world, that's how the light gets through. We thus forgive what only appears to be "wrong," now seeing the perfection in the seeming imperfection.

So the 7-year-old wounded inner child might feel: Mom, Dad, you really fucked up my whole life, I hate you (of course, didn't know the f-word at that point ;) The 44-year-old yoga guy, though, might acknowledge those childhood grievances, yet now be able to truly OWN it and forgive it, with the recognition that they were doing the best they knew how, just as he is. If he hates them or gets angry at them for anything, it is really only coming from how their judgment of him dredges up his own feelings of guilt, shame, unworthiness, etc. (in a word: Fear) Yet those feelings are not even truly his own feelings! They lie deeply embedded within us all as part of this shared collective unconscious ego-mind, including his parents! They might express themselves differently in each individual, yet ultimately they emanate from the same separate source.

I began to realize all of this even before getting involved with ACIM, mainly through yoga and working with the spirit medicine plants, which I feel prepared me for the Course. After one particularly revelatory evening of medicine work during which I had been really seeing and taking full responsibility for my own part in the whole drama with "Kali Ma" that erupted the night at the yurt, I felt the strong directive to write to my "persecutor" and finally bring some resolution to it all. Here is a just slightly edited version of my Facebook message to her:

Namasté Wanted to just check in with you to apologize about my reaction to what happened at the ceremony that night at the yurt. I was resisting the truth of what was coming through you to tell me, because it was too painful to look at... Instead of seeing what you did as wrong or inappropriate, it was really for me to surrender to the perfection of what was, and to receive the lesson with great humility—and I did, too, but not without a bit of a fight. And my reaction was perfect, too, because it was good for my sanity at that point to do that, my healthy ego boundaries needed to re-assert themselves, at least it felt that way, otherwise I would have been traumatized for much longer. Anyway, I feel now that really the appropriate response from me was/is to thank you (you as the instrument for that deep teaching) for facilitating that ego death process that night, and I am sorry for the fallout that occurred, and I also realize now that there's a sense in which one could say that you sacrificed yourself for my liberation, so I really feel the need to express my absolute gratitude for what you did. Anyway, that's all I wanted to say, felt that so strongly during my last session with the Mother Vine on the Solstice. Perhaps you already felt that from me, just putting it into words to make it more concrete...

When I wrote this, I had no idea of what the response would be—more of the same harshness I had experienced that horrific night, or what…? Yes, there was still a good bit of that ashamed child that feared more of the same chastisement from the Mother. And yet that fear, like all fear, was unfounded…

Namasté to you… I feel like a weight has been lifted off my shoulders. Your message means more than you know. The timing was perfect! I too must apologize for not being more loving and humble. Nothing happens by mistake in God's world. There is no good or bad, just learning curves. Sometimes our lessons can be painful, but is sometimes necessary for us to attain enlightenment. The ego is very cunning. The good news is that if we keep our focus on the divine, the ego doesn't stand a chance! So many lessons to be learned in this world. I've come to realize that the only thing that is truly real and everlasting is love. It sounds like your process is coming along beautifully. I am grateful to have been part of it. I think it has been healing for both of us. Being in "The Christ Consciousness" can be a challenging journey but it is the most rewarding! I was reading A Course in Miracles today and thought I would share this with you:

"I am here only to be truly helpful.

I am here to represent he who sent me.

I do not have to worry about what to say or do because he who sent me will direct me.

I am content to be wherever he wishes knowing he goes there with me.

I will be healed as I let him teach me to heal."

You have a great gift. You are a true healer who can make a difference in many lives. Remember to be humble and that you are a vessel that God works through. Love always…

As I just re-typed these words I had an "aha" moment. I realized that I had not re-read this message since it was written, and at that time I first read it, I really knew nothing about *A Course in Miracles* and so they did not mean as much to me as they do now. I also suddenly recalled that over the past couple of weeks of writing this, I had been considering including that very excerpt from the Course in this piece! Whoa! This to me is a sign of being led by Spirit to the Course and to this moment, and I also take it as a good indication it's probably a good time to shut up and let this all go, too. Yet before I do, just one more beautiful idea from the Course:

"The holiest place on earth is where an ancient hatred becomes a present love."

• • •

So much to say about all of this, and yet nothing at all! Isn't it ironic how writings that point to simplicity, unity, and emptiness can be long and convoluted? But perhaps they are complex because we have become so complex... and with so many complexes! As the saying goes, *the truth is simple, but it ain't easy*. A Course in Miracles is a 1200 page document that essentially makes the same holographic point over and over and over again just to drive it home to the heart of each student: Learn to see the other as yourself, for as you see and treat them, you see and treat yourself, so release all judgment, detach and stay in witness consciousness. I recently heard this great quote about listening to the voices in your own head: "Fire the judge and hire the witness."

Like yoga, for most of us it's a long, gradual process. Peeling an onion one layer at a time. So if I have repeated both *advice and warnings* here, it is because they are both warranted given the spiritual quagmire we find ourselves wallowing in.

Which brings me to something that has been an ongoing theme in my process, and an open question for me throughout: This idea of spiritual "shortcuts," as in shortcuts to enlightenment. Yes, we've all wondered about this, or at least, I am guessing at least all of you seekers who have come this far with me on this particular quest for understanding. And most of us here have probably heard the categorical response: "There are no shortcuts!" And: "There's no way around it, you've got to do the work!" "What? You think you can take ayahuasca and become one with God and that's it? Ha!"

Well, actually, there may be something to this, especially when you consider how deep the rabbit hole really goes (i.e., how stuck in the muck we are, and how many potential incarnations we might have left). This is why spiritual experiences are, when all is said and done, just experiences—they don't last, and yet they might just move us an inch forward, just to let in a pinpoint of light to illuminate the darkness of spiritual nescience, and in the process save us from that much more Maya-bound suffering. And this is perhaps why, beyond just the spiritual marketing, there may actually be truth behind claims to a given pathway being a shortcut.

Three of the main paths I have been on in my life have made such a claim to spiritual quickening: When I first received shaktipat initiation from a Kundalini teacher in the mid-'90s, I was informed that *moksha* (liberation) would occur within the next three births. Ten years later, the first night I received ayahuasca from the Shaman in this story, our group was told at the outset that this was the "quick path." And *A Course in Miracles* maintains that the miracle of love and the work of forgiveness can save a seeker thousands of years of stumbling in the dark.

So is there really any truth to these claims? Really no one stuck in the illusion can really say, yet the sensed feeling is: Yes, there is some truth. BUT we still need to do the work, there's no way around that, yet the yoke gets lighter, quicker and is that much more intense!

Certainly it was a good dose of ayahuasca that produced the most intense and profound experience of my life, next to my birth, which I don't consciously remember. This one experience alone feels like it has saved me a lot of time. There was so much of that night that I did not recount, and so much I don't recall, yet I do know that the medicine was moving me to speak and even shout through a good portion of it. Whether this was just recycled portions of my patterned mind, actual revelations coming through, or both, I will close here with just one message that seemed that night to be an ultimate one for me, and still feels so. A message most worthy of being shared. At a peak moment in my experience, when the medicine was very actively working in me, I recall sitting up and repeating over and over again:

The greatest lesson in this life is to be still!
The greatest lesson in this life is to be still!
The greatest lesson in this life is to be still!

The Last Word…

*"It is the wise and learned man, skilled in sorting out
the pros and cons of an argument who is really endowed
with the qualities necessary for self-realization."*

—Shankara

*"The journey to God is merely the reawakening of the knowledge
of where you are always, and what you are forever. It is a
journey without distance to a goal that has never changed. Truth
can only be experienced. It cannot be described and it cannot
be explained. I [Jesus] can make you aware of the conditions
of truth, but the experience is of God. Together we can meet
its conditions, but truth will dawn upon you of itself."*

—A Course in Miracles

*"Meditate like Christ—He lost himself in Love…
Love is the strongest medicine."*

—Neem Karoli Baba

If you are looking for the last word on the subject of this book, you've come to the right place. At least, this is my last word, for now.

I recognize that this is quite a long and involved study, and that few might actually have the time and interest to actually really delve deeply into what has been written on these pages.

And even those who have courageously read and understood what is admittedly a rather verbose and unwieldy tome may still be rightly wondering what the author's own simple views on this touch-and-go subject really are when all is said and done…?

If any of this applies to you, you've also come to the right place. And so without further ado…

I see this book now as essentially a spiritual "coming of age" tale that gives some deep insight into one soul's quest for truth and how that quest found some resolution, if not complete dissolution.

Clearly the quest began with a deep *quest*ioning process where anything and everything was fair game. In this process, even the greatest sacred cows of my formerly unquestioned faith were held to the light to see if they could truly see the light of day.

The quest ultimately found resolution with the help of one of the very things that was brought into question: Psychedelics. For as the last chapter made clear, the use of psychedelics, and Ayahuasca in particular, led me to a path that I had not formerly even remotely considered, and one which is surely to raise some eyebrows.

That path is that of A Course in Miracles (ACIM).

Upon reading an early manuscript of this book, a friend brought up the apparent discrepancy of writing a somewhat scholarly book on yoga and psychedelics and concluding with a chapter on finding a seemingly unrelated path…?

Ah, but is it really unrelated? It is not. In fact, my initial interest in ACIM was in no small part due to its strong parallels with Advaita Vedanta, which many view as the "crest jewel" of the yoga tradition, its highest philosophy. Reading centuries-old Advaita Vedanta texts like *Yoga Vasistha* or Shankara's *Viveka Chudamani* alongside ACIM makes for some very interesting reading indeed. Perhaps my next book will look at these parallels.

In any case, in light of these "findings," I will now make the following summation of the case:

"Paths are many, Truth is One."

There are very many spiritual paths, and it is my faith, based on much research and reflection, not to mention experiential glimpses of truth, that they all ultimately lead to the same One Reality.

Each person has their own unique path, even though they might not be aware of what that is, and so might not even consciously be on a spiritual path, per se. Even those who may be a member of a greater religious organization are on their own unique path, willy nilly, whether they know it or not.

The use of psychedelics with the intention of gaining spiritual awareness is its own valid path, one that will ultimately lead the sincere seeker to the truth they are seeking.

The path of Yoga, in its many forms and permutations, is also its own path, and also does not need anything else to bolster or support it.

And there is another path, too, with no doubt already many thousands of forms of it: The path of intentionally using psychedelics in the context of a yogic discipline. This, too, is a valid path, if practiced sincerely.

Now, if that was a bit too abstract and hedgy, I will say this: While these are all valid paths, some may be more capable of saving the seeker time than others. Those would be the paths that help one to look at one's identification with the ego, and thus to work through the greatest obstacle of all to enlightenment: Fear. Other paths will tend to be more roundabout, though again, they will all eventually lead the seeker home, without question.

In this sense, the unique path that I have put on the table throughout this book, namely that of Yoga AND Psychedelics, is a potentially potent one indeed, and one perhaps best suited for those who consider themselves "post-guru."

And yet one still needs a guide.

For some few souls, that guide will be their inner teacher. Yet for most, it will be an external teacher, though this teacher does not need to be human. Indeed, for me at this moment, the external teacher is a wonderful spiritual study guide known to millions worldwide as A Course in Miracles. It and Ayahuasca have greatly assisted me in looking at the ego and recognizing that I have a choice, in each moment, whether to identify with its illusions or not.

This does not mean that the plant spirit itself cannot be looked to as a teacher or guide. The only potential pitfall with this is the simple problem of interpretation: How does one interpret the vast array of information that one is given over the course of a psychedelic experience into a viable spiritual practice that will lead towards freedom and not away from it? Towards Spirit and not ego?

Although I am currently combining these various paths, the Course does counsel against all external aids, echoing the yoga sages' ageless counsel that nothing outside of ourselves can save us. It is only our choosing to change our minds and follow the promptings of Spirit and not the ego that will liberate us. Psychedelics, like any other form of external "medicine," are essentially irrelevant and could very well complicate the situation unnecessarily.

Which is not to counsel against taking medicines, if they help. It is just to say that while taking them, at the same time recognize the truth: In every instance that we take a medicine, it begins with a decision in our mind to choose health over sickness, enlightenment over endarkenment, and liberation over enslavement. Swami Satyananda Saraswati is right: Nothing else is needed but that firm *sankalpa*, that firm and unwavering intention for healing, for liberation, for Love. To do anything else is to belittle the greatest tool for health and Wholeness that we have at our disposal: Our own mind.

Interview with a Traditional Peruvian Shaman

Appendix A

Throughout this book I have mentioned my work with a traditional Peruvian shaman who also has spent time in India working with a guru and studying yoga. As a result, his teachings and ceremonies are an interesting hybrid of the yogic and shamanic perspectives. For example, he asks participants to sit up straight and sit still for as much of his ayahuasca ceremonies as possible, and to utilize the breath as a tool and ally in the process. Along with traditional *icaros* (medicine songs), he also chants Hindu mantras and counsels the ceremony participants to find the "undying Self" among the buzz and bloom of the ayahuasca experience. I personally found this approach to be most helpful, though very challenging.

I was so impressed by this shaman that I asked if he would be willing to be interviewed for this book. He assented and asked that I send him my questions via email. I did, and not long after received from him a 20-minute audio of his responses to all of my questions. What follows is the full interview, beginning with the shaman saying that he does not consider himself to be an expert, just someone who has been working with ayahuasca and yoga for some time and is searching for the truth just like me. I trust you will find this helpful...

• • •

The first thing that I would like to tell you is that I am going to try to answer these questions as well as I can, and I would like for you to understand that I am not an expert in any of these questions. I'm just a person like you who is trying to do my own work, and trying to learn from this master plan and advance in my spiritual evolution. So I can only tell you what I know, and I'm not going to try to tell you something that I don't really know. I'm going to tell you my truth, hoping that whatever I am saying to you or whatever you write in your book is going to be of help for you and for whoever reads the book that you are writing.

Q: In your ceremonies you combine traditional Peruvian shamanism with yoga chants, practices and teachings. Would you speak on what you see is the connection between sacred plant shamanism (particularly ayahuasca) and yoga?

A: *If we understand for yoga not only physical exercise, but the inner union with the Divine/Truth, and if we understand shamanism as the study of the Self through the plants, then I think that in what I just said, it's embedded how one relates to the other.*

In the higher states of spirituality, when we are deep in the profundities of the plant, or when yogis talk about their states in profound meditation, we realize that there is no separation between anything. For the Divine, there is only one, there is no separation of anything. There is not good, there is not bad, there is only this essence that is in absolutely everything.

The paths to this essence are many, but the goal, the Divine, it's only one.

From my understanding, concentration, and meditation, discovering the inner self and deepening our connection with ourselves are all really important. From this point of view, it's easy to realize that yoga, or meditation, and shamanism, specifically with the ayahuasca, are so complementary one with the other.

Because it's important that we can go deep into these realities, always knowing that it's important to do it at the hand of someone who is trained and who has the experience necessary to guide us through this trance in the proper way so that we are secure spiritually, energetically, mentally, emotionally, and even physically. And also, that the person that is guiding the experience is going to focus towards the truth; that the person who is going to take our hands through this trip is guiding the experience towards the true goal that is the Self-discovery, that is the self-study, and is the spiritual development of ourselves toward the Divine.

I think that when we look at our experiences with Mother Vine [ayahuasca] from this perspective, there is no difference between yoga and ayahuasca. I think that both of them have a common goal that bring us toward the same state. At the same time, I think that both of them are so complementary. They complement each other in a way that both together form a powerful way of Self-understanding and self-development.

Focusing the mind through exercises with Hatha Yoga, through the breath like with pranayama, and through meditation, develop certain states and certain inner practices that are going to be extremely helpful in our ayahuasca ceremonies. At the same time, developing certain practices inside of ceremony, like concentration, like focusing, like letting ourselves go, or surrender, and also developing the inner confidence necessary and the faith that we gain through certain ceremonies with ayahuasca are going to help us to deepen even more our inner practice with Hatha Yoga, meditation, etc.

Q: One of the things I found most interesting about your approach in your ceremonies is that you ask everyone to sit up straight and sit still for the whole ceremony if possible. Other shamans and traditions say it is ok to lie down, and I have observed that many people seem to find it more helpful (or at least comfortable) to lie down during the ayahuasca experience. Would you explain your reason for asking the participants to sit up?

A: *In ceremony it's really important to be able to process the energy inside. There are so many reasons for that. The way that we are sitting in ceremony and the way that we are processing the energy is affecting everything else, it's affecting the whole circle. When we have proper breath, good concentration, good posture, and we process the energy internally, movements of the body are not necessary.*

There are certain stages where a certain vibration is changing inside of ourselves. Some people have a tendency to move to adjust themselves with the new vibration, and there are moments when people are not induced to focus and process the energies through the breath, so then they need to express the process through movement.

In a good ceremony with ayahuasca, in a good personal process with shamanism, the energy is processed internally. I also want you to understand that I am talking specifically about ceremonies with the Mother Vine (ayahuasca), because you have not yet come to Peru to do a full dieta (ayahuasca retreat), you have not worked with me and other plants, so everything I am going to say has to do with everything we both have experienced together.

Kundalini Shakti in the base of our spine is so connected with our spiritual evolution, our concentration, our progress, and practice. Definitely there can be experiences of awakening the Shakti during ceremony.

I want to remind you once more that when we go deep into the experience with ayahuasca, it's so important that we are drinking with somebody that we trust and that we believe is focusing the experience towards the Divine. If the person that is guiding us through the experience is not focusing towards the Divine, there is not a single reason why we should be drinking. We don't have time to lose recreationally; we don't have time to lose for that. We need to advance as secure as possible in our own rhythm, in our own speed. The shaman needs to understand that and help each one in their own process without forcing, helping the person to evolve secure and in their own speed.

Q: **What path or system of yoga do you follow? Is it the 8-limbed path of Patanjali (Raja/Ashtanga Yoga), or something else? Also, what is your understanding of Samadhi ("mystical union" and the 8th limb of Patanjali's Ashtanga Yoga)? Can use of ayahuasca result in an experience of true Samadhi?**

A: *From my understanding, there are old codes that explain the right way of living. In India, in these ancient codes that teach us how we should live to have a righteous life, they call it "sanatana dharma." It explains how us humans should live on this earth correctly. What is my focus and my understanding and what I try to do with my own self and to teach my children is this ancient way of understanding the proper way of walking this earth.*

As for Samadhi, all that I can tell you is that Samadhi is not something that I can talk about. *My understanding about Samadhi is that it's not possible to explain in words, it's an experience. It's impossible to explain Samadhi. Ayahuasca can help us to attain Samadhi through developing ourselves; through working on ourselves and developing our inner self; developing concentration, cleansing, and healing our tendencies; becoming a pure vessel and developing deeper qualities such as concentration, compassion, love, and peace; calmness through our inner cleansing of tendencies and patterns that ayahuasca provides to us in ceremony.*

I definitely recommend the practice of Hatha Yoga asanas and a pranayama practice because it is especially useful for spiritual evolution.

I'm helping people with this medicine, with the Mother Vine, but my focus is not people having an experience with Mother Vine. My focus is with people connecting with their inner selves. That's my way of helping, but my desire is that everybody attain at least contact and awakening with themselves. So I definitely recommend yoga asana practice, pranayama, and meditation, because all of that is going to help in the spiritual evolution and is awakening themselves to the spiritual path.

Q: I have noted how much you emphasize the importance of "concentration" during your ceremonies. What does "concentration" mean to you and how does it assist one during the ayahuasca experience?

A: *If you really want to understand the meaning of concentration with me, you should come to retreat in Peru and experience it yourself. So many people ask me if there's any kind of technique that I recommend? There are so many different kinds of techniques. Definitely in ceremony I recommend to focus on the breath.*

In your daily life, there are people that like mantra, there are people that like icaros, there are people who like to pray or focus on an image or on a feeling. All kinds of practices for concentration and techniques are good to me. I don't believe there is one technique for everybody. I believe there are so many techniques, and one technique might be good for certain people. So you can come to Peru and have an experience of what I really mean. If you want me to help you to concentrate, just before you start your concentration, think of me for a little while and I will help you.

Q. What would you say to someone who says to you that they don't feel they need to try or use ayahuasca as they feel they already have a very good spiritual path and connection? Would you still recommend that they try ayahuasca, or to stay on their own path?

A: *If a person thinks that they have a powerful connection with the Divine, ayahuasca can still be so helpful for them. Ayahuasca has so many things to teach and the most important things that we have to learn with ayahuasca are not possible to understand with the mind, and definitely not something that we can attain with one* *ceremony. It is through constant practice and self-inquiry that we will go discovering.*

You can see people that are drinking for 5 or 20 years, and you can see people that are coming for the first time and notice a difference in their energy. I do not think that the goal is to attain liberation without drinking ayahuasca. The goal is attaining the Divine. The goal is to enter into contact with the higher realms and to live in those states, experience that. I cannot really judge if it's good or not until the end. I cannot really say that the goal is to not use it; I cannot say that. There are many saints in India who use several plants to be able to get contact with Shiva and they have attained certain states, even still using the plant. Because when we arrive at certain states, not even the use of the plant is important. So you can not use it or you can use it, it's not a problem. You are over that—over the plant, over the material things. So no matter what you do, everything is okay. We should not judge masters that use it or masters who don't use it, everything is good.

You are asking me if when someone has a strong connection to the Divine I would recommend that they drink ayahuasca, or would I tell them to stay on their own path? My answer is that that is so personal to the individual and I cannot give a general answer.

Q: There are some who refer to plant medicines and ayahuasca in particular as "plant teachers." Some have even said that the age of the guru is over and that we can learn the same if not more from plant teachers like ayahuasca than we could from a traditional guru. What are your thoughts on this?

A: *I am going to tell you that the guru, the real guru, is inside. We can put it in a plant, in a master, in a mountain, but the real guru is inside. Definitely ayahuasca can be your guru, because it's not the ayahuasca, it's God.*

Q: There seem to be many people who are afraid of ayahuasca and/or doubtful of its validity. I myself have been concerned about my own use of it, especially coming from a yogic tradition that does not condone the use of psychoactive plants for spiritual purposes. As I am sure you are aware, in India and elsewhere there are many who look down on such practices as cheating, black tantric arts, or worse. Would you speak to this?

A: *I feel that there are certain things for certain people. We should not judge anybody. We should not judge any practice and allow each one to experience this world, this reality, and themselves with complete and absolute freedom.*

Well, obviously I found what this shaman had to say very helpful as I did not erase it! Indeed, I was very glad to have found this interview after having thought I had lost it. I actually had some doubts about this shaman and wondered early on if I could really trust him, while at the same time being magnetically drawn to him. I questioned whether he might be getting caught up in the trap of guru/shaman worship. Clearly from his words, however, he seems very humble and clear and wanting to be truly helpful. In doubting him, was I just doubting myself? Was this all just an opportunity to see him just as an elder brother on the path, not enlightened (by his own admission) and struggling with the same egoic issues that I myself am?

These are rhetorical questions for me now. Yes, I do feel that the only path left is to let go of judgment and see that he is doing his best and does not have malicious intent, even if I sometimes might feel that from him. My understanding now is that if I feel that from him, it is only a projection onto him. And I can help him by seeing him in the light of true love and forgiveness, by which we both will remember who we truly are.

Faith Quest: The Mystery that is Nadi Astrology

Appendix B

"Passage to India!"
—Walt Whitman

"There are more things in heaven and earth, Horatio,
than are dreamt of in your philosophy."
—Shakespeare

For many, like myself, getting into yoga was like falling in love. Suddenly, it's like you've come home and it's so beautiful, you just can't get enough and your heart is full to overflowing. Yet the Honeymoon period doesn't last forever. Doubt begins to creep back in and the real work starts. If we were truly in touch with and honest about our feelings, we could look squarely at it and see that something just isn't working any more. At this point we could either jump ship, or try our best to plug that hole in the relation*ship*. For me, there was no question of jumping ship, because yoga had awakened something in me so deep in those first few years that there was never any way I could go back to my former life. The Beloved had rocked me awake from my slumber and had me knocking at Her door for further sailing.

In the realm of relationships, we have this curious expression in English of being "faithful" to our partner, and one of the greatest taboos in our society is to be "unfaithful" in the realm of love. In reality, how many marriages and relationships that remain intact do so while in a state of shipwreck. Again, is it more noble and courageous to stay with the sinking ship, or to swim for shore? Wisdom suggests that there are no wrong moves in this game of life, yet that wisdom also needs faith to support it and make it more than mere regurgitation of sage advice. In my case, I was left wondering when and where that faith would come from as I had always seemed to get so close, so close… only to have the Great Whale slip through my fingers, leaving me to tell the story of the big one that got away. In other words, I was on a quest for true, unshakeable faith in something that I could hold onto both as a guide and source of continual inspiration. My teachers alone, when I was honest with myself, still left me doubting. This book, and the story you are about to read in particular, is a document of my search for that Archimedean anchor point by which I could in a sense prove my faithfulness to my lover and myself.

• • •

When I was in Bangalore during my first India trip, my mentor, L, strongly suggested I go get a palm leaf reading. Now, like you most likely, I had no clue what a palm leaf reading was… "Is it like reading your palm?" I asked naively. L laughed and explained that thousands of years ago, in deep meditation, certain yogi sages were able to access the life information of souls who were to incarnate in the future. In other words, they were able to read what has now popularly known in New Age circles and beyond as the "Akashic Records," which is believed to be an etheric storehouse where all material impressions (karma) are archived. These great seers then recorded this information on palm leaves and the leaves were passed down from generation to generation via lineage with the knowledge of how to read and interpret them. [Endnote: Bhrigu Samhita]

So essentially, a palm leaf reading (known in India as "Nadi," or "lifestream" readings) is, at least in theory, a soul analysis done by a highly trained person who knows how to find, read, and interpret a person's individual leaf. The idea, as mind blowing as this sounds, is that if you go to a palm leaf reader, you're probably meant to, and your leaf has been there waiting for you for possibly thousands of years, collecting dust until that moment when you arrive to get your reading.

I can see some of you turning this off already, yet hang in there. While it is true there are all manners of frauds in India making one outrageous claim or another, if there is just one that is true, then it is worth examining these matters. Being a seeker myself and new to all of this, I was all for going to the Nadi Reader and seeing if my leaf was really there. I wasn't that naïve, however; I was trained in philosophy and did know how to think critically and ask questions. As with Paul Brunton, I wasn't going to be satisfied with anything more than exact details there on the leaf: names, numbers, past and future events foretold, etc. Having been in India for a couple of weeks already, though, I was realizing that this kind of certainty was going to be hard to come by. Still, I was hopeful and game, so off we went…

[What follows is a reliable reconstruction of the events based upon my journal, recollection, and notes I took during my Nadi reading.]

Praying to Ganesha all along, yet still there are obstacles… First thing that happens when we arrive at the Nadi reader's place is that it looks like he won't have time for me today, and after all, I haven't made an appointment. But we wait it out (my friend, at least, knows not to take "no" for an answer in India) and after an interminable wait with lots of mantras and attempts at meditation, we're finally led into his inner chamber, which is basically just a little office with a small room in the back of his desk housing the leaves.

This Nadi reader is very sweet, speaks good English and seems somewhat cosmopolitan. He's probably seen not a few Westerners like me, after all. He first asks me some basic questions about my life, which I have no idea why he needs really, but I obligingly answer everything he asks. Then he takes my thumbprint and goes into his little back room to look for my leaf. It isn't too long before he comes back and asks me a few more questions to narrow down his search. After another trip back into his inner chamber, he comes back with my leaf (or, at least, my reading). He asks me some more questions, and then proceeds to give me the contents of the leaf. He suggests that I take a pencil and paper and make notes as he would not be able to record what he says, which I do. What follows is a transcript of the shorthand notes I took.

My Nakshatra [astrological sign in the Vedic Astrology system] **is Chitra. This is the most mystical of signs. Overcoming sexual desire is a big thing, or can be. I was the third child. I was formed first and came last.** [I didn't understand this at first, but later guessed this meant that my fraternal twin is really the youngest, the fourth— something that the psychic in Jerusalem had already told me.]

I have "researching potential." I know 3 languages, Spanish being one of them [this is true to an extent—I am very familiar by this time with Hebrew and Sanskrit, too]. **I will be a writer, philosopher, and teacher. I will write a philosophy book that synthesizes psychology, Vedanta, and religion.** [While I have yet to do this, I have begun work on another book dealing with these subjects.]

I will do "unification work." I will also teach philosophy. I will be a traveler to learn. I want to meet my guru, but my guru is not alive. I will meet many masters, but find my own way. I will find the reality of knowledge and life. [This definitely all spoke to me.]

I am aware that I have some blockages inside. These blockages will go when I learn these "knowledges" and languages.

In my last life, I was born in India, and was a teacher of non-dualistic knowledge and Vikarana [Grammar—didn't know what it meant at the time.]

In this life, through the practices of Kundalini Yoga, I will learn all Vedanta and grammar. Patanjali's Yoga system will open my third eye, which will "give brightness in inner life." He also said: "Yoga will give strength for inner life."

I was born in Israel in Jesus' time, and had close contact with Jesus. I was a witness to Jesus' punishment at the time. [Ain't I special.]

I went to Nepal at the bottom of the Himalayas. I criticized my masters and gave away secrets to "non-permitted people." As a result, in this lifetime I have these certain blockages, and due to awareness of these, I am very careful about mistakes in this life. [In the margin of my notes, I wrote: "Is that so?" which is a question the

Nadi reader asked me in regard to making mistakes. I answered "yes" because I was becoming increasingly conscious and careful in regard to my every thought, word, and deed, making sure that I was truly living in accordance with the wisdom I was learning, though I certainly was making mistakes (or what felt like them).]

I will also have a lot of experiences in the region of the Himalayas—I will go in this lifetime. [Have yet to go].

I was born in Spain, but the land in which I was born no longer exists now. [I take it this meant in one of my past incarnations, which might explain my interest in Spanish and in studying abroad in Spain at one moment in college, but then again, it's too general and I wasn't that interested in any case.]

I have a desire to live in the countryside and do research. I will live in the Southeast of North America [I was then living in the Northeast, and am now in Florida, the Southeast].

The Nadi reader then asked if I have taught? I said that I have taught in High School. He said that I will teach languages in college. He later said I would do many kinds of work. [I have not taught officially at a college as of yet, though I do run a yoga school called "Yoga University."]

Health: Stomach is sensitive. Must eat slowly. Having a regular time of eating is best. May have an operation on stomach or throat [None such operations to date, though eating slowly has been a challenge]. Pranayama will give good health for me. Also, water therapy: Drink water in the early morning and 30 minutes prior to lunch and dinner.

Relationships: I am separated from my partner. I would marry second important girl in that year. I would find her in 19-20 months. My coming partner will be a good healer and counselor. We would have 1 child "if both minds permit." We would live together for many years, then marry. [Well, I was "separated" from my partner only in the sense that I was in India and she was in Philadelphia at the time, though it wasn't long before we were to go our separate ways, and that might have been about 19-20 months later. If that's what he was referring to, then he was right on, but I did not find someone new that year or in 19-20 months (you can see there were some contradictions there). I wasn't to get into a relationship for another 8 years, in fact.]

I was told to recite a certain mantra for jnana (wisdom, spiritual knowledge, gnosis). The Nadi reader wrote it on the page in both Sanskrit and English. I was to repeat it 30 minutes each day: 10 minutes in the morning, 10 in the evening, and 10 just prior to sleep. [I never kept up with this practice, partly due to doubts about all of this, and—so many practices, so little time!...]

The Nadi reader then asked if I had any questions? Yes, did I ever. First I asked him about meditation… He said I should do Patanjali's 8-limbed path like he said, and that path includes meditation.

What about music? Do it as a hobby, I was told.

Then I hesitantly expressed my doubts to the Nadi reader, telling him that while there were a lot of accurate things in the reading, some things were incorrect, such as his saying that the woman I am separated from is older than me (not to mention the fact that we weren't truly separated, though I did not say this). He had a ready response for that: You can read it that she is older than me in knowledge, or spiritually older, not in years. This didn't seem right, however, as originally he had said that she is one year older than me.

So overall I was not over-impressed, somewhat under-whelmed, yet nonetheless intrigued. Clearly there were some things that seemed pretty right on, yet this could be due to the initial questions he asked (which included my birth date, so he could have based a lot of it on astrology), educated guesswork, and his own intuitive powers. I was even more inclined to think this guy didn't have the goods when I found out my roommate from Australia got a very similar reading, which included the same curse and the same mantra to alleviate it. Good thing I only paid 850 rupees, or $17, I thought, though this was a good living for him and I'm sure if he was deceiving people, the placebo effect was in effect for many.

Later, though, I was to hear about another Nadi astrologer not too far away in the Chennai area. This guy apparently really was the real deal with a tradition going back to an ancient sage named Agasthya and whose palm leaves contain specific names and other details about one's incarnation. At the airport on my way back to the States, I ran into a fellow ashramite who had gone to see this particular Nadi reader. He was clearly sold and excitedly told me that his leaf contained the following information:

His Name
His Father's Name
His Mother's Name
His First Wife's Name
His Second Wife's Name
And more.

Mind you, this was all written in Tamil so he couldn't actually read the names himself, yet still… I was so blown away by this that I wanted to go see this guy immediately. My friend said he was going to both film him doing his readings and also try to bring him to the States. I doubt this ever happened, only because I haven't heard about it, and also because if more people knew about it and this was all more accessible, there would be droves getting readings and I doubt there are that many leaves. I am very glad to be wrong about this.

This is now all pretty ancient history, from way back in about 2001. Since then I have heard of a project to put all of the Nadi leaves onto a computer database that people can access (if they are meant to have a reading). I suspect the readings won't be as cheap as they are in India.

Also, since my last India trip in 2001, I have heard several more reliable first-hand reports about Nadi readers who certainly seem genuine, including a pretty convincing one on YouTube of a man who apparently went to see the same Nadi reader in Chennai [endnote]. This and the original blog posting containing this story from back in 2008 received several very interesting comments, both for and against. Some said that these astrologers are basically con men who are very skilled at the game of 20 Questions; essentially, you give them all of the information prior to their "finding" your leaf and then they just basically regurgitate that same information in an official and authoritative sounding way. While I would agree that this is no doubt true for some if not many of the Nadi readers, again, we must consider those few and far between cases that are not so easy to dismiss.

Some of the commentators on my original blog piece also begged to differ with those crying "fraud." On October 24, 2008, someone by the name of Robert Miller wrote in response to one of the comments on the thread that was critical of Nadi Astrology:

"Sorry dude, the permutations and combinations possible even with the info given by you are simply too much to just zero into the right name and date of birth. Try it yourself. As far as I am concerned, I went to a Nadi Astrologer in Kanchipuram. He gave me a different date of birth and insisted that he was correct and that my official date of birth is wrong. I went back home a month later and checked with my mother. My mother told me that the hospital officials gave a wrong date of birth. WOW. I was stunned as I was celebrating my birthday a day ahead for the first 25 years of my life... He [also] predicted that I will completely change direction of education and pursue higher studies abroad. All this apart from [author's note: I think he meant "including"] many family details and future predictions came true. I was a hardcore skeptic before this incident. Now I am not so sure about things we don't fully understand."

Another commentator similarly mentioned how her father went to a Nadi reader when she was 10-11 years old and all of the information told to her father was true, adding that *"a copy of the Tamil verses was given to us, which I was able to understand with some difficulty... I don't think they can cook up or come up with so much info on the fly."*

Another commentator wrote:

"Do not stamp the leaf as fraud. First one in Tambaram West in Chennai I found read out from the leaf that my younger brother was killed in a bomb attack as he was in public service. He did not ask me about my brothers and their jobs. My brother was killed in the bomb attack on RSS office in Chennai on 8/8/93. I consulted them on 19/8/93… Later in 2008 I consulted another Nadi [reader]. There it is written that I have opted for VRS and I was working in a financial institution. I did not give my date of birth in Tamil or Christian calendar yet he gave it to me in Tamil year and month. He also said my age now. How can he calculate my age without knowing my date of birth?"

While fairly convincing to me, especially in light of my other research and first-hand reports, this anecdotal evidence still would not be sufficient for the skeptic, and I, too, would still want to witness all of this for myself. In other words, I would still need to go see the Nadi Reader in question and see all of these things with my own eyes to really feel this was real, and even then there might still be questions in my mind. That said, recently I heard a report from a very reliable witness of the truth of Nadi Astrology, a report which I will relate to you momentarily. Before I do, I feel it will be interesting to present one other fascinating response to my initial blogpost on this subject, posted by one Debasish Sen in 2010. This commentator claims to have insider information on how Nadi Astrologers fool the public into believing that they are reading from ancient parchment when in reality they are contacting a "hereditary deity" who is reading your mind!

"Nadi Astrology: How it works… just read on…

"Recently I was under pressure from family members to visit a Nadi Astrologer. The procedure is that one has to give the thumb impression to the astrologer and answer to queries regarding details of siblings, parents, property owned, placement of letters in names, etc. etc. Such details are to be given by the person but the full names are not asked or revealed. The astrologer then says the full names of all persons and many details of the past which generally are 100 percent correct. He also mentions some of the incidents of the past life. Later he predicts the future and proposes to do some poojas (rituals to propitiate a deity) or yagna (fire ceremonies for same purpose) for 1 mandalam (48 days) or 2 in a far away place/temple inaccessible by the person and also gives an option or a shortcut for the pooja by giving the money directly to him. The accurate portrayal of the past generally overwhelms most persons and they happily agree to part with the money for the poojas and the costly service charges. One may find more about Nadi Astrology by surfing the net. This is another method to fool the person and encash his ignorance by bringing into the picture the great saint Agasthya.

"Demigods or lower gods also finds a place in creation. Some of the services of the lower gods are easily purchased for a so-called 'joint-venture.' The percentage of profit is agreed from the temple they purchase it and has to be given to the temple, failing which the results could be disastrous. It is not possible to cheat the demigods as the demigods are after all divine incarnations.

"When the victim approaches the astrologer for help, the astrologer asks various queries, as mentioned above. The answers of these queries are actually questions posed to the demigod to get the correct identity of the person. Once it is got, all other past details are easily available by the demigod. These details are only heard by the astrologer. This may sound unscientific but really is not.

"Demigods are unable to accurately predict the future and hence the predictions are mostly not correct. Astrologers, sooth-sayers, magicians also use demigods, fraudulent god-men who materialize processed goods from scratch, which is only shifting i.e., dematerializing, shifting and rematerializing.

"How I came to know about it?

"I have a friend who is an ardent Shiva devotee and who made a small portion of his house a Shiva temple. He has been a Shiva devotee and has been continuing for the past 25 years or so. But their hereditary god is a demigod. It seems the hereditary god also wanted to be revered and so he wanted a separate temple for it. He was also given the privilege of asking questions (or thinking and posing questions) to the demigod and he would get the answer about past incidents. But my friend never used this privilege for monetary gains. For those who come with a problem, he just queries it and suggests solutions for their well-being. He has helped me many times, such as when I misplaced a very important file in my office and also when my colleague created havoc by creating a bad name for me in the office. When I wanted to know about the practice of Nadi Astrology, I asked for his help and he let me know the actual functioning of it by querying it with the demigod.

"Sage Agasthya no doubt was a great sage. But it is ridiculous to say that he wrote the names and fate of persons 1200 years ago as if everything is destined and future generations do not have free will at all. I just wanted to share the information. It is the wish of the readers to believe or not. If at all you believe, please share the information and prevent the cheats from taking over."

Well, if these individuals truly can communicate with hereditary deities to gain information for their clientele, not only is this worthy of our attention, but we might even be able to overlook that they are fooling the public if their information is accurate and helpful. That's assuming that this alternative hypothesis about what Nadi readers do is really true. Obviously, if the information is written on a palm leaf in

Tamil that can be dated back to Sage Agasthya's time, then this explanation would be incorrect.

You will note that one commentator on my blog was given a copy of the Tamil verses, though she did not say that she was given a copy of the actual leaf, which means that they could have been written on the spot, however unlikely that sounds. In the video mentioned above, the man who received his reading brought with him someone who could read Tamil and who confirmed what was written on the leaf. This is rather strong evidence, unless what was written on the leaf was composed right there on the spot. It might be a question of to what extent the Nadi astrologers will go to in order to fool the public and keep themselves in business. For me, as with the subject matter of this book, this still remains an open question and a mystery that will perhaps never be completely unraveled in any satisfying way for everyone.

Postscript

I attended Bhakti Fest for the first time in the summer of 2014 and there had the pleasure to hear Dr. Manoj Chalam give a talk on the archetypes of the Hindu deities. During the course of that presentation, Dr. Chalam seemingly digressed to tell us the story of his going to visit that same Nadi reader that has been rocking people's world. Someone had told him about the astrologer and on a recent trip to India he just happened to be in the area, so...

Dr. Chalam's report was similar to the others: He was convinced beyond a reasonable doubt that the astrologer was not a fraud and had access to information that he not only did not give him, but which the man could not have gotten without access to either a higher power or psychic abilities. Not only did his leaf apparently have very personal details of his past and present, but the leaf also contained the exact time of his death. When the astrologer asked him if he wished to know the date, he said yes. Perhaps this is how some Indian gurus have known the date of their death. On the other hand, if the other explanation of the hereditary deities is correct, then this also explains why some gurus have incorrectly foretold the time of their death, as was the case with Sathya Sai Baba.

Yoga & Psychedelics:
A Select, Interpretive Chronology

Appendix C

Circa 1500 B.C.E. In the Vedas, the rishis (seers) extol Soma, a deity who was also some kind of a brew that was concocted from a "creeper" and supposed to confer immortality on the drinker.

Ancient times to the present: Shaivites have the tradition of using cannabis (*ganja*), datura, and other mind-altering substances as tools for their sadhana. Historically and mythologically, Shiva is the one who attracts this kind of person to his worship.

1954: Aldous Huxley publishes "The Doors of Perception," a book that is to exert a profound influence on the Baby Boomer generation, particularly the hippie/counterculture movement. The book's title is based upon a quote from the English prophet poet, William Blake. The rock group The Doors, who all (except lead singer Jim Morrison) originally met at a Transcendental Meditation meeting, take their name from Blake and Huxley's inspiration.

1958: Harvard Professor of Psychology Timothy Leary takes mushroom containing psilocybin ("magic mushrooms") with Maria Sabina in Mexico, claiming that he learned more about his mind in the 15 hours after taking the mushrooms than he had in the previous 15 years of studying psychology. (Note: A number of other elite artists, writers, and philosophers also take magic mushrooms at around this time, including Aldous Huxley, Gordon Wasson, and Allen Ginsberg.)

1959–1961: Leary and Dr. Richard Alpert conduct studies at Harvard using psilocybin. Harvard allows them to do these studies on the condition that they not give any psilocybin to undergraduates. They do end up doing this, however, and a young Andrew Weil (now well-known as Dr. Weil), who was an undergraduate at the time, discovers what they are doing and outs them in an editorial for the Harvard Crimson Review newspaper. Leary and Alpert are asked to resign. The two continue their studies, most famously at the Millbrook estate, where they begin to research LSD.

Early '60s: Meher Baba (self-proclaimed "Avatar of the Age") publishes the pamphlet "God In A Drug?" in which he categorically denounces LSD and other hallucinogenic drugs as having no spiritual value whatsoever, as well as extremely dangerous.

Famous followers of Meher Baba include Pete Townshend, lead guitarist and song-writer for the rock band The Who. The pamphlet has recently been re-published in a "*A Mirage Will Never Quench Your Thirst*," a collection of excerpts from Meher Baba's teachings on drugs.

1964: Dr. Richard Alpert, somewhat disillusioned with psychedelics (and Leary), writes a letter to Meher Baba, asking him for guidance regarding LSD and other psychedelics. Meher Baba writes back saying that Dr. Alpert's prodigious LSD use merely had the purpose of bringing Alpert to him, and that he no longer needed to use such things. Although to the best of my knowledge this correspondence has never been discussed publicly by Ram Dass, RD's writings, including his most recent book, *Polishing the Mirror* (2013), contain a number of Meher Baba references and quotes.

1966: The US government declares LSD a Schedule A drug, meaning it has no redeeming value whatsoever. LSD use gradually diminishes among the counterculture, to be replaced by harder drugs. Government-funded scientific research ceases.

1967–1968: Dr. Alpert goes to India, where he is led by Bhagavan Das to his guru, Neem Karoli Baba (NKB). Alpert allegedly gives a large dose of LSD to NKB with no noticeable effects. From this and other events that occur, Dr. Alpert becomes a devotee of NKB, who gives him the name "Ram Dass."

1967: Concurrently, the Beatles declare to the world that they are no longer using LSD but promoting meditation, and proceed to go on a meditation retreat in India with Maharishi Mahesh Yogi. They end up leaving the retreat early, however, because John believes the Maharishi was making advances on his then girlfriend Mia Farrow (John's song "Sexy Sadie" is about Maharishi). John ultimately parts ways with the yoga tradition, and George becomes a Hare Krishna.

1967: Gordon Wasson publishes "*Soma: Divine Mushroom of Immortality*," in which he claims that the original Soma of the Vedas was Amanita muscaria, a psychedelic Mushroom (familiarly recognized as the Alice in Wonderland mushroom).

August, 1969: Kundalini Yoga is taught at Woodstock by Tom Law, a former student of Yogi Bhajan, who tells the assembled hippies that yoga can do the same thing that drugs can do "only you don't have to score [drugs]" to get high. In the Woodstock movie, you can see Tom Law teaching his hippie brethren how to do a special type of yogic breathing meant to raise their Kundalini and get them high. Meanwhile, some of the greatest musical moments at Woodstock were inspired by psychedelics, and most of the half million at the festival peaked on one substance or another.

Late '60s, Early '70s: Terence McKenna visits India and is very disillusioned with what he finds, later writing that the religious culture of India is dead and dying, saying that the original Soma use had been replaced by the lifeless practices of chanting, meditation, and ritual. After India, McKenna travels to the Amazon Basin with his brother Dennis where they discover magic mushrooms. Terence goes on to be one of the most popular and vociferous proponents of using psychedelics as a tool for spiritual practice, though he is actually wary of using words like "spirit" and "entheogen," feeling these are loaded terms.

1970: Birth of the author.

1971: Ram Dass publishes "Be Here Now" in which he tells the story of meeting Neem Karoli Baba and giving him LSD. This is a huge publishing coup, and apparently for at least a little while after its initial publication, the book was second only to the Bible in sales. Whatever the case, the book had a profound influence on the hippies, including a young Steve Jobs, who both took psychedelics and practiced yoga. (McKenna, among others, doubted that NKB took the LSD, saying he probably palmed it and threw it over his shoulder. On his next trip to India, partly because of this kind of skepticism, Ram Dass gives a high dose of LSD once again to his guru, and again nothing happens, strengthening his story. Not too long after this, in 1973, NKB passes.)

1965–1972: At this time, numerous other swamis and gurus come to the United States and tell the young people (the hippie minions) that yoga can give them a steady high, higher than drugs. These teachers include some of the most well-known and influential to this day: Yogi Bhajan (3HO Kundalini), Maharishi Mahesh Yogi (Transcendental Meditation), Swami Prabhupada (Hare Krishna), Amrit Desai (Kripalu), Swami Sachidananda (Integral Yoga), BKS Iyengar (Iyengar), and Swami Rama (Himalayan Institute), among others. The hippie movement gradually shifts away from drugs and into meditation. At a Woodstock spinoff festival, a young David Williams is so inspired by Tom Law's presentation of yoga as an alternative to drugs that he goes to Mysore, India, finds his guru, Pattabhi Jois, and brings back one of the most highly influential forms of yoga in the West, Ashtanga Yoga.

1972: The Nixon Administration forms the DEA and begins its "War On Drugs" and later, "Just Say No" campaigns. Those of the generation after the Baby Boomers, Generation X, grow up with these messages, in addition to a yoga movement that is almost completely anti-drug across the board. The '70s and '80s see a movement away from the Utopian idealism about psychedelics and harder, non-psychedelic drugs (Cocaine, Heroin, Speed, etc) become more prominent in both the counter and mainstream culture. A kind of moratorium on psychedelics sets in.

Early 1990s: Dr. Rick Strassman conducts the first government-funded research on psychedelics in 20 years, administering DMT intravenously to subjects. The results are published in his now oft-cited book, *"DMT: The Spirit Molecule."* Dr. Strassman later determines that for the next study he does, he will use Ayahuasca instead of DMT.

1990s–Present: Western interest in shamanism increases, and the phenomenon of "eco-tourism" takes off. This period also sees the rise of the phenomenon of Ayahuasca and other plant medicine ceremonies both in South America and abroad. Gifted speakers like Terence McKenna play a large part in the "tribal revival."

2000: Huston Smith, who was also at Harvard during the Leary-Alpert period and who famously authored "The World's Religions," publishes *Cleansing the Doors of Perception: The Religious Significance of Entheogenic Plants and Chemicals.* The book is written for the layperson and brings the debate more into the popular discourse. Smith takes a scholarly, even-handed approach to his subject.

2002: Allan Hunt Badiner publishes *"Zig Zag Zen: Buddhism and Psychedelics,"* much of which had already been published in the mid-'90s in the Buddhist magazine Tricycle. The book is a fascinating dialogue on the subject by some of the top spiritual teachers in the West. (The book didn't last too long on the shelves, apparently because it was almost an art piece—a coffee table book, hard cover and with lots of pictures.)

January, 2007: World-renowned yoga teacher and founder of White Lotus Yoga, Ganga White, publishes "Yoga Beyond Belief" in which he talks positively about using the psychoactive brew Ayahuasca, traditionally used by shamans in the Amazon region. The widely popular book opens the public discourse even more, particularly in the yoga community.

2007–Present: "DMT" becomes a buzzword in the worldwide spiritual community, as does awareness of Ayahuasca and participation in sacred medicine ceremonies. There is a worldwide psychedelic renaissance, at least partly due to groups like the Multidisciplinary Association for Psychedelic Studies (MAPS).

Glossary of Terms and Personages

Note: The Glossary is meant to support the narrative of the book and is not intended to be comprehensive by any means. For more information on each subject, refer to the links included.

Ammachi (Mata Amritanandamayi): Also known as "The Hugging Saint," Ammachi is considered by her followers (who number in the millions) to be an avatar, or incarnation of the Divine. For more than 30 years, Amma (or "Mother," as she is lovingly called by her devotees) has spent most of her days giving hugs as a form of darshan (see entry below) to those who are called to her. Ammachi and the worldwide network she has inspired has done great charitable and disaster relief work, yet she is not without her critics.

Avatar: A "descent" of God into human form, or human incarnation of the divine. Well-known avatars of the Hindu tradition are Rama and Krishna, yet other teachers, like Buddha and Jesus, are also considered avatars. There is a teaching that we are all avatars, we just don't know it yet.

Ayahuasca ("Vine of the Soul"): An indigenous psychoactive plant medicine native to the Amazon region, which for the past 2 decades has seen an unprecedented worldwide rise in usage, partly due to the phenomenon of "eco-tourism," yet also due to the outreach efforts of traditional "ayahuasqueros," or Ayahuasca shamans.

Breathwork (see also "Pranayama"): Often used synonymously with the Sanskrit term "*pranayama*" (not exactly accurately), breathwork refers to exercises designed to bring greater awareness and control of the breath for the purpose of greater health, longevity, and spiritual awareness. There is a specific form of breathwork that this book considers (Holotropic and Transformational Breathwork, Rebirthing, etc.) that has been proven to give access to states similar to those engendered via psychedelic substances.

Darshan: A Sanskrit word meaning "vision," in the sense of seeing and being seen by a holy personage, which is believed to transmit their grace and/or blessing.

Wendy Doniger: An indologist (researcher of Indian tradition) who worked with R. Gordon Wasson on his book on Soma, and has over the past 40+ years written a number of scholarly books on India and Hinduism.

Dr. David Frawley (Vamadeva Shastri): One of the foremost scholars on Hinduism today, specifically in the realms of the Vedas, Jyotisha (Vedic Astrology), and Ayurveda. He has written a number of popular works on these subjects, and also offers trainings through his Institute of Vedic Studies.

Stanislav Grof: A pioneer in the study of LSD, Grof did hundreds of studies on LSD prior to it being made illegal in the late '60s, after which he developed his now famous system of Holotropic Breathwork (see entry below).

Hatha Yoga: A yogic path which emerged out of the Tantric world-view, with the understanding that the physical can be a doorway to the infinite. Though apparently the Sanskrit word "Hatha" literally means "forceful," it more figuratively is understood to be the processing of uniting (or "marrying") the Solar/Masculine (HA) and the Lunar/Feminine (THA).

Hatha Yoga Pradipika ("Light on Hatha Yoga"): A classic 14*th* Century manual detailing the practice of Hatha Yoga, attributed to Swatmarama, with instructions on asana, pranayama, mudra, bandha, and more, and is still referenced to this day.

Holotropic Breathwork: A system of breathwork developed by Stanislav Grof and his wife, Christina Grof, designed to bring one into similar space to what psychedelics engender. In the same family of breathwork systems as Transformative Breathwork (see below), Rebirthing, etc.

Aldous Huxley: One of the earliest and most influential writers on the subject of psychedelics, the two most popular being "The Doors of Perception" and his final work, the novel, "Island." Huxley first rose to prominence with the publication of his novel "Brave New World."

Meher Baba: The self-proclaimed "Avatar of the Age" who was especially influential in the '60s, and whose devotees included Pete Townshend, leader of the rock group The Who. Meher Baba expressed deep concern for the young Westerners who were getting involved with LSD and other psychoactive substances in his pamphlet "God in a Drug?" Correspondence with Dr. Richard Alpert apparently partly inspired Alpert to go to India to discover what yogis could tell him about LSD.

Judith Kravitz: The founder and developer of Transformational Breathwork, a trademarked system of breathwork designed to heal the individual of deep trauma (see entry below).

Ralph Metzner: Did research on psilocybin with Dr. Leary and Dr. Alpert while a graduate student at Harvard, and then continued the study of psychedelics with the two men at Millbrook once their positions at Harvard were terminated. Has since come into his own as one of the great contemporary voices on psychedelics.

Sri Karunamayi: Known by her devotees as Amma (Mother), and more formerly as Sri Sri Sri Vijayeshwari Devi, Sri Karunamayi rose to prominence in the early '90s after spending 12 years meditating in a remote forest in South India. One of the author's primary teachers on the path of Raja Yoga and Tantra.

Kundalini: Refers to a subtle energy that is said to lie dormant at the sacrum (base of the spine) coiled like a snake, until it is awakened via some internal or external force. For some, this force might be a special breathing exercise, for others a substance, and still others a teacher with the power of "awakening" this energy.

Kundalini Yoga (3HO Kundalini Yoga): A specific style of Kundalini Yoga developed by controversial Sikh guru Yogi Bhajan in the late '60s. Bhajan's yoga blends mantra, repetitive movement, and powerful breathwork together to create what for many is a very healing practice. Today, 3HO Kundalini is one of the most popular styles of yoga in the world.

Tom Law: In a sense, the man responsible for the rise of 3HO Kundalini Yoga (see above) as it was Law who exposed thousands of young hippies to it at Woodstock in 1969, a fact documented in the popular feature-length documentary "Woodstock" (1970). Law had a falling out with Yogi Bhajan, however, and did not continue to support his movement.

Dr. Timothy Leary: The self-proclaimed "High Priest of LSD," who famously/infamously counseled the Baby Boomers to "tune in, turn on, and drop out." This was after being fired from Harvard, along with his colleague, Dr. Richard Alpert, who subsequently found his guru in India and became Ram Dass. Unlike the latter, Leary championed psychedelics, not yoga, for the rest of his life.

Maharishi Mahesh Yogi: Founder of the widely popular meditation practice, Transcendental Meditation. Became internationally famous in the late '60s as the guru to the Beatles, and later Deepak Chopra, until a falling out with him in the early '90s.

Terence McKenna: One of the most outspoken and influential promoters of psychedelics, as well as critics of traditional Indian spirituality. Proposed the theory that Psilocybin mushrooms (as opposed to Amanita muscaria, see "Wasson") were the original inspirations for the Vedic revelations, and thus Hindu world-view.

Neem Karoli Baba: One of the most influential Indian gurus of the 20*th* Century, especially for Westerners, largely due to the work of Ram Dass (formerly Dr. Richard Alpert). Much of today's Bhakti Yoga and kirtan is due to Neem Karoli Baba's inspiration.

Daniel Pinchbeck: A member of the New York literary intelligentsia whose break out book on psychedelics, *Breaking Open the Head* (2003), helped to spark greater interest in psychedelics and spirituality. Pinchbeck's subsequent offering, *2012: The Return of Quetzalcoatl* (2007), went even further to cement his position as a voice of a generation. Pinchbeck went on to create the online literary journal, Reality Sandwich, and later Evolver, an online social network dedicated to "evolving consciousness" through connecting those sharing this intention.

Pranayama: A Sanskrit term meaning control or extension of the life force (*prana*) through specific breath exercises. A term that has gained much currency in the West is "breathwork," though this is not an entirely accurate translation of *pranayama*.

Dr. Richard Alpert/Ram Dass: Did psilocybin research with Dr. Timothy Leary at Harvard in the early '60s, was fired, and the two men continued their research (now also into LSD) at Millbrook and elsewhere until the mid-60s. In 1967, Alpert went to India, partly to research the effects of LSD on yogis, and in the process he met his guru, Neem Karoli Baba. In 1971, Alpert (now "Ram Dass"), published the groundbreaking book *Be Here Now*, which was highly influential in getting the hippie counterculture to move away from drugs and into spiritual practices like yoga. Ram Dass has continued this work and his devotion to his guru ever since.

Baba Rampuri: The first Westerner (American-born, of Jewish descent) to ever be initiated into the Naga Baba lineage of sannyasis (early '70s), which he wrote about in *Autobiography of a Sadhu: A Journey Into Mystic India* (2005). The author did an email interview with Rampuri for this book.

Shaman/Shamanism: A cross-cultural phenomenon in indigenous societies, wherein a man or woman would take on the role of intercessor with the spirit world in order to bring back knowledge or healing for the tribe. The term "Neo-Shamanism" has been used to describe the phenomenon as it has been adapted/adopted/co-opted in the West.

Dr. Huston Smith: Harvard professor of Religion (contemporaneous with Leary and Alpert) most well-known for his book *The World's Religions* (1958). A later book, *Cleansing the Doors of Perception* (2000), took a hard look at psychedelics in relation to the spiritual quest.

Soma: In the Vedas (see below), the name of a *deva* (god), and also the name for an apparently immortality-conferring psychoactive brew used by the *rishis* (sage-seers), whose exact identity is unknown.

Swami Satchidananda: A disciple of Swami Sivananda who came to the West in the late '60s and became famous as the "Woodstock Guru" after his appearance at the seminal rock festival in 1969. Founder of Yogaville (in Virginia) and his own style of yoga, Integral Yoga. Well-known followers include Dr. Dean Ornish and Carole King, among many others.

Swami Satyananda Saraswati & Shree Maa: Two highly revered and influential yoga preceptors of the Sri Ramakrishna Paramahamsa lineage, their Devi Mandir ashram is in Napa Valley, California. The author still considers them his teachers.

Dr. Rick Strassman: In the early '90s, Dr. Strassman carried out the first research in over 20 years on psychedelics, which he recounts in his now famous book, DMT: The Spirit Molecule.

Dr. Robert Svoboda: Ayurvedic physician and author most known for his *Aghora* series, which detail the teachings of Svoboda's left-handed tantric guru, Swami Vimalananda,

Transcendental Meditation: A system of meditation developed by Maharishi Mahesh Yogi, becoming a household term beginning in the late '60s when the Beatles went on retreat with Maharishi to learn the practice.

Transformational Breathwork: An intensive breathwork practice developed by Judith Kravitz (see above), similar to Holotropic Breathwork, Rebirthing, etc., though also unique.

R. Gordon Wasson: A successful banker who unwittingly became a mycophile (mushroom enthusiast) and developed a theory that the Soma of the Vedas was a concoction derived from the psychoactive mushroom Amanita muscaria. Subsequent research disproved the theory.

Ganga White: Director of the White Lotus Foundation and author of the book, *Yoga Beyond Belief* (North Atlantic Books, 2007), in which this self-titled "renegade yogi" makes a case for the use of Ayahuasca. White's book was partial inspiration for this one.

Vedas: The most ancient and revered sacred scriptures of the religious world-view that is now most widely known as "Hinduism." Some have used the term "Bible" (as in "Hebrew Bible") as an analogy to refer to both its similar antiquity, and also its impact.

Yoga: A philosophy and practice that ultimately stems from the Hindu Vedas (and perhaps even earlier), and has been recognized as India's greatest contribution to the world. There are many paths and styles of yoga, which can be confusing and frustrating to the neophyte; yet what appears to be shared by most if not all forms of yoga is a disciplined practice that leads to a more unified existence, however that might be understood. Yoga has in the past century become a worldwide, mainstream phenomenon that has reached well beyond its Indian roots.

Yogi Bhajan: Sikh Founder of "3HO Kundalini Yoga" in the late '60s, currently one of the most practiced yoga styles in the world. Bhajan was condemned by the Indian Sikh community for teaching their yoga to Westerners, and he remains a controversial figure even after his passing.

Bibliography

Aaronon, Bernard, & Osmond, Humphry. *Psychedelics: The Uses and Implications of Psychedelic Drugs*. Anchor Books. New York, 1970.

Adi Da. *The Knee of Listening*. Dawn Horse Press, 2004.

Arya, Pandit Usharbudh, D. Litt. *Superconscious Meditation*. Himalayan International Institute of Yoga and Science. Honesdale, PA, 1974.

Avalon, Arthur. *Shakti and Shakta*. New York: Dover Publications, Inc., 1978.

Baba Hari Dass. *Silence Speaks: From the Chalkboard of Baba Hari Dass*. Sri Rama Foundation, 1977.

Ball, Martin W, Ph.D. *Being Human: An Entheological Guide to God, Evolution, and the Fractal Energetic Nature of Reality*. Kyandara Publishing, 2009.

Ibid. *The Entheogenic Evolution: Psychedelics, Consciousness, and Awakening the Human Spirit*. Kyandara Publishing, 2008.

Ibid. *Mushroom Wisdom: How Shamans Cultivate Spiritual Consciousness*. Berkeley: Ronin Publishing, 2006.

Ibid. *Sage Spirit: Salvia Divinorum & The Entheogenic Experience*. Lulu.com, 1997

Beyer, Stephan. *Singing to the Plants: A Guide to Mestizo Shamanism in the Upper Amazon*. University of New Mexico Press, 2010.

Boyd, Doug. *Swami: Encounters with Modern Mystics*. Himalayan International Institute of Yoga Science and Philosophy: Honesdale, PA, 1995, 1976.

Buhner, Stephen Harrod. *Sacred Plant Medicine: The Wisdom in Native American Herbalism*. Bear & Company, 2006.

Campbell, Joseph. *Myths to Live By: How We Re-create Ancient Legends in Our Daily Lives to Release Human Potential*. Viking, 1972.

Cole, Krystle. *After the Trip: Thoughts on Entheogens, Spirituality, and Daily Life*. CreateSpace, 2008.

Cox, Harvey. *Turning East: Why Americans Look to the Orient for Spirituality— And What That Search Can Mean to the West*. Simon and Schuster, 1977.

Dobkin de Rios, Marlene. *The Psychedelic Journey of Marlene Dobkin De Rios: 45 Years with Shamans, Ayahuasqueros, and Ethnobotanists*. Rochester, Vermont: Park Street Press, 2009.

Eliade, Mircea. *Yoga: Immortality and Freedom*. Princeton, New Jersey: Princeton University Press, 1958.

Empty, Dean. *The Psychedelic Bible: The Other side of the Story*. CreateSpace, 2008.

Dodd, David G., and Spaulding, Diana. *The Grateful Dead Reader*. Oxford University Press, 2000.

Feuerstein, Georg. *Holy Madness: Spirituality, Crazy-Wise Teachers, and Enlightenment*. Hohm Press, 2006.

Forte, Robert, ed., Hoffman, Albert, Wasson, R. Gordon, et al. *Entheogens and the Future of Religion*. The Council of Spiritual Practices, 2nd ed., 2000.

Gaskin, Stephen. *Cannabis Spirituality*. 1996.

Goldberg, Philip. *American Veda: From Emerson and the Beatles to Yoga and Meditation—How Indian Spirituality Changed the West*. New York: Harmony Books, 2010.

Greer, Steven M., M.D. *Hidden Truth, Forbidden Knowledge*. Crossing Point Publications.

Grey, Alex. *The Mission of Art*. Boston: Shambhala, 2001.

Grob, Charles. *Hallucinogens: A Reader* (New Consciousness Reader). Tarcher, 2002.

Grob, Charles, and Walsh, Roger. *Higher Wisdom: Eminent Elders Explore The Continuing Impact Of Psychedelics*. SUNY Press, Albany, New York, 2005.

Grof, Stanislav. *The Cosmic Game: Explorations from the Frontiers of Human Consciousness*. SUNY Press, Albany, New York, 1998.

Ibid. *LSD: Doorway to the Numinous: The Groundbreaking Psychedelic Research into the Realms of the Human Unconscious*. Park Street Press, 2009.

Ibid. *LSD Psychotherapy: Exploring the Frontiers of the Hidden Mind*. Hunter House, 1980/1994.

Ibid. *The Ultimate Journey: Consciousness and the Mystery of Death*. Multidisciplinary Association for Psychedelic Studies (MAPS); 1st edition, 2006.

Ibid. *When the Impossible Happens: Adventures in Non-Ordinary Reality*. Sounds True, 2005.

Grof, Stanislav, and Grof, Christina. *Holotropic Breathwork: A New Approach to Self-Exploration and Therapy*. SUNY Series in Transpersonal and Humanistic Psychology, 2010.

Harner, Michael. *Hallucinogens and Shamanism*. Galaxy Books, 1973.

Harner, Michael. *The Way of the Shaman*. HarperSanFrancisco, New York, 1980.

Heinrich, Clark. *Strange Fruit: Alchemy and Religion, the Hidden Truth*. Bloomsbury Publishing, 1995.

Horgan, John. *Rational Mysticism*. Houghton Mifflin Company, New York, 2003.

Houston, Jean. *A Mythic Life: Learning to Live Our Greater Story*. HarperSanFrancisco, 1996.

Hunter, Kevin. *The Awakened Heart Path: Spiritual Transformation, Enlightenment, and Love*. The Awakened Heart Path, 2011.

Huxley, Aldous. *The Doors of Perception*. Harper & Row, 1954.

Irving, Darrel. *Serpent of Fire: A Modern View of Kundalini*. Samuel Weiser, York Beach, Maine, 1995.

Iyengar, BKS. *Light on the Yoga Sutras of Patanjali*. Thorsons Press: San Francisco, CA, 1966, 1996.

Jung, C.G. *The Psychology of Kundalini Yoga*. Princeton University Press, New Jersey, 1996.

Kalweit, Holger. *Dreamtime & Inner Space: The World of the Shaman*. Boston: Shambhala Books, 1984.

Krishna, Gopi. *Kundalini: The Evolutionary Energy in Man*. Shambhala Publications, Inc., 1967/1970.

Ibid. *Living with Kundalini: The Autobiography of Gopi Krishna*. Boston: Shambhala Publications Inc., 1993.

Kumar, Ravindra, and Larsen, Jytte Kumar. *The Kundalini Book of Living and Dying: Gateways to Higher Consciousness*. Weiser. Boston, MA, 2004.

Lama Surya Das. *Awakening the Buddha Within: Tibetan Wisdom for the Western World*. Bantam Doubleday Dell, New York, 1997.

Lang, Michael. *The Road to Woodstock: From the Man Behind the Legendary Festival*. Ecco/HarperCollins, 2009.

Lattin, Don. *The Harvard Psychedelic Club: How Timothy Leary, Ram Dass, Huston Smith, and Andrew Weil Killed the Fifties and Ushered in a New Age for America*. HarperOne, 2010.

Leary, Timothy. *Flashbacks*. Tarcher, 2007.

Ibid. *High Priest*, 2nd edition. Ronin, 1995.

Lilly, John. *The Scientist: A Metaphysical Autobiography*. Ronin Publishing, 3d edition, 1996.

Luna, Luis Eduardo, and Amaringo, Pablo. *Ayahuasca Visions: The Religious Iconography of a Peruvian Shaman*. Berkeley, California: North Atlantic Books, 1991/1999.

Masters, Robert, and Houston, Jean. *The Varieties of Psychedelic Experience: The Classic Guide to the Effects of LSD on the Human Psyche*. Park Street Press, 2000.

McKenna, Terrence. *Food of the Gods: The Search for the Original Tree of Knowledge A Radical History of Plants, Drugs, and Human Evolution*. Bantam, 1993.

McKenna, Terrence. *The Archaic Revival: Speculations on Psychedelic Mushrooms, the Amazon, Virtual Reality, UFOs, Evolution, Shamanism, the Rebirth of the Goddess, and the End of History*. HarperOne, 1992.

McKenna, Terrence. *True Hallucinations: Being an Account of the Author's Extraordinary Adventures in the Devil's Paradise*. HarperCollins, 1994.

Merkur, Dan. *The Psychedelic Sacrament: Manna, Meditation, and Mystical Experience*. Park Street Press: Rochester, Vermont, 2001.

Metzner, Ralph. *Ayahuasca: Human Consciousness and the Spirits of Nature*. Thunder Mouth Press: New York, 1999.

Metzner, Ralph. *Sacred Mushroom of Visions: Teonanácatl: A Sourcebook on the Psilocybin Mushroom*. Park Street Press, 2005.

Metzner, Ralph; Alpert, Richard; and Leary, Timothy. *The Psychedelic Experience: A Manual Based On the Tibetan Book of the Dead*. Citadel Press, 1995.

Metzner, Ralph. *The Unfolding Self: Varieties of Transformative Experience*. Origin Press, Novato, CA, 1986, 1998.

Mookerjee, Ajit, and Khanna, Madhu. *The Tantric Way: Art * Science * Ritual*. New York Graphic Society, 1977.

Narby, Jeremy. *The Cosmic Serpent: DNA and the Origins of Knowledge*. Tarcher, 1999.

Narby, Jeremy. *Intelligence in Nature: An Inquiry into Knowledge*. Tarcher, 2006.

Narby, Jeremy; Kounen, Jan; Ravalec, Vincent. *The Psychotropic Mind: The World According to Ayahuasca, Iboga, and Shamanism*. Rochester, Vermont: Park Street Press, 2008.

Neuhaus, Eve. Baumohl. *The Crazy Wisdom of Ganesh Baba: Psychedelic Sadhana, Kriya Yoga, Kundalini, and the Cosmic Energy in Man*. Inner Traditions, 2010.

Ott, Jonathan. *The Age of Entheogens & the Angel's Dictionary*. Natural Products Co., 1995.

Pinchbeck, Daniel. *Breaking Open the Head*. Three Rivers Press, 2003.

Ibid. *2012: The Return of Quetzcoatl*. Tarcher, 2007.

Ibid. *Notes from the Edge Times*. New York: Tarcher/Penguin, 2010.

Ibid. *Exploring the Edge Realms of Consciousness*. Chapter 6, "Prolegomena to a Guide for the Emerging Yoga Shaman" was included in this anthology.

Pinkham, Mark Amaru. *The Return of the Serpents of Wisdom*. Adventures Unlimited Press, 1997

Plotkin, Mark J. *Medicine Quest: In Search of Nature's Healing Secrets*. New York: Viking, 2000.

Radhanath Swami. *The Journey Home: Autobiography of an American Swami*. San Rafael, CA: Mandala Publishing, 2010.

Ram Dass. *Be Here Now*. Lama Foundation; Crown Books, 1971.

Ibid. *Be Love Now: The Path of the Heart*. HarperOne, 2010.

Ibid. *Miracle of Love*. Dutton, 1979; Hanuman Foundation, 1996.

Ibid. *Paths to God: Living the Bhagavad Gita*. Harmony, 2004.

Ibid. *Polishing the Mirror*. Sounds True, 2013.

Ram Dass, Metzner, Bravo. *Birth of a Psychedelic Culture: Conversations about Leary, the Harvard Experiments, Millbrook and the Sixties*. Synergetic Press, 2010.

Rampuri. *Baba: Autobiography of a Blue-Eyed Yogi*. Bell Tower, New York, 2005.

Razam, Rak. *Aya: A Shamanic Odyssey*. Icaro Publishing, 2009.

Schou, Nicholas. *Orange Sunshine: The Brotherhood of Eternal Love and Its Quest to Spread Peace, Love, and Acid to the World*. Thomas Dunne Books (St. Martin's Press), New York, 2010.

Schultes, Richard Evans, Hoffman, Albert, and Ratsch, Christian. *Plants of the Gods: Their Sacred, Healing, and Hallucinogenic Powers*. Healing Arts Press, Rochester, Vermont, 1992, 1998.

Singleton, Mark. *Yoga Body: The Origins of Modern Posture Practice*. Oxford University Press, 2010.

Smith, Huston. *Cleansing the Doors of Perception: The Religious Significance of Entheogenic Plants and Chemicals*. Jeremy P. Tarcher/Putnam: New York, 2000.

Stafford, Peter. *Psychedelics*. Ronin Publishing, 2003.

Steindl-Rast, David, Walsh, Roger N., Grof, Stanislav, et al. *Psychoactive Sacramentals: Essays on Entheogens and Religion*. The Council on Spiritual Practices, 2001.

Storl, Wolf-Dieter, Ph.D. *Shiva: The Wild God of Power and Ecstasy*. Inner Traditions, Rochester, Vermont, 2004.

Strassman, Rick, M.D. *DMT, The Spiritual Molecule: A Doctor's Revolutionary Research into the Biology of Near-Death and Mystical Experiences*. Park Street Press, Rochester, Vermont, 2001.

Strassman, Rick, M.D., Wojtowicz, Slawek, M.D., Luna, Luis Eduardo, Ph.D., Frecska, Ede, M.D. *Inner Paths to Outer Space: Journeys to Alien Worlds through Psychedelics and Other Spiritual Technologies*. Park Street Press, Rochester, Vermont, 2008.

Svoboda, Robert E. *Ayurveda: Life, Health, and Longevity*. Penguin Arkana, 1992.

Swami Prabhavananda and Christopher Isherwood, *How to Know God: The Yoga Aphorisms of Patanjali*. Vedanta Press, 1953.

Swami Rama. *Living with the Himalayan Masters*. Honesdale, PA., 2007.

Swami Satyananda Saraswati. *Kundalini Tantra*. Bihar School of Yoga, Munger, Bihar, India, 1984,1996.

Talbot, Michael. *The Holographic Universe*. HarperPerennial, New York, 1991.

Tart, Charles. *States of Consciousness*.

Tindall, Robert. *The Jaguar That Roams in the Mind: An Amazonian Plant Spirit Odyssey*. Rochester, Vermont: Park Street Press, 2008.

Walsh, Roger, M.D., Ph.D. *The World of Shamanism: New Views of an Ancient Tradition*. LLewellyn. Woodbury, Minnesota, 2007.

Wasson, R. Gordon, Stella Kramrisch, Jonathon Ott, and Carl A. P. Ruck. *Persephone's Quest: Entheogens and the Origins of Religion*. Yale, 1986.

Weil, Andrew. *The Natural Mind: A Revolutionary Approach to the Drug Problem*. Houghton Mifflin, 2004.

Weil, Andrew. *The Marriage of Sun and Moon: Dispatches From the Frontiers of Consciousness*. Boston: Houston Mifflin Company, 1980/2004.

White, David Gordon. *The Alchemical Body: Siddha Traditions in Medieval India*. The University of Chicago Press, 1996.

White, Ganga. *Yoga Beyond Belief: Insights to Awaken and Deepen Your Practice*. Berkeley, California: North Atlantic Books, 2007.

White, John (Ed). *Kundalini: Evolution and Enlightenment* (revised ed.). Paragon House, New York, 1990.

Zaehner, R.C. *Mysticism: Sacred and Profane*. Oxford, 1961.

Endnotes

1. See the movie "Woodstock: Three Days of Peace and Healing."

2. On this point, see, for example, R. R. Griffiths & W. A. Richards & U. McCann & R. Jesse, "Psilocybin can occasion mystical-type experiences having substantial and sustained personal meaning and spiritual significance," Psychopharmacology (2006) 187:268–283, The MAPS website has this and a number of other psychedelic research papers: http://www.maps.org/resources/papers/.

3. Ram Dass, *Paths to God: Living the Bhagavad Gita*, p. 100.

4. Jerry Garcia, quoted in *Rolling Stone*, November 30, 1989.

5. Carl Jung, *The Psychology of Kundalini Yoga*, Princeton University Press, USA, 1996, p. 26. Lecture 2, October 19, 1932.

6. From the poem, "The Perfect High," also known as "The Quest for Gimmesome Roy."

7. In his address to the crowd that day, the Swami most likely intentionally avoided the issue of drugs, knowing that would not be wise. Instead he spoke of the power of music and yoga to create peace, and how America was growing spiritually with the help of yoga. Here is a relevant excerpt from his address:

   "America leads the whole world in several ways. Very recently, when I was in the East, the grandson of Mahatma Gandhi met me and asked me what's happening in America and I said, "America is becoming a whole. America is helping everybody in the material field, but the time has come for America to help the whole world with spirituality also." And, that's why from the length and breadth, we see people—thousands of people, yoga-minded, spiritual-minded. The whole of last month I was in Hawaii and I was on the West Coast and witnessed it again… So, let all our actions, and all our arts, express Yoga. Through that sacred art of music, let us find peace that will pervade all over the globe. Often we hear groups of people shouting, "Fight for Peace." I still don't understand how they are going to fight and then find peace. Therefore, let us not fight for peace, but let us find peace within ourselves first." (Source: http://swamisatchidananda.org/woodstock-guru/)

8. A very engaging and insightful book on drugs and that period is Lee and Shlain's "*Acid Dreams: The Complete Social History of LSD: The CIA, the Sixties, and Beyond*." The authors do discuss Woodstock, but don't mention the scene with Law, nor do they discuss DMT very much, though it was used fairly widely in that era. It is, after all, primarily a book about LSD. Another very helpful book is Harvey Cox's "*Turning East: Why Americans Look to the Orient for Spirituality—And What That Search Can Mean to the West*" (Simon & Schuster, 1977), particularly the chapter "The Flesh of the Gods: Turning On and Turning East," pp. 32–51.

9. In Lisa Law's photo archive: http://americanhistory.si.edu/lisalaw/6.htm. Under this picture is the following quote from Lisa Law, Tom Law's first wife: "We stopped smoking marijuana and started getting high on breathing. Enough of being potheads. Now we could be healthy, happy and holy" (Lisa Law, 1987).

10. The filmmakers actually create a very fine transition from Law teaching yoga at the start of the festival, to where he is speaking to a smaller crowd of hippies away from the stage.

11. You can view the clip here: http://www.youTube.com/watch?v=Umh5FX5C1N0, or do a search on YouTube for "yoga and Woodstock."

12. Dr. Grof kindly offered some assistance and encouragement with this project, including sending me a PDF of his latest book, *Holotropic Breathwork: A New Approach to Self-Exploration and Therapy* (SUNY Series in Transpersonal and Humanistic Psychology), 2010. According to the book, Dr. Grof and his wife, Christina, developed Holotropic Breathwork in the mid to late Seventies, drawing upon the teachings and practices of many traditions and schools, both East and West.

13. The 14th century scripture, *Hatha Yoga Pradipika* ("Light on Hatha Yoga") discusses *bhastrika pranayama* in some detail (2.59–65). This pranayama is often taught in yoga classes these days (I teach it myself), though usually not as intensely or for the entire class. Also, it is interesting that the way Tom Law is doing the breath in the video very closely resembles the "Viking Breath" that is currently being taught by the Qi Gong teacher Jeff Primack. In the clip, we don't see anyone else breathing quite the same way as Law.

14. Consider the following quote from Jerry Garcia from the same year (1969) in the August 23rd edition of Rolling Stone. Garcia is talking about the early Acid Tests: "When it was moving right, you could dig that there was something that it was getting toward, something like ordered chaos. The Test would start off and then there would be chaos. Everybody would be high and *flashing* and going through insane changes during which everything would be demolished, man, and spilled and broken and affected, and after that another thing would happen, maybe soothing out the chaos, then another; it'd go all night 'til morning..." (italics mine.) Also, it's interesting to note that Tom Law's former wife, Lisa Law, produced an award winning documentary on the Sixties era called "Flashing on the Sixties."

15. Myra Friedman, from her biography of Janis Joplin, quoted just slightly out of context. In Lee and Schlain, "*Acid Dreams*," op. cit., p. 252.

16. Other rock bands, such as the Doors, had already been followers of the Maharishi from as early as 1966 (all the members except Jim Morrison, that is); the Beatles were just the most famous at the time and had the biggest influence.

17. From Lisa Law's photo archive: http://americanhistory.si.edu/lisalaw/6.htm.

18. Later we will consider Shri Brahmananda Saraswati's statement that psychedelics, pranayama, and Hatha Yoga asanas all fall into the same category of "*aushadha*" (see Yoga Sutras, 4.1)—things that produce chemical changes in the brain to induce a state of Samadhi.

19. Link: http://www.transformationalbreathing.com/. One other recent form of breathwork that involves something like hyperventilation is Sri Sri Ravi Shankar's "Sudarshan Kriya," which is the centerpiece of his Art of Being program, and supposed to be kept a secret except amongst those who do the seminar.

20. Online at www.maps.org.

21. One notable example is filmmaker David Lynch, who put on a TM benefit concert at Madison Square Garden in 2008. Lynch has been a faithful practitioner of TM for the past several decades (he meditates for 20 minutes, twice daily).

22. As cited above. A very interview with Garcia regarding his LSD use can be found in Lee Abbott's "Dead Reckoning and Hamburger Metaphysics," in Dodd and Spaulding, *The Grateful Dead Reader*, Oxford University Press, 2000, pp. 144–145. Garcia interestingly mentions how his LSD trips at the end took on a kind of "teacher-pupil relationship," a point which might connect with the discussion here of "plant teachers."

23. If I may here insert that classic line by Robin Williams: "Reality is just a crutch for people who can't cope with drugs."

24. It should be noted that there is a good deal of TM literature that wants to show how TM reduces drug use and abuse. For example, Denise Denniston's The TM Book: How to Enjoy the Rest of Your Life (Fairfield Press, 1975/1986), pp. 209–213, has a graph showing drug use before and after TM, with 50% using LSD and 40% "other hallucinogens" before, and only about 7% after. The book fails to mention, however, that prospective TMers were requested to stop taking psychedelics upon beginning their meditation practice. Jack Forem's Transcendental Meditation: Maharishi Mahesh Yogi and the Science of Creative Intelligence (Bantam, 1973/1976), pp. 140–151, delves deeper into the subject of drugs, devoting an entire chapter to it, "Without Chemical Crutches," which contains numerous first-hand reports and quotes of former psychedelic users turned TMers. The author says that he could "fill a whole volume" with before-and-after accounts, noting that "the one basic pattern that can be discerned in all the hundreds of reports concerning drug usage is that for whatever reason drugs were taken, whether in a conscious attempt to achieve a higher level of life, for "kicks" or for no particular reason, once the TM program was begun, fulfillment and happiness were experienced to such a degree that there was no desire to continue using drugs." (p. 144). The author also brings studies showing the deep drop in drug use among TMers, including a 1970 Harvard Medical School study by Drs. Herbert Benson and R. Keith Wallace. The results are certainly impressive, but again, there is no mention of the subtle and not-so-subtle pressure for new meditators to stop all drug use.

When I sent this to Edward for peer review, he made the following interesting comment: "As you quote, 50% had used LSD before starting TM, and if anything, probably more, as it was taboo and therefore not something quickly admitted, an astounding positive result of LSD use. For all the attempts to find research validating meditation's effectiveness in making a better person, here buried in those stats, from a slightly different perspective, is evidence that use of LSD promotes interest in spirituality—that LSD is a catalyst to the search for self awareness. A version of the famous Harvard psilocybin and mystical experience study Huston Smith took part in during the 1960's. See: http://www.druglibrary.org/schaffer/lsd/hsmith.htm."

25. Ram Dass had a suspicion he might have been duped the first time by his teacher, and was apparently criticized for being too gullible. When he returned to India the second time, it was Neem Karoli Baba who asked to do the "experiment" again, and Ram Dass took that as a sign that his guru knew of his doubts.

26. The reference is to the Shel Silverstein poem, "The Legend of Gimmesome Roy," quoted above.

27. Ram Dass did finally talk about his correspondence with Meher Baba in his 1977 book, Grist for the Mill (Santa Cruz: Unity Press), pp. 99–102. In answering the question from a student, "How does LSD affect the spiritual journey," Ram Dass relates some things that Meher Baba wrote to him in 1965, which I was not able to confirm through written sources (but don't have any reason to doubt). For example, Ram Dass interestingly relates that Meher Baba told him that he could take LSD three more times (p. 101), and Ram Dass says that he didn't listen but continued to take LSD regularly until he went to India in '67.

Ram Dass also recounts in brief the two stories of his giving Neem Karoli Baba LSD, with one notable difference: Instead of Neem Karoli Baba saying that "It would be much better to become Christ than just to visit him, but your medicine won't do that because it's not the highest Samadhi." Here Ram Dass has his guru saying, "because it's a false samadhi," which is a critical difference, because it's tantamount to saying that it's no samadhi at all, and that's exactly what Meher Baba had written to him in '65, Ram Dass notes. (Note: In Badiner's Zig Zag Zen, p. 212, Ram Dass has his guru saying "it's not the true Samadhi," something which is only a slight variation, but significant nonetheless. The difficulty lies in the fact that the guru's message was coming through translation.) Nevertheless, Neem Karoli Baba did add: "Though it's useful to visit a saint, it strengthens your faith," so a false samadhi, but not completely worthless. The guru added the now famous, "But love is a stronger medicine" (usually rendered, "Love is the strongest medicine.") Again, Ram Dass takes this as permission to use LSD, which he did, he says, once a year after that, and "every time was a profound experience." However, he ultimately realized that acid had "created a psychic blockage in my medulla, which made my spiritual work, for quite a while, more difficult, in terms of working with these incredible pressures in my head. It turns out that had I not ingested so much psychedelics I would have been able to get through that space much faster" (p. 101). He therefore concludes here that LSD might be helpful for some seekers, as it was for him, but isn't really necessary anymore given the spaces opened up for young people by the acid revolution.

One other notable difference in a later re-telling by Ram Dass of the original Neem Karoli Baba LSD story is interestingly found in Ram Dass' most recent book, *Be Love Now* (p. 132). In the earlier account, Neem Karoli Baba had mentioned that yogis had known about such medicines as LSD "a long time ago in the Kulu Valley," but for the first time in print that I am aware of, Ram Dass adds, "by yogis who would first do hatha yoga" before taking them. This is certainly a key addition to the story, implying as it does that Hatha Yoga was seen as a preparation for the psychedelic experience. See below for more.

28. There are a number of web sources detailing this connection, including a piece by Townshend himself, "In Love with Meher Baba," in *Rolling Stone* (issue # 71, 1970). His discussion of "Baba" and drugs bears including here:

"My Last Dope-Smoking Days"

It is on this basis that I approach another of Baba's most powerful and controversial statements:

"Drugs are harmful mentally, spiritually and physically."

I repeat these words parrot fashion, not knowing honestly whether I would have said it myself had Baba not said it first. One thing I do know, the last acid trip I took (on a plane coming back from the Monterey Pop Festival) would have been my last whether I had heard the above from Baba or not. Acid had taken me apart but not put me back together again, and it is clutching another of Baba's statements about drugs that I justify what I did to my brain:

"For a few sincere seekers, the use of hallucinogenic drugs may have instilled in them a state of longing that has brought them into my contact, but further injection would not only he harmful, but have no purpose."

"Somebody asked me if Baba ever took acid. That's where I have to walk away. It's clear that they can't act on the unqualified words of a stranger in India when they don't even accept that he is really the Avatar. If they accepted he was the Avatar they wouldn't ask if he had tried acid. So they keep on keeping on, and I try to stay cool. Even writing a piece like this makes me feel like a miniature Billy Graham.

"Pot was a little different. I never did make a personal decision that pot was screwing me up. For one thing I never used it to write on or play at the time I heard about Baba. I always got good buzzes from listening on it though, even if they got a bit clichéd... What I am trying to put across is that I still love the idea of getting stoned. I remember the days of colorful highs with acute nostalgia, I would be a fool to myself if I didn't allow myself the luxury of a past. The crux of it is, that I am now stoned all the time. It's hard to take, I know, but it's true. It's not a dizzy, smashed high, it's a fairly alert and natural one. Just about as natural as you can get. Everyone knows that there is such a thing as a natural high. Try thinking of it as the natural high..."

The piece concludes with these words: "I feel that never will I be able to stand back from myself and pretend anymore that God is a myth. That Christ was just another man. That Baba was simply a hypnotic personality. The facts are coming home to me like sledge hammers, not through the words I read in books about Baba, not through even his own words. But through my ordinary daily existence. Meher Baba is the Avatar, God Incarnate on our planet. The Awakener.

"As the river flows down outside my home, I look out and remember that eventually it will reach the sea. Each little stream that runs into the Thames feeding it and building it sustains the ocean. Retains the cycle of life that keeps our planet moist and airy. We too need sustaining; love is the only thing that can do it."

Link to the rest of this fascinating piece: http://www.thewho.net/?q=bibliography/articles/rs_1970.html.

29. Taken from "A Tapestry of Meher Baba's Connections with the West." http://www.ial.goldthread.com/Meher_Baba.html. This can also be found in the book *Lord Meher*, pp. 6398–6404.

30. *Ibid.*

31. Timothy Leary, *Flashbacks: An Autobiography*. J.P. Tarcher, Inc., 1983, p. 210.

32. There are two other interesting artifacts I would like to mention in regard to Leary's interest in India and yoga. The first is a story that Ram Dass has told about how Leary was in India two years prior to him and nearly met his guru, Neem Karoli Baba, through a fascination with his devotee, Baba Hari Dass (who we'll meet later).

The story was retold by Ram Dass in the film "Timothy Leary's Dead." The clip is also well worth watching as accompaniment to the text here: http://www.youTube.com/watch?v=vy-FnY9d42CI. Also, Leary's 1969 LP, "You Can Be Anyone This Time Around," particularly the title song, contains numerous references to India, with lines such as, "You can be Krishna this time around." Leary also says, "You can be God this time around—you've got to be God, this time around." Yet Leary was definitely not into the whole guru trip, not sure if that included himself or not!

33. For more about Alpert, Leary, and Metzner in this period, see also *Birth of a Psychedelic Culture: Conversations about Leary, the Harvard Experiments, Millbrook and the Sixties*, which quotes Leary's *Flashbacks* a number of times. There is also interestingly no mention of Meher Baba or the correspondence with him here, though Metzner does discuss how he and Leary went to India at least partly to discover what psychedelics were in light of the yoga tradition. Metzner notes there that Leary made fun of Alpert for his whole yoga/guru trip. Early on I did email Metzner for his assistance with this book, yet he did not seem interested. Of course, Metzner has done quite a lot of his own research into these areas over the past 5+ decades (and seems to have been more balanced overall than Leary or Alpert) and I would love to discuss these matters further with him. Also, there is a very interesting interview with Dick Anthony regarding Meher Baba, his guru, to be found in *Spiritual Choices: The Problem of Recognizing Authentic Paths to Inner Transformation*, Paragon House, 1987, pp. 153–191. This interview confirms for me even more the amazing personage that Meher Baba surely was, and still is for many. Was he "The Avatar of the Age" as he proclaimed to the world? Even if he was something else, he certainly was *something else*.

34. Ram Dass, op. cit., p. 101.

35. This was Tom's memory of that seminal moment in yoga's migration to these shores. After Danny Paradise looked at an early manuscript of this book, however, he wrote back with the following alternative account of what happened: "David Williams was at the Atlanta Rick Festival in 1969 [July, before Woodstock, which was in August] and Tom was the MC. Tom led 600,000 people there in a Yoga practice and David did the practice and that further led him on his search for Yoga. Eventually going to India after and finding KP Jois and Ashtanga Yoga. David and his wife Nancy Gilgoff brought the practices to the West… First in Encinitas around

1974/75, and then Maui in May, 1976, which was where I met them and learned from May 2nd, '76. David and his students brought KP Jois to the USA for the first time in '75, and Manju stayed and took over David's classes so he and Nancy were free to come to Hawaii."

For more about the Atlanta Pop Festival, see: http://en.wikipedia.org/wiki/Atlanta_International_Pop_Festival_(1969)

36. http://www.strippingthegurus.com

37. Dr. Paul Brunton, *A Search In Secret India*. Samuel Weiser, 1994/1934, p. 61.

38. Or, as Ganga White told me he rephrases the old chestnut, "When the student is ready, the teacher appears" to: "When the student is ready, the *teaching* appears."

39. The shaman in question very kindly agreed to an interview with me. The way we did it was, I emailed him some questions and then he did an audio of his answers and sent the file to me. It was very good stuff and would have added something to the discussion here. The thing was, my computer that was stolen had that file on it and it wasn't backed up. Since the time that all this was first written, a few years ago now, this particular shaman (who I have not seen in that time) has stopped offering Ayahuasca sessions and is now channeling a 5,000 year-old entity and offering *pujas*, ceremonies in which different deities are worshiped (Shiva, Kali, etc.) A yoga student who had done ceremony with him twice and who has been to see him recently told me all this and said she was really blown away by what he's doing now. Her Ayahuasca sessions were extremely transformational, she reported. Her last report is that he has now gone back to offering Ayahuasca ceremonies.

40. *Yage Letters*. Allen Ginsberg. Michael Harner's *Way of the Shaman*.

41. Ganga White, *Yoga Beyond Belief*, pp. 188–189.

42. Consider the following recent account of a student of the Diamond Heart school who says she felt shamed for taking Ayahuasca: http://www.elephantjournal.com/2012/09/diamond-heart-says-no-to-Ayahuasca-seeking-student/. I have also heard of Ammachi telling students not to take Ayahuasca, yet would need to inquire further into this.

43. Two representative quotes from Yogananda: "*Many uninformed persons speak of yoga as Hatha Yoga or consider yoga to be 'magic,' dark mysterious rites for attaining spectacular powers. When scholars, however, speak of yoga they mean the system expounded in Yoga Sutras (also known as Patanjali's Aphorisms): Raja ("royal") Yoga…*" "*Hatha Yoga [is] a specialized branch of bodily postures and techniques for health and longevity. Hatha is useful, and produces spectacular physical results, but this branch of yoga is little used by yogis bent on spiritual liberation…*" (Paramahamsa Yogananda, *Autobiography of a Yogi*, p. 254–255.)

44. This information is culled partly from the biographical material on Karunamayi's website, www.karunamayi.org.

45. You can read more about Karunamayi at her website: www.karunamayi.org.

46. One woman's first person account of witnessing such manifestations of kumkum and other sacred substances from Karunamayi can be found in *Sri Karunamayi: A Biography* (India: SMVA Trust, 1992/1999), pp. 82–85. Also, there is a fascinating account in Radhanath Swami's "*The Journey Home: Autobiography of An American Swami*" (pp. 134–137) about a sadhu, Balashiva Yogi, who demonstrated for the author and an assembled crowd, his ability to produce murtis and sacred ash out of thin air. The author reveals that he was actually most impressed not by the materialization, but by the sadhu's honesty in saying to those assembled, "I am not God nor is anyone else who performs such supernatural feats. I am just an ordinary man with some yogic powers." (135) If so, then a teacher's ability to demonstrate such things should not be the

a huge reason to follow or worship them. In fact, perhaps it is the teachers who demonstrate such things as somehow proof of their divinity that require the most scrutiny…

47. See *In Search of the Cradle of Civilization: New Light on Ancient India* by Georg Feuerstein, Subhash Kak, and David Frawley (Paperback, January 2, 2005).

48. Will have to find correct attribution, but for now, see the movie about Ram Dass called Fierce Grace, 2001; also in Zeitgeist Video. A similar sentiment can be found in a letter Leary wrote to Arthur Koestler, reprinted in Koestler's essay, "A Return Trip to Nirvana."

49. Smith, *Cleansing the Doors of Perception*, p. 46.

50. See the Schultes, Hoffman, and Ratschs' *Plants of the Gods: Their Sacred, Healing, and Hallucinogenic Powers*, pp. 82–85. The authors there say, "Amanita muscaria may be the oldest of the hallucinogens and perhaps was once the most widely used."

51. Op. cit., p. 48.

52. To be fair, Wasson did acknowledge this point at the outset of his presentation, saying: "It is in the nature of a hypothesis when once a man has conceived it, that it assimilates everything to itself, as proper nourishment, and from the first moment of your begetting it, it generally grows stronger by everything you see, hear or understand." pg. 18.

53. See Frawley, "The Secret of the Soma Plant," https://vedanet.com/2012/06/13/the-secret-of-the-soma-plant/.

Dr. Robert Forte, who has the fortune and distinction of having been both a student of Mircea Eliade and of Stanislav Grof, Facebook messaged me something very similar to what Frawley says: "*My own feeling… is that Soma was something used over a long period of time and over a vast geographical range. I bet there were many different somas in that pantherina, cannabis, etc, including morning glory flowers/seeds.*" In 2008, I completed Dr. Frawley's 300 Hour Advanced Yoga and Ayurveda correspondence course, which goes into some depth in regard to Agni and Soma.

54. Ibid.

55. Robert Svoboda, *Aghora*, p. 176, 1986/1998, Rupa & Co., Calcutta.

56. McKenna actually refers to this particular mushroom as Stropharia cubensis, which has been recently re-classified into the genus Psilocybe by the mycologist Rolf Singer, and some now refer to it as "*Psilocybe cubensis.*"

57. For the following, see McKenna, *Food of the Gods*, pp. 97–120.

58. Developed in the subsequent chapter, "Twilight in Eden," pp. 121–123.

59. McKenna, *Food of the Gods*, pp. 121–122. McKenna might have been relying here at least in part on Frits Staal's essay, "How a Psychoactive Substance Becomes a Ritual: The Case of Soma" (*Social Research. An International Quarterly of the Social Sciences*. Vol.68, Number 3, Fall 2001, pages 745–78) which concludes: "The case of Soma shows how a psychoactive plant was regarded as a God, inspired a mythology, and became a ritual. When the original Soma of the Rigveda became difficult or impossible to procure, Vedic peoples constructed a ritual edifice of unprecedented complexity, combining rites with chants and recitations. It happened around 1000 B.C., when their sociopolitical center shifted from the Indus Valley to the Kuru region near modern Delhi, between Indus and Ganges, where most of the other three Vedas were composed. The entire development demonstrates how ritualization increases as Soma decreases." However, Staal seemed a bit more wary of overgeneralizing than McKenna: "Is my story an illustration and confirmation of Karl Marx's statement that religion is the opium of the people?

It is to some extent and I am sure he had a point. It is less persuasive as a general theory about the origin of religion. Every psychoactive substance does not lead to a religion and every religion does not arise from such a substance. Ritualists possess a vast knowledge, but if we want to know the identity of the original Soma, we need botanists to find a psychoactive plant that grows in the high mountains of the Pamir watershed or similar surroundings, may be dried, and swells when put in water." Staal concludes: "Many mysteries and questions about Soma remain and cannot be solved by a single individual. We need teamwork between experts on psychoactive substances and human physiology, Vedic scholars, botanists familiar with high mountains, geographers, historians, chemists, pharmacologists and others. My contribution has been ritual but I hope that some readers will take up the identity of Soma in earnest." Source: http://fritsstaal.googlepages.com/soma2001.

It's also important to note here that Wasson was somewhat sympathetic to McKenna's view regarding what he saw as the devolution of sacred tradition, as he was critical of Eliade's opposing perspective—that the original practices were devotion, meditation, etc., and that use of plants to "force" ecstasy was a later degradation. In Shamanism, Eliade wrote, "In the sphere of shamanism, strictly speaking, intoxication by drugs (hemp, mushrooms, tobacco, etc.) seems not to have formed part of the original practice. For, on the one hand, shamanic myths and folklore record a decadence among the shamans of the present day, who have become unable to obtain ecstasy in the fashion of the "great shamans of long ago;" on the other hand, it has been observed that where shamanism is in decomposition and the trance is simulated, there is also overindulgence in intoxicants and drugs. In the sphere of shamanism itself, however, we must distinguish between this (probably recent) phenomenon of intoxication for the purpose of "forcing" trance and the ritual consumption of "burning" substances for the purpose of increasing "inner heat." (As quoted in Wasson's Soma, pages 338–339.)

60. Let me just add for the record that I feel that McKenna's essential argument that modern India is essentially spiritually bankrupt is no more to be given weight than Meher Baba's saying that there are no physical, mental, or spiritual benefits of taking LSD, and for the simple reason that such hyperbolic statements fly in the face of the experience of many people, including my own. But I'm still glad that he said it!

61. Terence McKenna, *Food of the Gods*, p.4.

62. McKenna as quoted in John Horgan's *Rational Mysticism*, p. 185.

63. This is a fascinating interview that is well worth watching in full. It will provide a good deal of insight into the debate in question here. Watch online: http://www.youTube.com/watch?v=RaY-8J3uf3w0.

64. The reader will also find interesting in this context, "Buddhism and the Psychedelic Society: An Interview with Terence McKenna," in Allan Hunt Badiner's *Zig Zag Zen: Buddhism and Psychedelics*, pp. 189–192. I excerpt from this interview below.

65. Grof, *When the Impossible Happens*, pp. 32–34. There is a very interesting story recounted by journalist Naosherwan Anzar about the second time he met Muktananda that is well worth mentioning here. As Anzar told it: "[It was at an] International Transpersonal Psychology Conference in 1980 in Bombay. Muktananda was the host for that conference. I was a panelist at the conference and gave a talk on Meher Baba's Universal Message. The transpersonal psychology conference was sponsored, along with Muktananda, by Stanislav Grof and a large number of spiritual leaders involved in transpersonal psychology. Mother Theresa and Dr. Karan Singh were there. The Dalai Lama spoke briefly. There were a number of people—Chilton Pearce and so on.

"[During the questions] Grof made some remarks about the use of LSD in a very positive way, saying that it could be beneficial. And immediately I sprang up and I chided him for being supportive of a drug which Meher Baba had categorized as deleterious physically, mentally, and spiritually. And the reason that I had that reaction was that he said that he had tried it several hundred times and that he was continuing to do so. And of course at the very moment when he saw that I had an angry retort, he retracted and said that it should not be used in an unsupervised way, but that it should be supervised medically, and that it should not be used recreationally; so he kind of backed off. Consequently, the next day it appeared in *The Times of India* that a young reporter from another paper had had a verbal battle with Stanislaf Grof." In "Muktananda and Meher Baba: Naosherwan Anzar's Meetings with Swami Muktananda, the Siddha Meditation Teacher, An Interview by Kenneth Lux." In *The Journal For Psychological and Spiritual Integration*, Spring 1993, Vol. VI; number 2, Copyright 1993 Winnie Barrett, Ken Lux and Jason Saffer, publishers.

66. From a phone conversation with Dr. Grof, December 19th, 2010. Dr. Grof also suggested I try to get in touch with Chidvilasananda (aka, Gurumayi), successor to Muktananda and current head of the SYDA Yoga movement. I said it seems like it would be a difficult task to get through, but I will give it a try. I still have not done so.

67. The PBS special, "The Story of India," starring Michael Wood, has Wood presenting a very interesting discussion of Soma. Because such a project has so much ground to cover, Wood was only able to go so deeply into the subject, but it is well worth watching.

68. Their website is www.shreemaa.org. Shree Maa was one of the four Indian saints that my mentor introduced me to in the late Nineties.

69. Frawley, op. cit.

70. In regard to this passage, it would be instructive to look at Wendy Doniger (O'Flaherty)'s discussion, "The Seed as Soma and Poison," in her ground-breaking work, *Siva: The Erotic Ascetic* (Oxford University Press, 1973/1981), pp. 277–279. There we see the sense in which the "seed" (male ejaculate) is sometimes equated with Soma, although generally the idea is that through the yogi's retention and drawing upward of his seed (*brahmacharya*), it becomes Soma in the brain, and from there, as per our discussion, it may be drunk via *khechari mudra*. I note this here as it seems that, according to the Hatha Yoga Pradipika, once this transmutation of the seed takes place, and the Soma has been partaken of, the yogi becomes immune to erotic arousal.

71. Link: http://www.yoga-age.com/pradipika/part1.html. Another very nice translation and commentary of the *Hatha Yoga Pradipika* is the one by Swami Muktibodhananda published by the Bihar School of Yoga, 1985/1993. It is also worth noting here that while there are very few reports of Westerners doing this practice of khechari mudra, Norman Paulsen (1929–2006), a direct disciple of Paramahansa Yogananda, was able to naturally do khechari mudra (i.e. without cutting the tongue), and Yogananda apparently told him this was due to work in past incarnations. Paulsen ultimately came to the conclusion that khechari mudra wasn't really necessary. For more on this, see Paulsen's *"Christ Consciousness,"* or various online sources, including this one: http://oaks.nvg.org/sunburst.html. See more in footnote lxxxv below.

72. From the Yoga Dork site: http://www.yogadork.com/yd-goes-to-yoga-school/yd-goes-to-yoga-school-week-10-hatha-yoga-pradipika-peck-of-pickled-peppers/.

73. I don't have the exact volume and page at hand now, but the passage in question is somewhere in the *Awaken Children* series published through Ammachi's M.A. Center organization.

74. A nice retelling of this story can be found online here: http://www.sanatansociety.org/indian_epics_and_stories/the_churning_of_the_ocean.htm.

75. In Rieker and Becherer (trans.), *Hatha Yoga Pradipika*, Aquarian Press, 1992, chapter 8, pp. 62–67. A free PDF download can be found online at: http://www.hermetics.org/pdf/HathaYogaPradipika.pdf.

76. In Ram Dass, *Paths to God: Living the Bhagavad Gita*, p. 191. See also Doniger O'Flaherty, op. cit., p. 279, where there is a discussion of how this ability of the yogi to drink poison, or to turn poison to nectar, can be traced back to Rudra in the Vedas, to Shiva in the puranic story in question, and even to the present day, where it would seem to be mainly a Shaivite practice, though here we see Neem Karoli Baba, on the surface more of a Vaishnava (as he worships Rama), apparently demonstrating this ability, though we should also keep in mind that if he was indeed Hanuman, an avatar of Shiva, then this would make sense.

77. "Few breatharians have submitted themselves to medical testing; of those that have, including a hospital's observation of an Indian mystic surviving without food or water for 15 days, [6] none have undergone peer review with results independently reproduced. In a handful of documented cases, individuals attempting breatharian fasting have died, [7] [8] and among the claims investigated by the Indian Rationalist Association, all were found to be fraudulent. [9]" From the Wiki article, "Inedia." Link: http://en.wikipedia.org/wiki/Inedia. See there for more on the Prahlad Jani case. See also the following websites: http://abcnews.go.com/Health/International/man-eat-drink/story?id=10787036; and http://chunriwalamaaji.blogspot.co.uk/.

78. Other sources to consider for further elaboration of this esoteric subject; Swami Sivananda, *Kundalini* (Divine Life Society, 10th edition, 1994).

79. I would also like to mention here again one well-known case of a Western teacher who succeeded in performing *khechari mudra* (without the incision of the tongue), and that was the late Norman Paulsen, who was a direct disciple of Paramahamsa Yogananda. In his book, *The Christ Consciousness: The Pure Self Within You* (Solar Logos Foundation, 1984), pp. 139–141, Paulsen told how he was able to perform the mudra the first time he tried it, finding that it did very much have the effect it was said to have: "It was true! I immediately felt a very deep consciousness pervading my mind; with closed eyes spectral lights flared around me… I began to practice Kriya Yoga with my tongue in this unique position experiencing tremendous results." (p. 140) Yogananda seems to have been very impressed by this, telling Paulsen, "You have been an adept in the past, this is why your karma has allowed you to perform the king of mudras." (p. 141) I would also note here what Paulsen says about the use of psychedelics on the spiritual path: "The higher flight path of the Ancients toward Divine Illumination stood firm against the very popular use of LSD, marijuana, and other mind-altering drugs." (p. 436)

80. Edward kindly allowed me to read and reference an unpublished paper he wrote on Soma for a Vedic Religion class at Columbia University in 2010, "Soma of the Rig Veda: A Review of Ancient and Modern Work in the Field."

81. McKenna's thesis that Soma was possibly an analogue of Ayahuasca (a brew containing DMT) has been supported more recently in the work of Dr. Matthew Clark. In an email correspondence, Dr. Clark told me that he has found a recipe in Iran of Peganum Harmala and Arundo Donax, the same ingredients of the analogue McKenna proposed. Dr. Clark wrote to me that since the publication of his essay, which makes a strong case that Soma was a form of ayahuasca, he has updated his thesis to suggest that "ephedra, cannabis and other plants were also used as additives to the main concoction." On a side note, but one central to this book, based on decades as a student and researcher of India and Yoga, Dr. Clark expressed skepticism both in regard to the Neem Karoli Baba LSD story, and that gurus can perform real miracles. His

words: "We have to be aware that Indian gurus are just full of tricks to beguile the willing."

82. McKenna makes this point both in his 1993 memoir, *True Hallucinations* (p.56), as well as in *Food of the Gods* (pp. 113–114), published around the same time. In the latter, he notes that this is "an area where further research is clearly called for."

83. My report of this experience is to be found in the Appendix.

84. From an interview with Dr. Strassman by Scotto and James Kent, source: http://www.tripzine.com/listing.php?id=strassman.

85. *DMT: The Spirit Molecule* (Inner Traditions, 2001), with further elaboration in its sequel, Inner Paths to Outer Space.

86. For more, see Dr. Strassman's website: http://www.rickstrassman.com/.

87. See White, Ganga: *Yoga Beyond Belief*, p. 219.

88. Some of Sri Karunamayi's discourses have been transcribed into book form, The Blessed Souls series (SMVA Trust, Inc., Bangalore/New York). In volume 3 of the series, pp. 103–109, there is a discourse entitled "Drink the Elixir of Rama's Name," translated to English from Sri Karunamayi's native language of Telugu. In it, Amma talks about the "*amrita valli,*" which she says is a creeper with 180 medicinal properties that is used in the Mrityunjaya Homa, or fire ceremony. Amma adds that there is another similar creeper called "*somalata*" which grows on the Vindhyavat Mountain in the Himalayas, noting that the crushed leaves of this creeper was the "*soma rasa*" used in ancient times, a brew which "cured blindness, developed intelligence, purified and increased healthy blood cells…" Amma adds that, "Whatever is in the cosmos is also in our bodies." Noting all of this, Amma is in agreement with Swami Vimalananda (see above), that the *rasa* or elixir of the divine name (Rama nama) is most delicious.

89. Strassman interview, op. cit.

90. In Rick Strassman, "DMT Dharma," published in *Zig Zag Zen: Buddhism and Psychedelics*, p. 112.

91. This chapter is a reworking of an essay entitled "Psychedelics in Light of the Yoga Sutras" featured on the Reality Sandwich website in January, 2009. In this revised piece, I have taken into account many of the very insightful and encouraging comments that RS readers made, and I want to thank them for their collaboration.

92. In the already mentioned *Yoga Body*, for example, Mark Singleton cautions, "Although the text has received an enormous amount of interest from modern scholars, even coming to be known as the "Classical Yoga," bear in mind that it is one among many texts on yoga and may not necessarily be the authoritative source for Indian yoga traditions, as is commonly supposed." (p. 26)

93. For an insightful look at the view of Hatha Yoga from within the tradition, see Mark Singleton, *Yoga Body: The Origins of Modern Posture Practice* (Oxford University Press, 2010).

94. This is largely based on BKS Iyengar's translation of the Yoga Sutras in "*Light on the Yoga Sutras of Patanjali,*" ("Patanjala Yoga Pradipika), Thorsons, Hammersmith, 1966/1996, p. 230.

95. A paraphrase of the story told by Ram Dass in *Be Here Now*, Lama Foundation, New Mexico, 1971.

96. As quoted in Swami Hariharananda Aranya, "*Yoga Philosophy of Patanjali,*" SUNY Press, 1983, p. 346.

97. Ibid, pp. 346–347.

98. Ibid.

99. Swami Satyananda Saraswati, "*Four Chapters on Freedom: Commentary on the Yoga Sutras of Patanjali*," Yoga Publications Trust, Munger, Bihar, India, 1976, 2000, pp. 307–308.

100. Swami Satyananda Saraswati, *Kundalini Tantra*, Bihar School of Yoga, Munger, Bihar, India, 1984/1996, pp. 33–34.

101. Swami Satchidananda, "*The Yoga Sutras of Patanajali: Commentary on the Raja Yoga Sutras*," Integral Yoga Publications, 1990, p. 207.

102. BKS Iyengar, op. cit., pp. 230–231.

103. In Huxley's last book, the Utopian novel, "*Island*," which we will be discussing at greater length in a later chapter. The "moksha medicine" in question are psilocybin ("magic") mushrooms.

104. R.C. Zaehner, *Mysticism: Sacred and Profane* (Clarendon Press, 1956/1969), p. 226. Writing around the same time, W.T. Stace is a bit more sympathetic to mystical experience as engendered by psychedelics in his *Mysticism and Philosophy* (Tarcher/St. Martin's Press, 1960; foreword by Huston Smith), pp. 29–30, noting that according to the principle of "causal indifference," if two experiences are phenomenologically similar in every way, they cannot be regarded as being of two different kinds; hence, Stace argues, the mescaline experience might well be the same as that of what a saint experiences, but only further studies might bear this out (studies, I might add, which have yet to be made!). Stace conjectures that "the drug-induced experience may perhaps in some cases indistinguishably resemble the extrovertive type of mystical experience, but it is unlikely that it resembles the far more important introvertive type." (p. 30) Stace's categories of "introvertive" and "extrovertive" mystical experiences are still in use to this day, as evidenced in the recent study of psychedelics done at Johns Hopkins university: Griffiths RR, Richards WA, McCann U, Jesse R (2006). Psilocybin can occasion mystical-type experiences having substantial and sustained personal meaning and spiritual significance. Psychopharmacology (Berl) 187: 268–83; discussion 284–292. http://www.maps.org/research-archive/w3pb/2006/2006_Griffiths_22780_2.pdf.

105. I.K. Taimni, *The Science of Yoga*. The Theosophical Publishing House, Wheaton, Illinois 1961/1999, p. 378.

106. *Ibid*, pp. 382–383.

107. Ibid.

108. T.K.V. Desikachar, *The Heart of Yoga: Developing a Personal Practice*, Inner Traditions International, Rochester, Vermont, 1995, pp. 203, 206.

109. Georg Feuerstein, *Yoga-Sutra of Patanjali: A New Translation and Commentary*. Inner Traditions International, 1979, 1989, p. 126.

110. Swami Prabhavananda and Christopher Isherwood, *How to Know God: The Yoga Aphorisms of Patanjali*, p. 203.

111. Pandit Rajmani Tigunait, Ph.D. *Inner Quest: Yoga's Answers to Life's Questions*. Himalayan Institute Press, Honesdale, Pa, 1995/2002, pp. 112–117.

112. Actually, the path I was following is called Sri Vidya, and it is, strictly speaking, a Tantric path, though right-handed Tantra, not left. See my further comments above.

113. From Dr. David Frawley's "*Advanced Yoga and Ayurveda Course*," pp. 116–117.

114. Dr. Robert Svoboda, "*Aghora: At the Left Hand of God*," p. 184.

115. Ibid.

116. Ibid, pp. 185–186.

Unfortunately, most of this evidence is anecdotal. For more on this, see Roger Walsh, M.D., Ph.D., "The World of Shamanism: New Views of an Ancient Tradition," Llewellyn Publications, 2007, pp. 223–234.

117. Alberto Villodo, Ph.D., *Yoga, Power, and Spirit: Patanjali the Shaman*, xxv.

118. *A Postscript in Light of Reality Sandwich*: After this piece was published by Reality Sandwich in January, 2009, there were many who made comments, some of which included very helpful feedback that have enabled me to tighten and expand my findings a bit. Before I go into the content of this feedback, I would first like to thank all those in the Reality Sandwich community and beyond who freely offered their critiques and support, I have learned much from our online dialogue.

One point which is certainly applicable here is from Padmani, a yoga teacher and Ayahuasca journeyer in Toronto who wrote a RS piece entitled "Insects, Yoga, and Ayahuasca," in which she noted that "practices such as *pranayama* (breath control) and *asana* (physical exercise)—the two most important components of modern yoga practice in the West—are considered chemical means ["*aushadhi*"], according to Shri Brahmananda Sarasvati, because they work by causing biochemical changes in the body and mind."

Later I requested the relevant passage from Padmani, and she readily supplied it:

"Perfection by chemical means is produced by chemical, biochemical, and biological changes in body tissue. Breathing exercises, postures, asanas, and various powerful drugs are included in this group."

This suggests that we are indeed inducing changes in brain chemistry via the practice of Hatha Yoga, which is one reason why more and more people are becoming "addicted"—for better and/or for worse.

Another entire book could surely be written on how in fact Hatha Yoga affects the biochemistry of the human organism, and how this might relate to the "various powerful drugs" that are listed. Certainly alternatives to psychedelics, such as the intensive breathwork practices mentioned in the first chapter, demonstrate the validity of what Shri Brahmananda Saraswati says—that these profound, "non-ordinary" states of consciousness certainly can be induced by breathwork, ecstatic dance, and various other methodologies.

One of the things that was mentioned in a lot of the comments was the whole issue of *siddhis* and aren't they a distraction, and why did I (and yogis in general) seem to be so obsessively fixated on the quest for "powers"?

One RS member wrote:

"All very interesting, however, is not Yoga about becoming independent? The siddhis, may well be a by-product of our effort towards a certain goal, but should not become the reason we practice or a distraction from discovering our true nature. Relying on certain plant remedies to achieve a certain level of clarity does not promote independence, only dependence…"

To which I responded:

Yes… the goal is to be independent, and I hope the readers of this piece get that most of the commentators on Sutra 4.1 seem to be in agreement that drugs/herbs are but a means to that greater end.

I felt that this was a given, but a few individuals expressed great disapproval of such an idea, one writing:

Independence? Yoga means UNION, there is no independence!

This reader continued:

The very idea that we need each other and each thing, that the journey inward and upward IS dependent on our union with each other, with medicines, ideas, and sutras and positions is YOGA because YOGA means UNION.

It does not matter how you achieve UNION, what matters is what you are doing to prevent union, like speaking nonsense about independence and not needing ANYTHING or ANYONE.

I felt this was misunderstanding what was being said, namely that until one reaches a certain level, sure we may need certain "ways and means" of getting there, but ultimately it seems, and some few masters have demonstrated this, once you are in a state of Yoga/Union, there is not much need for external supports, so to speak. That said, given that maybe 99.99% of us will go our entire lives without fully realizing a state of complete "self-reliance," to use Emerson's phrase, I do agree that such a lofty goal, if even desirable, might be a bit unrealistic and ultimately disillusioning, so I would provisionally agree with this comment.

Another apparent critique from a Reality Sandwich subscriber came with the title, "*This need for POWER!*" and included the following:

This sitting and self-absorption, and wanting power.

Whereas for me, the essential meaning of psychedelics and experience is not "getting powers"—whatever they be. BUT understanding relationship with nature. Understanding the power of nature! And us feeling into this cyclic changing natural power.

And also encouraging the power to see what is going on in the world, and find ways to actively change things for the better. This must need seeing through all forms of power-mongering.

One of the biggest gaffes in debate is the tendency to over-generalize, and this argument is guilty of that, as well as perhaps being a bit too self-congratulatory. To say that all yogis are only meditating to attain "powers" is simply too categorical a statement. Some yogis seek powers, and some meditate purely to seek Yoga, or Union, and some do both. In any case, there are enough checks and balances in the system to keep yogis honest (or at least the honest ones!). As one commentator put it:

It is actually like a "main clause" in all bona-fide yogic texts that the achievement of "siddhis" are actually a distraction from the ultimate goal of unified consciousness with all.

This is a point made in the Yoga Sutras itself (see below), and is interestingly confirmed in a revealed "yogic" scripture of more recent vintage: A Course in Miracles (more on this in a later chapter).

Another reader wrote me privately:

As regards siddhis, attainment has nothing whatsoever to do with psychic talents or gifts. Until one has come into one's heart… and then gone beyond the heart, such gifts are parlor tricks when applied without consciousness—manipulative. It seems to me that enlightenment cannot be attained without meditation, and that the deeper the meditation, the deeper the love. To be concerned with these powers or these powers in others or what others think kinda misses the point. I have known many people who do have these gifts, with and without the higher chakras being activated, but then, they are not my concern. I have observed the gamut of use and abuse. My concern is about knowing who I am. Each person encounter teaches me that, as does my aloneness.

And one final comment:

Seeking siddhis is a distraction, and likely damaging to the progress to freedom. Exercising cogni-

tive powers that result in powers are one thing, as is taking herbs for healing, but pursuing powers for powers is not an exercise in removing egoism, but in strengthening it.

Yes, though I didn't really talk about this much in my essay, a careful reading of the Yoga Sutras does suggest that for Patanjali, the *siddhis* are in fact a distraction from *Samadhi*.

I actually wasn't exactly clear about this point when I first wrote the piece, but became clearer through email correspondence with Salvatore Zambito, a scholar of yoga who has written a book on the Yoga Sutras, *The Unadorned Thread of Yoga: The Yoga-Sûtra of Patañjali in English*, which presents each of the 196 sutras, with text analysis and twelve authoritative translations. What follows is a bit of our correspondence…

AL: One question that comes to mind right now: Granted that the *siddhis* are obstacles to *Samadhi*, but for Patanjali, are they not also byproducts of *Samadhi/Samyama*?

SZ: *Short answer—No.*

Explanation:

Patanjali answers this Sutra III.38: While the siddhi-attainments appear as magical powers in the objective world, they are actually perfections of an exhibitive mind operating on the subtle level; as such they are additional obstacles to samaadhi. (Zambito translation)

He is very clear—siddhis are mental operations and the outcome of mental operations—NOT samaadhis which are states beyond mind. Having evolved beyond mind, samaadhi does not produce mental by-product, which is lower vibration. By Patanjali's understanding, siddhi is a significantly less evolved state than samaadhi. This can be difficult for the externalized Western mind to grasp.

All of Patanjali's opinion/instruction about obstructions involve dissolving them: I.12, I.29, I.32, II.2. No sutra advises initiating or strengthening obstructions (kleshas, vrrtis, vishesas, siddhis, etc.); on the contrary, we are advised to dissolve them. II.11 is quite adamant: The vrttis are to be dissolved thru meditation. This is not a suggestion.

AL: And so would the *siddhis* be a necessary stage (or perhaps even a kind of test) through which the yogi must go on the way to the highest Samadhi? Put another way: Are the siddhis not an indispensable part of this whole process?

SZ: *Patanjali gives no opinion in either direction; he had no chatterbox DNA. We can take as a hint that he only gives antidotes to obstructions to basic samaadhi. We might speculate that siddhis are a common state, but nothing in the Sutra implies that they are inevitable or indispensable. The general view is, given the Y-S context, that his listing is a warning, not a suggestion. The ego is tricky, hence the warning to siddhi-sadhakas: III.51: We should not respond with pleasure or pride to the alluring of celestial beings, because this will obstruct progress, and it is always possible to fall. While many Masters exhibit siddhis, they are regarded as obstructions to overcome on the Path, not tools of transcendence.*

This only summarizes Patanjali. There is no intellectually honest way to cite Patanjali as advising siddhi pursuit. This is not to say that siddhis do not have some lessons; it's just that they are detours on the path to samaadhi and not proposed as practice in the Yoga-Sutra. Perhaps other texts may give the support you seem to be seeking.

I guess I never suspected I would be suspected of seeking a textual support for the validity of acquiring *siddhis*! That was not my intention, though as I noted, early on I was interested in obtaining experiences and powers as a confirmation that "something" was happening. I do sense, however, that the *siddhis* are an important milestone, shall we say, that lets the yogi/ni know that he/she is on the right path (see Dr. Villodo's comments, noted above). And if psychedelics give one such powers, at least temporarily, it also seems to suggest that there is something similar going on to what happens in deep meditation.

In any case, it seems our interest in all of this is far more remedial. Meaning that, for example, many of us in our Western materialist culture need to see/experience things for ourselves to understand or believe them. Consider the following response from a reader:

"Just wanted to thank the author for a beautiful, and well researched, article on a very important topic. I practiced yoga and meditation years ago, greatly desiring to experience an altered, greater state of awareness. But I didn't know what I desired to attain; I could not comprehend what a super conscious state meant. How can we seek to become or attain something we cannot define? Although super conscious states and siddhis attained through the use of psychedelics are not as lasting as those gained through meditation and sincere sanyasa, they can serve as a step through the door to higher awakening. I do find myself wanting to return to Yoga and meditation more than ever, because I have experienced those higher states first through psychedelics, and now understand that Yoga offers an experience more lasting and powerful than that! I think first, to get to where we want to be, we need to know where we're going. And psychedelics, taken in a spirit of gratitude, can do that. They can only open the door to Yoga; we have to walk through it. Thanks so much for this article, it answered a lot of questions I had about the relationship between Yoga and these different states.

Others I have spoken with share this sentiment. As Yogi Berra is said to have said (he said a lot of things he didn't really say, apparently), *"If you don't know where you're going, you might not get there."* Well, might this not be true on the spiritual journey? As already noted, the psychedelic experience has provided many with an inside view of things that they had only read or heard about, and once granted, there is a profound impetus for beginning a discipline like yoga. Consider Ram Dass' words from a Buddhist dialogue on psychedelics 15 years ago:

"What I've noticed in my own life over the thirty-five years since my first ingestion, is that when I reenter (i.e., come back from the psychedelic experience), the habits come back in. But what I have in addition to habits is the memory of the experience, the sense of knowing that it's possible. Knowing that it's possible changes the meaning of all spiritual practice that follows because you go in with a perspective that's not just from here, but from there as well."

It seems to me that this point alone, aside from all the other positives that might accrue from a safe, guided psychedelic session, is certainly worthy of our attention.

119. This essay was originally featured on the Reality Sandwich website as "Prolegomena to a Guide for the Emerging Yoga Shaman." Link to the original piece: http://www.realitysandwich.com/ yoga_shaman. Please keep in mind this was written for a specific audience, and I would not necessarily put things now as I did then. For example, re-reading the excerpt from Wilber quoted, it is overall a fair and balanced perspective.

120. Georg Feuerstein, *The Yoga Tradition*, (Hohm Press, 2001), p. 35.

121. I have been in email contact with Baba Rampuri, an American born initiate into the Naga Babas and Yoga Shaman. For more on Rampuri, go to https://rampuri.com and in particular, watch the video of his address to the World Psychedelic Forum in Basel, Switzerland, 2008 (see also the footnote below).

122. See Stanislav Grof, M.D., *"Ken Wilber's Spectrum Psychology,"* at http://primal-page.com/ grofken.htm. Another wonderful book by Grof which is really a must read for those interested in these subjects is Grof's recent offering, *When the Impossible Happens: Adventures in Non-Ordinary Reality.* Sounds True, Incorporated, 2005. Particularly interesting are Grof's accounts of his meeting with Swami Muktananda, as well as his chapter on his experience with 5-MeO-DMT.

123. Here's but one website dedicated to **Ramana Maharishi** (or, "Maharshi"): http://www.srirama-namaharshi.org. One book which I would highly recommend that everyone read or re-read is Yogananda's *Autobiography of a Yogi*, particularly the chapter entitled "The Resurrection of Sri Yukteswar," as that goes into some detail about what the "subtle" (astral) and "causal" planes are like. Not that we should take this is as the last word on the subject, but just to familiarize ourselves with one highly influential view.

124. Grof quotes John Perry: "True mystics occasionally reactivate regressive complexes on their way to mature unity states," and goes on to say: "In spite of the fact that Ken acknowledges frequent mysterious invasion of transpersonal insights in psychotic patients, mysticism remains for him miles apart from psychosis. It represents for him a purely trans-egoic progression, whereas psychosis is primarily characterized by a regression to early infancy in the service of the ego." (op. cit.)

125. I would add that I'm not sure if any of my Indian teachers even attained to the same level as Ramana Maharishi, though they all fulfilled the role of the shaman for their communities.

126. At this point I would like to make a special note of 5-MeO-DMT as being potentially the one entheogen that just might give more consistent access to the Causal planes, and even beyond that to Source (God, Void, Brahman, etc.). I would like to make special mention of James Oroc's new book, *Tryptamine Palace: 5-MeO-DMT and the Sonoran Desert Toad* (Inner Traditions, 2009), in which the author argues that 5-MeO-DMT is really the only true entheogen in that it provides a direct experience of Source (or God). Another new proponent of 5-MeO-DMT, Hal Lucius Nation, the spiritual head of the Temple of Awakening Divinity (T.O.A.D.) and longtime practitioner of Raja Yoga, refers to this particular substance as "Samadhi," a Sanskrit word which he translates as "Union with God" or "Union with the Divine." Martin Ball, Ph.D. has also written a book which is largely about and inspired by 5-MeO-DMT, entitled *The Entheogenic Evolution: Psychedelics, Consciousness, and Awakening the Human Spirit*, and has interviewed both James Oroc and Hal Lucius Nation. Both interviews are available for free download at http://entheogenic.podomatic.com/.

127. See Ken Wilber, *The Eye of the Spirit: An Integral Vision for a World Gone Slightly Mad*. Shambhala, 1998, pp. 165–185. In these pages, Wilber confronted Grof's criticisms of his work for the first time in publication. This needs to be read along with Grof's essay in response (see above). Also, a video where he talks about Ayahuasca: https://www.youtube.com/watch?v=-Z3j7laY2lI.

128. I doubt whether Wilber was thinking of Grof when he said that. In an early book, *No Boundary: Eastern and Western Approaches to Spiritual Growth* (Shambhala, 1979), p. 124, Wilber suggested that the "urge to transcendence occasionally takes on bizarre or exaggerated forms, such as black magic, occultism, misuse of psychedelic drugs, and cultic guru worship." There was clearly enough of these things happening in that era of the late Seventies for Wilber to note this, and there had already been enough of a backlash against psychedelics in spiritual circles for him to recommend reading Grof's *Realms of the Human Unconscious*, with the words: "Don't dismiss Grof's work as being data from 'acid hallucinations.'" Dr. Grof is among the most brilliant of psychologists now living, and his work is always carefully researched, skillfully presented, and intelligently discussed." (p. 139)

129. There's a discussion of what might have been the cause of Terence's death at http://www.shroomery.org/forums/showflat.php/Number/1696452.

130. This is also a critique that Baba Rampuri, an American-born initiate into the Naga Babas, made at the World Psychedelic Forum in Basel, Switzerland, March, 2008. Rampuri's words: *"It was very curious for me to find that the vast numbers of professional explorers of alchemically or botanically induced altered consciousness, including their own, seem to have gone only to the edge of*

the Western paradigm in order to find a knowledge that crosses all paradigms. But, the border is the border, and very few are willing to cross the line. Whether an anthropologist or a psychologist, few are willing to let go long enough to explore Magic, i.e., Consciousness on ITS OWN TERMS." See https://rampuri.com/ for Rampuri's writings, videos, pictures, etc.

131. From email correspondence with White and from speaking with one of his students, I understand that even though White made that statement, he still has been rather guarded about what he makes public about his use of plant sacraments. He apparently will only talk about it with his students when the subject is broached. I sense that this will all change in the next couple of years, that there will be far more openness in the yoga community about these subjects.

132. You can watch the video of their dialogue, "Asanas and Ayahuasca," at http://www.realitysandwich.com/asanas_and_Ayahuasca. You will also want to read all of the comments posted. My own view of what some called a "fiasco," is that it might have gone over better if Daniel had been dialoguing with a shaman yogini like Padmani, who wrote the RS essay, "Insects, Yoga, and Ayahuasca,"—http://www.realitysandwich.com/insects_yoga_and_Ayahuasca, and who is both a yoga teacher and a regular user of plant sacraments like Ayahuasca.

133. I also sense that it is precisely those of us who have been perhaps overly physically-oriented in our life and yoga practice that actually need a high dose of something, anything to bust through the layers of egoity. This idea will take a good deal of unpacking and I'll leave that for a separate piece.

134. Here is a link to DeGracia's study: http://csp.org/practices/entheogens/docs/kundalini_survey.html.

135. Ok, about that LSD experience with Zen (see, careful reading has its rewards—this is your reward)… We sat by the fire all night after a brief stint in a little cave. We hadn't taken a high enough dose to really go full-on, and as a result I was kind of stuck in this loop where I would almost keep dying, but then not be able to, if that makes sense. And I kept talking, was finding it very hard to just be still. It was a low grade torture, a kind of hellish realm. I was not feeling good about anything. I noted my general tendency to disempower myself by mistakenly seeing certain others as better or more advanced, leading also to jealousy, which was definitely happening with Zen. There's more to share, but maybe another time.

136. Gopi Krishna, *Living with Kundalini*, pp. 120–121.

137. Irving, Gopi Krishna, *Serpent of Fire*, p. 182.

138. William James, *The Varieties of Religious Experience*. I made this the centerpiece of a course I gave on mysticism and religion in Naples, Florida in 2003. Amongst older, retired Neapolitans, a longtime ayahuasquero showed up for it and it was interesting to see the interchanges that took place. I had hardly heard of Ayahuasca myself and had to ask the man how to pronounce it. You can read more about this in one of the appendices.

139. From *The Psychotropic Mind* (2009), conversations between Jeremy Narby, Jan Kounen, and Vicent Ravalec on ayahuasa, iboga, and shamanism.

140. See Alain Danielou, *Gods of Love and Ecstasy: The Traditions of Shiva and Dionysus* (Inner Traditions).

141. From the 1969 *Rolling Stone* interview with Jerry Hopkins. http://tinyurl.com/klgkbtd.

142. Aldous Huxley, *Doors of Perception 1963*, p. 18.

143. Excerpted from the book, *The Ecstatic Adventure*, found online @ http://www.psychedelic-library.org/books/ecstatic22.htm.

144. Stephen Gaskin, *Amazing Dope Tales*, Ronin, 1980/1999, p. 90.

145. It's interesting to note that Dr. Timothy Leary first met with Swami Satchidananda in 1967 and his theory of the "8 circuits" might have been influenced by the Swami.

146. http://www.luminist.org/archives/psychedelic.htm. A number of different sites have now posted this essay, no doubt in an effort to do as the author requested.

147. Lennon's song "Tomorrow Never Knows" is heavily based upon Leary's book (which by the way, was co-written by Richard Alpert, aka Ram Dass, and Ralph Metzner). See for example, Martin A. Lee and Bruce Shlain's book, *Acid Dreams: The Complete Social History of LSD: The CIA, The Sixties, and Beyond*. New York: Grove Press, 1985, 1992, pp. 182–183.

148. Ibid, p. 181.

149. Ibid. p. 184.

150. http://www.rollingstone.com/music/news/john-lennon-remembered-20101208

151. For more on this, see *Dharma Lion*.

152. See http://www.dandavats.com/?p=1494.

153. Listen to the very first meeting between John, Yoko, George Harrison and Swami Bhaktivedanta here: http://krishna.org/george-harrison-john-lennon-and-yoko-ono-from-the-beatles-talk-with-srila-prabhupada-mp3-audio/. This interview was actually published in the 1992 edition of "Chant and Be Happy" (for which George Harrison wrote the Forward), which the cover says has "exclusive interviews with George Harrison and John Lennon," yet the interview, as we have seen, is not exactly supportive of the Hare Krishna mission.

154. http://www.rollingstone.com/music/news/john-lennon-remembered-20101208

155. From "An Interview with 'Deepak Chopra' in South Africa," in The Observer, August 17, 2008.

156. http://www.guardian.co.uk/lifeandstyle/2008/aug/17/healthandwellbeing.familyandrelationships

157. http://krishna.org/science-defined-mp3-audio-morning-walk-with-srila-prabhupada/
http://www.drweil.com/drw/u/QAA401630/Can-Ayahuasca-Relieve-Depression.html

158. Here's a yoga demo from about 15 years later: https://www.youTube.com/watch?v=51BJoofI-3lo.

159. Ram Dass, *Be Love Now*, p. 162.

160. I was interested to find a news piece online about Brian: http://www.littleindia.com/arts-entertainment/1250-searching-east.html. Here is the relevant excerpt: "Within days, Greenwald was hooked to this yoga, where all he had to do was sit calmly and meditate on his kundalini energy, residing at the base of the spine. A few weeks later, a friend took him to a rock concert where they consumed LSD. As soon as the drug hit him, he started hallucinating. Out of curiosity, he tried to meditate on his Kundalini energy and immediately the halucinations vanished. He felt in control and sober even though LSD typically takes anywhere from 8 to 10 hours to wear off."

161. Source: http://www.gratefulness.org/resource/lay-monasticism/.

162. Ibid.

163. There are several versions of this story. See appendix for the textual variants.

164. See Bhagavan Das, *It's Here Now (Are You?): A Spiritual Memoir*, pp. 157–159. "Maharajji took enough LSD to make an elephant grow wings and fly over Mr. Everest. And absolutely nothing happened." (p. 158)

165. In Horgan, *Rational Mysticism*.

166. In Ram Dass, *Paths to God*, p. 190. Originally published in a later book, *The Only Dance There Is* (1974), which is a collection of Ram Dass' lectures at the Menninger Foundation in the early '70s. Note: There are several versions of this story, this is for the most part the one floating around the Internet. See Appendix for variants.

167. Anyone who truly wants to get a better sense of what it was like to be around Neem Karoli Baba (at least in his later years) should read Ram Dass' anthology of stories, *Miracle of Love: Stories About Neem Karoli Baba* (E. P. Dutton, New York, 1979). The chapter "About Drugs" (pp. 225–237) is especially relevant to this discussion.

168. This was not the case: A few of the Westerner devotees of Neem Karoli did speak Hindi. See Ram Dass, *Miracle of Grace*, p, 105. Rampuri's point is still well-taken.

169. Lama Surya Das: "I fondly remember my first guru, Neem Karoli Baba, taking three tabs of Ram Dass's Sandoz Laboratiry acid in the late Sixties and then throughout the day asking Ram Dass if and when it was going to have some effect. It's really Ram Das who went on a trip that day. It didn't seem to change Neem Karoli Baba's consciousness much." See Hunt Badiner's *Zig Zag Zen*, p. 185. Bhagavan Das also confirms the story in his "It's Here Now (Are You?)."

170. In Feuerstein, *The Mystery of Light: The Life and Teaching of Omraam Mikhael Aivanhov*, p. 51, Integral Publishing, 1998.

171. Boyd, *Swami*, pp. 296–297.

172. Ram Dass, *Be Here Now*, 1971.

173. Bhagavan Das, *It's Here Now (Are You?)*, p. 143.

174. Bhagavan Das, *It's Here Now (Are You?)*, pp. 88–90.

175. For more about Bhagavan Das, go to www.bhagavandas.com.

176. Timothy Leary was also quite taken with Baba Hari Dass—two years prior to Ram Dass' first trip to India! His interest almost led him to the door of Neem Karoli Baba—almost, but not quite. (See endnote above, or watch the movie "Timothy Leary's Dead" online.)

177. You'll recall that this is not too dissimilar from Meher Baba's message to the hippie counter-culture.

178. In the magazine *What is Enlightenment*, January–March, 2007, p. 21.

179. Lama Surya Das, *Awakening the Buddha Within*, pp. 214–215.

180. Ibid, p. 214.

181. Ibid, p. 214.

182. See Smith, *Cleansing the Doors of Perception*.

183. Lama Surya Das mentions only once in his book, and it is to note Neem Karoli Baba's ecumenicism, how he always admonished his devotees to learn from everyone—all true teachers. I wonder if this might not also mean from certain "plant teachers," as well? If Ram Dass' story is true, the answer is the affirmative.

184. *Tricycle*, Fall/Winter, 1995.

185. Jack Kornfield, from an interview with Robert Forte, in *Tricycle*, Fall/Winter 1995.

186. Rick Strassman in *Tricycle*, Fall/Winter, 1995.

187. Op. Cit.

188. Ibid. For a very helpful dialogue between Dr. Robert Forte and Jack Kornfield on these subjects, see "Psychedelics and Spiritual Practice: A Buddhist Perspective," available online here: http://www.lycaeum.org/nepenthes/Misc/buddhism.html. Here Kornfield very clearly and succinctly deals with most of the issues of concern in this book, and in my mind, though there is not the tradition of taking psychedelic substances in the Buddhist tradition as there is in its parent tradition, Hinduism, what Kornfield says here seems to me to equally well apply to both traditions.

189. Ibid; this is a point also made by Kornfield in the piece noted directly above.

190. Krishna Das, *Chants of a Lifetime* (Hay House, 2010), p. 6.

191. Ibid, p. 7.

192. Ibid, p. 9.

193. See http://www.krishnadas.com/about, as well as the recent documentary about Krishna Das, "One Track Heart."

194. Interview with Shyamdas published in *Hinduism Today* magazine, May, 1986.

195. At the point of this writing (2014), I feel I must make note of the great controversy surrounding Mata Amritanandamayi, something that shocked me upon first hearing about it. At this moment, I am reading Gail Tredwell's memoir/exposé of Ammachi and the movement (*Holy Hell*, 2013) and find it hard to discount the seriousness of her allegations.

196. An example of this is the Andrew Cohen, "guru," Ken Wilber, "pandit," dialogue in *What is Enlightenment?* magazine.

197. This did not originate with Mike Myers' "The Love Guru," by the way, or even by Deepak Chopra, who repeats it quite often in his talks and interviews and is who Mike Myers based his character on (it is not trademarked, the "TM" is from the movie). Ganga White suggested it might have been original to his teacher, Swami Venkates, who used to say this in his lectures in the Sixties.

198. For a traditional understanding of the guru from a text I myself on several occasions have chanted, please see the Guru Gita. Here is one English translation of it: http://www.yogalifesociety.com/GuruGita.html.

199. "Shortcut to False-Samadhi": http://o-meditation.com/2010/04/21/lsd-a-shortcut-to-false-samadhi-osho/.

200. Boyd, *Swami*, pp. 296–297.

201. Alan Wattts, *Does It Matter? Essays on Man's Relation to Materiality*. New York: Vintage Books, 1971. The excerpt in question is from chapter 5, "Psychedelics and Religious Experience," pp. 78–95. Highly recommended to read the whole piece!

202. http://www.avatarmeherbaba.org/erics/drugs01.html

203. Ram Dass, *Paths to God*.

204. Ram Dass, *Paths to God*, pp. 304–305.

205. Bhagavan Das, *It's Here Now (Are You?)*, pp. 88–90.

206. As quoted in *Birth of a Pyschedelic Culture*, p. 214.

207. http://en.wikiquote.org/wiki/Timothy_Leary.

208. Swami Muktananda, *I Have Become Alive*, 1985/1992, pp. 93–95. This was Muktananda's last book.

209. From "Marijuana and Kundalini Yoga," by Nihal Singh, on spiritvoyage.com. Note that marijuana has the potential to initiate a psychedelic experience if taken in sufficient dosage.

210. Yogi Bhajan, *Kundalini Yoga: The Flow of Eternal Power*, p. 104.

211. From the lecture "Self-Reverence" given by Yogi Bhajan on July 26, 1996. See 3HO.org.

212. As quoted in Eve Neuhaus' forthcoming biography of Ganesh Baba.

213. For the full interview, try www.oprah.com.

214. Excerpted from Rabbi Schacter-Shalomi's essay, "The Conscious Ascent of the Soul," found in Chapter 10 of Ralph Metzner's *The Ecstatic Adventure*. http://www.psychedelic-library.org/books/ecstatic10.htm.

215. 4th Public Talk, Brockwood Park, 1971; Book: Awakening of Intelligence, Part IX. CD-rom code: br71t4; http://www.katinkahesselink.net/kr/drugs.html.

216. http://www.luminist.org/archives/psychedelic.htm

217. Originally quoted in Tricycle Review, Fall, 1995, and reprinted in Allan Badiner Hunt's *Zig Zag Zen*.

218. From a question and answer session at the 1966 Kumbha Mela.

219. Ibid, p. 181.

220. *The Beatles Anthology* (2000), p. 177.

221. Ibid. p. 184.

222. Excerpted from a 2001 interview between Wilber and Piers Clement.

223. By Hayagriva Dasa, http://krishna.org/matchless-gifts/. Also, see Sasvarupa Dasa Swami's book, *Planting the Seed, New York City 1965–1966: A Biography of His Divine Grace A.C. Bhaktivedanta Swami Prabhupada* (Bhaktivedanta Book Trust, 1980/82), pp. 141, 216, et all.

224. Terence McKenna, *Food of the Gods*, p.4.

225. McKenna as quoted in John Horgan's *Rational Mysticism*, p. 185.

226. From a Tripzine.com interview with McKenna.

227. Swami Satyananda Saraswati, *Bhakti Yoga Sagar*, p. 233.

228. http://www.maps.org/news-letters/v21n1/v21n1-33to34.pdf.

229. Sting, *Broken Music* (Random House, 2009). See also: https://www.youTube.com/watch?v=Sx-axvC3W6CQ.

230. Transcribed from the Gaiam documentary, "Titans of Yoga." http://yogamonth.org/titansofyoga/.

231. From *Shamanic Medicines & Eco-Consciousness: A Conversation with Dennis McKenna, Ph.D.*, by Dennis McKenna, Ph.D., and David J. Brown, in Maps Bulletin, volume xix, number 1, pp. 35–36.

232. Two notable books I read at that time were Dr. Samuel H. Sandweiss' *Sai Baba: The Holy Man and the Psychiatrist*, (San Diego: Birth Day Publishing Company, 1975), and Howard Murphet's *Sai Baba: Man of Miracles* (London: Frederick Muller Ltd, 1971).

233. A good piece on the storm of controversy is Mick Brown's "Divine Downfall," (in The Daily Telegraph, October 27, 2000), which notes that Jeff Young, the father of Sam Young, the young man who initially made the Web allegations, first got into yoga, and then Sai Baba, through an exploration of psychedelics in the '70s.

234. Rodarmor, William (1983). "The Secret Life of Swami Muktananda." *CoEvolution Quarterly*. http://www.leavingsiddhayoga.net/secret.htm. See also Lis Harris' New Yorker piece, "O Guru, Guru, Guru," Nov. 14th, 1994. The above website, leavingsiddhayoga.net, also contains a good deal of information on the controversy.

235. Ram Dass, *Be Love Now*.

236. Ram Dass' Naropa talks were finally transcribed and published in *Paths to God: Living the Bhagavad Gita* (Three Rivers Press, 2004), and the passage in question is on p. 131.

237. The documentary about Ram Dass, "Fierce Grace" has a snippet of Ferguson playing his trumpet up on the roof at Millbrook. For the Maynard-Sai Baba connection: http://sathyasaibaba.wordpress.com/2008/06/29/sri-sathya-sai-baba-maynard-ferguson/; also: http://sathyasaibaba.wordpress.com/2009/03/23/maynard-ferguson-meets-sathya-sai-baba/.

   Because Ferguson went to India in '68, he might well have been influenced by Dr. Richard Alpert (Ram Dass), who was there in '66–'67.

238. See ex-devotee Robert Priddy's blog: https://robertpriddy.wordpress.com/.

239. http://robert-priddy-exposed.blogspot.com/2007/03/robert-priddy-psychedelic-drug-years.html

240. Ibid. For a fuller account of this experience, see: http://robert-priddy-exposed.blogspot.com/2007/03/robert-priddys-lsd-trip-beyond-mind.html.

241. http://www.sriprembaba.org/biography.

242. From private communication with Padmani, although Padmani did not feel at liberty to say, I at first guessed that the celebrity yoga teacher was Ganga White. I later discovered that it was Danny Paradise. When I was in Bali I was able to pose a question to Danny relating to plant medicine in the context of a talk he gave at the Bali Spirit Festival in Ubud.

243. http://entheogenic.podomatic.com/.

Made in the USA
Columbia, SC
26 January 2022

54196470R00220